Automotive Industrialisation

This book looks at the industrial policies of Southeast Asian economies in their motor vehicle industries from early import substitution to policy-making under the more liberalised WTO policy regime.

The book examines how inward automotive investment, especially from Japan, has been affected by policies, and how such investment has promoted industrial development in the late-industrialising economies within ASEAN (Association of Southeast Asian Nations). It provides insights into the automotive industry of Southeast Asia in terms of production volumes, sales volumes, market structure, and trade. Through country case studies, the book is a useful reference and illustrates how industrial policies in Southeast Asia have affected the spread of automotive development in the region.

It will appeal to policy-makers and researchers interested in the automobile industry, industrial policies in the industry, and the spread of development from foreign investors to local firms.

Kaoru Natsuda is a professor, College of International Management, Ritsumeikan Asia Pacific University, Japan, and visiting professor, Budapest Business School. He was formerly a visiting scholar at Charles University, Prague. He obtained his PhD in economics from the University of Sydney, Australia, and his MA in international development studies from the University of Bradford, UK. He has published papers including in *Review of International Political Economy, European Journal of Development Research, Canadian Journal of Development Studies,* and *Asia Europe Journal.* He serves as a senior associate editor of *PSU Research Review* and editorial board member of *International Journal of Development Issues.*

John Thoburn holds a PhD degree from the University of Alberta, Canada, and is Emeritus Reader in Economics, School of International Development, University of East Anglia, UK. After retiring from East Anglia, and after six months as a visiting professor at Kobe University, Japan, he became Professor of Development Economics, Ritsumeikan Asia Pacific University, and then a visiting professor until 2017. He is the author of five books on development, and published articles including in *Oxford Economic Papers, Oxford Bulletin of Economics and Statistics, Journal of Development Studies, Review of International Political Economy,* and *Journal of the Asia Pacific Economy* (on whose editorial board he serves).

Routledge-GRIPS Development Forum Studies

Edited by Kenichi Ohno and Izumi Ohno, National Graduate Institute for Policy Studies, Japan

1 **The Rise of Asian Donors**
Japan's Impact on the Evolution of Emerging Donors
Edited by Jin Sato and Yasutami Shimomura

2 **Learning to Industrialize**
From Given Growth to Policy-aided Value Creation
Kenichi Ohno

3 **Eastern and Western Ideas for African Growth**
Diversity and Complementarity in Development Aid
Edited by Kenichi Ohno

4 **Inequality, Inclusive Growth, and Fiscal Policy in Asia**
Edited by Donghyun Park, Sang-Hyop Lee and Minsoo Lee

5 **Mismanaging Innovation Systems**
Thailand and the Middle-income Trap
Patarapong Intarakumnerd

6 **Health Rights of Older People**
Comparative Perspectives in Southeast Asia
Edited by Long Thanh Giang and Theresa W. Devasahayam

7 **Automotive Industrialisation**
Industrial Policy and Development in Southeast Asia
Kaoru Natsuda and John Thoburn

For more information about this series, please visit: www.routledge.com/Routledge-GRIPS-Development-Forum-Studies/book-series/GRIPS

Automotive Industrialisation

Industrial Policy and Development in Southeast Asia

Kaoru Natsuda and John Thoburn

Routledge
Taylor & Francis Group
LONDON AND NEW YORK

First published 2021
by Routledge
2 Park Square, Milton Park, Abingdon, Oxon OX14 4RN

and by Routledge
52 Vanderbilt Avenue, New York, NY 10017

Routledge is an imprint of the Taylor & Francis Group, an informa business

British Library Cataloguing-in-Publication Data
A catalogue record for this book is available from the British Library

Library of Congress Cataloging-in-Publication Data
A catalog record for this book has been requested

ISBN: 978-1-138-33441-0 (hbk)
ISBN: 978-0-429-44535-4 (ebk)

Typeset in Galliard
by codeMantra

MIX
Paper from responsible sources
FSC™ C013985
FSC
www.fsc.org

Printed in the United Kingdom
by Henry Ling Limited

Contents

Figures

Tables

Appendices

Preface and acknowledgements

The last two decades have seen major shifts in the location of the production of motor vehicles towards Asia. While China is the best known beneficiary of these trends, Southeast Asia also has seen large increases in automotive production, concentrated in countries in ASEAN (Association of Southeast Asian Nations). The 'ASEAN-5' countries – Thailand, Indonesia, Malaysia, Vietnam, and the Philippines – had a combined 2018 world share of vehicle production of 4.6%, only a little behind that of Germany's, and larger than that of Mexico, a country also a beneficiary of relocation trends.

We have been conducting research on the Southeast Asian automotive industry since 2010, based at Ritsumeikan Asia Pacific University (APU) in Japan, with Natsuda as a full-time professor and Thoburn as a regular visiting professor. We carried out fieldwork in Thailand (2010 and 2011), Malaysia (2012), Indonesia (2013), the Philippines (2014 and 2015), and Vietnam (2015). We (but mainly Natsuda) also have later worked on the automotive industry in Eastern and Central Europe, principally Czechia, the largest producer in the region. This was mainly done while Natsuda was a visiting scholar at the Institute of East Asian Studies, Charles University in Prague (October 2015–March 2016); and also in Hungary as a visiting professor, Faculty of International Management and Business, Budapest Business School(from March 2019 until September 2020). We have introduced some comparisons with Czechia in this book where we think they provide useful perspective on developments in Southeast Asia.

For finance for our research, we gratefully acknowledge the support of the Japan Society for the Promotion of Science: KAKENHI Grants No.22730153 (2010–2012), No.15K03496 (2015–2018), and No.17KK0059 (2018–2020), and of Ritsumeikan Asia Pacific University.

In the time this book has been in preparation, we have become indebted to many individuals for comments or discussions: in Japan, Kozo Otsuka and Hidetaka Yoshimatsu (APU), Noriyuki Segawa (Kindai University), Kenta Goto (Kansai University), Tetsuo Abo (University of Tokyo),Yoko Ueda (Doshisha University), and Kenichi Ohno and Patarapong Intarakumnerd (National Graduate Institute for Policy Studies, Tokyo); in the United Kingdom, Rhys Jenkins, Chris Edwards, and Leonardo Lima Chagas (University of East Anglia); in Thailand, Takashi Tsukamoto (Thammasat University); in Malaysia, Rajah

Rasiah (University of Malaya); in the Philippines, Rafaelita Aldaba (Department of Trade and Industry); in Vietnam, Pham Vu Thang (Vietnam National University) and Adam McCarty (Mekong Economics); in Czechia, Jan Sykora, Jiri Blazek, and Takashi Hosoda (Charles University, Prague); in Poland, Tomasz Olejniczak (Kozminski University); in Hungary, Magdolna Sass, Lazlo Csonka, Katalin Antaloczy, and Csaba Moldicz (Budapest Business School); in the United States, Richard Doner (Emory University); in Turkey, Murat Yulek (OSTIM Technical University) and Mustafa Erdogdu (Marmara University); and in Australia, Gavan Butler and Dilip Dutta (University of Sydney).

We also would like to express our gratitude to the following government and international organisations, industry associations, and universities for assisting in our research. In Thailand, the Thai Board of Investment, Thai Automotive Industry Association (TAIA), Thai Auto-Parts Manufacturers Association (TAPMA), and Thammasat University; in Indonesia, the Ministry of Trade, Ministry of Industry, BKPM (Investment Coordinating Board), GAIKINDO (Association of Indonesia Automotive Industries), GIAMM (Indonesian Automotive Parts & Components Industries Association), the Japanese Embassy in Indonesia, and JETRO Jakarta Office; in Malaysia, the Ministry of International Trade and Industry of Malaysia, Malaysian Automotive Institute (MAI), Malaysian Automotive Association (MAA), Malaysian Automotive Component Parts Manufacturers Association (MACPMA), Japanese Embassy in Malaysia, JETRO Kuala Lumpur Office, the University of Malaya, and the Malaysian-Japan International Institute of Technology; in the Philippines, the Department of Trade and Industry, Board of Investment, Chamber of Automotive Manufacturers of the Philippines (CAMPI), Motor Vehicle Parts Manufacturers Association of the Philippines (MVPMAP), Philippines Automotive Competitiveness Council, Philippine Institute for Development Studies (PIDS), Asian Development Bank, and JETRO Manila Office; in Vietnam, the Ministry of Industry and Trade, Institute for Industrial Policy and Strategy, Development and Policies Research Center, Mekong Economics, UNIDO Hanoi Office, JETRO Hanoi Office, JICA Hanoi Office, and Vietnam National University; in Japan, the Japan Automobile Manufacturers Association (JAMA); in the Czech Republic (Czechia), Czech Invest and Czech Automotive Industry Association, JETRO Prague Office, and Charles University in Prague.

Last but certainly not least, we should like to thank very warmly the many automotive assemblers and component manufacturers who willingly provided us with information.

Our earlier research findings have been published as a series of journal articles. Where we have reproduced material from these articles, we should like to acknowledge copyright permissions as follows:

- Kaoru Natsuda, Noriyuki Segawa, and John Thoburn (2013) Liberalization, Industrial Nationalism, and the Malaysian Automotive Industry. *Global Economic Review*, 42(2): 113–134, copyright ©Institute of East and West Studies, Yonsei University, Seoul, reprinted by permission of Informa

UK Limited, trading as Taylor & Francis Group, www.tandfonline.com on behalf of Institute of East and West Studies, Yonsei University, Seoul.

- Kaoru Natsuda, Kozo Otsuka, and John Thoburn (2015) Dawn of Industrialization: The Indonesian Automotive Industry. *Bulletin of Indonesian Economic Studies*, 51(1): 47–68, copyright ©Indonesia Project ANU, reprinted by permission of Informa UK Limited, trading as Taylor & Francis Group, www.tandfonline.com on behalf of Indonesia Project ANU.

We express our thanks too to Noriyuki Segawa and Kozo Otsuka, respectively, for their kind permission to use extracts from these two articles that they co-authored with us.

In addition, we thank Taylor & Francis for their kind permission also to reproduce extracts from some of our other articles, as follows:

- Kaoru Natsuda and John Thoburn (2013) Industrial Policy and the Development of the Automotive Industry in Thailand. *Journal of the Asia Pacific Economy*,18 (3): 413–437
- Kaoru Natsuda and John Thoburn (2014) How Much Policy Space Still Exists under the WTO? A Comparative Study of the Automotive Industry in Thailand and Malaysia. *Review of International Political Economy*, 21(6): 1346–1377.
- Kaoru Natsuda and John Thoburn (2018) Industrial Policy and the Development of the Automotive Industry in the Philippines. *Canadian Journal of Development Studies*, 39(3): 371–391, copyright © Canadian Association for the Study of Development reprinted by permission of Taylor & Francis Ltd, http://www.tandfonline.com on behalf of Canadian Association for the Study of Development.
- John Thoburn and Kaoru Natsuda (2018), How to conduct effective industrial policy: a comparison of automotive development in the Philippines and Indonesia. *Journal of the Asia Pacific Economy*, 23(4): 657–682.

Of course, no person or organisation mentioned here necessarily agrees with any view expressed in this book, and any errors are our own.

Kaoru Natsuda and John Thoburn
April 2020

Selected abbreviations

AAF	ASEAN Automobile Federation
ADF	Automotive Development Fund (Malaysia)
AEC	ASEAN Economic Community
AEM	ASEAN Economic Ministers
AEMICC	AEM-MITI/METI Economic and Industrial Cooperation Committee
AFC	Asian Financial Crisis (of 1997)
AFTA	ASEAN Free Trade Area
AIC	ASEAN Industrial Complementation scheme
AICO	ASEAN Industrial Cooperation
AOTS	Association for Overseas Technical Cooperation and Sustainable Partnerships (of Japan)
APEC	Asia Pacific Economic Cooperation
ASEAN	Association of Southeast Asian Nations
ATIGA	ASEAN Trade in Goods Agreement
BBC	Brand-to-Brand Complementation scheme
CARS	Comprehensive Automotive Resurgence Strategy (the Philippines)
CAMPI	Chamber of Automotive Manufactures of the Philippines
CBU	Completely Built-Up
CEPT	Common Effective Preferential Tariff (of AFTA)
CKD	Completely Knocked Down
CLMV	Cambodia, Laos, Myanmar and Vietnam
CV	Commercial Vehicle
EEV	Energy-Efficient Vehicle
EPA	Economic Partnership Agreement
ERP	Effective Rate of Protection
EU	European Union
EV	Electric Vehicle
FDI	Foreign Direct Investment
FTI	Federation of Thai Industries
FTA	Free Trade Agreement
GAIKINDO	Association of Indonesian Automotive Industries

GIAMM	Indonesian Automotive Parts and Components Industries Association
GATS	General Agreement on Trade in Services (of WTO)
GATT	General Agreement on Tariffs and Trade (forerunner of WTO)
GM	General Motors
GPN	Global Production Network
GVC	Global Value Chain
HS	Harmonised System (of trade classification)
HEV	Hybrid Electric Vehicle
IAP	Industrial Adjustment Fund (Malaysia)
IKD	Incompletely Knocked Down (Indonesia)
ILP	Industrial Linkage Programme (Malaysia)
IMF	International Monetary Fund
IMV	Innovative International Multipurpose Vehicle
ISI	Import-Substituting Industrialisation
ISO	International Organization for Standardization
JAMA	Japan Automobile Manufacturers Association
JETRO	Japan External Trade Organization
JICA	Japan International Cooperation Agency
JODC	Japan Overseas Development Corporation
JV	Joint Venture
LC	Local Content
LCE	Low Carbon Emission
LCGC	Low Cost Green Car (Indonesia)
LCR	Local Content Requirement
MAA	Malaysian Automotive Association
MACPMA	Malaysian Automotive Components Parts Manufacturers Association
MAJAICO	Malaysia-Japan Automotive Industry Cooperation
MDP	Mandatory Deletion Programme
METI	Ministry of Economy, Trade and Industry (Japan)
MFN	Most-Favoured Nation (tariff)
MIT1	Ministry of International Trade and Industry (Japan, replaced by METI)
MNC	Multinational Corporation
MPV	Multipurpose Vehicle
MVPMAP	Motor Vehicle Parts Manufacturers Association of the Philippines
NAFTA	North American Free Trade Agreement
NAP	National Automotive Plan (Malaysia)
NCP	National Car Project (Malaysia)
NEP	New Economic Policy (Malaysia)
NIEs	Newly Industrialised Economies
NRP	Nominal Rate of Protection
NTB	Non-Tariff Barrier
OBM	Original Brand Manufacturer

ODA	Official Development Assistance
ODM	Original Design Manufacturer
OEM	Original Equipment Manufacturer
OICA	Organisation Internationale des Constructeurs d'Automobiles
PHEV	Plug-in Hybrid Electric Vehicle
PV	Passenger Vehicle
R&D	Research and Development
SAP	Structural Adjustment Programme
SCMs	Agreement on Subsidies and Countervailing Measures (of WTO)
SMEs	Small and Medium Sized Enterprises
SUV	Sport Utility Vehicle
TAIA	Thai Automotive Industry Association
TAPMA	Thai Auto-Parts Manufacturers Association
TRIMs	Agreement on Trade-Related Investment Measures (of WTO)
TRIPs	Agreement on Trade-Related Intellectual Property Rights (of WTO)
UNCTAD	United Nations Conference on Trade and Development
USBTA	United States Bilateral Trade Agreement (with Vietnam)
VAMA	Vietnam Automobile Manufacturers' Association
VDP	Vendor Development Programme (Malaysia)
VW	Volkswagen
WTO	World Trade Organization

1 Introduction

The global automotive industry

The automotive industry[1] is the archetypal way in which many developing countries have tried to move beyond simple labour-intensive activities, such as garments and textiles, towards ones which require – and generate – higher levels of technology and labour skills. The industry, which started as automotive assembly based on imported kits of parts, now offers opportunities for further industrialisation through the use of locally produced parts instead of imported ones. Since the late 1980s, global automotive production and exports have grown rapidly in association with foreign direct investment (FDI) from automotive multinational corporations (MNCs) in developing countries.

Global automotive production increased by over 37 million between 2000 and 2018, reaching a total of 95.6 million vehicles (Table 1.1). During this period, a striking global shift occurred in the industry. Firstly, in North America, Western Europe, and Japan, vehicle demand has become saturated and reliant on replacement purchases. In fact, all developed countries showed negative growth in the period 2000–2018 (see Table 1.1). Although the USA (–12%), Japan (–4%), Germany (–7%), Spain (–7%), and UK (–12%), to some extent, have maintained their vehicle production, France (–32%), Italy (–39%), and Canada (–32%) have seen significant falls in their global production shares.

Secondly, automotive production has been growing rapidly in developing countries, particularly in Asia. Automotive MNCs have been relocating to emerging economies in order to reduce transport costs, to take advantage of lower-cost labour, and to service their rapidly growing markets. Remarkable growth of automotive production has occurred in China, India, Mexico, Thailand, Turkey, Iran, the Czech Republic, Indonesia, and Slovakia. Among them, China, India, Turkey, Iran, and Indonesia, with large populations, have developed in order to meet their rapidly growing domestic demand. In this context, the automotive industry first developed as a domestically oriented industry. In Mexico and Thailand, in contrast, the automotive industry is based on both a large domestic market and on export. In Mexico, from the 1980s, American automotive MNCs in particular have relocated to build export platforms for North American markets, and this regional division of labour accelerated under the North American Free

Table 1.1 Total Vehicle Production and Shares of Top 20 Countries and ASEAN Producers, 2000–2018

	2018			2000			2000–2018	
Country	*Rank*	*Production*	*Share (%)*	*Rank*	*Production*	*Share (%)*	*2018: 2000*	*Growth (%)*
World	–	95,634,593	100	–	58,374,162	100	1.64	64
China	1	27,809,196	29.1	8	2,069,069	3.5	13.44	1,244
USA	2	11,314,705	11.8	1	12,799,857	21.9	0.88	-12
Japan	3	9,728,528	10.2	2	10,140,796	17.4	0.96	–4
India	4	5,174,645	5.4	15	801,360	1.4	6.46	546
Germany	5	5,120,409	5.4	3	5,526,615	9.5	0.93	–7
Mexico	6	4,100,525	4.3	9	1,935,527	3.3	2.12	112
South Korea	7	4,028,834	4.2	5	3,114,998	5.3	1.29	29
Brazil	8	2,879,809	3.0	12	1,681,517	2.9	1.71	71
Spain	9	2,819,565	2.9	6	3,032,874	5.2	0.93	-7
France	10	2,270,000	2.4	4	3,348,361	5.7	0.68	-32
Thailand	11	2,167,694	2.3	19	411,721	0.7	5.26	426
Canada	12	2,020,840	2.1	7	2,961,636	5.1	0.68	-32
Russia	13	1,767,674	1.8	13	1,205,581	2.1	1.47	47
UK	14	1,604,328	1.7	10	1,813,894	3.1	0.88	-12
Turkey	15	1,550,150	1.6	18	430,947	0.7	3.60	260
Czech Rep.	16	1,345,041	1.4	17	455,492	0.8	2.95	195
Indonesia	17	1,343,714	1.4	25	292,710	0.5	4.59	359
Iran	18	1,095,526	1.1	27	277,985	0.5	3.94	294
Slovakia	19	1,090,000	1.1	30	181,783	0.3	6.00	500
Italy	20	1,060,068	1.1	11	1,738,315	3.0	0.61	-39
Malaysia	23	564,800	0.6	26	282,830	0.5	2.00	100
Vietnam	–	237,000	0.2	–	6,862	0.01	34.54	3,354
The Philippines	–	79,763	0.1	–	41,840	0.1	1.91	91

Source: OICA (website: www.oica.net) for 2000, and 2018 production is from Fourin (2019: 61).

Note: Number of vehicles.

Trade Agreement (NAFTA) since 1994 (Humphrey and Memedovic 2003). In Central and Eastern Europe, the two largest producers –the Czech Republic and Slovakia – both have small domestic populations, and hence the automotive industry has grown as an export-oriented activity, selling to Western Europe, taking advantage of lower-cost labour and of their geographical proximity to the market. In particular, both countries have specialised in passenger vehicle (PV) production with the privatisation of state-owned enterprises in the early 1990s, and have later attracted FDI from European, Japanese, and Korean automotive MNCs in the 2000s (Natsuda *et al.* 2020b).

In Asia, China, and to a lesser extent India, have been the most obvious beneficiaries of these global shifts – China's vehicle output increased more than 13-fold between 2000 and 2018 and India's by nearly 6.5-fold. In Southeast Asia, the major vehicle producers within the membership of the ASEAN are the 'ASEAN-4' (Thailand, Indonesia, Malaysia, and the Philippines), joined more recently by Vietnam. Thailand and Indonesia were ranked in the top 20 producing countries in the world in 2018. Thailand (at 11th) produced over 2.1 million vehicles and Indonesia (at 17th) was producing over 1.3 million in 2018. Malaysia (at 23rd) produced over 0.5 million, followed by Vietnam (over 0.2 million) and the Philippines (only 79,736 vehicles).

Global automotive producers

Table 1.2 shows major automotive producers in the world in 2000 and 2017. The global production of vehicles has increased 1.7-fold during this period. We can identify some important features in the global automotive industry. Firstly, a relatively small number of automotive MNCs dominate the industry. The top five producers in the world accounted for 49.7% production in 2000 and 42.6% in 2017, and the top ten producers for 72.2% in 2000 and 66.8% in 2017. Although the share of top producers slightly decreased between 2000 and 2017, it remained still high. Indeed, the top 20 firms produced 87.7% of global production in 2017.

Secondly, most automotive MNCs in developed countries have increased their output, while only three firms (GM, Ford, and Mitsubishi) decreased their production between 2000 and 2017. In response to this, these firms have needed to conduct harsh restructuring. General Motors (GM) announced about 15,000 job cuts with the closing down of five factories in North America in November 2018.[2] In the case of Ford, it announced global lay-offs of 7,000 white-collar employees (saving US$600 million) in May 2019,[3] and additionally there were 12,000 job-cuts in Europe with the closing down of six factories by the end of 2020, announced in June 2019.[4] In the case of Mitsubishi, it was merged with Nissan in October 2016 and integrated into the Renault-Nissan alliance.

Thirdly, firms from emerging countries, particularly China and India, have been growing rapidly. Five Chinese firms were included among the top 20 firms in 2017. These firms started taking over well-established brands in the developed countries. For instance, China's Geely took over Volvo (in Sweden) in 2010. Similarly, India's Tata (the 23rd largest producer in the world in 2017) took over British Jaguar Land Rover in 2008. These two locally owned automotive firms from emerging countries have started playing a major role in the global automotive industry in recent years.

Fourthly, and despite the falls in the shares of the production of the top five and the top ten firms between 2000 and 2017, the industry has become more concentrated as mergers and acquisitions (M&A) have accelerated. Some dozen large companies like Toyota and Volkswagen (VW) dominate, and often such large companies have grown through absorbing many previously independent brands. For instance, the Toyota group (Japan) consists of three firms: Toyota, Daihatsu for small PVs, and Hino for commercial vehicles (CVs). By the same token, the VW group consists of VW, Audi, and Porsche (Germany); Seat (Spain); Skoda (Czech Republic); Bentley (UK); and Buggati (France) for PVs, and Man (Germany) and Scania (Sweden) for CVs. The other type of change is the formation of strategic alliances such as the Renault-Nissan-Mitsubishi alliance and

Table 1.2 Major Global Automotive Producers, 2000 and 2017

		2017			*2000*			*2000–2017*	
Group	*Country of Origin*	*Rank*	*Production*	*Share (%)*	*Rank*	*Production*	*Share (%)*	*2017:2000*	*Growth (%)*
World	–	–	96,922,080	100	–	58,392,376	100	1.66	66.0
Toyota	Japan	1	10,466,051	10.8	3	5,954,723	10.2	1.76	75.8
Volkswagen (VW)	Germany	2	10,382,334	10.7	4	5,106,749	8.7	2.03	103.3
Hyundai	Korea	3	7,218,391	7.4	11	2,488,321	4.3	2.90	190.1
General Motors (GM)	USA	4	6,856,880	7.1	1	8,133,375	13.9	0.84	–15.7
Ford	USA	5	6,386,818	6.6	2	7,322,951	12.5	0.87	–12.8
Nissan	Japan	6	5,769,277	6.0	8	2,628,783	4.5	2.19	119.5
Honda	Japan	7	5,236,842	5.4	10	2,505,256	4.3	2.09	109.0
Fiat-Chrysler	Italy/USA	8	4,600,847	4.7	7	2,641,444	4.5	1.74	74.2
Renault	France	9	4,153,589	4.3	9	2,514,897	4.3	1.65	65.2
PSA	France	10	3,649,742	3.8	6	2,879,422	4.9	1.27	26.8
Suzuki	Japan	11	3,302,336	3.4	13	1,457,056	2.5	2.27	126.6
SAIC	China	12	2,866,913	3.0	n.a.	n.a.	n.a.	n.a.	n.a.
Daimler AG	Germany	13	2,549,142	2.6	4*	4,666,640	8.0	0.55	–45.4
BMW	Germany	14	2,505,741	2.6	15	834,628	1.4	3.00	200.2
Geely	China	15	1,950,382	2.0	n.a.	n.a.	n.a.	n.a.	n.a.
Changan	China	16	1,616,457	1.7	20	203,127	0.3	7.96	695.8
Mazda	Japan	17	1,607,602	1.7	14	925,876	1.6	1.74	73.6
Dongfeng Motor	China	18	1,450,999	1.5	24	157,038	0.3	9.24	824.0
BAIC	China	19	1,254,483	1.3	25	124,824	0.2	10.05	905.0
Mitsubishi	Japan	20	1,210,263	1.2	12	1,827,186	3.1	0.66	–33.8
Others	–	–	11,886,991	12.3	–	6,020,080	10.3	1.97	97.5

Source: OICA (website: www.oica.net).

Note: Number of vehicles, * including Chrysler, n.a. (not available). Daimler output fell only because link with Chrysler ended.

Fiat-Chrysler alliance. Most Recently, Fiat-Chrysler and PSA (Peugeot and Citroen) announced the plan of the merger between two firms to create the fourth largest automotive company in December 2019.[5] It is important to note that international M&A and alliances are increasingly important for automotive producers in order to reduce the heavy costs of new vehicle development and R&D activities. Many groups and alliances including Nissan and Renault share the same platform for different models. In addition, original equipment manufacturer (OEM) arrangements between manufacturers are an increasingly important strategy. For instance, Toyota contracts their affiliate Daihatsu to produce and share the same model but using a different brand name. Furthermore, their R&D centre has been established jointly for the development of their models in Southeast Asia (see Chapter 4).

It is worth noting too that new automotive technologies such as the development of electric vehicles (EVs) and autonomous driving (AD) systems have been forcing automotive producers to form new alliances. In Japan, Toyota has been very active in forming capital and technological alliances with relatively small independent producers like Mazda, Subaru and Suzuki since 2017.[6] Toyota, Mazda, and Denso jointly established a firm, 'EV C.A. Spirit' in September 2017, in order to develop electric PVs, sport utility vehicles (SUVs), and small trucks by combining *Toyota New Global Architecture*, Mazda's ***model-based development*** skills, and Denso's electronics technology.[7] In addition, Toyota and Mazda undertook capital cooperation by partially exchanging equity (Toyota took 5.05% of Mazda's equity, and Mazda took 0.25% of Toyota's equity) in August 2017.[8] In addition, Toyota and Subaru (20% of whose equity has been held by Toyota since 2005) agreed in June 2019 to jointly develop electric SUVs. They are planning to develop common platforms as the first step and to release a model under both brand names in the early 2020s.[9] Similarly, Toyota and Suzuki agreed to set up capital and technical cooperation in August 2019.[10] In terms of capital cooperation, Toyota took 4.9% of Suzuki's equity, while Suzuki acquired 0.2% of Toyota's equity. In terms of technical cooperation, Toyota provides its hybrid electric vehicle (HEV) system to Suzuki and jointly develops EV and AD technology with Suzuki. In Germany, Audi joined BMW and Mercedes to form formal collaboration for AD technology in August 2019. In addition, VW collaborated with Ford for AD technology.[11]

Global automotive suppliers

Another important structural change in the global automotive industry involves the supply chain networks of automotive producers. In the past, the US and European assemblers used to employ market linkages (market competition) with suppliers. Typically, Ford and GM used market competition among their suppliers in order to lower their input costs, typically switching suppliers with little advance notice (Sturgeon *et al.* 2009). By contrast, Japanese assemblers have long been using long-term, captive relationships with their suppliers, with several tiers of suppliers in their vertically oriented supply chain networks (Thoburn and Takashima 1992: ch. 5). In competition with Japanese producers, in the 1980s and 1990s, the assembler-supplier relationship in the US and European firms has significantly changed, with the reduction of in-house production levels and the transfer of design functions to their leading suppliers (Humphrey and Memedovic 2003). In this context, automotive assemblers have become more and more focussed on assembly alone, buying-in most of their components. The production of components is organised in a series of tiers in Western countries and Japan nowadays, and also increasingly in developing country automotive producers. Many Tier-1 suppliers, like Denso from Japan or Bosch from Germany, have become major multinationals in their own right – 'mega-suppliers' – and they help organise the smaller, lower-tier producers who make simpler parts. Such Tier-1 suppliers often 'follow-source' the assemblers for whom they work, setting up component production in the countries where the assemblers have established vehicle assembly.

Table 1.3 shows the top 20 automotive suppliers in the world in 2017. Bosch (in Germany) is the largest supplier, followed by Denso (in Japan) and Magna (in Canada). Of the top twenty suppliers, seven firms are from Japan, six firms from Germany, three firms from North America, two firms from France, and one firm each from Korea and China. Of the top 100 suppliers in the world, five firms are

Table 1.3 Top 20 Automotive Parts Suppliers in the World, 2017

Ranking	*Firm*	*Country of Origin*	*Global OEM Automotive Parts Sales*	*Share North America*	*Share Europe*	*Share Asia*	*Share Others*
1	Bosch	Germany	47,500	16	45	37	2
2	Denso	Japan	40,782	23	13	63	1
3	Magna	Canada	38,946	54	38	7	1
4	Continental	Germany	35,910	25	49	22	4
5	ZF	Germany	34,481	27	48	21	4
6	Aisin	Japan	33,837	17	10	72	1
7	Hyundai Mobis	Korea	24,984	20	14	62	4
8	Lear	USA	20,467	38	40	18	4
9	Valeo	France	19,360	21	47	30	2
10	Faurecia	France	19,170	26	50	17	7
11	Adient	USA	16,200	31	26	43	0
12	Yazaki	Japan	15,754	26	17	52	5
13	Panasonic Automotive	Japan	14,995	30	14	56	0
14	Sumitomo Electric	Japan	14,872	23	n.a.	n.a.	n.a.
15	Mahle	Germany	14,441	26	48	20	6
16	Yanfeng	China	14,278	19	12	69	0
17	Toyota Boshoku	Japan	13,444	14	5	79	2
18	JTEKT	Japan	12,709	19	16	59	2
19	ThyssenKrupp	Germany	12,591	25	65	8	2
20	BASF	Germany	12,157	24	45	22	9

Source: Crain Communications (2018).

Note: US$ Million, share (%), n.a. (not available).

from China, and one firm each is from India and Mexico (Crain Communications 2018). Unlike the assembly industry, emerging countries seem to be rather limited in their presence in automotive parts.

New technology movements in the automotive industry

Due to rapid advances in technological innovation, the global automotive industry seems to be entering a turning point. Sometimes described under the heading of '*CASE* (Connected, Autonomous, Shared, and Electrified)' technologies, a number of new developments are expected to be the used in the next generation of vehicles.[12] Of the various new technologies, three – Industry 4.0 and robotics, electric mobility, and AD systems – are highly relevant in the Southeast Asian context. Firstly, Industry 4.0 and robotics have been increasingly becoming an important set of technologies not only for developed countries but also for emerging countries in recent years. With regard to global robot sales of 381,335 units in 2017, the top five purchasing countries – China (137,900 units and 36.2% of the total), Japan (45,566 units and 11.9%), Korea (39,732 units and 10.4%), USA (33,192 units and 8.7%), and Germany (21,404 units and 5.6%) – account for a total share of over 72% of world purchases (IFR 2018: 14–15). In particular, the automotive industry has become the largest customer for industrial robotics since 2010 due to its demand for automation technology, accounting for approximately 125,700 units (and 33%) in 2017. Indeed, the sales of robots have increased by 14% on average per year over the period 2012–2017 (ibid.: 16). In emerging countries, for instance in the Central European region, MNCs, which looked for low-cost labour, are currently facing rapid wage rises and labour shortages. In such countries, the use of automation technology is one of the most effective solutions (see Natsuda *et al.* 2020a). In Southeast Asia, Vietnam, perhaps surprisingly, has become the seventh largest customer in the world: its purchases jumped from about 1,600 units to 8,300 units in 2017, though this was thanks to the growth of its electronics rather than its automotive industry. Thailand accounted for 3,400 units in 2017 (IFR 2018: 15). Indeed, demand for robotics in Thailand is surging in the automotive industry.[13]

Secondly, electric mobility is another new force for change in the automotive industry.[14] Among the above-mentioned three technologies, electric mobility is particularly important in terms of this book, because it is already integrated as part of the latest automotive industrial policies in Thailand, Indonesia, and Malaysia. There are three types of electric mobility technologies: HEVs, plug-in hybrid electric vehicles (PHEVs), and EVs. HEVs have been available in the market since the late 1990s (Toyota's Prius model is probably the best known), followed by the mass production of PHEVs and EVs starting in the 2000s (e.g. Renault's Elect'road, Kangoo model in 2003, and Tesla in 2004). Due to environmental concerns, the electric mobility movement will be one of the key issues in the automotive industry in the future.[15] In July 2017, France announced that a ban on sales of gasoline and diesel engine vehicles would be implemented by 2040,[16] and similar moves have been followed by the UK[17] and others. In Southeast

Asia, the Thai government announced an EV action plan (2016–2036) in 2016 to enhance the production of EVs and PHEVs, with a target to have 1.2 million such vehicles in use by 2036 (Fourin 2017: 42–43, also see Chapter 5 of this book). In Malaysia, the government promoted energy-efficient vehicles (EEVs) under its National Automotive Plan (NAP) in 2014 (see Chapter 7). However, it was not only to facilitate electric mobility but also to target standards for gasoline, diesel, and LPG engine vehicles with low emissions (Fourin 2017: 88–89). Similarly, the Indonesian government encourages various types of low emission vehicles including electric mobility technology under the low carbon emission (LCE) scheme of 2013 (ibid.: 66, also see Chapter 6 of this book). In this context, it is apparent that a gradual shift to electric mobility will occur in Southeast Asia over the next 20 years.

Thirdly, AD technology is the latest technology in the automotive industry. It is still under development by major vehicle producers such as Audi, BMW, Ford, GM, Honda, Mercedes, Tesla, Toyota, and VW in collaboration with leading IT-related firms like Apple, Baidu, Google, and Uber (Chang *et al.* 2016: 5). The development of AD technology includes two challenges: (1) standardisation of safety assurance and (2) scalability (engineering solutions that lead to high costs will not scale to millions of vehicles) (Shalev-Shwartz *et al.* 2017). In the introduction of AD technology in Southeast Asia, Thailand, the largest automotive producer, faces three barriers: (1) incompatibility between Thai regulations and the AD system, (2) infrastructure (poor urban planning), and (3) not yet strong-enough market demand for the system. In Indonesia, traffic congestion is one of the major challenges. In the Philippines, regulation reform is necessary. In Malaysia, however, REKA (a research and development firm) commenced a project on the AD system. Furthermore, the Vietnamese government is said to be keen on the technology in alignment with Industry 4.0.[18]

Themes and aims of this book

Developing countries have used active industrial policy to accelerate automotive development faster than reliance on free market forces could achieve. Active industrial policy was strongly advocated in the 1950s–1970s period, and principally consisted of import substitution of both imported vehicles and of parts – parts production being made easier by the fact that a typical car has several thousand individual components. Such substitution was reinforced by local content requirements (LCRs), and sometimes by mandatory deletion programmes (MDPs), where certain imported parts had to be 'deleted' from imported kits of components and produced locally. Assembly itself was protected by high import tariffs, usually higher than the tariffs on components, thus generating often far higher levels of *effective protection* (that is, protection on value-added) than the nominal tariffs indicated. Industrial policy went out of fashion in the 1980s and 1990s under the influence of the so-called 'Washington consensus' view of development through free-market forces, but since then it has made a substantial comeback, and its importance is now widely accepted.

As a consequence of the tariff protection of automotive production under import-substituting industrialisation (ISI) policies, automotive MNCs wishing to penetrate ASEAN or other developing country markets have set up local assembly. Within ASEAN, such assembly often dates back to the 1950s and 1960s, predating the more recent large increases in production and exports from ASEAN. Nowadays, as automotive assemblers have grown larger and more powerful, Japanese assemblers have come to dominate production within the ASEAN motor industry. The bulk of Japanese automotive production growth in recent years has taken place outside of Japan, and ASEAN is now a key part of Japanese automotive assemblers' regional production networks. As ISI fell out of favour in international development thinking after the 1970s, and particularly in the 1990s, ASEAN countries have been moving towards trade liberalisation. Then, from 2000, new rules from the WTO, especially under its TRIMs (trade-related investment measures) provisions, outlawed LCRs and MDPs. Moves towards trade liberalisation within ASEAN were strongly reinforced by the ASEAN Free Trade Area (AFTA), under which trade in vehicles and components within most countries in the region became free from 2010,[19] and later by the ASEAN Economic Community (AEC) in 2015.

Not only is the ASEAN automotive industry worth studying in its own right, it also provides rich lessons for how industrial policy can be conducted in the context of global and regional value chains and production networks. Looking at industrial policy, both under past import substitution and in the more recent context of trade liberalisations, the book considers how far inward automotive investment, especially from Japan, has been affected by policies, and how far such investment has promoted local automotive development in the late-industrialising Southeast Asian host economies.

The aims of this book are as follows. Firstly, the book aims to examine the development of the automotive industry in five ASEAN countries (Thailand, Indonesia, Malaysia, the Philippines, and Vietnam) in historical perspective. Until the 1980s, the production volume of the automotive industry was very similar in each of ASEAN countries (except Vietnam, whose production was very small). However, from the 1990s the automotive industry has developed differently in different ASEAN countries. Thailand and Indonesia have grown rapidly, while Malaysia has been stagnating, and the Philippines has failed to grow. Vietnam has joined as a significant new vehicle producer in the region. This book analyses what are the main drivers of success or failure in the automotive industry in the region. We seek to answer this question by comparing the main five ASEAN vehicle producers.[20] Historically, Malaysia has pursued a strong state-led development model by using a direct method of market intervention – creating *national car producers* in cooperation with foreign capital as a source of technology. By contrast, Thailand, Indonesia, and the Philippines have facilitated the development of the industry by attracting automotive MNCs. In addition, Vietnam entered into commercial automotive production in the 1990s. Although the methods of state intervention differed between Malaysia and the other countries in Southeast Asia, all countries used industrial policy for the development of their automotive industries. As a result, local supporting industry was established. However, in the late 1990s and early 2000s, when liberalisation policy was enforced in the ASEAN automotive industry under the WTO, there resulted some significant changes in strategy for the industry.

The second aim of this book is to explore automotive industrial policies in ASEAN countries by analysing how each country employed its policies and then adjusted them in response to the new WTO rules. Before the liberalisation period, all ASEAN-4 countries used 'hard' (directive) industrial policies such as LCRs in their early stages of post-war ISI, along with MDPs, often encouraging further inward FDI by component manufacturers. The component production stimulated by LCRs and MDPs, however, outlasted their outlawing under the WTO from the early 2000s. Since liberalisation, the ASEAN-4 countries have introduced new automotive industrial policies: Automotive Master Plans (AMPs) in Thailand, the Low Cost Green Car (LCGC) project in Indonesia, the National Automotive Plan (NAP) in Malaysia, and the Comprehensive Automotive Resurgence Strategy (CARS) in the Philippines. In addition, this book investigates how Vietnam has been adjusting its automotive development policy in relation to AFTA and, more recently, under the AEC.[21]

The third aim of this book is to examine the role of Japanese automotive MNCs in Southeast Asia. Japanese automotive MNCs control over 80% of vehicle production in the region. They have used various strategies in order to acquire and maintain their market share. In addition, they have played a role as one of the main actors in ASEAN regional integration. We explore the relationship between Japanese automotive MNCs, the Japanese government, and ASEAN governments from the perspective of regional integration arrangements in ASEAN. In addition, the book also explores how local supporting industry in ASEAN was established in association with foreign capital firms, again, particularly Japanese automotive MNCs.

The structure of this book

With the main aim of analysing the historical and current development of the automotive industry in Southeast Asia, with particular reference to industrial policy, this book first considers the theoretical context for industrial policy debates and global value chains (GVCs) in terms of the automotive industry. It then provides an overview of the industry in Southeast Asia, Japanese automotive MNCs, and Japanese government policy towards Southeast Asia, including regional integration arrangements within the region. The study further sets out case studies of five countries (Thailand, Indonesia, Malaysia, the Philippines, and Vietnam). An outline of specific chapter content follows.

Chapter 2 examines theoretical approaches which account for the development of the automotive industry in Southeast Asia. It begins with industrial policy debates between neoliberal and statist views of economic (industrial) development. The first issue is whether Southeast Asian countries are developmental states or not. Although Southeast Asian countries seem to be rather different from Northeast Asian developmental states, the former can be classified as neo-developmental states in the sense that they have been employing vertically oriented hard industrial policies for their development. The second issue concerns 'policy space' debates in international political economy. With the rise of the WTO, moves towards a more strongly free-market policy stance have been affecting developing countries by reducing their policy options. There is no doubt that policy space has diminished in the automotive industry in Southeast Asia. Nonetheless, policy options are not as constrained as might first appear: some policy options can be still available. Secondly, this chapter examines the global value chain concept in relation to the automotive industry. The GVC concept is strongly interested in issues of industrial upgrading. In automotive assembly operations, there are several stages of industrial upgrading. With regards to assembler and supplier relations, some studies are optimistic about the industrial upgrading of local suppliers, while other studies are rather negative, claiming that the emergence of global mega-suppliers and tendencies towards long-term collaborative relationships between assemblers and such suppliers hinder upgrading opportunities for locally owned firms. In addition, more recently, the GVC literature has started to pay attention to the role of industrial policy to enhance industrial upgrading by local suppliers, as well as dealing with lead firms in the context of the growth of regional production networks.

Chapter 3 presents an overview of the automotive industry in Southeast Asia. The industry in Southeast Asia (particularly in Thailand and Indonesia) has been growing rapidly in the last few decades. This chapter then explores the production, sales, and R&D activities of major automotive producers of Japanese, US, European, Korean, and local origin in the region. Some Japanese automotive multinational corporations have been increasingly strengthening cooperation with their affiliated firms or strategic partner firms in the region. Important US automotive MNCs have restructured their regional operations by centralising their production operation on Thailand in recent years. Korean and European firms both depend on small-scale subcontracting arrangements with local firms in the region for assembling their completely knocked down (CKD) kits. In addition, local firms are operating as assemblers in Malaysia and Vietnam. The third issue is the role of locally owned firms in the region's automotive component supply industries. Thailand has the largest number of suppliers in the region, followed by Indonesia, Malaysia, and the Philippines. Local business groups have formed various joint venture (JV) firms with foreign-owned suppliers and diversified their operations in the domestic market. This chapter also shows that some local automotive suppliers in Thailand and Malaysia have upgraded themselves to become multinational suppliers within regional or global production networks. Lastly, the trade performance of the automotive industry in Southeast Asia is examined.

Chapter 4 explores the political economy of the automotive industry in Southeast Asia by analysing the relations between Japanese automotive MNCs, the Japanese government, and ASEAN countries, in order to demonstrate how the regional industrial and trade policies have been shaped. Japanese MNCs, accounting for over 80% of market share in the region, have introduced various production, location, local business, and technology transfer strategies in order to maintain their presence in Southeast Asia. At a multilateral level, the Japanese government assists Japanese MNCs to establish region-wide industrial networks in association with the ASEAN governments. There is an active ASEAN-Japan working group on the automotive industry[22] designed to identify problems and to facilitate automotive regional development, such as the fostering of supporting industries and the promotion of the regional automotive part complementation scheme. In the automotive industry, Japanese automotive MNCs in association with the Japanese government have been playing a significant role in the establishment of the regional arrangements in Southeast Asia. The first successful scheme was the Brand-to-Brand Complementation (BBC) scheme in the late 1980s, followed by the ASEAN Industrial Cooperation (AICO) scheme and AFTA in the 1990s, and most recently the AEC. This chapter examines Toyota's regional production and export strategies as a case study.

Chapter 5 provides an historical perspective on the development of the Thai automotive industry. The Thai automotive development can be classified into five phases. The first phase (1960–1970) is associated with ISI policy. The second phase (1971–1977) is characterised by policy for localisation. The third phase (1978–1990) is associated with policy for strengthening further localisation of the industry. The fourth phase (1991–1999) is characterised by the first liberalisation of the industry. The fifth and latest phase (2000 to the present) is characterised by WTO-compliant policy-making. Since the abolition of LCRs in 2000, now outlawed under the WTO rules, the Thai government has been successfully adjusting to the new environment by shifting its policy orientation towards using effective fiscal policy along with selective state intervention. Policy has focussed on selecting national *product champions* (picking a winning type of vehicle) and, by setting lower excise tax rates for such vehicles, helping to create a particular market demand by domestic consumers. At the same time, the government has provided tax concessions, such as low corporate tax, for attracting investors into national product champion production. Furthermore, sector-specific 'soft' (facilitative) industrial policy such as technology transfer and human resource development also effectively helped to enable the development of the automotive industry in Thailand. Consequently, Thailand has joined the major vehicle producers of the world and has become the most significant vehicle exporter in ASEAN.

Chapter 6 provides an historical perspective on the development of the Indonesian automotive industry. The Indonesian automotive development can be classified into five phases. The first phase (1928–1968) was the early stage of the industry. The second phase (1969–1992) is characterised by the policy for localisation under ISI. The third phase (1993–1998) is associated with an unsuccessful national car project. The fourth phase (1999–2012) is characterised by the liberalisation of the industry under WTO rules. The fifth and latest phase (2013 to the present) is characterised by the new industrial policy of the LCGC project. Until the late 1990s, the development of the industry was slow. After the liberalisation forced by the conditionality of the International Monetary Fund (IMF) and by the WTO, the Indonesian automotive industry has developed steadily, finally producing over a million vehicles in 2012. However, issues such as increased political stability may well have been more important drivers of expansion than simple liberalisation or particular policies, though such policies have become more influential as the investment climate has improved and become 'good enough', and the impact of policies on the attraction of automotive FDI from Japan has been especially important. Although Indonesia lacks effective soft industrial policies, the automotive growth trend is expected to continue with future domestic market growth, and also partly due to Indonesia's new automotive industrial policy in the form of the LCGC project.

Chapter 7 gives a historical account of the development of the Malaysian automotive industry. Malaysian automotive development can be split into three phases. The first phase (1967–1982) is associated with ISI policy. The second phase (1983–2003) is characterised by the state-led national car projects. The third phase (2004 to the present) is characterised by liberalisation of the industry under WTO rules. The Malaysian government actively employed a state-led automotive development policy in the 1980s and 1990s by establishing national car producers. During this time, the Malaysian government provided various discriminatory and protective industrial policies in order to foster the development of the national car producers, especially Proton. The Malaysian policy measurements included the provision of favourable tariff rates and excise duties for national car producers. In addition, the Malaysian government encouraged many *bumiputra* (indigenous, mainly ethnic Malay) entrepreneurs into the automotive industry through the Vendor Development Programme in order to rapidly expand the supporting sector, with provision of subsidies to Proton in particular. However, such strong industrial policy measures in Malaysia needed to be changed in the 2000s under the WTO. The Malaysian government implemented its first liberalisation policy in the automotive sector by lowering tariffs, abolishing local content requirements and discriminatory measures for national car producers, and later introducing the National Automotive Policy in 2006. However, the Malaysian government still has some controversial protectionist policies, such as the Industrial Adjustment Fund (IAF) and the Industrial Linkage Programme (ILP), linked with local content provisions and non-tariff barriers, such as the manufacturing licensing (ML) and Approval Permit (AP) systems.

Chapter 8 considers the historical development of the automotive industry in the Philippines. The Philippines' automotive development can be classified into four phases. The first phase (1951–1972) is associated with ISI policy. The second phase (1973–1995) is characterised by localisation policies such as the Progressive Car Manufacturing Programme (PCMP) in 1973 and the Car Development Programme (CDP) in 1987. The third phase (1996–2002) is characterised by liberalisation of the industry. The fourth phase (2003 to the present) is characterised by the Automotive Export Programme (AEP) in

2003, and, the most recent, the CARS programme in 2015 under WTO rules. The Philippines' series of automotive development policies including PCMP and CDP used various performance requirement policies for assemblers, which now would violate current WTO rules. The Philippines government also was obliged under World Bank conditionality to liberalise the automotive industry by reducing tariffs and abolishing import bans on vehicles, and later by removing foreign exchange requirements in 2001. Local content requirements were abolished under the WTO in 2003. The industry declined throughout the 2000s. Despite the lack of success of industrial policies in the Philippines in terms of automotive assembly, certain types of automotive component production, particularly transmissions, which were established under earlier local content provisions and foreign exchange requirement policies, have become internationally competitive and serve as export platforms within Southeast Asia. The Philippines' other main automotive component export, wiring harnesses (an electrical item), however, possibly owes more to the country's abundance of low-cost but educated labour than to policies *per se*. In 2015, the Philippines' new industrial policy, the CARS programme, hoped to develop the automotive industry further by 2022, with an intended domestic output of over 500,000 vehicles. Certainly the Philippines' economy is expected to grow in the future, but the CARS programme faces various challenges such as low LC ratios, competition from imported second-hand vehicles, and from cars imported under free trade agreements (FTAs).

Chapter 9 provides a historical perspective on the development of the Vietnamese automotive industry. The Vietnamese automotive development can be classified into three phases. The first phase (1990–2006) is the era before joining the WTO. The second phase (2007–2017) is after joining the WTO. The third phase (2018 to the present) is under AEC. Vietnam is a latecomer in the automotive industry in Southeast Asia. Although there was state production of military vehicles in the country from the 1950s, the modern automotive industry dates only from the early 1990s, some 30–40 years behind the other ASEAN vehicle producers. Following the introduction of Vietnam's *doi moi* programme of extensive economic reforms in 1986, and the country's subsequent opening to foreign investment, a substantial number of foreign automotive assemblers started making investment in Vietnam in the early and mid-1990s. By the time Vietnam joined the WTO in 2007, it had already committed itself under AFTA to reducing all its tariffs on imports from its ASEAN neighbours progressively, finally to zero in 2018. The WTO membership involved various rules outlawing the use of LCRs and other TRIMs and also required 'national treatment' for foreign investors, outlawing the imposing of different rates of tax on them compared to domestic producers. In such an environment, the Vietnamese government in 2018 started using a complicated set of non-tariff barriers in order to protect their domestic automotive industry. At the time of writing, there are signs of significant expansion by a large domestic vehicle producer.

Chapter 10 presents our conclusions in terms of the three main aims set out in the present chapter, and ends with discussion of the challenges and prospects for the ASEAN automotive industry.

Notes

1 We do not cover the motor cycle industry in this book, which we regard as a rather separate research topic.
2 *Reuters* (5 February 2019): https://www.reuters.com/article/us-gm-layoffs/gm-cutting-4000-workers-in-latest-round-of-restructuring-idUSKCN1PT21Z [accessed on 2 September 2019].
3 *Business Insider* (20 May 2019): https://www.businessinsider.com/ford-is-cutting-7000-white-collar-jobs-2019-5 [accessed on 2 September 2019].
4 *AP NEWS* (27 June 2019): https://www.apnews.com/e7acce1cc9b14508bc642a4c6a4446fd [accessed on 2 September 2019].
5 *The Guardian* (31 October 2019): https://www.theguardian.com/business/2019/oct/31/fiat-chrysler-and-psa-peugeot-agree-35bn-merger [accessed on 8 January 2020].
6 These firms are not included in Toyota's consolidated accounting.
7 See Toyota's website: https://global.toyota/jp/detail/18839949 [accessed on 30 August 2019].
8 *Chunichi Shinbun* (29 August2019): https://www.chunichi.co.jp/article/front/list/CK2019082902000065.html [accessed on 30 August 2019].
9 *Nikkei Shinbun* (6 June 2019): https://www.nikkei.com/article/DGXMZO45764850W9A600C1000000/ [accessed on 30 August 2019].
10 *Nikkei Shinbun* (28 August 2019): https://www.nikkei.com/article/DGXMZO49090300Y9A820C1000000/ [accessed on 30 August 2019].
11 *Reuters* (25 August 2019): https://www.reuters.com/article/us-volkswagen-audi-bmw-daimler/audi-to-join-mercedes-bmw-development-alliance-paper-idUSKCN1VC0YT [accessed on 16 September 2019].
12 See https://www.automotiveworld.com/articles/c-s-e-future-industry/ [accessed on 16 September 2019].
13 *Bangkok Post* (19 February 2018): https://www.bangkokpost.com/business/1414350/japanese-firm-hails-thai-embrace-of-robotics [accessed on 29 August 2019].
14 In writing this section, we have benefitted particularly from reading Davies *et al.* (2015).
15 Note, however, that electric vehicles do not lessen, and may indeed worsen, urban traffic congestion and pressure on parking space, and they raise problems of the adequacy of countries' electricity generation. Also, electric mobility is not confined to motor vehicles: electrically assisted bicycles are becoming important, particularly in China (Nieuwenhuis and Wells 2015). Public (land) transport too, of course, now often electrically driven, increases mobility and reduces the need for motor vehicles use.
16 *The Guardian* (6 July 2017): https://www.theguardian.com/business/2017/jul/06/france-ban-petrol-diesel-cars-2040-emmanuel-macron-volvo [accessed on 29 August 2019].
17 *The Guardian* (25 July 2017): https://www.theguardian.com/politics/2017/jul/25/britain-to-ban-sale-of-all-diesel-and-petrol-cars-and-vans-from-2040 [accessed on 29 August 2019].
18 CIO's website: https://www.cio.com/article/3309917/the-state-of-autonomous-vehicles-in-southeast-asia.html [accessed on 29 August 2019].
19 Note that from 2010, AFTA became formally known as ATIGA, the *ASEAN Trade in Goods Agreement*; although the term AFTA remained widely used.

20 Some minor assembly of vehicles now is also taking place in some poorer ASEAN countries such as Cambodia (see Chapter 9).

21 Vietnam (along with Cambodia, Myanmar, and Laos) was not subject to intra-ASEAN tariff-free trade until the start of 2018, compared to 2010 for the other members of AFTA.

22 This working group is known as WG-A1. It was set under the auspices of the ASEAN Economic Ministers' (AEM) and the Japanese Ministry of Economy, Trade and Industry's (METI) jointly established *AMEICC*, the AEM-METI Economic and Industrial Cooperation Committee. See https://www.ameicc.org/site/about for an introduction to the origins of AMEICC, and http://www.jama-english.jp/asia/news/2017/vol69/article1.html for its relation to the automotive industry in ASEAN [both accessed on 17 September 2019].

2 Industrial policy, global value chains, and the Southeast Asian automotive industry

Introduction

The focus of this book is on industrial policy in ASEAN's automotive producers. Views on industrial policy have changed considerably over the period since the Second World War. Until the 1970s, industrial policy was strongly associated with import-substituting industrialisation (ISI). In the face of the perceived failure of ISI in many countries, such interventionist industrial policies were replaced in the 1980s by heavily free-market policies, which became known as the 'Washington Consensus', named after the institutions in Washington – the World Bank, the International Monetary Fund (IMF), and the US Treasury Department – which strongly supported them.[1] It has later been recognised that the interventionist policies of countries such as South Korea and Taiwan during the same period, following the earlier lead of Japan – the 'developmental states' – have been rather effective in pushing industrialisation faster than market forces alone would have allowed.[2] Indeed, these policies have been emulated by two other very successful growth performers in the world economy: China from the 1980s, and Vietnam from the 1990s. Nowadays, as Weiss (2016) has noted, industrial policy is 'back on the agenda'. Industrial policy options for developing countries – their 'policy space' – have been constrained, though, by new rules set out under the auspices of the World Trade Organization from the late 1990s and implemented widely in the 2000s (Natsuda and Thoburn 2014).

It also is now widely recognised that, in recent decades, successful exporting by developing countries has required their firms to gain access to global value chains (GVCs) (Gereffi 2014a).

GVCs have helped producers in Southeast and East Asia to grow their exports of labour-intensive products such as garments and footwear. In such products, control (often referred to as 'governance') typically is exercised by global buyers in rich countries, where 'rents' (excess profits) are located mainly at the retail end. In addition to such 'buyer-driven' GVCs, there are also 'producer-driven' GVCs, such as electronics or vehicles, where governance is carried out by the producers (and nowadays also by their global suppliers). The structure of governance influences the possibilities for firms in a GVC to upgrade their products, production processes, and functions – a key concern of the GVC approach.

While the explanatory power of the GVC framework fits buyer-driven chains quite closely, our understanding of producer-driven chains is also facilitated by the Global Production Networks (GPN) approach (Henderson *et al.* 2002, Kimura and Obashi 2011), which stresses horizontal as well as vertical production relations. The GPN approach can also be used to look at *regional* production networks, increasingly common in the automotive industry.

At first sight rather surprisingly, writers on industrial policy on the one hand, and on GVCs and GPNs on the other, have tended to go their separate ways. The GVC literature has stressed 'upgrading' as a fundamental policy objective in a seemingly self-contained analysis. But now, mainly from the 2010s, GVC researchers have started to relate their work to industrial policy issues directly (Gereffi 2014b, Milberg *et al.* 2014, UNIDO 2018). New developments in GVC analysis reflecting the effects of global tensions (*The Economist*, 13 July 2019) and technological developments (World Bank 2017 and 2019) are also in evidence.

This chapter does not attempt a thoroughgoing literature review. Instead we try to pull out various aspects of industrial policy, 'policy space', and GVC/GPN analysis that clarify events in the automotive industry, particularly as they concern ASEAN. Our first section sets out industrial policy issues, starting with how far ASEAN countries can be considered to be developmental states, given that they exhibit many differences from those in East Asia, and moving on to issues of industrial policy and policy space. The next section considers GVC and GPN analysis and how it relates to industrial policy. The third section offers brief conclusions.

Industrial policy

State capacity: Southeast Asia countries as neo-developmental states

Some 30 years ago, various critics of the then 'mainstream' approach to development noted the importance of state guidance and intervention in East Asian economic development, particularly with regard to industrial policy, referring to East Asian countries as *developmental states* (see Amsden 1989, Evans 1995, Johnson 1982, Wade 1990, Weiss 1995, Woo-Cumings 1999). In their view, East Asian industrialisation was brought about not only by market-led growth but also by the role of the state in cooperation with private capital. Economic development in East Asia was achieved by management of the market, industrial strategies, public investment and export strategies in accordance with state-business cooperation. Among these critics, some took a *statist* approach, emphasising the authoritarian aspect of state capacity (Amsden 1989, Johnson 1982, Wade 1990). Others, with a more *institutionalist* approach, acknowledged the 'limits of state strength' (Doner 1992) and stressed the interdependence of state and business (institutional arrangements) – so-called, 'embedded autonomy' (Evans 1995) or 'governed interdependence' (Weiss 1995). One of the most important characteristics of developmental states was their industrial policy. East Asian states targeted particular industries to be developed, the 'picking winners' strategy, which fostered firms to grow from being local champions to becoming global players.

This set of critical analyses was based on empirical studies of Northeast Asian countries: Japan, Korea, and Taiwan. However, there are some important differences between Northeast Asia and Southeast Asia, the regional focus of our work. Booth (1999: 313) has shown that Northeast Asian countries have used state intervention not just for removing policy-induced distortions but also for coordinating and subsidising private investment. In contrast, Southeast Asian countries have sometimes used subsidies for either political cronyism or to achieve non-economic goals, such as the promotion of indigenous (e.g. non-ethnic-Chinese) business. In this sense, it seems difficult to sustain entirely the argument that industry policy has been used systematically for development purposes throughout Southeast Asia. In the view of Phongpaichit, it is difficult to fit Thailand, for example, into the developmental state model, with the country's notoriously weak development planning; yet it is also wrong to assume that the Thai government did nothing to facilitate industrial expansion, even though the Thai economy seemed to expand without the need for the 'prodding' of a strong 'developmental state'. Therefore, it can be described as neither wholly state-interventionist nor *laissez-faire*. In comparison with Northeast Asia, Southeast Asian countries seemed to adopt relatively less state-interventionist policies because they have not established the political and administrative conditions of a strong state. Nonetheless, their willingness to pursue state-led economic development continues (Phongpaichit 1996: 373–381). Rock (2001) acknowledged the significant role of the Thai government, claiming that selective (or 'vertical') industrial policy in the vehicle export industry in Thailand was used systematically and effectively in collaboration with foreign investors.

It is true that Southeast Asian countries have implemented less elaborate, less efficient and less effective industry policies in the sense that state intervention in Southeast Asia has been far more abused, and often seriously compromised, by political and influential business interests (Suffian 2020). At the same time, the role of industrial policy in Southeast Asian countries is undeniable, and their structural transformation and industrialisation have gone beyond what would have been achieved by relying exclusively on market forces (Jomo 2001a: 9, 2001b: 480–481). In this context, Kim and Lee (2000: 89) explained that Southeast Asian countries were not able to reduce the role of the state in their economy. State-intervention has been an effective and necessary way of escaping from being 'dependent peripheral' economies. Their motivation for economic liberalisation and participation in globalisation has been based not on the creation of a purely *laissez-faire* market, but in bidding for more foreign investment in their countries. Similarly, Jomo *et al.* (1997: 157) argued that industrial policies in Southeast Asia, by promoting foreign investment inflows, compensated for weaknesses in national economies such as deficiencies in terms of having a local industrial entrepreneurial community, managerial expertise, technological capacity, and international marketing networks.

Similarly to Northeast Asia, then, Southeast Asia's economic development has not been based on a *laissez-faire* market economy. The governments in both Northeast Asia and Southeast Asia have played an active role in industrialisation and pursued economic development based on common *developmentalism*. To this extent, Southeast Asian countries could be regarded as 'neo-developmental states'. In the automotive industry in Southeast Asia, each country has been introducing active industrial policy in order to upgrade the industry since the 1960s. Chapters 5–9 of this book explore automotive industrial policies in five ASEAN countries from a historical perspective.

Industrial policy debates[3]

Warwick (2013: 16) defines industrial policy as

> any type of intervention or government policy that attempts to improve the business environment or to alter the structure of economic activity toward sectors, technologies or tasks that are expected to offer better prospects for economic growth or societal welfare than would occur in the absence of such intervention.

With regard to state intervention, Justin Lin and Ha-Joon Chang provide an influential and useful debate (Lin and Chang 2009). Although both agree on the need for government support, their views on the role of the state are significantly different. In Lin's view, there needs to be a 'facilitating state' that will intervene in the economy to take account of externalities and market imperfections, but will encourage industries according to the country's comparative advantage, which will change gradually over time as capital accumulates and technology is acquired. Lin contrasts his own approach with *comparative advantage-defying* strategies, which he attributes to advocates like Chang (Lin and Chang 2009: 487). Lin emphasises the role of state in supporting innovation and industrial upgrading, and correcting for short-term market failures within a (broadly) neoclassical approach. Chang's view is far stronger in relation to state intervention, with the emphasis on active state roles and selective industrial policy.

Since the Second World War, industrial policy was used by many countries in order to promote dynamic structural change – from agriculture to labour-intensive industry – and then to upgrade to capital- and technology-intensive industries faster than market forces alone would do (UNIDO 2013: ch.7). In the early stages of industrialisation, many developing countries used import-substituting industrialisation policies to foster local infant industries by using combinations of tariffs, import quotas, and quite often subsidies – policies, which Chang (2002) observes, also were used by most industrial countries in their own industrialisation. While East Asia continued to achieve significant economic development – and international competitiveness in exporting – by using industrial policy, such policy largely fell out from the development agenda of many countries due to the rise of the free-market fundamentalism of the Washington Consensus in the 1980s and 1990s.

A significant event during this period was the establishment of the World Trade Organization (WTO).

The WTO rules

The WTO agreements have lessened the policy space, or range of policy options, in developing countries in recent years (Chang 2002, Gallagher 2005, Khan 2007, UNDP 2005, Wade 2003). In this context, some researchers, such as Lee and Han (2006) and Moon and Rhyu (2000), are pessimistic in relation to the role of the state in the WTO era, arguing that such policy reforms resulted in the virtual closing of policy space and the end of East Asian style developmental states. In contrast, others such as Amsden and Hikino (2000), Rasiah (2005), Rodrik (2004), Shadlen (2005), UNCTAD (2006), and Natsuda and Thoburn (2014) argue that developing countries still have policy space for development, although a narrower range of policy options is available today.

The WTO was established in 1995 as a result of the Uruguay Round (1986–1994) trade negotiations held under the auspices of the General Agreement on Tariffs and Trade (GATT). Under the WTO, a new set of agreements on 'trade-related' activities was introduced – the Agreement on Trade-Related Intellectual Property Rights (TRIPs), the General Agreement on Trade in Services (GATS), Trade-Related Investment Measures (TRIMs), and also the Agreement on Subsidies and Countervailing Measures (SCMs) – moving beyond GATT's traditional trade barrier reduction agreements. Our chapter focusses primarily on TRIMs and, to a lesser extent, on SCMs. While TRIPs are relevant background, and are discussed briefly here, we do not find them to be of direct importance in Southeast Asian automotive examples.[4]

In the case of GATS, WTO-compliant policies, in principle, could impinge on the motor industry, for example with regard to foreign firms being allowed to offer engineering consultancy services; however, we have not found evidence of this, and we do not consider GATS further in this chapter. Important features of the WTO regime too are 'most favoured nation treatment' (continued from the earlier GATT arrangements), under which a government in its tariff policy must treat all WTO members equally (except those with which it has free trade agreements or customs union or economic union arrangements); and 'national treatment', in which a government must treat equally both foreign (WTO members') firms operating in its country and domestic firms (Wade 2003: 629). These are relevant, especially with regard to the automotive industry in Southeast Asia.

In more detail, the WTO agreements include the following:

- *the Agreement on Trade-Related Investment Measures (TRIMs)* relate a country's investment policy to the core rules of the multilateral trading regime by identifying measures that are inconsistent with national treatment and outlawing applications of performance requirements and quantitative restrictions, such as local content requirements (LCRs), trade balance requirements, foreign exchange balancing requirements, and export restrictions (Brewer and Young 1998, UNCTAD 2006). In the past, many developing countries have employed performance requirements in order to enhance backward linkages from foreign firms to local firms. For instance, LCR, which placed an obligation on foreign investors to source components locally, was one of the commonly used policies, aiming to increase domestic value added, job creation, and technology transfer. Similarly, trade balance requirements, which obliged foreign investors to include sufficiently high levels of domestic input in exports to offset imported inputs, were used as a means of integrating the affiliates of the host country into global production networks (Shadlen 2005, UNCTAD 2006). Under TRIMs, such performance requirements are banned. When the TRIMs agreement was to be implemented by developing countries in 2000,[5] a total of 26 developing country WTO members gave notice that they still had TRIMs-related policies in place, mostly relating to the automotive industry (or agro-foods). These policies were overwhelmingly LCRs, although there were foreign exchange balancing requirements too. Indeed, LCRs and foreign exchange balancing requirements have been the only two commonly acknowledged TRIMs (Brooks *et al.* 2003: 15 and 19). In the case of Southeast Asia, it is LCRs that were the key tool among TRIMs-related policies, although, as we shall show later in the book (Chapter 8), the Philippines used a form of foreign exchange balancing requirement effectively to promote domestic production of some key automotive components for export.

- *the Agreement on Subsidies and Countervailing Measures (SCMs)* establishes multilateral disciplines for regulating the provision of subsidies, but covers only goods (not services). 'Prohibited' subsidies, which are considered to be distorting international trade and adversely impacting other countries, include export subsidies (to encourage recipients to meet certain export targets) or local content subsidies (to encourage recipients to use domestic inputs rather than imported inputs).[6] There are also 'actionable' subsidies that are not necessary illegal but can be declared as such if another country demonstrates proof of injury. Additionally, 'permissible (non-actionable)' subsidies to promote R&D (up to 75% of research costs and 50% of pre-competitive development), regional development (assistance to disadvantaged regions or unemployment), and environmental objectives (assistance to introduce plant and equipment for new environmental regulations) existed until December 1999, which are now integrated into the actionable subsidies category (Dunkley 1997: 59–60, UNCTAD 2006: 170).
- *the Agreement on Trade-Related Intellectual Property Rights (TRIPs)* established the protection of intellectual property rights (IPRs), such as trademarks, copyrights, industrial designs, and patents. In principle, strong protection of IPRs could encourage increased flows of FDI and facilitate technology transfer to developing countries, consequently stimulating local innovation capacity. However, the UNDP argues that the TRIPs agreement

has rather been widening the technological gap between developed and developing countries (UNDP 2005: 135). From an historical perspective, today's developed countries, including the United States, European countries, and Japan, employed industrial and technology policies to promote domestic industrialisation: reverse engineering, imitating, and copying technologies developed were critical elements in the process of economic catch-up (Chang 2002). By the same token, East Asian late-industrialising countries have successfully upgraded local industries by borrowing technology (Amsden 1989). Under the WTO regime, current developing countries cannot pursue the same policies as the current developed countries and East Asian countries did in the past, because TRIPs limit developing countries' access to technology and knowledge. In other words, the policy space for such technology policies has been shrunk, and the ladder up towards development partly has been kicked away, at least partially (Chang 2002).

Horizontal-vertical and hard-soft industrial policy

Industrial policy can be categorised according to two broad divisions: horizontal-vertical and hard-soft. Horizontal industrial policy is oriented towards the whole economy, while vertical industrial policy is designed for a specific sector or industry. Hard industrial policy is essentially *directive* – requiring economic actors to take certain actions – and includes the establishment of state-owned enterprises (SOEs), provision of selective subsidies, protection for domestic firms/industries, and performance-related policies on firms/industries that are closely connected with vertically oriented policy. By contrast, soft industrial policy is *facilitative* or *supportive*, designed for the promotion of science, technology and innovation, human resource development, and infrastructure development, based on market-conforming methods. Soft policies are normally also horizontal ones, although, in principle, vertical soft policies could be conceived, for example, the establishment of R&D institutes mainly for research to help some particular activity like the automotive industry.

In terms of policy choice, Hausmann and Rodrick assert that state interventions should be as horizontal as possible and as sectoral as necessary, because horizontal industrial policy targets the fostering of a wide range of industries, and thus its influence can be wider. At the same time, they recognise that sectoral policy might be required to foster a particular sector under some circumstances (Hausmann and Rodrick 2005: 79). In fact, horizontal and soft industrial policies are perfectly compatible to the WTO rules, as set out earlier. In this context, there is no contradiction in terms of policy implementation. On the other hand, vertical industrial policy might include risks in terms of policy implementation. Weiss (2016: 140) classifies vertical industrial policy into four types: (1) to support any firm possessing a specific technology, (2) to support any firm in particular sectors with the potential for significant productivity growth and spillover, (3) to support individual firms either as key foreign investors or national champions operating in an area with potential growth, and (4) to support sectors or individual firms in relation to restructuring. Among all these, support to individual firms might be controversial. In principle, such support should be equally distributed to all economic actors (no discriminatory allocation of resources). In other words, a ***picking winners*** strategy in terms of particular firms is no longer permissible.

It is also worth noting that although competition policy is often viewed as a part of industrial policy, such policies are fundamentally in contradiction with each other. Competition policy aims to promote rivalry between firms in a sector. In contrast, industrial policy offers a market advantage over competitors in a favoured domestic sector, and subsequently conflicts might occur in the case of the new entry of firms or of competition between domestic and foreign firms. However, if industrial policy aims at sectors rather than particular firms, such policies can have a complementary relationship (UNIDO 2013: 139).

With regard to the implementation of industrial policy, we can find a clear regional difference. For instance, in Europe, industrial policies are based primarily on horizontal policies, consisting of competition, promoting innovation, supporting SMEs, and attracting FDI. The European Commission introduced the first common industrial policy in 1990, designed for the improvement of competitiveness of European industry through innovation and technological development, and targeted the European Community as a whole. The European industrial policy was strictly based on a microeconomic approach by using firms and competition policies and predominantly horizontal intervention for the creation of favoured business environments. This approach was elaborated into the Lisbon Strategy in 2000 and, most recently, the Europe 2020 Strategy in 2010 (UNCTAD 2014: 95). In the EU, the existence of the state aid rule of the Treaty on Functioning of the EU – to be precise, Article 107 of the Treaty[7] – limits sectoral industrial policy in the EU members (ibid.: 96). In this context, industrial policy has shifted to innovation policy in Europe (Soete 2007). On the other hand, Southeast Asian countries have been using vertically oriented industrial policies, including those towards the automotive sector.

Automotive industrial policy and policy space

Before discussing policy space, a fundamental issue is whether interventionist industrial policies– and trade policies relating to industrialisation – are themselves effective or desirable, whatever the policy space available. This issue has long been debated, and the 'Washington Consensus' views of the 1980s were, for a time, thought to have killed off the case for industrial policies along with other forms of state intervention. More recently, following widespread disillusion with the experience of 'Washington Consensus' market-fundamentalist policies, the pendulum has swung back somewhat in favour of interventionist industrial policy: a wide range of externalities in the industrialisation process could justify policy intervention (Noland and Pack 2003: 16–18).[8]

We take the view that industrial policy still has a role to play in moving an economy towards more dynamic activities at a rate faster than the market by itself could achieve (Rodrik 2004).[9] Although externalities to be addressed by policy, such as the learning by doing associated with the argument for protecting infant industries, often do not arise directly in the trade sphere (Bora *et al.* 2001: 168–169), trade-related policies such as tariff protection or LCRs are often used in practice, seeming to be easier or cheaper to administer than more direct measures.

The Southeast Asian automotive industry has been moving the region's industrialisation beyond simple labour-intensive production into activities requiring more advanced technology and engineering. The industry was attractive also in the sense that, even if set up by foreign investors and dependent on imported components initially, the industry offers scope for the progressive import-substituting of a very wide range of automotive components by local firms. This production of local components was promoted by LCRs in both countries initially, now outlawed by the WTO under TRIMs. In an interesting take on this issue – and in a paper otherwise broadly sceptical about the value of industrial policy in general and trade-related industrial policy in particular – Bora, Lloyd, and Pangestu refer to the example of the Australian motor industry, where LCRs had been used to develop local component supply. They note that the industry became more efficient after liberalisation and a period of structural adjustment, but that it could be argued that local supply might not have come into existence if local content policies had not been used in the first place (Bora *et al.* 2001: 175). Certainly, several developing countries believe that many WTO rules – of which the restriction on LCRs under TRIMs is an important one – do not work in their favour and that more special and differential treatment for developing countries is required (Hoekman 2005: 414).

Table 2.1 shows automotive industrial policies in the ASEAN-4,[10] before the liberalisations of the 1990s and (particularly) the 2000s, as set out in our later chapters. All four countries shown in the table used hard industrial policies, such as local content requirements, in their early stages of post-war ISI, along with MDPs, often encouraging further inward FDI by component manufacturers. In general, too, the component production stimulated by LCRs and MDPs outlasted their outlawing under the WTO from the early 2000s. An interesting policy addition is the Philippines' introduction of requiring assemblers to earn themselves some foreign exchange that they needed to import kits. This was one of the country's few automotive successes, leading to the development of exports of automotive transmissions,[11] whose production, like that resulting from LCRs and MDPs, has continued into the 2000s and beyond, under post-2000 TRIMs (Natsuda and Thoburn 2018, Thoburn and Natsuda 2018). Malaysia and Indonesia also used market controls and some preferential tariff treatment for foreign producers. Although Indonesia is listed as having a national car project, this programme, introduced in the 1990s, was very short-lived and unsuccessful (Natsuda *et al.* 2015a), whereas Malaysia's national car projects (Proton and Perodua) resulted in the development of vehicle production, which, though highly protected and inefficient, has continued to the present. Similarly, Malaysia's Vendor Development Programme has used preferential treatment to encourage the

Table 2.1 Automotive Industrial Policy before Liberalisation in Southeast Asia

Aim	*Automotive Industrial Policy*	*Country*
Performance requirements	Local content requirement (LCR)	ASEAN-4 countries
	Mandatory deletion programme (MDP)	ASEAN-4 countries
	Foreign Exchange balancing requirement	Philippines
Market control	Control of manufacture license, models imported vehicles	Thailand, Malaysia
	Preferential (discriminatory) treatment tariff for foreign producers	Malaysia, Indonesia
Business development	National car projects	Malaysia, Indonesia
	Vendor (supplier) development programme	Malaysia

Source: Natsuda and Thoburn (2013, 2014, 2018), Natsuda *et al.* (2013 and 2015a), Thoburn and Natsuda (2017).

development of a local supply chain, the efficiency of some of whose firms is in doubt (Natsuda and Thoburn 2013 and 2014, Otsuka and Natsuda 2016, Segawa *et al.* 2014). Although Malaysia still exercises control of manufacturing and importing vehicles, and its national car projects, all the policies in Table 2.1 were abolished by the early 2000s under the WTO.

There are several further issues in relation to policy space under WTO rules. Firstly, one of the biggest changes is in relation to ownership – domestic versus foreign firms. Policies based on favouring local firms are no longer allowable. But as long as governments treat domestic and WTO members' firms equally, policy space still exists. In addition, FDI-regulating measures that do not violate national treatment or impose quantitative restrictions continue to be consistent with the WTO rules (UNCTAD 2006). This is related to the second feature: development policies related to science and technology, regional development, environment, infrastructure, human capital, and capacity building are still usable under the WTO regime. In other words, soft industrial policy is still applicable. In this regard, governments can require foreign firms to transfer technology by specifying a certain proportion of R&D activity locally or licensing a specified technology to a local firm (UNCTAD 2006: 169), and can also influence foreign firms' employment practices with the aim of enhancing human capital and skills (Shadlen 2005: 759). Similarly, Amsden and Hikino (2000) argue that developing countries can continue to support their own particular industries by providing government assistance in the name of science and technology. For instance, countries such as Korea, Taiwan, China, and India have recently established science parks and targeted industries, including biotechnology, by providing subsidies, tax incentives, and special loans to catch-up with more advanced countries. Thirdly, in relation to performance requirements and fiscal policy, Dunkley (1997: 67–68) asserts that TRIMs can be classified into 'positive' (e.g. tax concessions to attract investment) or 'negative' (various requirements imposed on foreign investors) policies. In fact, governments can control foreign participation in a particular sector's economy though the provision of tax incentives (Shadlen 2005: 759). In Southeast Asia, Thailand and Malaysia tactically use tax incentives to promote (or protect) their automotive industry. Indonesia and the Philippines seem be less sophisticated in their tax incentive system (see later chapters).

Additionally, as Mayer (2008: 15) notes, under SCMs, some subsidies tacitly have been allowed, and member countries have not challenged them. Also, of course, a more standard restriction of policy space, dating from GATT, is that tariffs have been reduced and 'bound' to maximum levels after successive negotiation rounds, reducing the scope to protect favoured sectors like vehicles from import competition. In Malaysia's and Thailand's cases, though, such trade liberalisation has been driven more by ASEAN Free Trade Area (AFTA) and ASEAN Economic Community (AEC), than by GATT or the WTO. It is also worth noting that the extent to which Thailand, Malaysia, and the Philippines have adhered to new WTO rules, involving the abolition of some hard industrial policies, has been on a voluntary basis. It does not seem to be the case that these countries have been pushed into observing the WTO commitments as they relate to the automotive industry, as a result of complaints by fellow WTO members,[12,13] however, TRIMs related to Indonesia's auto industries have been the subject of complaints (Brooks *et al.* 2003: 15).

Some policy space, therefore, is still open. In sum, the WTO rules still allow developing governments to select strategic industries or particular operations and functions (such as R&D, human resource development, regional headquarters) for industrial development. This can be still done by employing discretionary power in providing subsidies or positive tax incentives. We examine automotive industrial policies in Thailand, Indonesia, Malaysia, the Philippines, and Vietnam in pre- and post-WTO era in Chapters 5–9.

Global value chains

The GVC concept

The concept of the GVC was developed by Gereffi (1994, 1999) and was influenced by various existing approaches, such as Porter's value chain concept,[14] the French *filière* approach,[15] and Wallerstein's concept of world-systems theory.[16] GVC analysis delineates the various stages of production activity, from raw material production to the final retail sales. GVCs represent a process of vertical specialisation where individual developing countries can enter manufacturing exporting by producing a single stage in the production chain rather than an entire vertically integrated product. GVC activities cover design, production, marketing, distribution, and logistics in bringing the product or service from the producer to the final consumer. The theory focusses not only on input–output relations of the chain across countries but also on the exercise of control (governance) within the chain.

There are two types of GVC: the *buyer-driven value chain* and the *producer-driven value chain*. The former is common for labour-intensive industries such as the garment, footwear, and toy industries, where governance is exercised at the retail end (see Alam and Natsuda 2016, Azmeh and Nadvi 2014, Bair and

Gereffi 2001, Frederick and Gereffi 2011, Gereffi and Memedovic 2003, Goto *et al.* 2011, Nadvi and Thoburn 2004, Natsuda *et al.* 2010, Schmitz 2006, Tokatli and Kizilgum 2004, Zheng and Sheng 2006).[17] In contrast, the latter is characterised by technology and capital-intensive activities such as the automotive, electronics, and aircraft industries, where power is exercised at the production end (see Bamber and Gereffi 2013, Humphrey 2000, Humphrey and Memedovic 2003, Kawakami 2011, Kishimoto 2004, Ozatagan 2011, Sturgeon *et al.* 2008, Sturgeon and Kawakami 2011, Sturgeon and Van Biesebroeck 2011, Sturgeon *et al.* 2009). In later versions of GVC analysis, five types of governance structure (*market*, *modular*, *relational*, *captive*, and *hierarchy*) are identified (Gereffi *et al.* 2005: 86–87). *Market* linkages are typically based on price-based competition in markets or trade – characterised by products with easily codified and simple product specification. Suppliers provide a wide range of standard products to the many buyers. Under the chain, price is the most important factor (Gereffi *et al.* 2005, Humphrey 2003, Sturgeon 2002). *Modular* linkages allow suppliers to take full responsibility for competencies to supply full packages and modules, when technical standards simplify interactions by reducing parts variation and unifying components, products, and process specification (Gereffi *et al.* 2005, Sturgeon *et al.* 2008). Under these linkages, suppliers specify their own processes and use their own technology to manufacture components or modules in response to the design specification provided by lead firm (Ozatagan 2011). *Relational* linkages are typically characterised by mutual dependence between buyers and suppliers due to exchange of tacit knowledge. Under these linkages, highly competent suppliers provide a strong motivation for lead firms to outsource to gain access to complementary competencies (Gereffi *et al.* 2005, Sturgeon *et al.* 2008). Such relations are often based on reputation, social and spatial proximity, or family or ethnic ties (Gereffi *et al.* 2005). Under relational linkages, buyers or lead firms typically maintain strong relations with suppliers who are involved in the design and product-development (Ozatagan 2011). *Captive* linkages are based on low levels of supplier capability (where small suppliers typically rely on large buyers). Under these linkages, suppliers conduct specific tasks, following detailed instructions provided by their buyers or lead firms that are responsible for product design (Gereffi *et al.* 2005, Sturgeon *et al.* 2008). *Hierarchy* linkages are based on vertical integration. When lead firms cannot find suppliers, they tend to develop and manufacture in-house by controlling resources, including intellectual property (ibid.). Under such governance structures, lead firms effectively control their suppliers by integrating them into their production networks or restructuring them (Blazek *et al.* 2018).

One of the most significant aspects of the GVC concept is related to the issue of *industrial upgrading*. Local producers in buyer-driven chains may receive advice and technological and financial support from their global buyers on how to improve their production processes to help them attain consistency and high quality (Humphrey and Schmitz 2002). Moreover, Kaplinsky and Morris (2001) also argue that firms can upgrade their position through participating in a GVC. In particular, they argue that local firms can be upgraded in the following four areas: (1) ***process upgrading*** by raising efficiency in transforming inputs into output through introducing modern production systems and technology, (2) ***product upgrading*** which can be conducted by development of new products or improving existing ones, (3) ***functional upgrading*** by shifting from lower value-added activities to higher value-added activities. This typically involves a transition from Original Equipment Assembly (OEA) to Original Equipment Manufacturer (OEM), to Original Design Manufacturer (ODM), and finally to Original Brand Manufacturer (OBM), (4) ***inter-sectoral upgrading,*** using the knowledge acquired in particular chain functions to move into different sectors (Humphrey and Schmitz 2002, Schmitz 2006). In addition to these four areas, Palpacuer *et al.* (2005) have identified ***volume-based upgrading*** by achieving economies of scale and diversifying export markets by providing insightful information regarding emerging markets.

With regard to industrial upgrading within GVCs, Gereffi (1994) and Van Grunsven and Smakman (2001) stress the importance of *institutions*, including the national and international policies that shape the globalisation process. From their perspective, states are able to assist local firms or industries through institutional support, infrastructure, and the capacity to positively influence elements of local production to upgrade the positioning of local firms or industries within the value chain ladder (Gereffi 1994: 100–101, Van Grunsven and Smakman 2001: 175). Barnes and Morris's study of the South African automotive industry stresses the importance of industrial policy in shaping the national industry's insertion into GVCs (Barnes and Morris 2008). We discuss the role of industrial policy in relation to the thinking of leading GVC researchers later in this chapter.

GVCs and the automotive industry

The automotive industry exemplifies the idea of a *complex* global value chain, where value-added crosses borders many times and there are re-exports of imported inputs (World Bank 2017: 2, 83–85). The concept of the GVC then, though now well-known and widely employed, is still very useful as a setting within which to understand Southeast Asian automotive industrialisation, although we do not try to force all our discussion into a GVC framework. As noted in the previous section, a particular focus of much GVC analysis is whether domestic firms within a chain can upgrade their products, processes, and functions to achieve higher productivity and (sometimes)[18] a larger share of value-added (Humphrey and Schmitz 2002). Beyond the GVC literature's usual emphasis on the upgrading of firms' activities, there is also an issue of upgrading the whole industrial structure (Lauridsen 2009) – in this case, the entire network of local production. Governance is exercised by a small number of large multinational motor companies in an industry where it is thought that the size of a *firm* with output of at least five million vehicles is necessary for a mass market vehicle-maker to achieve necessary economies of scope and to finance the high level of R&D necessary to remain competitive (Nolan 2012: 25). The minimum efficient size of an automotive *plant* necessary to achieve economies of scale is very much smaller, though, depending on the degree of vertical integration (Thoburn and Natsuda 2017: 33).

One limitation of the GVC concept for our purposes is its apparent neglect of horizontal relations between economic actors in the chain. This shortcoming is addressed in the global production network (GPN) approach (Henderson *et al.* 2002) and in other research on production networks (Athukorala 2011, Kimura and Obashi 2011). These approaches give insights into how different components can be produced in different locations, often within the networks of automotive multinationals, and internationally (or, more often, intra-regionally) traded. The tendency towards interregional specialisation is strengthened by some components, such as engines and transmissions, being subject to large economies of scale, more so than assembly.

The formation of GVCs (and GPNs) has been facilitated by the growing ability of producers to fine-slice (vertically disintegrate) production into different stages, which can be carried out in different locations. A result of this – the subject of some new work on GVCs – is that where a country exports a good within a GVC, the good's production may be highly import-intensive and so the gross export value overstates the country's value-added contribution. Of some 42 industries identified as heavily involved in GVC activity, the automotive industry was second only to electronics in the high share of non-domestic value-added[19] in total exports – around 35%, compared to 45% of electronics (UNCTAD 2013: 129). This high trade-intensity of production implies there is a lot of choice as to what is produced locally, and also indicates considerable scope for global and regional specialisation in the production of the thousands of components needed for a vehicle. Note though that some recent works find that automotive production is actually much less network-trade intensive in the Asian context than is electronics production. Athukorala (2011: 76–77) attributes this, in part, to the lower trade intensity within automotive production networks due to the low value/weight ratio of auto components, and he notes that localisation policies to increase domestic value-added in automotive production also are trade-reducing.

As mentioned earlier, the automotive industry is seen as a *producer-driven* GVC, where major multinational vehicle assemblers exercise control over the chains. Vehicle assemblers have been governing this highly capital and technology-intensive chain by controlling core technologies, production processes, research and development (R&D), human resources, finance, and marketing from upstream to downstream operations through their supplier networks (Barnes and Morris 2008).

Relations between assemblers and their networks of suppliers have been transformed in the world automotive industry, particularly since the 1980s, when Western producers moved away from their earlier more vertically integrated Fordist-style production with market-based linkages with their production networks (Humphrey 2003), towards the system the Japanese had developed in the

1960s. Under the Japanese system, there were flexible, long-term buyer-supplier relationships within *keiretsu* (business groups).

Assemblers, suppliers, and industrial upgrading in the automotive industry

Assemblers

Sturgeon *et al.* (2008) have presented a strong case for the GVC approach as a focus of analysis for the automobile industry, with its structure of a small number of powerful, oligopolistic assemblers, and tiers of suppliers. They note that, unlike some other global industries such as garments and electronics, the automotive industry has maintained strong regional aspects: production often being located near consumer markets both as a result of political pressure (as in the USA) and for locational reasons such as transport costs and lower unit-cost labour. They highlight the way that multinational (first tier) 'mega-suppliers' – about whom more in the next subsection – have grown in importance in terms of employment and sales (Sturgeon *et al.* 2008: 306–307) relative to the assemblers, and how (often at the behest of the powerful assemblers) global mega-suppliers have undertaken the production and designing of modules and subassemblies. Trade in components has become more global than the pattern of vehicle trade, which is more regional. We shall note later in the book that some component exports (e.g. wiring harness exports from the Philippines or Vietnam) are essentially global in their markets, where other component exports (e.g. the Philippines exports of transmissions) are more regional. Sturgeon *et al.* (ibid.) stress the importance of clustering to gain agglomeration economies (particularly in terms of specialised labour markets and the exchange of tacit knowledge), but also that the global auto industry is more than a collection of integrated clusters and that tacit knowledge is, to some extent, spread internationally. Such spreading of tacit knowledge is aided by the 'follow sourcing' (co-location) strategies of mega-suppliers in countries where the automotive companies have set up assembly operations.

The Southeast Asian automotive assembly industry has upgraded through six stages of industrial development since the Second World War (see Table 2.2). In the case of Thailand, the automotive industry commenced with the importation of completely built-up (CBU) vehicles and then into the repair business at stage 2. The first vehicle assembly firm was established in 1961 as a result of 'Industrial Promotion Act' in 1960, by shifting from stage 1 to stage 2. In the period of 1973–1999, localisation policies (such as LCRs) were employed by targeting to increase LC ratios gradually. During this period, the assembly industry has shifted from stage 2 to stage 3, and to stage 4. With regard to R&D activity of stage 5, the first R&D centre – Isuzu Technical Center of Asia – was established in 1991 (Fourin 2017: 39). It is also important to note that Japanese vehicle producers have developed Asian strategic vehicles in response to local market conditions by modifying popular models in Japan since

Table 2.2 Industrial Upgrading of Vehicle Production in Southeast Asia

Stage	*Vehicle Production Activities*	*Thailand*	*The Current Status*
1	Import and repairing: Importation of CBUs	1950s	–
2	Assembly level 1: Vehicle assembly with imported CKD kits	1960s	Vietnam (M)
3	Assembly level 2: Vehicle assembly with low LC ratios, localisation of autoparts production based on OEM of lower value-added or bulky parts	1970s	Malaysia (L) Philippines (L) Vietnam (L) Indonesia (M)
4	Assembly level 3: Vehicle assembly with high LC ratios, localisation of auto parts production based on OEM of higher value-added parts	1980s–1990s	Thailand (M) Indonesia (M)
5	R&D level 1: R&D for localisation of vehicles and production process	1990s	Thailand (L, M) Indonesia (L, M)
6	R&D level 2: R&D for vehicle development and design (plus coordination functions such as marketing, procurement)	2000s	Thailand (L) Indonesia (L) Malaysia (N)

Note: L (leading multinational assemblers, such as Toyota, in the country), M (major multinational assemblers, such as Mazda, in the country), N (national producers).

the mid-1990s (see Table 4.1 in Chapter 4). Most recently in 2017, four firms – Isuzu, Toyota (in 2005), Honda (in 2005), and Nissan (in 2011) – have their own R&D centres for vehicle development and for coordination of regional markets, which is considered the highest stage of industrial upgrading (see Table 3.6 in Chapter 3 and Fourin 2017: 39). In the current regional situation, leading multinational assemblers in Thailand and Indonesia and national car producers in Malaysia have reached the highest stage of R&D, while leading multinational assemblers in Malaysia, the Philippines, and Vietnam are still placed at stage 3, by assembling their vehicles with relatively low LC ratios. We investigate how industrial policy has influenced assembler's decisions, and their suppliers who have responded to them; and how Southeast Asia has progressed through the stages.

The stress on the upgrading of products, production processes, and functions in the GVC literature focusses on the abilities and willingness of economic actors higher in the chain to upgrade those lower down the chain. *Upgrading* is also used here more generally to refer to improving 'the capacities of firms to use and to improve technology' (Lauridsen 2009: 412). The motor industry is one which can be initiated in a developing country using assembly operations, with all components imported as CKD kits. Over the industrialisation process, individual components can be 'deleted' from the kits as local component production develops. Although some local component production may start as a result of market forces, more often developing countries have used industrial policy to foster such component production with special measures. These include MDPs and LCRs, though, as already noted, since 2000, these have been outlawed under WTO rules. The development of component supply is seen as a crucial aspect of automotive development since there are thousands of different components in a motor vehicle. Component production offers opportunities for local firms to develop through 'backward linkage' and thereby spread industrialisation as well as improve the balance of payments by replacing imported components. However, as has long been known, there can be 'bad' as well as 'good' linkages (Thoburn 1973) in the sense that production promoted by policy measures will not always meet the eventual goal of being internationally competitive. It is also noteworthy at this point that a simplistic desire to increase the local content of automotive production should take account of the fact that global suppliers may achieve highly efficient production through economies of scale in locating certain components in a small number of international locations and then shipping them to the location of assemblers (Sturgeon *et al.* 2008: 306). Even the most efficient of vehicle assemblers in developed countries are quite import-intensive. Also, to recall an 'anti-linkage' argument of the 1960s, some component supply, in principle, could start as an export activity, not dependent on any local assembler's backward linkage demand, as, to some extent, in the Philippines (see Chapter 8). Indeed, even from the 1990s, vehicle assembly was no longer necessarily regarded as an ideal point of entry into automotive production, and starting by producing labour-intensive components for export was recommended by some authorities on the industry (Aswicahyono *et al.* 2000, Auty 1994).

In the highly oligopolistic context of the global motor industry, where technical change is very rapid (Nolan 2012: 25), an independent national producer may face difficulties. These particularly relate to attempting to export, where they may have to develop retail outlets and marketing in the face of an industry that has been suffering from excess capacity in relation to the North American, European, and Japanese markets (Abe 2009). In other words, a national producer can easily be inserted into the production end of the automotive GVC by a determined government, but it still has to cope with the fact that the parts of the chain outside of the country, particularly at the retailing end, are governed by major foreign assemblers.

Foreign assemblers in joint ventures may exercise their governance by controlling their JV partners' exports or prohibiting them from exporting altogether.[20] Where there is majority foreign control over vehicle production, exports occur where a firm decides to use a particular country as a global or (more often) regional base from which to feed its production into its global or regional sales outlets. In this sense, different countries – such as Malaysia or Thailand – may find themselves in competition with each other in using policy to try to influence such decisions. If the foreign partner has minority ownership, the help that it is willing to offer for exporting may be limited, yet with several producers serving the domestic market, exports may be essential to achieve economies of scale. A further difficulty for a national producer attempting to develop its own supply network is that economies of scale in component supply have increased, so for some items such as engines and gearboxes, efficient production may require a million units or more annually. Suppliers of such items may well have higher technological capabilities than a new national producer such as Proton in Malaysia.

Suppliers

The automotive industry can be seen as a typical example of quasi-hierarchy where lead firms control the chain through their market power. Assembler-supplier relations in the automotive industry have been transformed over time. Ford developed its mass production system for the famous Model-T for the first time in 1908 by forming a vertically integrated production system, with hierarchical governance in the United States. Up to 1980s, the US and European assemblers formed *market linkages* (Humphrey 2003). The second revolution in the automotive manufacturing system was developed by Toyota in Japan, introducing in the 1960s its *Just-in-time* (JIT) system, the Toyota Production System (TPS), or so-called *lean production.* The Japanese *keiretsu* system enabled Japanese automotive assemblers to establish flexible and long-term assembler-supplier relationships. Under this system, Japanese automotive assemblers typically have established a vertical, three-layer subcontracting system under OEM arrangements. Automotive assemblers (OEMs) directly source finished components only from Tier-1 suppliers, which subcontract lower value manufacturing activities to lower-tier suppliers (Thoburn and Takashima 1992: ch. 5).[21] In the post-Second World War period, Japanese lead firms relied on suppliers, often with equity ties – essentially 'captive' linkages. Such relationships have shifted to more *relational* ones, as supplier competence has increased (Sturgeon *et al.* 2008). Under such relationships, lead firms and suppliers jointly develop the components for particular vehicles. Suppliers are responsible not only for producing components according to the lead firm's specification but also for designing solutions, adapting basic designs to customers' specific requirements, or designing modules or subsystems using their own technology (Ozatagan 2011).

As indicated earlier, a major change in recent years has been the growth and increasing global reach of Tier-1 automotive mega-suppliers such as Denso and Aisin from Japan, Bosch and Continental from Germany, and Magna from Canada. In parallel to the relocations of automotive assembly to overseas locations, automotive assemblers, particularly the Japanese, have required their Tier-1 suppliers to follow them. Assemblers and global mega-suppliers need to have global reach, innovation capabilities, and design capabilities, as well as considerable financial resources (Humphrey and Memedovic 2003: 21–22). As a result of having these capabilities, the drivers of automotive GVCs have come to include mega-suppliers as well as assemblers, and the opportunities for domestic firms to enter and later to upgrade depend more on Tier-1 suppliers – and less on assemblers – than they did in the past. The industry's move towards a modular system has allowed some higher value-added activities to be transferred from assemblers to mega-suppliers (Doran 2004, Takeishi and Fujimoto 2001). In this sense, the automotive GVC is no longer entirely producer-driven, and major Tier-1 suppliers are important 'drivers' too (Wad 2008). Vehicle assemblers now take their international location decisions in consultation with large Tier-1 suppliers (Busser 2008: 34) and devolve various supply chain management tasks to them (Humphrey and Memedovic 2003). In concert with the rise of mega-suppliers, local Tier-1 firms are often pushed down into lower tiers or need to form partnerships with global suppliers (Humphrey 2000: 254–271).

With regard to assembler and supplier relations, some studies are optimistic about the positive benefits of participation for local firms in relation to industrial upgrading, asserting that local firms are gradually able to upgrade their technological and management capabilities through assembler-supplier relations (Contreras *et al.* 2012, Gentile-Ludecke and Giroud 2009 and 2012, Ivarsson and Alvstam 2004 and 2005, Kaplinsky and Morris 2001, Okada 2004); other studies claim that the process is not so simple (see Bair and Gereffi 2001, Kishimoto 2004, Ozatagan 2011, Pavlinek and Zenka 2011, Tokatli and Kizilgum 2004, Van Grunsven and Smakman 2005). Humphrey and Schmitz (2002: 1023) assert that a quasi-hierarchical value chain provides favourable conditions for process and product upgrading, but hinders the functional upgrading of participating firms in the chain. Some automotive GVCs argue that the emergence of global mega-suppliers and the tendencies towards long-term collaborative relationships between assemblers and suppliers hinder upgrading opportunities for indigenous firms. Thus, subsequently, indigenous firms remain in lower value activities or sometimes are pushed down to lower value activities by global mega-suppliers due to lack of competence to meet the cost, flexibility, and quality requirements of their customers (Humphrey and Schmitz 2002, Sturgeon and Lester 2004, Wad 2006). In short, the relationships with lead firms, whose core competences include branding, marketing, retailing, and product development, can create adverse effects on the functional upgrading of local firms. Even in the buyer-driven value chains, local firms in low-income countries are typically excluded from such high-return activities. For instance, Bair and Gereffi's study of the blue jeans industry in Mexico suggests that core competencies such as product development, marketing, and retailing predominantly remain in the United States, making it practically difficult, if not impossible, for Mexican firms to develop their own apparel brands in the United States' market (Bair and Gereffi 2001). In the same vein, in the automotive industry, Ozatagan's study in Bursa, Turkey, concluded that although parts suppliers in Bursa have acquired design and product-development competences through MNCs, cutting-edge innovation activities such as marketing and branding continue to remain the domain of the lead firms (Oztagan 2011). Pavlinek and Zenka (2011) reveal that industrial upgrading in the Czech automotive industry was highly selective and uneven. Process upgrading, product upgrading, and functional upgrading (R&D) were limited to higher-tier suppliers. Similarly, Rugraff (2010) asserts that locally owned firms in the Czech Republic have failed to upgrade to produce innovative-intensive products due to price-driven subcontracting. In short, process and product upgrading of suppliers is enhanced through process and product standards imposed by lead firms in quasi-hierarchy networks. In this context, JIT and lean production systems apparently facilitate process upgrading of suppliers. However, these production systems are unlikely to encourage functional upgrading of suppliers (Isaksen and Kalsaas 2009).

Interestingly, where GVC specialists have started to comment on industrial policy issues in relation to GVCs, their particular stress has been on industrial policy to enhance industrial upgrading by local suppliers, as well as dealing with lead firms in the context of the growth of regional production networks (Milberg *et al.* 2014: 155, 157). Similarly, Gereffi (2014b) stresses upgrading as an industrial policy, and also highlights the role of global suppliers, who are making many of the new investments in developing countries. He notes though that economic upgrading does not necessarily preclude simultaneous social downgrading, in the sense of worsening conditions of employment (Gereffi 2014b: 452 and 455–456). However, David Dollar (in World Bank 2017: ch. 1) notes that a lack of gain for unskilled workers from GVC participation is more a feature of developed countries like the United States than of developing countries, and that unskilled workers in China have seen their incomes rise, though less than those of more skilled workers.

It is also worth noting that the Japanese literature highlights the analysis of detailed subcontracting relations between assemblers and suppliers. There are four outsourcing methods in assembler and supplier relations in the automotive industry: (1) *Taiyo-zu*, a *drawing-supplied* system (or *captive linkages* in GVCs), where suppliers produce components according to the blueprint provided by assemblers, (2) *Shonine-zu*, a *drawing approval (black box parts)* system (closer to *relational linkages*), where suppliers conduct a design and production of components according to basic specifications provided by assemblers and receive approval from the assembler (but the patent of the blueprint is owned by a supplier)[22]; (3) *Itaku-zu*, a *drawing contracted* system (closer to *modular linkages*), which is similar to drawing approval system, but the patent is owned by an assembler, paying a design fee to the supplier, and (4) a *supplier propriety parts system* (or *market linkages* in GVCs), where suppliers produce and design generic or standard products in a catalogue, in which assemblers select products from the catalogue (Asanuma 1997, Fujimoto 1997). According to Clark and Fujimoto (1991), the US assemblers are heavily dependent on the *drawing-supplied system*, accounting for approximately 81% of outsourcing parts in value, European assemblers for 54%, and Japanese assemblers for 30%. Japanese assemblers employed more the *drawing approval system*, accounting for 62%, the US for 16%, and European for 39% in the 1980s (Clark and Fujimoto 1991: 143–146). In their analysis, the vertical nature of the US linkages (typically based on the *drawing supplied* system) seems to prevent suppliers from conducting R&D and thus hindering improvements in their engineering capability, making supplier-OEM relations more of a zero-sum game, with communication and interactions occurring at arm's length and the parties behaving as adversaries. The level of involvement of parts suppliers in R&D activities was much lower than Japanese counterparts. In the total engineering works in the vehicle development, the US firms accounted for only 7% of suppliers' involvement in comparison with Japan for 30% and Europe for 16% (ibid.: 136–137). More recently, in a survey of 141 automotive supplier firms in Japan in 2003, in all, 69.5% of suppliers were contracted under the ***drawing approval system***, 16.3% were using the drawing contracted system, and only 9.9 % were using the ***drawing-supplied system*** (Fujimoto *et al.* 2006: 6). In this context, Japanese assemblers appear to offer more scope for their suppliers to upgrade their products and functions by establishing more relational or modular linkages. The issue here, though, is clouded by the fact that these relations tend to be with Tier-1 suppliers, which are very often also foreign-invested (and usually Japanese) firms. The assemblers' main concern would be to have sales sufficient to achieve economies of scale and to induce their Tier-1 suppliers to join them. Although automotive mega-suppliers enter a country, they may push local Tier-1 firms down to lower tiers; they may also, especially the Japanese, offer technical help to their local lower-tier suppliers (Natsuda *et al.* 2020a: 92, Natsuda and Thoburn 2013: 416 and 431–432).

It is also worth noting that three changes in the relation between assemblers and suppliers have occurred in the West in response to Japanese automotive and parts producers. First, there has been a shift of design activity from assemblers to suppliers. Second, there has been a shift towards the supply of complete functions (modules, systems, or sub-assemblies rather than individual components). In this context, Tier-1 suppliers have become responsible not only for the assembly of parts but also for the management of Tier-2 suppliers. The third change has been characterised by assembler's involvement in the specification of the production and quality systems of their suppliers as a result of increasingly importance of Japanese JIT system and total quality management (TQM) in the automotive industry (Humphrey 2000: 249–250).

Developments in GVC research

Work on GVCs continues apace. The World Bank's two *GVC Development Reports* (2017 and 2019), produced jointly with several other organisations including the WTO and the OECD, provide convenient overviews, as does the World Bank's 2020 *World Development Report*, devoted to 'trading for development in the age of GVCs' (World Bank 2020). The 2017 GVC report highlights the importance of recent work on the value-added content of trade to show that figures for gross exports and imports can be misleading, and that GVC analyses are made clearer by thinking in terms of value-added when the import content of vehicle exports is typically high. Also highlighted is the service content of manufacturing export value-added. (Non-tariff) trade costs as well as labour costs are important in determining the possibilities of GVC entry, even where they are non-monetary such as bureaucracy or inefficient customs clearance. The World Bank suggests that these costs can be reduced by entering into 'deep' trade agreements than have wider provisions than mere tariff-cutting. Such agreements are even better if they are regional, as some trade costs incurred by a country may be generated by neighbouring countries. In Southeast Asia, the ASEAN Economic Community (AEC) agreement seems to fall into this category.

The World Bank (2019) GVC report, noting that two-thirds of world trade now occurs through GVCs, discusses the impacts of new technological developments such as the Internet of Things, as well as 3-D printing and further developments in robotics. It comments in this context that these so-called *Industry 4.0* developments are leading to the reorganisation of supply chains in GVCs, and some technological changes are reducing the incentive to locate to lower-wage countries.[23] The Bank's 2020 *World Development Report* notes that growth in GVC trade, which grew rapidly in the 1990s and earlier 2000s, has slowed since the 2008 world financial crisis. It highlights the need for better trade infrastructure and the importance of better mutual trade facilitation policies between trading partners, while needing more policy intervention to prevent rising wage inequality and negative environmental impacts. The Report's stress on the importance in GVCs of large firms engaged in both exporting and importing (World Bank 2020: ch. 2) seems to fit neatly the automotive industry with its major multinationals.

Changes in global sourcing patterns in GVCs may change in the light of recent (2018–2019) trade disputes between the United States and China (The Economist 2019). Also, UNIDO's recent report on global value chains and industrial development notes that 'although GVC participation can improve industrial competitiveness, there is a strong reverse causality; a pre-existing competitive industrial sector may be a prerequisite for GVC participation', although these conclusions are mainly drawn from case studies of the garment and electronics industries (UNIDO 2018). It also stresses that 'GVC upgrading occurs in environments favourable to development and not independently of such environments' (ibid.: xvi, xvii).

Conclusions

This chapter has tried to pull together key issues relating to industrial policy and global value chains relevant to the automotive industrialisation of Southeast Asia, which is the book's main concern.

Views on industrial policy among policy-makers, international agencies, and scholars have undergone great changes since the Second World War. Until and into the 1970s, industrial policies were widely promoted in the content of import-substituting industrialisation, in the belief that developing countries needed to move away from reliance on primary commodities for their export earnings, but where export prospects for manufactures seemed unfavourable (Thoburn 1977 and 1984). Widespread experience of the failure of ISI policies led to their replacement by the highly free-market policies of the so-called Washington Consensus in the 1980s and 1990s. Various writers recognised, however, that some economies in East Asia – first Japan, then South Korea and Taiwan – had grown rapidly through highly state-interventionist industrial policies, including successful import-substitution. These countries became known 'developmental states'. Southeast Asian countries typically have had less effective state structures and bureaucracies, often being plagued by corruption and cronyism. Nevertheless, they have been able to conduct some effective industrial policy-making, and have been often described as 'neo-developmental states'. Indeed, particularly because of East and Southeast Asian experiences, industrial policy issues are now firmly back on the agenda.

During the ISI period, all the main Southeast Asian automotive-producing countries used 'hard' (directive), 'vertical' (sector or industry-specific) policies to foster vehicle and component production, such as local content requirements and mandatory deletion policies. Following the start of operations of the World Trade Organization in 1995, such policies were banned from 2000 under prohibitions against trade-related industrial policies, particularly trade-related investment measures (TRIMs). These restrictions considerably reduced the 'policy space' (the range of policy options) that could be used by automotive producers, but, as we shall show in later chapters, some countries, particularly Thailand, have been able partially to circumvent such restrictions by imaginative measures.

In recent years, countries whose producers wish to export have needed to enter global value chains, where control ('governance') over entry and operations is exercised either by global buyers (as in garments) or by major producers (as in motor vehicles or electronics). Rather surprisingly, academic thinking about industrial policy, on the one hand, and GVCs, on the other, has tended to develop quite separately. In the 2010s, though, these separate strands have started to come together. Key GVC writers now are presenting one of their most important concerns – how domestic firms in developing countries can 'upgrade' their products, processes, and functions – in terms of industrial policies. Such policies also need to include policies towards major multinational component suppliers ('mega-suppliers') who exercise governance over smaller suppliers of components. Other new work on GVCs has recognised the importance of focusing on 'value-added trade' within GVCs, which recognises that many industrial exports, including motor vehicles, are highly import-intensive, with key components sourced from overseas, either on a global or a regional basis.

Notes

1 See Williamson (1990), Stiglitz (1998) and Rodrik (2006) for more details.
2 See *The Developmental State* edited by Woo-Cumings (1999) for more details.
3 This subsection draws heavily on Natsuda and Thoburn (2014).
4 Alavi (2005: 3) notes that Malaysia has complied with high standards of intellectual property protection since the 19th century, so complying with TRIPs within the stipulated five-year period up to 2000 caused few problems. She is of the opinion, though, that in the automotive industry TRIPs may limit future policy actions.
5 Least developed countries had a further two years beyond 2000.
6 Least-developed countries and developing countries with per capita income below US$1,000 were exempted from this prohibition.

7 Article 107 states that

> Save as otherwise provided in the Treaties, any aid granted by a Member State or through State resources in any form whatsoever which distorts or threatens to distort competition by favouring certain undertakings or the production of certain goods shall, in so far as it affects trade between Member States, be incompatible with internal common market.

See http://ec.europa.eu/competition/state_aid/legislation/provisions.html [accessed on 11 February 2019]

8 However, in their fair-minded and comprehensive study of work on industrial policies in South Korea, Taiwan, and Japan, Noland and Pack (2003: ch. 5) tend towards the view that other factors such as stable macroeconomic and real exchange rate policy, technology transfer policies, and infrastructural and education policies were of more importance. This was particularly so in the period from the 1970s onwards, whilst they concede more importance to industrial policy in those countries in their earlier post-war development.

9 Rodrik, in an innovative paper written for the United Nations Industrial Development Organization, UNIDO, proposes considerable updating of industrial policy too. He stresses the need for a policy architecture which 'embeds private initiative in a framework of public action that encourages restructuring, diversification, and technological dynamism beyond what market forces on their own would generate' (Rodrik 2004: 1). He stresses the need not so much to 'pick winners' as to identify losers quickly among the range of activities selected for help and to withdraw support. He notes, engagingly, that during the Washington Consensus years of the 1980s and1990s, actually a lot of industrial policy was conducted, mainly to encourage exports and inward FDI.

10 Vietnam, the other ASEAN automotive producer, is a special case since it did not incur full trade liberalization under AFTA until 2018, and until 2016 (when it overtook the Philippines), it was Southeast Asia's smallest producer of vehicles. More on Vietnam is in Thoburn and Natsuda (2017), and our Chapter 9.

11 The Philippines' other success was the development for export of wiring harnesses, an increasingly important component in vehicles with the increased use of electronics. However, this seems to have owed more to the product's basic labour-intensity of production and skill requirements than to policy (Natsuda and Thoburn 2018, Thoburn and Natsuda 2018).

12 According to the WTO *Trade Policy Review* (TPR) for Thailand in 2011 (p. 41, see www.wto.org), Thailand had been involved in 16 disputes going back to 1995, but only in three of these as a respondent, and none of the disputes was related to the automotive industry. In the case of Malaysia, successive TPRs (1997, 2001, 2006, 2010) indicate that Malaysia had not been involved in any trade disputes in the preceding five years where solution has been sought within the WTO framework (Natsuda and Thoburn 2014: 26).

13 However, note that a WTO ruling did require Thailand to eliminate various foreign investment incentives by 2004 as violating SCM subsidy restrictions (Brooks *et al.* 2003: 14)

14 The concept emphasizes value-added activities through the sequential and interconnected structure of economic activities (see Henderson *et al.* 2002, Porter 1990).

15 The approach focusses particularly on agricultural commodity chains from production to consumption by identifying agent and activities, but, in general, the analysis is based on the domestic value chain (see Kaplinsky and Morris 2001, Raikes *et al.* 2000).

16 The theory stresses how a hierarchical commodity chain is organised by identifying actors and activities across space (see Bair 2005, Hopkins and Wallerstain 1986).

17 For a useful overview of recent thinking in GVC research, see Satoshi Inomata in World Bank (2017: ch. 1).

18 See UNCTAD (2013: 172) for a discussion of some trade-offs between increasing value-added, on the one hand, and upgrading, on the other.
19 Non-domestic here refers to value-added originating overseas. Value-added originating in foreign-owned firms operating in the domestic economy is treated as domestic.
20 Our interview evidence suggests this is also done by some Japanese component firms in Malaysia with their associated companies.
21 Some component-makers in the automotive industry are outside this system, not being OEM (*original equipment manufacturer*) producers but makers of *replacement equipment* (like replacement tyres and batteries). Some Tier-1 suppliers make ODM (*original design manufacture*) products.
22 The drawing approval system is generally employed by Tier-1 suppliers, not by Tier-2 and 3 suppliers in Japan (Fujimoto *et al.* 1994).
23 This would be in terms of lower unit labour costs (wages adjusted for productivity), rather than lower wages *per se.* World Bank (2017: iv) summarises considerable evidence that low unit labour costs are not closely associated with actual lower wages in a variety of developing countries.

3 Overview of the automotive industry in Southeast Asia

Introduction

The automotive industry in Southeast Asia has been growing rapidly in the last few decades. The aim of this chapter is to provide an overview of this industry. It begins by discussing regional vehicle production and market trends, then explores the production, sales, and R&D activities of automotive producers – Japanese, US, European, Korean, and local capital firms in the region. Third, the chapter investigates the automotive and parts industry by examining capital accumulation, with a particular focus on local business groups in Southeast Asia. Fourth, the chapter examines Southeast Asia's vehicle and parts trade performance. It then offers some brief conclusions.

Vehicle production, sales, and market trends in Southeast Asia

Vehicle production in Southeast Asia has grown rapidly in the last few decades. Total production in the region was nearly 1.4 million units before the Asian financial crisis (AFC) in 1997–1998, at which point it dropped sharply to 427,372 units in 1998. The production volume increased rapidly throughout the 2000s, reaching over 2 million units in 2005, 3 million in 2010 and 4 million in 2012 (see Figure 3.1). According to Fourin (2019: 11), vehicle production in the region was 4,356,578 units in 2018, which was approximately 4.6% of the total world production, 95.6 million vehicles (OICA website).

Thailand is the largest producer in the region, accounting for over 2 million units in 2018, followed by Indonesia, Malaysia, Vietnam, and the Philippines. The Philippines was overtaken by Vietnam in the early 2010s. With regard to domestic sales, Indonesia is the largest market in Southeast Asia, with sales of over 1.1 million vehicles in 2018, followed by Thailand, Malaysia, the Philippines, and Vietnam. Table 3.1 gives an overview of the major ASEAN car producing countries during the period 1996–2018. Thailand and Indonesia are the only net exporting countries in terms of vehicle numbers (production more than domestic sales). With regard to the motorisation ratio, Malaysia shows the highest ratio of 439 vehicles per 1,000 members of the population in 2015, followed by Thailand,

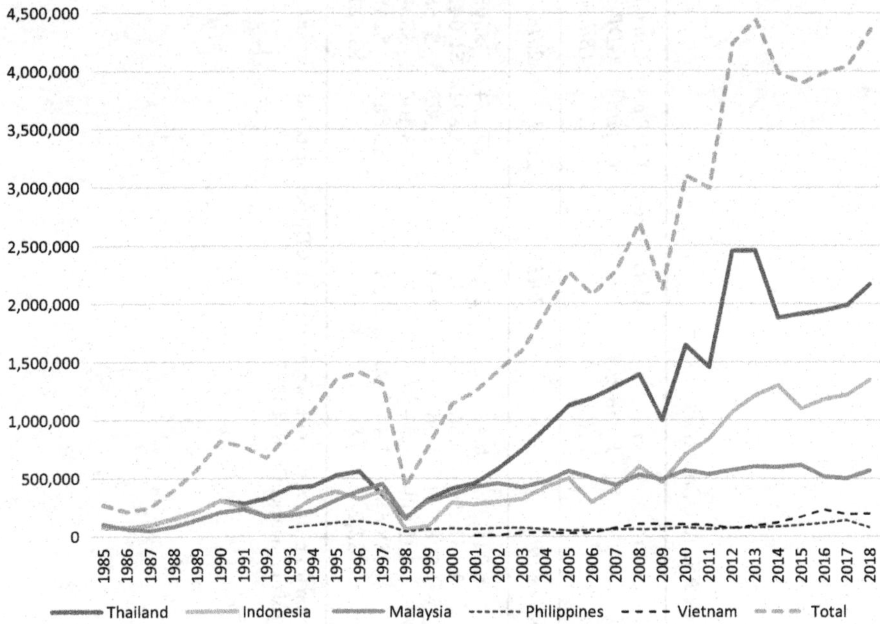

Figure 3.1 Vehicle Production in ASEAN-5 Countries 1985–2018.
Source: Adapted from Fourin (2017, 2019). Note: Number of Vehicles.

Indonesia, the Philippines, and Vietnam. Indeed, Malaysia has already overtaken Korea (417) and Taiwan (327) in terms of vehicle ownership (OICA website), so there may not be strong prospects there for the continued rapid growth of the domestic market (although Japan, with a ratio of 609, showed that there is still some potential for domestic market growth for vehicles). On the other hand, Indonesia, the Philippines, and Vietnam have a vast domestic market potential. In general, a GDP per capita of US $3,000 (measured at market exchange rates) is considered to be the starting point for motorisation (replacing motorcycles with cars). Indonesia reached US $3,000 in 2015, and the Philippines did so in 2018; Vietnam is expected to reach this threshold in the near future.

Table 3.2 gives an overview of the production structure of the automotive industry in Southeast Asia. In Thailand, there were 18 assemblers and 1,599 suppliers in 2017, accounting for a total employment of approximately 525,000 people. The leading producers in the country are Toyota, followed by Mitsubishi and Auto Alliance Thailand (AAT), which is a joint venture (JV) firm between Ford and Mazda. In Indonesia, there were 20 assemblers and approximately 1,550 suppliers in 2014, with total employment of 445,000 people. In addition, 14,000 authorised sales service and spare parts firms created 380,000 jobs, and 42,000 non-authorised sales service and spare parts firms generated 5,004,000 jobs (Fourin 2015: 89). The leading producers of the country are Daihatsu, followed by Toyota and Honda. Daihatsu produces several vehicles under Toyota's

Table 3.1 Overview of Production, Sales, and Motorisation Ratios in Major ASEAN Countries

	Production					*Sales*	*Sales / Production*	*Motorisation Ratio**	*GDP per Capita*	*Current GDP (Billion)*
	1996	*2008*	*2018*	*2018:1996*	*2018:2008*	*2018*	*2018*	*2015*	*2018*	*2018*
Thailand	559,428	1,393,742	2,167,694	3.87	1.56	1,041,739	0.48	228	$7,274	$505.0
Indonesia	325,495	600,628	1,343,714	4.13	2.24	1,151,291	0.86	87	$3,894	$1,042.2
Malaysia	390,609	530,810	564,971	1.45	1.06	598,714	1.06	439	$11,373	$358.6
Philippines	136,556	63,621	79,763	~~1.05~~ 0.58	~~1.82~~ 1.25	401,809	~~3.07~~ 5.4	38	$3,103	$330.9
Vietnam	n.a	107,918	200,436	n.a	1.86	288,683	1.44	23	$2,567	$245.2
Total	1,412,088	2,696,719	4,356,578	3.09	1.62	3,482,236	0.80	–	–	$2,481.9

Source: Production & (Domestic) Sales from Fourin (2017, 2018, 2019), Motorisation from OICA (website: www.oica.net), GDP per capita and Current GDP from World Development Indicator (Online). 1996 chosen as the years before the Asian Financial Crisis of 1997.
Note: Unit is the Number of Vehicles,
* vehicles per 1000 population,
n.a (not available)

JT corrected

Table 3.2 Overview of Production Structure of the Automotive Industry in Major ASEAN Countries

		Number of Assemblers	*Number of Parts Suppliers*	*Employment of Assemblers and Parts Suppliers*	*Main Producers (Production Number, Share)*
ASEAN-5	Thailand	18	1,599 Tier 1: 462 Tier 2: 1,137	525,000 Assembler: 100,000 Tier 1: 250,000 Tier 2: 175,000	1. Toyota (596,533: 27.5%) 2. Mitsubishi (385,192: 17.8%) 3. AAT (262,229: 12.1%) 2,167,694 units in 2018
	Indonesia[a]	20	1,550 Tier 1: 550 Tier 2&3: 1,000	445,000 Assembler: 45,000 Tier 1: 220,000 Tier 2&3: 180,000	1. Daihatsu (546,541: 40.7%) 2. Toyota (184,969: 13.8%) 3. Mitsubishi (164,107: 12.2%) 1,343,714 units in 2018
	Malaysia	27	641 Tier 1: 200 Tier 2&3: 441	709,457 including 53,001 firms in after service	1. Perodua (237,037: 42.0%) 2. Honda (108,531: 19.2%) 3. Proton (54,103: 9.6%) 564,971 units in 2018
	Philippines[b]	10	256 Tier 1: 124 Tier 2&3: 132	66,800 Assembler: 6,800 Suppliers: 60,000	1. Toyota (55,026: 47.1%) 2. Mitsubishi (22,008: 18.8%) 3. Honda (8,913: 7.6%) 116,868 units in 2016
	Vietnam[c]	21	n.a.	n.a.	1. Toyota (57,036: 24.2%) 2. Kia (52,866: 22.4%) 3. Mazda (32,108: 13.6%) 236,161 units in 2016

Source: Production data in Thailand, Indonesia, Malaysia from Fourin (2019), Philippines and Vietnam from Fourin (2017).

Note: n.a. (not available).

a assemblers and supplier information are based on 2014 (Fourin 2015).

b employment numbers: Interview with CAMPI (6 February 2015) and MVPMAP(10 February 2015).

c Kia and Mazda have a production subcontracting arrangement with Thaco.

OEM arrangement. Therefore, Toyota's market share in Indonesia is larger than that of Daihatsu.

Although the automotive production of Malaysia is much smaller than the above two countries, there are 27 assemblers. In this regard, most assemblers in Malaysia cannot utilise economies of scale. Indeed, the third-largest producer, Proton, produced only 73,400 units in 2016. Furthermore, the supporting industry is also relatively small, with approximately 641 suppliers (200 Tier-1 and 441 Tier-2&3 firms) in 2016. Perodua (a JV between Daihatsu and local capital) and Proton are regarded as Malaysia's national car producers. It is estimated that the automotive and related industries, including after-service employment, generated 709,457 jobs. Similarly, in the Philippines and Vietnam, all assemblers are facing difficulty in achieving economies of scale. In Vietnam, a local firm, Thaco (Truong Hai Auto), owns the largest production capacity of 71,000 units. They achieved this by forming JVs or subcontracting arrangements with foreign producers, such as Kia, Mazda, Peugeot, and Hyundai. Furthermore, Thaco produces buses and trucks under its brand name.

Automotive producers in Southeast Asia

Table 3.3 shows the production and market shares of major vehicle producers in Southeast Asia in 2016. Automotive assemblers can be categorised into five main types of capital (Japanese, US, Korean, Europe, and local) in Southeast Asia. First, Japanese assemblers show a significant presence: they accounted for a market share of over 80% in the region in 2016.

Toyota, particularly, shows the strongest regional presence, with over 936,000 units of production and sales, accounting for 23.3% of production and 29.0% of regional market shares.[1] In addition, Toyota's affiliate, Daihatsu (the third-largest producer in the region), accounted for 12.5% (17.8%, including Perodua) of production and a market share of 5.9% (12.3%, including Perodua).[2] In this context, over 40% of production and sales in Southeast Asia is controlled by the Toyota group. Table 3.4 shows the sales of the top five vehicle brands and market shares in Southeast Asia in 2016. Toyota was the most popular brand in all countries except Malaysia. It established its first assembly factory in the Philippines in 1962, followed by ones in Thailand in 1964, Malaysia in 1968, Indonesia in 1971, and Vietnam in 1995.[3] Until the 1980s, Toyota produced vehicles according to individual demands in Southeast Asia; each country has different types of demand for vehicles, typically one-ton pick-up trucks with diesel engines (Hilux model) in Thailand, multipurpose vehicles (MPVs) with gasoline engines in Indonesia (the Kijan model), and PVs in Malaysia and the Philippines. In the 1990s, Toyota introduced a special model for Southeast Asia, the Soluna, which was developed based on the Japanese Tercel model. In the past, Japanese automotive producers converted their models which were popular in developed countries into ones for use in emerging countries to adjust to local needs (Kamo 1999). However, since local demands are very different between developed and emerging countries, merely adjusting to emerging countries'

Table 3.3 Production and Market Shares of Major Producers in Southeast Asia, 2016

Rank	*Company*	*Country*	*Production*	*Share (%)*	*Sales*	*Share (%)*
1	Toyota	Japan	936,107	23.3	937,311	29.0
2	Honda	Japan	511,458	12.7	453,036	14.0
3	Daihatsu	Japan	501,831	12.5	190,625	5.9
4	Mitsubishi	Japan	402,796	10.0	197,477	6.1
5	Isuzu	Japan	284,606	7.1	210,417	6.5
6	Perodua	Malaysia	212,724	5.3	207,280	6.4
7	Nissan	Japan	193,409	4.8	153,095	4.7
8	Mazda	Japan	178,643	4.4	104,054	3.2
9	Suzuki	Japan	177,212	4.4	140,195	4.3
10	Ford	USA	166,148	4.1	112,657	3.5
11	Proton	Malaysia	73,400	1.8	73,034	2.3
12	Thaco	Vietnam	71,000	1.8	27,247	0.8
13	Hyundai	Korea	67,915	1.7	127,869	4.0
14	GM	USA	64,953	1.6	34,960	1.1
16	BMW	Germany	26,584	0.7	27,063	0.8
17	Daimler	Germany	23,349	0.6	39,980	1.2
18	VW	Germany	3,824	0.1	10,595	0.3
–	Other Japanese	Japan	92,915	2.3	105,018	3.2
–	Others	–	31,214	0.8	83,489	2.6
	Total		4,020,088	100	3,235,402	100

Source: Adapted from Fourin (2017).

Note: (1) Production is based on the ASEAN vehicle producing countries, Market share is based on all ASEAN countries except for Cambodia and Myanmar; (2) In Vietnam, Production figure is production capacity, and Sales figure is based on only VAMA member firms; (3) In Singapore, Sales figure is based on the number of registration of new vehicles; (4) Other Japanese firms include Hino, Fuso (Mitsubishi), UD, and Subaru.

markets turned out to be not enough to expand market share and profits. Consequently, in the 2000s, Toyota started to employ two vehicle development strategies: global common models and regionally specific/strategic models. In 2004, they established production and sales of 'Innovative International Multipurpose Vehicles' (IMVs, which can be considered as region-specific models) outside of Japan. Toyota chose Thailand as a major R&D and production base for IMV operations, producing 5 IMV models in 12 countries, including Indonesia, South Africa, Argentina, and Egypt (Ito 2014). For IMV's production in Southeast Asia, the Hilux model (one-ton pick-up truck) is mainly produced in Thailand, and the Fortuner and Innova (MPV) models are mainly produced in Indonesia. Furthermore, it is important to note that Toyota has successfully introduced its vehicles according to government policies in Southeast Asian countries – the Hilux model under the Detroit of Asia plan in Thailand, the Vios model under the Eco Car project in Thailand, and the Agya model in association with Daihatsu under the Low Cost Green Car (LCGC) project in Indonesia that has been in operation since the late 2000s.

Daihatsu has been associated with Toyota's regional strategy in Southeast Asia most recently. For instance, in Thailand, Toyota restructured its regional operation headquarters – Toyota Motor Asia Pacific Engineering and Manufacturing

Table 3.4 Sales of the Top Five Vehicle Brands and Market Share in Southeast Asia, 2016

Country	*Brand*	*Sales Unit*	*Market Share (%)*	*Country*	*Brand*	*Sales Unit*	*Market Share (%)*
Thailand	1. Toyota	245,087	31.9	[a]Singapore	1. Toyota	24,468	22.9
	2. Isuzu	143,170	18.6		2. Honda	19,349	18.1
	3. Honda	107,342	14.0		3. Nissan	10,852	10.2
	4. Mitsubishi	55,409	7.2		4. Mazda	7,091	6.6
	5. Nissan	42,677	5.6		5. Mercedes-Benz	6,945	6.5
	Others	175,103	22.8		Others	37,937	35.6
	Total	768,788	100.0		Total	106,642	100.0
Indonesia	1. Toyota	381,570	35.9	Brunei	1. Toyota	2,430	19.1
	2. Honda	199,364	18.8		2. Suzuki	1,665	13.1
	3. Daihatsu	189,683	17.9		3. Kia	1,486	11.7
	4. Suzuki	92,950	8.8		4. Hyundai	1,482	11.6
	5. Mitsubishi	66,443	6.3		5. Mitsubishi	834	6.6
	Others	131,725	12.4		Others	4,833	38.0
	Total	1,061,735	100.0		Total	12,730	100.0
Malaysia	1. Perodua	207,110	35.7	Laos	1. Toyota	11,651	39.5
	2. Honda	91,830	15.8		2. Hyundai	5,465	18.5
	3. Proton	72,290	12.5		3. Daehan	3,264	11.1
	4. Toyota	63,757	11.0		4. Kia	1,769	6.0
	5. Nissan	40,706	7.0		5. Howo	628	2.1
	Others	104,431	18.0		Others	6,717	22.8
	Total	580,124	100.0		Total	29,494	100.0
Philippines	1. Toyota	158,058	39.1	Myanmar			
	2. Mitsubishi	59,480	14.7				
	3. Hyundai	33,695	8.3				
	4. Ford	33,688	8.3		n.a.	n.a.	n.a.
	5. Isuzu	27,361	6.8				
	Others	91,774	22.7				
	Total	404,056	100.0				
[b]Vietnam	1. Toyota	58,701	21.6	Cambodia			
	2. Kia	52,866	19.4				
	3. Mazda	32,108	11.8				
	4. Ford	29,011	10.7		n.a.	n.a.	n.a.
	5. Thaco	27,247	10.0				
	Others	71,900	26.5				
	Total	271,833	100.0				

Source: Adapted from Fourin (2017).

Note: n.a. (not available).

a The number of registration of new vehicles.

b VAMA member firms only (total sales: 30,4427 units).

(TMAP-EM) – by integrating Daihatsu's operation and changing the name to 'Toyota Daihatsu Engineering and Manufacturing (TDEM)' in order to utilize Daihatsu's know-how with regards to the production of low cost, economical vehicles in 2017 (Fourin 2017: 165). In Indonesia, Daihatsu produces various Toyota-brand vehicles, such as the Agyo, Calya, Rush, and Town Ace models under OEM arrangements. Daihatsu's OEM production for Toyota was 196,935 units in 2011, increasing to 316,500 units in 2016. These OEM arrangements include not only selling to the domestic market but also exporting within the region as well as to the Middle East and Japan (Fourin 2017: 178–180). In 2016, Toyota manufactured 555,907 vehicles in Thailand, 218,720 in Indonesia, 56,454 in Malaysia, 55,026 in the Philippines, and 57,036 in Vietnam, while Daihatsu produced 501,831 units in Indonesia (Fourin 2017: 16). Both firms performed well in relation to actual production volume and capacity (see Table 3.5).

Nissan (the seventh-largest producer in Southeast Asia) and ***Mitsubishi*** (the fourth) formed the other main Japanese alliance network in 2016. Nissan also entered into an alliance with Renault in the late 1990s, making Nissan-Renault-Mitsubishi the second-largest car producer in the world and helping to save Nissan from failure.[4] Due to Mitsubishi's misrepresentation of fuel efficiency problems in April 2016,[5] Nissan took over Mitsubishi in October 2016. Mitsubishi manufactured 368,795 vehicles in Thailand, 22,008 in the Philippines, 6,113 in Vietnam, 3,452 in Indonesia, and 2,428 in Malaysia, while Nissan produced 113,197 vehicles in Thailand, 35,843 in Indonesia, 33,669 in Malaysia, 8,520 in the Philippines, and 2,180 in Vietnam in 2016 (Fourin 2017: 216 and 224). In Southeast Asia, Mitsubishi's operations are larger than those of Nissan. Indeed, Mitsubishi was a pioneer of Japanese automotive production in Asia. It employed strategic alliances with other Asian automobile producers, working with Hyundai in Korea in 1976, Proton in Malaysia in 1983, and Vina Star Motors in Vietnam in 1994 as JV partners (see Erdogdu 1999, Hatch 1995, Jomo 1994). As a part of its regional strategy, Mitsubishi uses its Thai operation as an export platform for its global markets. In 2016, 307,623 units out of 368,795 units of production was exported to Asia (87,248 units and 28.4%), Europe (79,060 units and 25.7%), North America (57,400 units and 18.7%), Oceania (37,001 units and 12.0%), South America (22,585 units and 7.3%), and others (2,429 units and 7.9%) (Fourin 2017: 224). In particular, Mitsubishi commenced the production of its Mirage model with the establishment of a third factory in 2012, exporting to the Japanese market (Nishimura and Kobayashi 2016: 33). In the Philippines, Mitsubishi formally acquired Ford's former factory, which has a 50,000-unit production capacity, and announced its participation in the Comprehensive Automotive Resurgence Strategy (CARS) programme in 2016 (Natsuda and Thoburn 2018).

However, in 2016, Mitsubishi produced only 402,000 vehicles out of its 805,500 production capacity, and Nissan used only 25.6% of its production capacity (see Table 3.5). In Indonesia, Nissan introduced its strategic brand name in emerging economies, 'Datsun'[6]; nevertheless its market share still decreased from 6% in 2012 to 3.6% in 2016 (Fourin 2017: 211–212). In response to this, Nissan attempted to strengthen its strategic network with Mitsubishi by arranging OEM-supply from Mitsubishi and expanding its range of products.[7] Nissan owns local partners in Southeast Asia: Siam Motors in Thailand, Indomibil in Indonesia, Tan Chong Motor in Malaysia, and Univation Motor in the Philippines. In Vietnam, TCIE Vietnam was established by its Malaysian partner, Tan Chong Motor (sic), in 2013 and produced 2,180 units of its Sunny model in 2016. Similarly, in Myanmar, Tan Chong Motor (Myanmar) was established by

Table 3.5 Production Capacity of Major Vehicle Producers in Southeast Asia, 2016

Firm	*Type*	*Thailand*	*Indonesia*	*Malaysia*	*Philippines*	*Vietnam*	*Total*
Toyota	CBU factory: number	5	3	2	1	1	12
	CBU: production capacity	700	256	76	50	46	1,128
	Parts factory: number	1	3	1	1	–	6
Daihatsu	CBU factory: number	–	2	2			4
	CBU: production capacity	–	530	430	–	–	960
	Parts factory: number	–	3	1	–	–	4
Mitsubishi	CBU factory: number	1	2	1	1	1	6
	CBU: production capacity	414	240	100	50	1.5	805.5
	Parts factory: number	1	1	–	1	–	3
Nissan	CBU factory: number	2	2	2	2	1	9
	CBU: production capacity	370	250	100	30	6.5	756.5
	Parts factory: number	2	–	–	–	–	2
Honda	CBU factory: number	2	2	1	1	1	7
	CBU: production capacity	420	200	100	15	10	745
	Parts factory: number	–	1	1	1	–	3
Isuzu	CBU factory: number	2	1	1	1	1	6
	CBU: production capacity	466	52	12	15	94	639
	Parts factory: number	3	1	–	1	–	5
Suzuki	CBU factory: number	1	2	–	–	1	4
	CBU: production capacity	100	265	–	–	5	370
	Parts factory: number	–	–	–	–	–	0
Proton	CBU factory: number	–	–	2	–	–	2

Firm	*Type*	*Thailand*	*Indonesia*	*Malaysia*	*Philippines*	*Vietnam*	*Total*
	CBU: production capacity	–	–	360	–	–	360
	Parts factory: number	–	–	1	–	–	1
Ford	CBU factory: number	2	–	1	–	1	4
	CBU: production capacity	290	–	30	–	14	334
	Parts factory: number	–	–	–	–	–	–
GM	CBU factory: number	1	–	–	–	1	2
	CBU: production capacity	180	–	–	–	30	210
	Parts factory: number	1	–	–	–	–	–
Hyundai	CBU factory: number	–	2	3	1	2	8
	CBU: production capacity	–	20	80	10	90	200
	Parts factory: number	–	–	–	–	–	–
Mazda	CBU factory: number	2	–	1	–	1	4
	CBU: production capacity	140	–	20	–	10	170
	Parts factory: number	2	–	–	–	–	2
Total	CBU factory: number	17	17	16	7	9	66
	CBU: production capacity	3,080	1,813	1,308	170	307	6,678
	Parts factory: number	10	9	4	4	–	27

Source: Adapted from Fourin (2017).

Note: (1) Production capacity: unit-1000 vehicles; (2) OEM assemblers are included in factory number; (3) Parts factory: majority owned factory by assemblers; (4) Perodua is included in Daihatsu; and (5) Hyundai includes Kia and 50,000 units of Thaco's capacity in Vietnam.

Tan Chong Motor in Malaysia in 2017, planning to assemble 10,000 units of the Sunny model in 2019 (Fourin 2017: 216–217).

Honda is the second-largest producer in the region (see Table 3.3). They manufactured 200,004 units of vehicles in Thailand, 195,095 units in Indonesia, 96,414 units in Malaysia, 11,032 units in Vietnam, and 8,913 units in the

Philippines in 2016 (Fourin 2017: 2000). Its production capacity utilisation is also relatively high. In terms of sales, Honda has a strong presence in Thailand, Indonesia, and Malaysia (see Table 3.4). In particular, Honda has expanded its Thai operation with the opening of a new plant with a 120,000-unit production capacity in 2016.[8] ***Isuzu*** is the fifth-largest producer in Southeast Asia. They located its main operations in Thailand and Indonesia. In 2016, they produced 243,016 vehicles in Thailand, 14,062 in Indonesia, 12,420 in Malaysia, 8,295 in the Philippines, and 6,813 in Vietnam (Fourin 2017: 249), and its main products are one-ton pick-up trucks and medium- and large-sized commercial vehicles (trucks and buses). Previously, Isuzu developed its Panther and D-MAX models (pick-up trucks) jointly with GM under GM's capital tie-up with Isuzu from 1971. Although the capital tie-up ended in 2006, Isuzu and GM developed the current D-MAX model in Isuzu's R&D centre in Thailand in 2010 (Nishimura and Kobayashi 2016: 35). However, this alliance seems to have ended. In the development of new one-ton pick-up trucks (expected to be introduced in 2020), Isuzu announced (1) termination of joint development with GM and (2) OEM supply to Mazda (Fourin 2017: 245). In this context, Isuzu is planning to achieve economies of scale in production by supplying to Mazda.

Mazda (the eighth-largest producer) utilises its full production capacity in Southeast Asia, producing 178,643 vehicle, compared to its production capacity of 170,000 in 2016. Mazda manufactured 135,787 vehicles in Thailand, 32,108 in Vietnam, and 10,748 in Malaysia in 2016 (Fourin 2017: 237). Its regional strategy is based on JVs and subcontracting. Ford, which had been the largest equity holder in Mazda since 1979, is still one of its JV partners in Southeast Asia, even though Ford sold all its shares of Mazda in 2015.[9] Auto Alliance Thailand (AAT), established in 1998 between Ford and Mazda, has two factories in Thailand. The second, established in 2009, has a 100,000-unit production capacity and is used for only Mazda production. In the first factory, 40,000 units out of 140,000 units were used for Mazda after 2015. In Malaysia, Mazda contracted local assembler Inokom in 2013, assembling 8,308 units of the CX-5 model and 2,440 units of the Mazda 3 model in Malaysia. In Vietnam, Mazda uses the local firm Thaco for the assembly of 32,108 vehicles, under an OEM arrangement (Fourin 2017: 237).

Suzuki (the ninth-largest producer) is planning to develop its strategy in Southeast Asia as a global production and supply hub, after Japan and India.[10] Its main focus in the region is on Indonesia and Thailand. In 2016, it manufactured 113,243 vehicles in Indonesia, 56,275 in Thailand, and 7,694 in Vietnam (Fourin 2017: 231). In Indonesia, in 1976, Suzuki established its factory in association with a local partner, the Indomibil group. More recently, in 2015, Suzuki expanded its production capacity with the establishment of a new plant with a 120,000-unit capacity. In Thailand, Suzuki's operation is relatively new; Suzuki established its factory and commenced its vehicle production with a 10,000-unit production capacity in 2012 (Fourin 2015: 264). In 2016, Suzuki produced 56,275 vehicles in Thailand (Fourin 2017: 230–231). In Malaysia, it subcontracted Proton to assemble its vehicles but withdrew from the market upon the termination of the arrangement in 2015. In Vietnam, Suzuki established a factory with a 5,000-unit production capacity in 1996, much earlier than it did in Thailand, producing 7,694 vehicles in 2016. It is also worth noting that Suzuki established a factory with 10,000 units of production in Myanmar in 2016, planning to assemble vehicles in 2018 (ibid.).

In addition, major US producers ***Ford*** (the tenth-largest producer in the region) and ***GM*** (the fourteenth) have each conducted a major restructuring of production operations in Southeast Asia. In terms of automotive production history in Southeast Asia, GM commenced its assembly operation in Indonesia in 1928 (Sato 1992). In Thailand, Ford established the first assembly firm, the Thai Motor Company, with local capital in 1961 (TAI 2008). Although both companies formed a strong tie with Japanese partners (Ford-Mazda and GM-Isuzu), these alliances are becoming less significant. Consequently, both firms have been restructuring their operations in Southeast Asia. Ford had been a leading vehicle producer in the Philippines for a long time but withdrew from production in the country in 2012 (Natsuda and Thoburn 2018). Furthermore, in 2015, it closed its production and sales operations in the rapidly growing market of Indonesia due to a mismatch between its products and market demands.[11] The Indonesian market demands small MPVs (which can accommodate relatively large families) and small PVs under the LCGC project of 2015. However, Ford did not produce these types of vehicles in Indonesia and, as a consequence, moved its management to Thailand (Fourin 2017: 284). At the moment, Ford owns two production operations: AAT with Mazda (100,000 units of production capacity for Ford production) and Ford Thailand, with a 150,000-unit production capacity, producing vehicles (166,148 units) only in Thailand. Thus, Ford uses Thailand as a regional export platform. Similarly, GM withdrew from the Indonesian market in 2015. It currently owns two production operations in Thailand and Vietnam, producing 55,227 units and 9,726 units, respectively, in 2016. Although GM is planning to downsize its Thai operation, GM's affiliate in China, SAIC-GM, is planning to establish a production facility of 150,000 units in Indonesia (Fourin 2017: 278–283).

Meanwhile, the Korean ***Hyundai*** group (Hyundai and Kia) shows relatively high market shares in the countries with relatively small automotive market demand, such as the Philippines, Vietnam, Brunei, and Laos (see Table 3.4). Hyundai (the thirteenth-largest producer) produced 67,915 vehicles and sold 127,869 in 2016 (Table 3.3), even though it owns 200,000 units of production capacity in the region (Table 3.5). In Hyundai, the group's strategies are characterised by (1) subcontracting to local assemblers in the region and (2) trade (exporting from Korea) rather than its own local production (Nishimura and Kobayashi 2016: 38). Hyundai operates its own factory of 10,000 units of production capacity in Indonesia and set up subcontracting arrangements with Inokom and Naza Automotives in Malaysia, Columbian Autocar in the Philippines, and Thaco and Thanh Cong in Vietnam; in this way 510 vehicles were produced in Indonesia, 4,933 in Malaysia, and 62,472 in Vietnam in 2016 (Fourin 2017: 276–277). In the Philippines, Hyundai was interested in the CARS programme (see Natsuda and Thoburn 2018) but gave up due to the requirement to produce 200,000 vehicles over the six-year period specified in the policy. In Vietnam, a local partner, Thaco, has been assembling Kia models since 2007. Hyundai also made a subcontracting arrangement for passenger vehicle production with the Thanh Cong group in 2011, upgrading the arrangement into a JV firm in 2017. Hyundai and Thanh Cong also established another JV firm for commercial vehicle production in the same year (Fourin 2019: 139). Although the Hyundai group has been slowly expanding its production capacity in the region, the FTA (Free Trade Agreement) with ASEAN is becoming increasingly important for Korean assemblers. Korea established the ASEAN–Korea FTA in 2007 at a multilateral level and formed a bilateral FTA agreement with Vietnam in 2015.[12]

Fourth, European producers are virtually non-existent in Southeast Asia. The world's leading producer, ***Volkswagen* (VW)**, produced a mere 3,828 vehicles in Southeast Asia in 2016. The VW group had been interested in a production operation in Southeast Asia for a long time, but this was not successful. In Malaysia, VW tried – and failed – to take over Proton (Athukorala and Kohpaiboon 2010, Nizamuddin 2008, Natsuda *et al.* 2013). VW also applied to join the Eco Car project in Thailand and the LCGC project in Indonesia, and received approval but then gave up trying to set up full production operations. In Thailand, in 2007, VW could not meet the requirements of the Eco Car scheme due to its weak supplier networks in Southeast Asia. In Indonesia, in 2013, they announced the establishment of a new factory with a 50,000-unit production capacity (Natsuda *et al.* 2015a), but in 2016 announced the discontinuation of the project during its chaotic fuel-efficiency misrepresentation problem. VW also eventually abandoned applying for the CARS programme in the Philippines. It is currently conducting small scale OEM production through DRB-Hicom in Malaysia and the Indomobil group in Indonesia. Hence, its currently strategy depends on exporting to the region. In contrast, ***BMW*** and ***Daimler* (*Mercedes-Benz*)** show more presence than their competitor ***Audi*** (a member of the VW group) in the upper market segment of Southeast Asia. In general, European assemblers contract local assembly firms to assemble SKD (semi-knocked down) or CKD kits for their production.

Fifth, local car producers, such as ***Proton*** and ***Perodua***, have over 50% of the market share in Malaysia. In 1983, the Malaysian Prime Minister Mahathir initiated the first National Car Project under HICOM; then Proton was established as a joint venture between HICOM and the Mitsubishi group. Subsequently, the Prime Minister conducted the second national car project, with the establishment of Perodua as a joint venture between Daihatsu Motors and Malaysian firms in 1993 (Jomo 1994, Machado 1994). Proton is the eleventh-largest producer in Southeast Asia. It was a leading vehicle producer in Malaysia for a long time, but its production dropped by one-third, from 232,000 units in 2002 to 73,000 units in 2016. Mitsubishi, which had been a JV partner, sold its equity of Proton due to Mitsubishi's financial problems in Japan and the diminishing sales of Proton in Malaysia in 2004 (Natsuda *et al.* 2013, Segawa *et al.* 2014). After Mitsubishi's withdrawal from Proton, there were many rumours about acquisition plans by VW, Honda, etc., but in 2017, the Chinese automotive producer Geely took over 49.9% of the equity from Proton's share holder DRB-Hicom.[13]

Unlike Proton, under Daihatsu's management, Perodua has steadily been expanding its production from 139,544 vehicles in 2011 to 207,110 in 2016. In fact, Perodua is the sixth-largest assembler in Southeast Asia.

Thaco, a state-owned enterprise in Vietnam, established in 1997, was ranked as the twelfth-largest vehicle producer in the region in 2016. Thaco produces its own CVs – buses and trucks – and has been increasingly subcontracting PV assembling operations with foreign producers, including Mazda, Hyundai, and the PSA Group (formerly PSA Peugeot Citroën). In its own CV production, Thaco receives technical assistance from Foton in China (Nishimura and Kobayashi 2016: 44–45).[14] In Southeast Asia, there are many local assembling firms, such as Thonburi Automotive Assembly (for Mercedes) and Bangchan General Assembly (for TATA) in Thailand, Tan Chong Motor (for Nissan, Renault, Mitsubishi, and Subaru) and Hicom Automotive Manufactures (for VW and Mercedes) in Malaysia, Indomibil (for Suzuki, Nissan, Hino Volvo, and Renault) in Indonesia, and Columbian (for Kia) in the Philippines. These firms specialise in assembling operations for foreign producers under subcontracting agreements. Lastly, it is worth noting that Asian emerging vehicle producers, such as Geely, Chery, SAIC from China, and TATA from India, are slowly expanding their presence in the region.

R&D in Southeast Asia

Thailand is the leading automotive producer in the region, and its R&D capacity has been strengthened by four firms – Toyota, Honda, Nissan, and Isuzu – engaging in R&D activities. With regards to R&D centres, the leading producer in the country, Toyota, set up its 'Toyota Technical Centre Asia Pacific' in 2003. In 2007, this was integrated with some of the regional headquarters functions of Toyota Motor Asia Pacific in Singapore, renamed 'Toyota Motor Asia Pacific Engineering and Manufacturing (TMAP-EM)', and put in charge of R&D and regional procurement.[15] In 2017, TMAP-EM was renamed Toyota Daihatsu Engineering and Manufacturing (TDEM) in collaboration with Daihatsu, utilising the latter's know-how in terms of the production of low cost and economical vehicles. TDEM employed approximately 2,550 people in one of the largest R&D centres in Thailand (Fourin 2017: 39). In response to Thailand's 'product champion' policy, Toyota relocated all its production as well as the R&D of the Hilux model (a pick-up truck) from Japan to Thailand. Consequently, Toyota's Thai operation has become its IMV development location and the base for its global production networks. In addition, Toyota has been expanding the development of small passenger vehicles in association with Daihatsu. Isuzu established the first R&D centre, 'Isuzu Technical Centre of Asia', in 1991, employing 271 people in 2017. Like Toyota, Isuzu relocated its main R&D operation for pick-up trucks from Japan to Isuzu Technical Centre of Asia in 2010. Furthermore, Isuzu Global CV Engineering Centre (which employed 159 people in 2017) was established in 2014 in order to develop low cost medium- and large-sized commercial vehicles (previously done in Japan)

Table 3.6 Main R&D Facilities of Assemblers in Southeast Asia

Firm	*Country*	*Function*	*Est. Year*	*R&D Organisation*
Toyota	Thailand	R&D/ RHQ	2017 (2003)	Toyota Daihatsu Engineering and Manufacturing
Daihatsu	Indonesia	R&D	2017	Astra Daihatsu Motor Karawang factory
(Perodua)	Malaysia	R&D	n.a.	Perodua Manufacturing Rawang factory
Honda	Thailand	R&D	2005	Honda R&D Asia Pacific
	Indonesia	R&D	2013	Honda R&D Indonesia
Nissan	Thailand	R&D/ RHQ	2011	Nissan Motor Asia Pacific
Isuzu	Thailand	R&D	1991	Isuzu Technical Center of Asia
	Thailand	R&D/ RHQ	2014	Isuzu Global CV Engineering Center
Proton	Malayasia	R&D	n.a.	Proton Shah Alam factory

Source: Adapted from Fourin (2017).

Note: n.a. (not available).

and procure components locally (ibid.). Meanwhile, Honda's R&D function initially targeted the body design of its models in the Asia Pacific region and later expanded to include all R&D operations except for powertrain development. Also, Nissan Motors Asia Pacific (NMAP) is in charge of R&D and Regional Headquarter (RHQ). In addition, NMAP developed testing functions for all vehicles produced in Southeast Asia, exporting to over 90 countries (ibid.). In Indonesia, Daihatsu started R&D operations and established its R&D centre in 2017; this centre is in charge of the design and evaluation of all vehicles produced in Indonesia (ibid.: 185). In 2013, Honda also established an R&D centre in Indonesia for supporting the operation of its models (ibid.: 203). In Malaysia, the two national car producers own R&D centres (Table 3.6). Proton, particularly, carries out R&D functions not only in Malaysia but also in its affiliated company, Lotus, in the UK (ibid.: 268).

The local automotive and parts industry in Southeast Asia

The ASEAN countries initially launched the development of their automobile industries by adopting import substituting industrialisation (ISI) policies in the 1960s. However, significant differences emerged among the ASEAN countries. Malaysia launched the first national car project in the early 1980s, originally in collaboration with Mitsubishi, protecting its domestic market directly until 2004 and indirectly into the present (see Chapter 7 on Malaysia). In contrast, Thailand, Indonesia, and the Philippines depended almost entirely upon the production of automotive MNCs, particularly Japanese producers. The automotive industry in Thailand, Indonesia, and the Philippines was gradually liberalised through regional trade agreements in the 1990s, and the liberalisation of the industry under the WTO was completed in the early 2000s. In the early years of the automotive industry in ASEAN, capital accumulation in the industry was made in conjunction with foreign producers, particularly Japanese MNCs, though stipulating local content requirements, at least until WTO rules outlawed such requirements around 2000. One of the motives in forming alliances with foreign producers lay in Southeast Asia's technological backwardness. Where Southeast Asian entrepreneurs were involved they employed foreign technology to develop the automobile industry under government protection. However, the recent development of local components industries in Southeast Asia seems to have followed a somewhat different path than the assembly sector. Indeed, a number of Tier-1 suppliers in Southeast Asia, particularly in Thailand, have grown from ISI types of business operations into more regionally and globally oriented operations by upgrading into internationally operating firms. This section first examines how local business groups helped create the automotive industry in Southeast Asia, contrasting Siam Motors in Thailand with Proton in Malaysia during the early stages of capital accumulation. Both companies were linked with Japanese assemblers, but their development approaches were different. Second, this section investigates leading local automotive parts suppliers in Thailand, Indonesia, Malaysia, and the Philippines, and examines their status in global production networks.

Local capital in assembly

The Siam Motors group (SMG) in Thailand is one of the most prominent cases to demonstrate the process of local capital accumulation alongside foreign capital in Southeast Asia.[16] Thawon Phornprapha established Siam Motors by importing and distributing Nissan trucks and commercial vehicles in 1952 (Suehiro 1989). After the implementation of the tariff system in 1962, Thawon established Siam Motors & Nissan to assemble Nissan cars domestically instead of importing them (Phongpaichit and Baker 1995: 136). The success of Siam Motors led Thawon to diversify his manufacturing businesses using Japanese corporations. He set up Siam Yamaha with Yamaha Motor and Prince Motors Thailand with Prince Motors[17] in 1964. After 1966, he developed his business with the automobile parts manufacturing industry in cooperation with the Nissan group. In addition to the automobile industry, in 1991, Thawon formed a joint venture with Hitachi for an elevator business and another with Komatsu on construction machinery production in 1995. Suehiro (1989: 237) has noted three characteristics in the development of SMG. First, its major business was centred in the core industry of automotive production, and most of its commercial activities were related to the importation or distribution of cars. In addition, its financial business has assisted consumer credit for automobile customers. In short, SMG's business activities diversified both vertically and horizontally on the basis of its automobile business. Second, SMG was fully assisted by the Japanese both financially and technologically. Third, almost all of Thawon's manufacturing firms were supported by the Thai government, with privileges such as tax exemption. In SMG, its development strategy was, to some extent, characterised by an ISI type of development model, diversifying its businesses in the domestic market in association with MNCs.

In contrast, Malaysia launched national car projects. Perusahaan Otomibile Nasional Sendirian Bhd (Proton) was established as a JV firm between Mitsubishi Motors and Mitsubishi Corporation (holding 15%, RM 75 million equity each) and the Heavy Industries Corporation of Malaysia (HICOM), and was placed under the Minister of Trade and Industry (holding 70%, RM 490 million equity) in May 1983[18] (Machado 1994: 300–301). Malaysia's first national car, the Proton Saga, a slightly modified Mitsubishi Lancer, was initially planned to be produced for the domestic market at a capacity of 5,000 vehicles in the first year, 1985 (Abdulsomad 1999: 278). The project aimed to foster the development of the automotive industry, in particular, encouraging related industries, such as the parts and components industry, and other supporting industries. This led to a greater utilisation of locally made components to facilitate the upgrading of technology, engineering and technical skills, and increase *bumiputra* (indigenous, mainly local Malay) involvement in the automobile industry, in which foreign capital and local ethnic-Chinese capital had long dominated (ibid.). In order to secure Mitsubishi's participation and financial viability for the project, the Malaysian government guaranteed its market dominance and offered a special incentive by exempting it from a newly imposed 40% import duty on CKD kits. In addition to this, the 50% excise duty, which was reduced to 25% for the Proton Saga, was imposed on the net sales price for all other vehicles (Torii 1991a). Low interest rate loans were provided to encourage civil servants to purchase the Proton Saga (Abdulsomad 1999: 279). In 1993, the Malaysian government launched a second national project, a joint venture, Perusahaan Otomobile Kedua Sdn. Bhd. (Perodua),[19] established with Daihatsu. It began to produce a mini-car called 'Kancil' based on Daihatsu's Mira model as government officials believed that lower income buyers might switch from motorcycles to mini-cars (Fujita and Hill 1997: 314). The Malaysian government employed a protectionist industry policy in the automobile industry over a long period, finally liberalising under the WTO and AFTA in 2004. Regarding the development of the automotive industry, the Malaysian approach seems to be characterised by a sort of developmental state model. However, although Malaysia developed its own national car companies, overall in Southeast Asia automotive MNCs have played a critical role in the development of the automotive industry in terms of capital accumulation and technology transfer. Furthermore, local assembling subcontractors also depend on automotive MNCs.

Local Tier-1 suppliers

Doner and Wad (2014: 668–669) note that Southeast Asia's automotive industrialisation is based on the dominance of foreign capital firms, in comparison with Northeast Asia, where the local automotive industry has successfully developed in association with national vehicle assemblers by sourcing locally produced parts. There is no doubt that the Southeast Asian automotive industry depends on foreign capital more heavily than its Northeast Asian counterparts. Nevertheless, it is difficult to sustain the argument that the Southeast Asian automotive industry, in particular, the automotive parts industry, entirely depends on foreign capital – for example, in comparison with rapidly growing Central and Eastern Europe (CEE), whose automotive industry depends almost entirely on foreign-owned Tier-1 firms as a result of the rapid liberalisation policies in CEE transitional economies (see Egresi 2007, Natsuda *et al.* 2020a, Natsuda *et al.* 2020b, Pavlinek 2002, Pavlinek and Janak 2007).[20] In contrast to the CEE automotive parts industry, Southeast Asia's automotive parts industry has developed and upgraded itself by linking local capital to foreign technology. Moreover, a number of local suppliers in Thailand and (to some extent) Malaysia have grown into multinational automotive suppliers in recent years.

In the ASEAN-4 countries, there are over 4,000 automotive parts suppliers. Of these, 40% are located in Thailand, 38% are located in Indonesia, 16% are located in Malaysia, and 6% are located in the Philippines. Of these firms, 1,336 (or 33%) are classified as Tier-1 suppliers. In Thailand, there were 1,599 parts suppliers in 2017. Of 462 Tier-1 firms, 31% were wholly foreign-owned firms, 27% were foreign majority JV firms, 3% were 50% local JV capital firms, 16% were local majority JV firms, and 23% were Thai-owned firms. Of 1,137 Tier-2 firms, 31% were wholly foreign-owned firms, 12% were foreign majority JV firms, 15% were local majority JV firms, and 42% were Thai-owned firms (Fourin 2017: 35). In Indonesia, there were 1,550 suppliers (550 Tier-1 and 1,000 Tier 2&3 firms) in 2015 (Fourin 2015: 89). With regard to types of capital, of 161 member firms in GIAMM (Indonesian automotive parts association) in 2012, 91 firms were foreign or JV firms (69 were Japanese), and 65 firms were local capital (Interview with GIAMM, 20 February 2013). In Malaysia, there were 641 suppliers: 200 Tier-1 firms and 441 Tier-2 or -3 firms (Fourin 2017: 89). Due to Malaysia's vendor development programme, local-capital firms play an important role in its automotive supply chain networks. In the Philippines, of 256 suppliers in 2014, 90 were Tier-1 suppliers (of which were 60% were JV firms, 30% were foreign firms, and 10% were local capital firms), and 176 firms Tier-2 suppliers, owned by local capitals (Interview with MVPMAP, 10 February 2015). All multinational 'mega-suppliers' of parts, such as Denso and Aisin from Japan, Bosch and Continental from Germany, and Delphi and Johnson Control from the US, are engaged in supplying components to assemblers in the region. With regards to sourcing by mega-suppliers (all Tier-1), one of the leading Japanese mega-suppliers sourced from 260 Tier-2 suppliers in Thailand in 2011. Of these, approximately 30% were purely local Tier-2 suppliers, and the rest were to some extent related to Japanese capital in Thailand.[21] The other leading Japanese mega-supplier sourced 50–60% of sub-components from purely local Tier-2 suppliers and the rest from Japanese-related Tier-2 suppliers in Thailand.[22] It is worth noting that as a result of a massive FDI by Japanese Tier-1 suppliers into Thailand's Eco Car project after 2010, local Tier-1 suppliers were divided into two categories: large local Tier-1 suppliers, which remain in the production networks as Tier-1 suppliers, and smaller local Tier-1 firms, which shifted down to Tier-2.[23]

As we noted in Chapter 2, some studies claim that assemblers have a positive influence on technology and management transfer to local suppliers in the automotive industry, while others assert that automotive MNCs do not always upgrade local suppliers, although MNCs do bring in their technology and managerial skills. In this context, Humphrey investigated five firm strategies and trajectories of local automotive parts suppliers in their relations with automotive MNCs in Brazil and India: (1) growing as a multinational Tier-1 supplier (expansion to outside of the country but on a relatively small scale from a global perspective); (2) developing an alliance with a leading global component manufacturer; (3) becoming a national Tier-1 supplier; (4) moving to a profitable niche in the Tier-2 segment; and (5) specialising as the global supplier of a particular product (Humphrey 2000: 266–267).

With regard to assembler-supplier relations in Southeast Asia, local executives in the automotive industry identified some differences between Japanese and US/European assemblers in terms of procurement. In its view, Japanese assemblers organise Japanese-like *keiretsu* systems of procurement/production networks in Southeast Asia. On the one hand, Japanese procurement systems provide stable and long-term business relationships based on trust, guarantee of technical support, and flexibility of production and quantity. On the other hand, Japanese production networks often prevent the new entry of firms.[24] In this context, US/European assemblers employ a market-based system and are thus more open to new suppliers. However, in extreme cases, they compare the price of local components of Southeast Asia with those of imported components from China and India. If imported components are more competitive, assemblers tend to use imported components.[25] In relation to technical assistance, US and European assemblers force local suppliers in Southeast Asia to purchase the latest machinery in order to meet its requirement of quality, cost, and delivery (QCD). In this regard, it is very difficult for local suppliers to make large investments for a short-term supply contract under the US/European system.[26] By contrast, Japanese assemblers encourage them to conduct *kaizen* activities in order to improve their technological capability and achieve their QCD standard. From a cost perspective, a Japanese approach is more favourable for local suppliers.[27]

Thailand

In the local automotive parts industry of Thailand, the government's localisation policy was very effective for the creation of backward linkages in the automotive industry. Local automotive suppliers benefited from the policy, and many local entrepreneurs developed automotive parts businesses in cooperation with foreign capital (particularly from Japan) and diversified their businesses (Ueda 2009). First is the case of SMG, which can be seen as a typical example of type (2), described above, developing an alliance with a leading global component manufacturer in the automotive parts sector. SMG has developed not only an assembly business with Nissan but also automotive parts production. It has established SNN Tools and Dies, Nissan Power Train, and Siam Nissan Body in association with Nissan (see Table 3.7). SMG also diversified its parts production by establishing over 20 JVs, along with foreign producers, such as Yuasa, NSK, Riken, Calsonic, KYB, and Hitachi from Japan; Valeo from France; and Bosch and Mahle from Germany.[28]

Table 3.7 Major Local Automotive Parts Producers in Thailand, 2018

Group Name	*Main Affiliates*
Siam Motors Group in 1952	SNN Tools and Dies, Nissan Power Train, and Siam Nissan Body (with Nissan), Siam GS Battery, Siam Yuasa Siam Industry (with Yuasa, Japan), Siam NSK Steering Systems, NSK Bearings Manufacturing, NSK Bearings (with NSK, Japan), Mahle Siam Filter Systems, Mahle Siam Electric Drives (with Mahle, Germany), Valeo Siam Thermal Systems (with Valeo, France), Siam Riken Industrial (with Riken, Japan), Siam NGK Spark Plug (with NGK, Japan), Siam Carsonic (with Carsonic, Japan), Siam Hitachi Automotive Product (with Hitachi, Japan), Siam Chita (with Chita, Japan), Bosch Automotive (with Bosch, Germany), KYB Thailand (with KYB, Japan), Nittan Thailand (with Nittan, Japan), etc.
Somboon Group in 1962 Core firm: Somboon Advance Technology (originally Somboom Spring)	• Direct subsidiaries: Somboom Malleable Iron Industrial Company, Bangkok Spring Industrial Company, and International Casting Product, Somboon Forging Technology • JVs: Tsuchiyoshi Somboon Coated Sand (with Tsuchiyoshi, Japan), Yamada Somboon (with Yamada, Japan), Nisshinbo Somboon Automotive (with Nisshinbo, Japan), Somboon Sonic Manufacturing (Sonic Ishikawa, Japan)
Thai Rung Group in 1967 Core firm: Thai Rung Union Car	• Direct subsidiaries: Thai Rung Tools&Dies, Thai Auto Press parts, Thai VP Auto Service, and Thai Ultimate Car • JVs: Thai Auto Conversion (with Toyota Autobody, Japan), Delta Thai Rung (with Delta, Japan), Kyowa Thai Rung (with Kyowa Sangyo, Japan), and Trex Thai Rung (with Nippon Trex, Japan)
Summit Group: in 1972 Core firms Summit Auto Seats Industry (SAS) in 1972 Summit Auto body Industry (SAB) in 1986	• Thailand: Modern Products Industry, Summit Engineering Center, Auto Advance Material Manufacturing, Summit Laemchabang Auto Seats Manufacturing, Auto Interior Products (under SAS), Summit Auto Tech Industry, Summit Laemchabang Auto Body Work, Summit R&D, Summit Auto Body Skill Development Center (under SAB) • JVs in Thailand: SAS - Johnson Control & Summit Interior (with Johnson Control, US), Thai Steel Cable Industry (with Hilex, Japan), Thai Seat Belt (with Tokai Rika, Japan), STB Textile Industry (Toyota Boshoku, Japan), etc. (under SAS); Showa Autoparts (with Showa, Japan), Hiruta & Summit, Bangkok Eagle Wings (with Hiruta Kogyo, Japan), Sankei Summit (with Sankei Giken Kogyo, Japan) etc.(under SAB); Summit Showa Manufacturing (with Showa, Japan), and other 7 firms (under SAS and SAB) • Overseas: Summit Auto Seats Industry (Guangzhou and Wuhan), Summit Auto Seats Alliance in China, Summit Auto Seats Industry in Delhi India, Summit Auto Seats Industry in Hanoi Vietnam, SAB-PT Summit Adyawinsa (Indonesia) under SAS • Overseas JV in Vietnam: SAS Marubishi Summit Industry (with Marubishi, Japan) under SAS

(*Continued*)

Group Name	*Main Affiliates*
AAPICO Hitech Group in 1996 Core firm: AAPICO Hitech Public Company	• Direct subsidiaries: AAPICO Hitech Parts, AAPICO Amata, AAPICO Forging, AAPICO Hitech Tooling, AAPICO Structural Products • JVs: AAPICO Lemtech (with Fujikura), AAPICO Mitsuike (with Mitsuike, Japan), AAPICO Sodecia (with Sodecia, Portugal), Able Sanoh (Sanoh Industry, Japan), Edscha APPICO Automotive (with Edscha, Germany), Sumino AAPICO (Sumino, Japan), etc. • Overseas: Jackspeed in Singapore; Kunshan Chaitai-Xincheng Precision Forging in China
Thai Summit Group in 1977 Core firm: Thai Summit Auto Parts Industry	• Thailand: (Direct subsidiaries): TS Interseats and Thai Summit Harness, • JVs: Thai Summit PKK (with PKK, Japan), Thai Summit Hirotec (with Hirotec, Japan), MCI & TSH (with Mitsubishi Cable, Japan), etc. • Overseas: Ogihara in Japan; Thai Summit America in US; Fuzhou Ogihara Thai Summit in China; Oriental Summit Industry in Malaysia; PT Indonesia Thai Summit Auto in Indonesia; Thai Summit in Vietnam; Thai Summit Neel Auto in India

Source: Adapted from Fourin (2012) and Website of Siam Motors, Somboon, Thai Rung, SAS, SAB, AAPICO Hitech, and Thai Summit.

Second, the Somboon group is characterised by a mix of type (2) developing an alliance with a leading global component manufacturer and type (3) becoming a national Tier-1 supplier. Somboon group is comprised of wholly owned core firms and JV firms with foreign capital. Somboon Spring was established in 1962 and later restructured as Somboom Advance Technology. It owns four direct subsidiaries – Somboom Malleable Iron Industrial Company, Bangkok Spring Industrial Company, International Casting Product and Somboon Forging Technology – as well as four JVs with Japanese capital firms.[29] The Somboon group is also actively engaged in R&D activities. The R&D section employs about 30 Thai engineers and conducts joint research with local universities and the National Science and Technology Development Agency (NSTDA) in Thailand (Kuroiwa *et al.* 2016: 108).

Third, the Thai Rung group is characterised by a mix of type (2) developing an alliance with a leading global component manufacturer, type (3) becoming a national Tier-1 supplier, and type (4) moving to a profitable niche in the Tier-2 segment. Thai Rung was established in 1967 in response to the Thai government's localisation policy in the automotive industry. Thai Rung Union Car is a core firm in the Thai Rung Group; the group consists of four direct affiliates and four JVs.[30] Thai Rung group plays a role as both Tier-1 and Tier-2 suppliers. As a Tier-1 supplier, the Thai Rung group supplies flat deck, stamping inner parts, and door assemblies to such assemblers as Nissan, GM, Isuzu, and Ford. It also provides, as a Tier-2 supplier, stamping chassis parts, and body inner parts to Tier-1 suppliers. Finally, the Thai Rung group owns R&D functions, consisting of two fields. The first conducts new product development. The second conducts R&D in association with government institutions, including NSTDA (Kuroiwa *et al.* 2016: 111–112).

Fourth, some local Thai suppliers, such as the Summit group, Thai Summit group, and the AAPICO Hitech group, upgraded their supplier status from being local Tier-1 firms into being multinational automotive parts producers. These groups are characterised by a mix of features: (1) becoming a multinational Tier-1 supplier, (2) developing an alliance with a leading global component manufacturer, and (3) being a national Tier-1 supplier. At a multinational level, the Summit group and the AAPICO Hitech group are limited to regional operations in Southeast Asia, China, and India, while the Thai Summit group's business operations take place not only at a regional level but also at the global level for leading global automotive producers in Japan and the US. The Summit group consists of two main companies: Summit Auto Seats Industry (SAS, established in 1972, with over 6,500 employees in 2011) and Summit Auto Body Industry (SAB, established in 1986, with over 5,300 employees in 2011).[31] SAS not only have its own factories and R&D centre in Thailand but also have five overseas plants (three in China and one each in India and Vietnam). SAS also formed ten JVs with foreign firms, including Johnson Controls in the US (Johnson Controls & Summit Interiors, established in 1999). Similarly, SAB has four factories, an R&D centre, and a Training centre in Thailand; one overseas factory in Indonesia; and 12 JVs.[32] In addition, SAS and SAB formed eight JVs with foreign capital, including the Showa Corporation from Japan (Summit Showa Manufacturing, established in 1993). In AAPICO Hitech Group, the original firm, Able Autoparts Industries Company, was established in order to assemble and distribute Ford cars in 1985. AAPICO Hitech group was involved in manufacturing (OEM auto parts, jigs, stamping dies, and car navigation) and dealership activities. The group consists of 40 firms, including those in China and Singapore.[33] Probably the Thai Summit group is the most globally oriented supplier based in Thailand, pursuing a range of active overseas business operations. This was developed on the basis of Thai Summit Auto Parts Industry, established in 1977. Thai Summit group has two wholly owned firms, over 40 subsidiaries in Thailand, and seven overseas subsidiaries. It took over one of the leading global stamping-die producers, Ogihara Corporation, in Japan in 2009, which now operates in six countries: Malaysia, Indonesia, Vietnam, China, Japan, and the US.[34] Moreover, the Thai Summit group also has R&D functions – Thai Summit R&D Next Technology.

Malaysia

In Malaysia, of 641 suppliers in 2017, over 200 firms were Tier-1 suppliers. It is important to note that the majority of Tier-1 suppliers were locally owned firms, and many of these were developed under the Malaysian government's Vendor Development Programme (VDP). In the case of Proton, there were 287 suppliers in Malaysia in the mid-2000s. Of 287 local suppliers, local *bumiputra* firms, local non-*bumiputra* firms, and local foreign capital (including unknown) firms accounted for 108 firms, 56 firms, and 128 firms, respectively (Anazawa 2006: 307). Leading automotive parts suppliers in Malaysia are characterised by a mix of three types: (1) multinational Tier-1 suppliers, (2) developing an alliance with a leading global component manufacturer, and (3) national Tier-1 suppliers. DRB-HICOM, one of the largest business groups in Malaysia, is engaged in various business sectors, including the automotive industry. Although DRB-HICOM owns an overseas operation, its operations in the automotive sector are more oriented towards type (2), (developing an alliance with a leading global component manufacturer). DRB-HICOM was established from Diversified Resource Berhad (DRB) and Heavy Industries Corporation of Malaysia Berhad (HICOM) in 2000. In the automotive industry, DRB-HICOM assembles various vehicle brands, including Suzuki, Mercedes Benz, Volkswagen, TATA, Ssang Yong, and Fuso through HICOM Automotive Manufacturing; and Proton with Geely, Isuzu, and Honda through JV firms. DRB-HICOM directly owns Tier-1 automotive parts suppliers and various JV Tier-1 suppliers.[35] PHN Industries, which has two affiliates – HICOM Mechatronics (wholly owned by PHN Industries) and Oriental Summit Industries (a JV between Summit group in Thailand and PHN Industries) – is wholly owned by DRB-HICOM. In its overseas operations, DRB-HICOM owns HICOM Automotive Plastics in Thailand (see Table 3.8).

The Delloyd group and Ingress Corporation group seem to be more active in overseas operations. Their overseas operations are associated with two types of foreign partners: local partners or multinational firms from Japan and Europe. The Delloyd group, established in 1984, is involved in automotive parts productions, vehicle distribution, and plantation sectors.[36] In the automotive manufacturing-related sector, the Delloyd group owns eight firms, including an R&D operation in Malaysia and four overseas operations in Thailand and Indonesia. Delloyd is also engaged in R&D activities consisting of (1) the development of new products and (2) researching new technology by using approximately 3% of sales output. Approximately 5% of Delloyd's sales output came from its export to GM factories in Latin America and Europe in 2014 (Interview with Delloyd, 17 September 2014). In this context, it can also be categorised as type (5), specialising in the global supply of a particular product. The Ingress Corporation, starting with the establishment of Ingress Engineering in 1991, operates in three sectors: automotive parts production, automotive dealerships, and energy and railways. It owns six firms in Malaysia and five firms in Thailand, Indonesia, and Indonesia in the automotive parts sector.

The APM group has more wholly owned firms and overseas operations than the others. Originally, it was a spin-off in 1997 from Nissan's JV partner in Malaysia, Tan Chong Motor.[37] APM Automotive has three divisions – suspension, heat exchange and electrical, and interior and plastic of the production of automotive parts – holding over ten direct affiliates and four JV firms with Japanese, Korean, and Australian capital firms in Malaysia.[38] APM is a leading automotive parts firm, with overseas operations, including

Table 3.8 Major Local Automotive Parts Producers in Malaysia, 2018

Group Name	*Main Affiliates*
DRB-HICOM	• Assemblers: HICOM Automotive Manufacturing, Proton (with Geely, China), Isuzu-HICOM (with Isuzu, Japan), Honda Malaysia (with Honda, Japan) • Direct subsidiaries: DRB-HICOM Diecasting, PHN Industries • JVs: HICOM-Teck See Manufacturing (with Teck See Plastic, Malaysia), HICOM Mechatronics (owned by PHN Industries), Oriental Summit Industries (with Summit group in Thailand and PHN Industries), HICOM HBPO (with HBPO, Germany), Faurecia HICOM Emission Control Technology (Faurecia, France) • Overseas: HICOM Automotive Plastics in Thailand
Delloyd Group in 1984	• Malaysia: Delloyd Industries, Delloyd Auto Parts Manufacturing, Delloyd Electronics, Delloyd R&D, Delloyd C&C, Delloyd Auto Parts, GMI Mould Industries, Wemaz Auto Technology • Overseas: Delloyd Industries Thailand, Delloyd-TIMS (with TIMS Thailand), and Brose Delloyd Automotive (with Brose, Germany) in Thailand; Asian Auto International, Murakami Delloyd Indonesia (with Murakami, Japan) in Indonesia
Ingress Corporation Group in 1991	• Malaysia: Ingress Engineering, Ingress Precision (with Katayama Kogyo, Japan), Ingress Katayama Technical Centre (with Katayama), Ingress Technologies (with Perodua, Malaysia), Ingress Industrial, and Talent Synergy • Overseas: Ingress Autoventures (with Katayama and Yonei, Japan) and Fine Components in Thailand; Ingress Malindo Ventures (with Tidar Adyagiri Sakti, Indonesia) and Ingress Technologies in Indonesia; Ingress Autoventures in India
APM Automotive in 1997	• Malaysia: APM Shock Absorbers, APM Springs, SPM Coil Springs, APM Aluminium Castings, APM Auto Electronics, APM Climate Control, Auto Parts Manufacturers, APM Seatings, APM Plastics, APM Automotive Modules, APM Auto Safety Systems • JVs: APM Tachi-S Seating Systems (with Tachi-S Japan), Fuji Seats (with Fuji Seats, Japan), APM-Coachair (with Coach Air, Australia), APM Tinnos (with Tinnos, Korea) • Overseas (wholly owned): APM Auto Components in Thailand; APM Auto Components Indonesia and APM Armada Suspension in Indonesia; APM Auto Components Vietnam and APM Springs Vietnam in Vietnam; Auto Components Myanmar in Myanmar; Auto Components USA in US; McConnell Seats Australia and Locomotive Seats Australia in Australia • Overseas (JVs): Armada Johnson Control (with Jonson Controls, US), APM Armada Autoparts (with Mekar Armada Java, Indonesia) in Indonesia; IAC APM Automotive Systems (with International Automotive Components group, Luxemburg) in Thailand; APM-TS BV (with TS-Automotive Netherlands) in the Netherlands

Source: Adapted from Fourin (2012) and Website of DRB-HICOM, Delloyd, Ingress Corporation, and APM Automotive.

those in Southeast Asia, the US, and Europe. APM owns nine wholly owned affiliates and four JVs abroad.

Indonesia

In Indonesia, of approximately 1,550 automotive parts suppliers, 550 firms are classified as Tier-1 suppliers. Unlike Thai and Malaysian leading automotive parts firms, Indonesian suppliers have not yet regionalised. Even Indonesian leading suppliers are oriented only towards the domestic market. The largest automotive-related firm is Astra group (see Table 3.9). Using our earlier classification, the group firms are characterised by type (2) (developing an alliance with a leading global component manufacturer) or type (3) (being a national Tier-1 supplier). The Astra group was established in 1957 as a trading firm and has diversified into various sectors, including automotive, finance, mining, agriculture, and infrastructure. It is one of the largest business groups in Indonesia. In the automotive assembling sector, Astra International formed out of various JVs with foreign assemblers, such as Toyota (Astra Toyota Motors), Daihatsu, Honda, Isuzu, BMW, and Peugeot-Citroen. In the automotive parts sector, Astra Otoparts is the core firm; it directly owns 18 automotive parts suppliers and established 32 JVs with foreign capital firms (most of which are Japanese).[39] Another leading local automotive group is IndoMobil under the Salim group. In the automotive sector, Indomobil Sukses International is a core firm in the group. Like the Astra group, Indomobil Sukses International formed various JVs with foreign assemblers, such as Suzuki, Nissan, Hino, Volvo, Renault, VW, and Audi. In the automotive parts industry, Indomobil formed various JVs with Japanese firms.

Table 3.9 Major Local Automotive Parts Producers in Indonesia, 2018

Group Name	*Main Affiliates*
Astra Group in 1956 Core firms: Astra International Astra Otoparts	• Automotive Parts: Astra Otoparts • Direct affiliates: PT Menara Terus Makmur, PT Indokarlo Perkasa, and other 16 firms • JVs: PT Aisin Indonesia (with Aisin, Japan), PT Denso Indonesia (with Denso, Japan), PT Toyoda Gosei (with Toyoda Gosei, Japan), PT Astra Daido Steel (with Daido steel, Japan), PT Nusa Keihin Indonesia (with Keihin Seimitsu, Japan), PT GS Battery (with Yuasa, Japan), PT Kayaba Indonesia (with Kayaba, Japan), PT Astra Nippon Gasket (with Nippon Gasket, Japan), PT Astra Visteon Indonesia (with Visteon, US), and 22 other firms
IndoMobil Group in 1976 Core firm: Indomobil Sukses International	• Assembler: Indomobil Sukses International • Automotive Parts: PT Autotech Indonesia (with Fuji Kiko, Japan), PT Indomatsumoto Press&Dies (with Matsumoto Kogyo, Japan), PT Jideco Indonesia (with Mitsuba, Japan), PT Sumi Indo Wiring (Sumitomo Electric, Japan), and more than ten other firms

Source: Adapted from Fourin (2012) and Website of Astra and Indomobil.

The Philippines

In the Philippines, there were 256 suppliers in 2015. Although 124 of these suppliers are classified as Tier-1, in general the size of suppliers in the Philippines is relatively small, consisting mostly of SMEs (small and medium sized enterprises) (Ofreneo 2016). Automotive parts exported from the Philippines are largely limited to wire harnesses and transmissions produced by MNCs, though such exports are substantial. The local parts industry is extremely limited in relation to backward linkages (Aldaba 2007). One of the leading parts suppliers is Yazaki-Torres, which is the top wire harness producer and exporter of the country. Yazaki-Torres Manufacturing was established in 1974 by the Torres family (holding 60% of equity) and the Japanese Yazaki (40%). In the Philippines, most Tier-1 suppliers can be categorised as type (2) (developing an alliance with a leading global component manufacturer) or small scale type (3) (becoming a national Tier-1 supplier).

Automotive and parts trade in Southeast Asia

It is also important to view trade performance in terms of competitiveness in the region's automotive industry. In the last few decades, FTAs and Economic Partnership Agreements (EPAs) have played an important role in the development of the automotive industry in Southeast Asia. FTAs and EPAs have influenced the firm strategies of the automotive producers not only at the regional level but also at the global level, although automotive producers have also been operating regionally and globally prior to formal FTAs and EPAs. There are three types of agreement: regional integration arrangements, including the ASEAN Free Trade Area (AFTA) and, most recently, the ASEAN Economic Community (AEC) within Southeast Asia; agreements with regional groupings or individual countries outside the region on a multi-lateral (ASEAN) basis; and bi-lateral agreements (see Table 3.10). In relation to regional integration arrangements,

Table 3.10 FTAs/EPAs in Major ASEAN Countries

Country/Area	*Partners*
Southeast Asia	ASEAN (1967), AFTA (1993), AEC (2015)
ASEAN	China (2005), Korea (2007), Japan (2008), India (2010), Australia/ New Zealand (2010), TPP (2010)
Thailand	Australia (2005), New Zealand (2005), Japan (2007) Peru (2011), Chile (2015)
Indonesia	Japan (2008), Pakistan (2013)
Malaysia	Japan (2006), Pakistan (2008), New Zealand (2010), India (2011), Chile (2012), Australia (2013), Turkey (2015)
Philippines	Japan (2012), EFTA (2016)
Vietnam	Japan (2009), Chile (2014), Korea (2015), EEU (2016)

Source: Fourin (2017: 18–19).

Note: EFTA-European Free Trade Area, EEU-Eurasian Economic Union, TPP-Trans Pacific Partnership.

Kimura and Urata (2016: 64–68) explain the impact of trade policy in Southeast Asia on the automotive industry as follows. Until 1990, ASEAN countries erected high tariff barriers to protect their domestic automotive industries under ISI. During this period, although Southeast Asian automotive assemblers could not achieve the minimal scale of efficiency, they enjoyed certain benefits under government protection. This situation dramatically changed as a result of the AFC in 1997–1998. First, automotive assemblers in Thailand started employing an exporting strategy due to the lack of domestic demand caused by the crisis, then utilising the low business costs also caused by the crisis. Second, ASEAN countries accelerated trade liberalisation under AFTA and under the ASEAN Industrial Cooperation (AICO) scheme due to fears of FDI withdrawal from the region after the crisis. At the same time, tariff rates on CBUs from outside AFTA were only reduced gradually. In short, automotive assemblers were attracted to two benefits in Southeast Asia. The first was fewer obstacles in the regional operations of Southeast Asia. The second was the protection of ASEAN markets from competition outside the region. These factors encouraged automotive FDI in the region as well as intra-regional trade in Southeast Asia.

Among many bi-lateral agreements in Southeast Asia, in 2005, the Thai-Australian Free Trade Agreement (TAFTA) significantly influenced automotive assemblers' firm strategies and enabled the Thai automotive industry to enjoy rapid automotive industrialisation in association with the relocation of the automotive assembly industry from Australia to Thailand. Australia had one of the longest histories of automotive production, dating back to the 1890s (Stanford 2017). As a result of TAFTA, the tariff on Thai produced vehicles was reduced to 5% in January 2005 and 0% in January 2010. Vehicle output in Australia was 394,713 units in 2005 – coming from four assemblers: Ford (established in 1925), Holden (GM, established in 1931), Toyota (established in 1963), and Mitsubishi (established in 1980) – but dropped to only 98,632 units in 2017 (OICA website), which was expected to fall to zero in 2018. There were harsh restructurings in the Australian motor industry during this period. Mitsubishi ceased its assembly operation in Australia in March 2008, followed by Ford in October 2016, Toyota in October 2017, and Holden in October 2017, due to high labour costs and the lack of an industrial policy established by the government (see Darby 2009, Stanford 2017). Instead of producing in Australia, the country's vehicle producers expanded their assembly operations in Thailand and started exporting Thai-made vehicles to Australia. From 2004–2017, Thai exports to Australia in HS87 (Vehicles and Accessories) increased 7.8 fold 3 from US $786 million to US $6.1 billion. Indeed, Thailand became the second-largest exporter to Australia after Japan (which accounted for US $7.7 billion) in 2017 (Global Trade Atlas database). Furthermore, bi-lateral agreements with Japan have played an important role in creating a regional division of labour between Southeast Asia and Japan. For instance, in many companies Thai-made Eco cars are exported to the Japanese market, replacing Japanese domestic production. In addition, the automotive parts trade between Southeast Asia and Japan is increasingly important in the supply chain networks of both regions (see Table 3.11).

Table 3.11 Directions of Automotive Trade in ASEAN: Indonesia and the Philippines, 2016

	(US $ mil)		*Japan*							*ASEAN*	*ASEAN+JAPAN*
		Total	*Japan*	*% of Total*	*Philippines*	*Thailand*	*Malaysia*	*Vietnam*	*All ASEAN*	*% of Total*	*% of Total*
INDONESIA											
Export Destinations											
Vehicles, parts, and accessories	HS87	5,868	489	8.3	1,468	849	436	200	2,953	50.3	58.7
Motor cars	HS8703	2,566	116	4.5	1,071	174	93	46	1,384	53.9	58.5
Vehicles for transport of goods	HS8704	121	34	28.1	21	–	6	20	47	38.8	66.9
Parts and accessories of motor vehicles	HS8708	1,981	256	12.9	101	506	278	75	960	48.5	61.4
Gear boxes and parts	HS870840	730	3	0.4	13	216	87	15	331	45.3	45.8
Wiring harnesses for vehicles	HS854430	793	534	67.3	–	40	4	–	44	5.5	72.9
Import Sources											
Vehicles, parts, and accessories	HS87	5,298	1,612	30.4	85	1661	95	115	1956	36.9	67.3
Motor cars	HS8703	1,190	290	24.4	–	634	19	–	653	54.9	79.2
Vehicles for transport of goods	HS8704	397	23	5.8	–	203	–	–	203	51.1	56.9
Parts and accessories of motor vehicles	HS8708	2,594	1,189	45.8	81	723	57	74	935	36.0	81.9
Gear boxes and parts	HS870840	545	473	86.8	32	19	–	–	51	9.4	96.1
Wiring harnesses for vehicles	HS854430	85	17	20.0	7	7	5	9	28	32.9	52.9

(*Continued*)

	(US $ mil)		Japan							ASEAN	ASEAN+JAPAN
		Total	*Japan*	*% of Total*	*Philippines*	*Thailand*	*Malaysia*	*Vietnam*	*All ASEAN*	*% of Total*	*% of Total*
PHILIPPINES											
Export Destinations											
Vehicles, parts, and accessories	HS87	1,418	405	28.6	67	320	–	–	387	27.3	55.9
Motor cars	HS8703	27	9	33.3	1	11	1		13	48.1	81.5
Vehicles for transport of goods	HS8704	–	–	–	–	–	–	–	–	–	–
Parts and accessories of motor vehicles	HS8708	1,318	389	29.5	60	308	–	–	368	27.9	57.4
Gear boxes and parts	HS870840	252	15	6.0	23	165	–	–	188	74.6	80.6
Wiring harnesses for vehicles	HS854430	2,001	816	40.8	19	105	–	4	128	6.4	47.2
Import Sources											
Vehicles, parts, and accessories	HS87	7,608	1,580	20.8	1,527	2,736	29	34	4,326	56.9	77.6
Motor cars	HS8703	3,959	422	10.7	1,152	1,823	–	–	2,975	75.1	85.8
Vehicles for transport of goods	HS8704	1,063	259	24.4	17	603	–	–	620	58.3	82.7
Parts and accessories of motor vehicles	HS8708	509	204	40.1	35	105	–	–	140	27.5	67.6
Gear boxes and parts	HS870840	33	17	51.5	7	3	–	–	10	30.3	81.8
Wiring harnesses for vehicles	HS854430	72	18	25.0	4	11	2	2	19	26.4	51.4

Source: From Thoburn and Natsuda (2018: 666), data from comtrade.un.org/db [accessed on 26 October 2017].

Note: items marked – less than US $1 million; ASEAN's here refers only to the five automotive producing countries.

Trade in the automotive sector in Southeast Asia has been rapidly increasing in the last two decades. The export value of HS87 has increased fifteen-fold from US $2.5 billion in 1998 to US $38.2 billion in 2017 in the ASEAN-4 countries, while the import value has increased ten-fold, from US $2.8 billion in 1998 to US $29.7 billion in 2017. Indeed, until 2004 imports of HS87 in value in the ASEAN-4 exceeded that of their exports, but this trend has reversed since 2005. The export surplus in the ASEAN-4 was US $8.5 billion in 2017. Thailand is the largest exporter in the region, followed by Indonesia, while Malaysia and the Philippines have automotive trade deficits (see Table 3.12). Thailand's major export destinations in 2017 were Australia, the Philippines, Indonesia, China, Malaysia, and Japan. In the case of Indonesia, the major export destinations were the Philippines, followed by Thailand, Japan, Saudi Arabia, Vietnam, and Malaysia. In these countries, intra-ASEAN exports accounted for US $7.6 billion (26.6%) for Thailand and US $3.8 billion (55.2%) for Indonesia in 2017. In the case of Vietnam, import dependence on ASEAN for vehicles was considerable, with almost 58% of HS8703 imports coming from Indonesia and Thailand in 2017, in almost equal amounts. However, Vietnam's import dependence on ASEAN was much lower in the case of components, HS8708, where only Thailand was a significant supplier (13.7%), and two-thirds were from Korea, Japan, and China. For Vietnam's automotive exports, automotive components and wiring harnesses were the only important categories. Of HS8708 only 9.1% were sold to Thailand, while over half went to Japan, China, and Korea. Regarding wiring harnesses (HS 854430), only 1.7% were sold to Thailand among ASEAN countries, whereas two-thirds went to Japan and a further fifth went to China.[40] In this context, though, note that it is not unusual for export destinations to differ considerably between a country's automotive products. For example, the Philippines exports of transmissions are mainly within ASEAN and to Japan, whereas its wiring harness exports are mainly to North America and Japan, not to ASEAN (refer back to Table 3.11)

In Southeast Asia, HS87 consists mainly of two large sub-codes - HS8703 (Motor Cars) and HS8708 (Parts and Accessories of Motor Vehicles), accounting for 67.6% in 2017. In HS8703, Thailand has expanded its exports rapidly since 2005, playing an export platform role in Southeast Asia. Similarly, Indonesia has been increasing its export capacity since 2007. In both Malaysia and the Philippines, the import of vehicles is much larger than their export. With regard to the auto parts trade (HS8708), Thailand is the largest both exporter and importer in the region, accounting for a US $1.4 billion trade surplus. In the case of Indonesia, the import of auto parts is much larger than the export, accounting for a US $1.1 billion trade deficit. Similarly, Malaysia has trade deficits in components, while the Philippines has a trade surplus. It is worth noting that among the ASEAN countries the Philippines is also one of the largest exporters of wiring harnesses, which are categorised as an electronics product (HS8544), accounting for US $2.2 billion in export in 2017, and matched in value only by Vietnam.

Table 3.13 shows intra-ASEAN Trade in the ASEAN-4 in HS8703 (cars) and HS8708 (components). Intra-ASEAN exports increased rapidly in the

Table 3.12 Automotive and Parts Trade in ASEAN-4, 1998–2017

HS87 (Vehicles, Parts and Accessories)

Export	*1998*	*1999*	*2000*	*2001*	*2002*	*2003*	*2004*	*2005*	*2006*	*2007*	*2008*	*2009*	*2010*	*2011*	*2012*	*2013*	*2014*	*2015*	*2016*	*2017*
Thailand	1,321	1,968	2,497	2,758	2,996	4,143	5,955	8,135	10,103	13,751	16,673	11,943	18,587	17,978	24,175	25,765	25,765	26,540	27,225	28,507
Indonesia	314	428	492	465	532	629	935	1,298	1,664	2,111	2,819	1,958	2,900	3,329	4,857	4,567	5,214	5,419	5,868	6,834
Malaysia	481	456	436	339	396	464	659	830	950	1,161	1,346	1,135	1,507	1,567	1,813	1,875	1,949	1,783	1,702	1,717
Philippines	386	504	642	688	858	1,165	1,426	1,611	1,529	1,808	2,214	1,568	1,861	2,226	1,954	1,446	1,660	1,429	1,418	1,168

Import	*1998*	*1999*	*2000*	*2001*	*2002*	*2003*	*2004*	*2005*	*2006*	*2007*	*2008*	*2009*	*2010*	*2011*	*2012*	*2013*	*2014*	*2015*	*2016*	*2017*
Thailand	570	1,339	2,050	2,068	2,317	3,156	3,672	4,036	3,918	4,850	5,792	4,721	7,910	8,701	12,505	11,471	8,338	8,048	8,834	9,180
Indonesia	957	748	1,914	1,868	1,663	1,890	2,423	3,061	2,447	2,779	6,656	3,151	5,737	7,603	9,757	7,915	6,254	5,343	5,298	6,693
Malaysia	741	1,364	1,776	1,583	1,736	1,960	2,599	3,118	3,125	3,220	4,032	3,851	5,728	5,874	7,125	7,160	6,497	6,077	5,798	5,479
Philippines	589	814	1,026	999	1,082	1,199	1,096	1,229	1,353	1,733	1,972	1,945	2,719	2,703	3,362	3,444	3,644	4,644	7,291	8,368

HS8703 (Motor Cars)

Export	*1998*	*1999*	*2000*	*2001*	*2002*	*2003*	*2004*	*2005*	*2006*	*2007*	*2008*	*2009*	*2010*	*2011*	*2012*	*2013*	*2014*	*2015*	*2016*	*2017*
Thailand	66	118	213	671	526	780	1,125	2,148	2,917	4,139	5,288	4,074	7,030	6,199	5,653	6,523	6,458	9,393	11,633	10,879
Indonesia	17	9	7	6	20	30	141	246	366	839	1,234	629	1,027	1,337	2,264	2,085	2,642	2,429	2,566	3,096
Malaysia	185	142	92	49	88	51	100	104	154	174	194	146	230	184	237	307	322	182	216	242
Philippines	4	1	1	2	25	156	154	170	88	63	95	94	127	81	56	35	106	38	27	7

Import	*1998*	*1999*	*2000*	*2001*	*2002*	*2003*	*2004*	*2005*	*2006*	*2007*	*2008*	*2009*	*2010*	*2011*	*2012*	*2013*	*2014*	*2015*	*2016*	*2017*
Thailand	128	434	286	191	184	390	376	342	253	281	480	469	814	894	1,443	1,364	1,293	975	950	824
Indonesia	54	20	192	183	99	283	581	586	455	782	1,150	656	1,406	1,764	2,728	2,231	1,481	1,165	1,190	1,144
Malaysia	437	887	1,047	897	950	976	1,157	1,281	1,353	1,275	1,558	1,579	2,507	2,532	2,824	2,743	2,144	1,911	1,847	1,498
Philippines	123	160	191	140	166	215	225	304	399	654	918	905	1,428	1,186	1,596	1,624	1,654	2,217	3,819	4,389

HS8708 (Parts and Accessories of Motor Vehicles)

Export	*1998*	*1999*	*2000*	*2001*	*2002*	*2003*	*2004*	*2005*	*2006*	*2007*	*2008*	*2009*	*2010*	*2011*	*2012*	*2013*	*2014*	*2015*	*2016*	*2017*
Thailand	232	341	504	489	628	965	1,410	2,115	2,506	3,646	4,139	2,992	4,156	4,535	5,831	6,254	6,722	6,714	6,926	7,720
Indonesia	89	145	222	255	288	381	533	758	909	923	1,088	843	1,171	1,115	1,477	1,449	1,620	1,834	1,981	2,052
Malaysia	71	104	135	130	151	212	276	373	426	542	596	556	764	827	870	882	831	770	775	783
Philippines	337	442	568	625	755	929	1,172	1,355	1,372	1,672	2,052	1,423	1,670	2,069	1,414	1,344	1,472	1,307	1,318	1,072
Import	*1998*	*1999*	*2000*	*2001*	*2002*	*2003*	*2004*	*2005*	*2006*	*2007*	*2008*	*2009*	*2010*	*2011*	*2012*	*2013*	*2014*	*2015*	*2016*	*2017*
Thailand	238	677	1,329	1,493	1,623	2,126	2,491	2,736	2,589	3,047	3,451	2,877	5,127	5,563	8,422	7,866	5,321	5,301	5,897	6,290
Indonesia	356	297	1,137	936	826	952	986	1,251	904	840	2,547	981	1,963	2,277	2,982	3,218	2,908	2,457	2,594	3,165
Malaysia	111	203	298	269	333	472	618	1,018	1,013	1,109	1,311	1,185	1,603	1,681	2,115	2,129	2,316	2,402	2,275	2,332
Philippines	153	211	215	246	289	384	364	389	313	279	289	253	350	395	409	400	407	395	475	423

Source: Global Trade Atlas (database).

Note: US $ Million.

Table 3.13 Intra-ASEAN Trade of Automotive and Parts, 1998–2017

(a) Export from ASEAN-4 to ASEAN and to World, 1998–2017

HS8703 (Motor Cars)

Export	1998	1999	2000	2001	2002	2003	2004	2005	2006	2007	2008	2009	2010	2011	2012	2013	2014	2015	2016	2017
ASEAN	27	37	81	57	90	576	1,164	1,394	1,350	1,704	2,369	1,784	3,023	2,831	4,071	3,488	3,732	3,648	4,885	4,782
Total (%)	9.9	13.7	25.9	7.8	13.7	56.6	76.6	52.2	38.3	32.7	34.8	36.1	35.9	36.3	49.6	39.0	39.2	30.3	33.8	33.6
World	272	270	313	728	659	1,017	1,520	2,668	3,525	5,215	6,811	4,943	8,414	7,801	8,210	8,950	9,528	12,042	14,442	14,224

HS8708 (Parts and Accessories of Motor Vehicles)

Export	1998	1999	2000	2001	2002	2003	2004	2005	2006	2007	2008	2009	2010	2011	2012	2013	2014	2015	2016	2017
ASEAN	108	233	390	443	611	815	1,047	1,594	1,535	2,046	2,721	2,176	2,996	3,027	3,676	3,725	3,838	3,788	3,747	3,778
Total (%)	14.8	22.6	27.3	29.6	33.5	32.8	30.9	34.6	29.4	30.2	34.6	37.4	38.6	35.4	38.3	37.5	36.1	35.7	34.1	32.5
World	729	1,032	1,429	1,499	1,822	2,487	3,391	4,601	5,213	6,783	7,875	5,814	7,761	8,546	9,592	9,929	10,645	10,625	11,000	11,627

(b) Export Destinations in ASEAN-4, Japan and World, 2017

HS8703 (Motor Cars)

Export	*Thailand*	*Indonesia*	*Malaysia*	*Philippines*	*Japan*	*World*
Thailand	–	390	68	1,738	209	10,879
Indonesia	177	–	83	1,203	135	3,096
Malaysia	197	12	–	2	2	242
Philippines	1	0	1	–	1	7
Japan	153	364	596	400	–	93,398

HS8708 (Parts and Accessories of Motor Vehicles)

Export	*Thailand*	*Indonesia*	*Malaysia*	*Philippines*	*Japan*	*World*
Thailand	–	833	708	336	752	7,720
Indonesia	501	–	252	114	941	2,052
Malaysia	81	61	–	14	58	783
Philippines	276	54	17	–	217	1,072
Japan	2,569	1,626	607	263	–	34,557

Source: Global Trade Atlas (database).

Note: US$ Million, ASEAN Total - all member countries, ASEAN-4 are Thailand, Indonesia, Malaysia and the Philippines.

ASEAN-4 over the period of 1998–2018. Both HS8703 and HS8708 reached over US $1 billion for the first time in 2004, then US $2 billion in 2007–2008, on to US $3 billion in 2010–2011. In 2017, intra-ASEAN exports accounted for US $4.78 billion in HS8703 and US $3.78 billion in HS8708. With regard to the share of ASEAN in world trade, intra-ASEAN exports accounted for 33.6% of total ASEAN-4 exports to the world in HS8703 and 32.5% in HS8708 in 2017. In terms of both CBUs and components export, ASEAN countries are important trade partners in Southeast Asia. With regard to export destinations within ASEAN, the Philippines constituted the largest export destination for Thailand and Indonesia in 2017, indicating the current weakness of the automotive industry in the Philippines. Unlike HS8703, in HS8708, in 2017, Japan is the most important export destination for ASEAN countries – the largest exporting destination for Indonesia, the second-largest for Thailand and the Philippines, and the third-largest for Malaysia. It seems that ASEAN-4 countries are integrated into Japanese automotive supply chain networks in Japan, although Japan's export to ASEAN-4 countries (US $ 5.07 billion) was much larger than its import from the ASEAN-4 (US $ 1.97 billion). In this context, interdependence between Japan and Southeast Asia is increasing.

Conclusions

This chapter has provided an overview of trends in production and sales in the automotive industry of ASEAN, focussing in some detail on the development of producers in ASEAN countries. It has shown the preponderance of foreign companies in assembly in all except Malaysia. It has also highlighted the way in which local auto component supplying companies, particularly, but not only, in Thailand, have formed effective partnerships with foreign companies and succeeded, in a number of cases, in going multinational themselves. It has shown the development of intra-ASEAN automotive trade, facilitated by AFTA, although this differs somewhat according to particular automotive products, with some, such as transmissions, having a strong regional orientation. The chapter aims to form a background for the discussion of policies in the main producing countries in Chapters 5–9. The predominance of Japanese companies in the region has also been made clear and is examined further in Chapter 4.

Notes

1 Calculated from Fourin (2017). Note: (1) Calculation of production share is based on the actual production volume of the ASEAN-4 countries (Indonesia, Malaysia, Thailand, and the Philippines) and the production *capacity* of Vietnam in 2016. (2) Market share is based on all ASEAN countries, except for Cambodia and Myanmar; however, Singapore is based on the number of registration of new vehicles, and Vietnam is VAMA member firm's figure only. Thus, market share is based on actual sales figures of 7 ASEAN countries and registration number in Singapore in 2016.
2 Calculated from Fourin (2017).

3 Toyota's website: https://www.toyota.co.jp/jpn/company/history/75years/data/automotive_business/sales/activity/asia/index.html#other [accessed on 3 September 2019].

4 However, the alliance's chairman, Carlos Ghosn, who had been a key figure in the rescue of Nissan from problems in 1999, was unexpectedly arrested in Japan in 2018 on what he claims were trumped-up charges of fraud. Ghosn hit newspaper headlines in January 2020 by making a dramatic escape from Japan to his native country of Lebanon. See *The Guardian* (4 January 2020): https://www.theguardian.com/business/2020/jan/04/carlos-ghosn-renault-nissan-mitsubishi-electric-cars [accessed on 4 January 2020].

5 Mitsubishi supplied its vehicles to Nissan under an OEM arrangement. Its false reporting of efficiency problems thus spread to Nissan.

6 The Datsun brand is produced only in Russia, India, and Indonesia.

7 *Nikken Shinbun* (20 October 2016): https://www.nikkei.com/article/DGXLASFL20HRC_Q6A021C1000000/ [accessed on 29 September 2019].

8 Honda's website: https://www.honda.co.jp/group/manufacturing-facilities/index.html [accessed on 3 September 2019].

9 *Nikkei Shinbun* (14 November 2015): https://www.nikkei.com/article/DGXLASDZ13I2G_T11C15A1TI1000/ [accessed on 3 September 2019].

10 Suzuki's website: http://www.suzuki.co.jp/ir/library/forinvestor/pdf/suzukinext100.pdf [accessed on 3 September 2019].

11 *The Jakarta Post* (26 January 2016): http://www.thejakartapost.com/news/2016/01/26/ford-exits-indonesia-japan.html [accessed on 3 September 2019].

12 Korean Custom Services: http://www.customs.go.kr/kcshome/main/content/ContentView.do?contentId=CONTENT_ID_000002320&layoutMenuNo=23225 [accessed on 29 August 2018].

13 *The Straits Times* (25 May 2017): https://www.straitstimes.com/asia/se-asia/malaysias-mahathir-slams-proton-acquisition-by-chinese-carmaker [accessed on 3 September 2019].

14 The emergence of VinFast, a new producer in Vietnam, is discussed in Chapter 9.

15 Interview, 5 March 2010.

16 Siam Motors was founded by Thawon Phornprapha, who began importing hardware during the Second World War. Just after the Second World War, he paid attention to Japanese cars, even though the Japanese automotive industry was still in its infancy. During a trip to Japan, he approached several business leaders and managed to set up a business network with Nissan (Phongpaichit and Baker 1995).

17 Price Motors merged into Nissan in 1966.

18 In October 1981, Malaysian Prime Minister Mahathir visited Mitsubishi Corporation, talked with the president, Mimura, and obtained a verbal agreement regarding Mitsubishi's commitment to the Malaysian national car project, and in February 1982, Dr Kubo, a chairman of Mitsubishi Motors, visited Malaysia to discuss the project with Prime Minister Mahathir, who announced that Malaysia would launch the first national car project in Southeast Asia in October 1982 (Jomo 1994: 268–269).

19 The ownerships involved Daihatsu in Japan (20%); Daihatsu Malaysia Bhd – local distributor in Malaysia (5%); Mitsui Co. in Japan (7%); Permodalan Nasional Bhd. (PNB), a public investment house intended to advance *bumiputera* shareholding (10%); UMW Holdings Bhd., the local Toyota assembler and distributor, in which PNB holds a controlling interest (38%); and Med-Bumikar MARA Bhd, a subsidiary of MARA, a public agency for advancing *bumiputera* participation in the economy (20%) (Machado 1994: 311).

20 For instance, in the case of the Czech leading vehicle producer Skoda (under the VW group after privatisation in 1991), of Skoda's 232 suppliers in 2004, only three firms were Tier-1 majority Czech-owned firms (Pavlinek and Janak 2007: 140). In the case of one of the major Japanese multinational assemblers in Czechia, of 88 Tier-1 firms,

only one firm was Czech-owned, 31 firms were Japanese-owned firms. and 56 firms were foreign-owned firms. In addition, the firm sourced components from another 152 firms in the EU in 2016 (Interview, 20 September 2016).

21 Interview, 24 February 2011.
22 Interview, 25 February 2011.
23 Interview, 16 February 2011.
24 Interview in Indonesia, 20 February 2013.
25 Interview in Thailand, 16 February 2011.
26 Interview in Malaysia, 17 September 2014.
27 Ibid.
28 Siam Motors' website: https://www.siammotors.com/en/ [accessed on 3 September 2019].
29 Somboon's website: http://www.satpcl.co.th/About/Profile.php [accessed on 3 September 2019].
30 Thairung's website: http://www.thairung.co.th/en/investor24.php [accessed on 3 September 2019].
31 The number of employed did not include JVs and overseas factories (Interview on 17 February 2011); see Summit's website: http://www.summit.co.th [accessed on 3 September 2019].
32 8 firms overlapped with SAS.
33 AAPICO Hitech's website: http://www.aapico.com/about.php [accessed on 3 September 2019].
34 Thai Summit's website: http://www.thaisummit.co.th/en [accessed on 3 September 2019].
35 DRB-HICOM's website: https://www.drb-hicom.com/ [accessed on 3 September 2019].
36 Delloyd's website: http://www.delloyd.com/v2/overview/ [accessed on 29 August 2018].
37 Tan Chong Motor's website: http://www.tanchonggroup.com/corporate-information/history-and-business/; and Financial Times: https://markets.ft.com/data/equities/tearsheet/profile?s=APM:KLS [accessed on 3 September 2019].
38 APM Automotive's website: http://www.apm.com.my/ [accessed on 3 September 2019].
39 Astra's website: http://www.component.astra.co.id/default.asp [accessed on 29 August 2018].
40 Note that in 2017 under AFTA, intra-ASEAN tariff-free trade did not yet apply to Vietnam, which had a derogation until 2018, along with Cambodia, Myanmar, and Laos.

4 Japanese automotive MNCs and ASEAN

Introduction

As we showed in Chapter 3, Japanese automotive MNCs have a strong presence in the region. This chapter explores the regional strategies of Japanese automotive MNCs, which involve the Japanese government in relation to ASEAN regional integration. The chapter first explores strategies employed by these MNCs in Southeast Asia. It then examines the role of the Japanese government in association with Japanese automotive MNCs in the ASEAN context. Third, the chapter investigates ASEAN regional integration, with particular emphasis on the Brand to Brand Complementation (BBC) scheme and the ASEAN Industrial Cooperation (AICO) scheme, established as a result of the negotiation between a Japanese automotive MNCs–government alliance and the ASEAN governments, and the more recent ASEAN Economic Community (AEC).[1] Also, Toyota's operations in Southeast Asia are presented as a case study, and a final section offers a brief conclusion.

Japanese automotive MNCs in Southeast Asia

Japanese automotive MNCs have been employing various strategies in order to maintain their high market share in Southeast Asia. This section examines, first, their marketing and production strategies; second, their locational strategies within Southeast Asia; third, their local business strategies; and finally, firm-level technology transfer in the region.

Marketing and production strategies in Southeast Asia

Car strategy in Asia in the 1990s

With regard to local marketing strategies in Southeast Asia, the US company Ford introduced the Fiera model as long ago as 1971, presenting it as a low cost model (at approximately US $1,100) against the local Jeepney in the Philippines; it was followed by some Japanese models – Toyota's Tamaraw model in the Philippines in 1976 and the Kijang model in Indonesia in 1977

(Hashiya and Jiang 2010). Except for these models, previously, automotive MNCs in general had introduced old popular models into Southeast Asian markets. In particular, in order to reduce costs, until the 1990s Japanese automotive MNCs would select a model, first produced for the mass market in Japan, to sell in Southeast Asian markets, using main components imported from Japan (Kamo 1999). Since the mid-1990s, Japanese automotive MNCs have been employing a new marketing strategy in Southeast Asia by developing special models for the Asian market in response to local market conditions, thereby introducing 'Asian Cars' into the region. The price of the 'Asian Car' was set lower than that of popular models in Japan in order to accommodate local purchasing power. For instance, Toyota introduced the 'Soluna' as an affordable family car which was situated one rank below the Corolla (previously Toyota's cheapest and most popular passenger model). One of the main reasons for the introduction of the 'Asian Car' was to enhance price competitiveness against Korean low-cost rivals (Guiheux and Lecler 2000). In other words, Japanese automotive MNCs were keen on maintaining their market share in the region.

The development of the 'Asian Car' involved three features. First, the development of original parts production plants in the region. For instance, Honda initially planned to use 80% of the components from its existing Civic model for the production of its Asian Car. However, it realised that the production method for their components in Japan was complicated, making it difficult and expensive for its affiliates in the ASEAN region to produce such components. Hence, Honda decided to develop the moulds for the components of its Asian Car from scratch. By doing so they could achieve a 30% cost reduction and use 22% of the components of the existing 'Civic' model. The second feature involved designing components to reduce transportation costs. A number of components have been transferred across the region under the BBC scheme (later the AICO scheme); these components were designed for easy transportation. For instance, in Honda's Asian car, bumpers were divided into three parts instead of single parts because this uses container space more efficiently. The third feature involved developing models according to local needs, such as transportation conditions, weather, and taste. Japanese automotive MNCs changed the air conditioning system and eliminated the heater, changed the height of the body, and made leak-proof doors to withstand heavy rain. They also developed a special body form to cope with strong sunshine and adapted to the local taste for body colours (Kamo 1999: 191–192).

Table 4.1 shows some Japanese strategic 'Asian Cars'. Toyota and Honda developed a passenger vehicle as their Asian strategic vehicle; in contrast, Nissan and Mitsubishi introduced a commercial vehicle as their Asian strategic vehicle. Honda was a leading producer of Asian Cars. It established a new factory in Ayutthaya, Thailand, in 1996 and encouraged clustering of their parts suppliers; subsequently, a local content ratio for the Civic model of 70% was achieved (Hashiya and Jiang 2010: 89).

Table 4.1 Overview of Asian Cars, 1990s

Producer	*Toyota*	*Honda*	*Nissan*	*Mitsubishi*
Model name	Soluna	City	AD Resort	Delica
Base model	Tercel	–	Sunny California AD Van	Delica
Model	PV with 4 doors	PV with 4 doors	CV(pick-up and wagon)	CV (mini van)
Engine	1,500 cc	1,300 cc 1,500 cc	1,600 cc	2,100 cc
Start of sales	1997	1996	1993	1997
Location of production	Thailand Indonesia	Thailand Malaysia Indonesia Philippines Taiwan	Thailand Malaysia Philippines Taiwan	Taiwan
Local content ratio	70%	70%	65%	70%

Source: Adapted from Kamo (1999: 191).

Export and global production strategies since the late 1990s

Most of the Asian Car models were introduced over the period of 1996–1997, but then the Asian financial crisis (AFC) hit Thailand in 1997 and spread across the region in 1998. As a consequence, Japanese automotive MNCs faced difficulties as local demand in Southeast Asia sharply decreased. For instance, vehicle sales in Thailand dropped to only 24.5% of their previous level, from 589,126 units in 1996 to 144,065 units in 1998 (Fourin 2017: 35). Since the domestic markets in Southeast Asia shrunk after the crisis, Japanese automotive MNCs found it necessary to change their firm strategy from domestically oriented operations in Southeast Asia to more export-oriented operations, utilising unused production capacity. Furthermore, localisation of production, particularly utilising local intermediate products, was another important strategy due to the depreciation of local currencies in the region. In the case of Thailand, vehicle exports increased by approximately 9-fold over the period 1996–1999, accounting for 14,020 units in 1996 and 125,702 units in 1999. This export-oriented strategy continued throughout the 2000s and eventually accounted for 1.19 million units in 2016 (ibid.).

In the 2000s a new marketing strategy was employed by Toyota in Southeast Asia. Since local demands are very different between developed and emerging countries, merely adjusting to emerging countries' market conditions was not enough to expand market share and profits. Consequently, Toyota started to employ two vehicle development strategies: global common models and regional specific/strategic models. In 2004, it established production and sales of 'Innovative International Multipurpose Vehicles' (IMVs), which are thought of as regional specific models outside of Japan, and decided on Thailand as a major R&D and production base for IMV operations. Toyota produces five IMV models in twelve countries, including Thailand, Indonesia, South Africa, Argentina, and Egypt (Ito 2014). This strategy was also employed in association with the Thai government's *Detroit of Asia* plan as a pull factor. In the early 2000s, the Thai government targeted the development of the one-ton pick-up truck segment as the country's product champion (see Chapter 5 for more details). Similarly, Isuzu followed Toyota's strategy. Isuzu jointly developed its D-Max model (a one-ton pick-up truck) with General Motors (GM) in Thailand and started exporting to other Asian countries and Australia. It also produced the model in North America and South America under the GM brand. Isuzu relocated its export production of pick-up trucks from Japan to Thailand in 2004. This was in accordance with the centralisation of component production in Thailand due to the fact that the Thai market has the second-largest demand for pick-up trucks in the world, after the US. Isuzu's Asian strategy was to locate production close to market demand. In 2006, Mazda and Ford also started producing their BT-50 model (Ranger model under Ford, Original Equipment Manufacturer (OEM) from Mazda) and their Everest model under the Ford brand in Thailand, and exported them all over the world. Similarly, Mitsubishi started producing its new Triton model in Thailand in 2005, exporting to all over the world, including Japan (Hashiya and Jiang 2010).

ASEAN automotive industrial policies since the 2000s

In recent years, Japanese automotive MNCs have needed to develop their vehicles, technology, and components in the context of ASEAN governments' industrial policies (vehicle development plans) in exchange for access to incentives. For instance, Thailand's *product champion* strategy became one of the most significant automotive industrialisation models under the WTO system of restrictions on trade-related investment measures. The nation introduced the second *product champion*, the Eco-car, in 2007 (see Table 4.2). The Thai government selected a model to be developed in the country and set what was to be produced locally for the model. In addition, it reduced excise tax on the model, which encouraged consumers to purchase it. The Thai government introduced its second Eco-car project in 2013 (see Chapter 5 for more details). Following Thailand, the Indonesian government introduced its low cost green car (LCGC) project in 2013. In this case, incentives were not as attractive as they had been in Thailand. Most recently, the Philippines introduced its comprehensive automotive resurgence strategy (CARS) in 2015. Unlike Thailand and Indonesia, the CARS programme does not target a particular model to be developed in the Philippines, allowing assemblers to make their choice of model. Instead, the CARS programme concerns the expansion of assembly operations with the provision of incentives. In Malaysia, the government started promoting energy efficient vehicles (EEVs). Table 4.2 provides an overview of automotive industrial policy in the ASEAN-4.[2] Most participants in the projects are Japanese automotive MNCs.

Table 4.2 Overview of Automotive Industrial Policy in ASEAN-4, 2017

Country	*Thailand*	*Indonesia*	*Malaysia*	*Philippines*
Project Name	2nd Eco Car	LCGC	EEV	CARS
Model	Small PV	Small PV	PV/SUV/MPV	Any
Mileage	More than 23.3 km/L	More than 20 km/L	Depend on models Small PV: More than 20 km/L	–
Engine Displacement	Gasoline: less than 1,300 cc Diesel: less than 1,500 cc	Gasoline: 980–1,200 cc Diesel: less than 1,500 cc	–	–
Min Investment	6.5 billion Bhat	–	–	–
Min Production	100,000 units per year (within 4 years after the first production)	–	–	Total of 200,000 units in the period of 6 years, after the first production
Local Production Requirement/ Recommendation	More than four out of five engine component items must be produced locally (cylinder head, cylinder block, and crankshaft are compulsory, and camshaft and/or connecting rod).	Recommendation for localizing the following parts: engine, and parts of transmission, clutch, body, chassis, steering, break, and suspension	–	Required for body shell assembly (press parts and large plastic parts) and Recommendation for common/ strategic parts, which are not produced in the Philippines
Benefits	Exemption of corporate tax for 6 years (max of 8 years for extension) Exemption of import duty for machineries and intermediate materials Favoured excise tax rate of 12% or 14% for vehicles	Exemption of luxury tax of 10% for vehicles	Individual negotiation with MIDA (based on local content ratio)	Two incentives: production (PVI) and equipment and machinery (FIS), Max of 9 billion Peso per model/firm
First Production (Model)	Mazda (Mazda 2) in Jan 2016	Toyota (Agyo) Daihatsu (Ayola) in Sep 2013	Perodua (Axia) in Sep 2014	Mitsubishi (Mirage G4) in Feb 2017
Participants (including plan)	Mazda, Nissan, Honda, Toyota, Mitsubishi, Suzuki Ford, CP-SAIC	Toyota, Daihatsu Suzuki, Honda, Nissan	Perodua, Toyota, Honda (and others)	Mitsubishi, Toyota

Source: Fourin (2017: 12).

Locational strategies in Southeast Asia

Until the 1980s, each ASEAN country implemented different automotive development policies and requirements for local content regulations. The automotive MNCs initially manufactured relatively small numbers of vehicles in each market, so it was difficult for them to enjoy economies of scale within ASEAN. By the end of the 1980s, however, new ASEAN industrial policies opened an opportunity for Japanese automotive MNCs to take the lead in the region. Since the ASEAN governments adopted the BBC scheme; then the AICO scheme; and, most recently, the AEC, Japanese automotive MNCs developed extensive production networks under these schemes. They have started consolidating intra- and inter-firm linkages involving their affiliates across the region in order to enjoy the economies of scale of production according to each nation's demands, industrial policy, and competitive advantages. In order to rationalise production operations in the relatively small markets in Southeast Asia, Japanese automotive MNCs have specialised in terms of vehicle assembly and parts production in specific countries. Thus, they are able to achieve economies of scale, despite the smallness of individual markets, by exchanging vehicles and parts between countries through their regional production networks.

Thailand

In Thailand, one-ton pick-up trucks (which can be used for agriculture, business, and passenger transport) have long been the most popular vehicle; hence, their selection as the country's first ***product champion*** in the mid-2000s. In 2016, one-ton pick-up trucks accounted for 43.1% (331,593 units) of total vehicle sales (768,788 units) in Thailand. The second-most popular type of model is small PVs, including their second ***product champion***, Eco cars, which accounted for 23.3% (179,611 units) in 2016 (Fourin 2017: 48–49). With regard to these vehicles, Thailand has been playing an important role for Japanese automotive MNCs as a strategic production base. With regard to parts production, the Thai government mandated assemblers to manufacture diesel engines that were used for one-ton pick-up trucks in 1989 (Natsuda and Thoburn 2013: 425). Consequently, many Japanese automotive MNCs, such as Toyota, Nissan, and Isuzu, own their own diesel engine factories in Thailand and export to other countries.

Indonesia

In Indonesia, MPVs (with three rows of seats), such as Toyota's Innova (Kijang) model, have long been the most popular type of vehicle due to the large family size in Indonesia. In 2016, MPVs accounted for 40.6% (431,294 units) of the total domestic vehicles sales (1,061,735 units) in the country. In recent years, small PVs under the Indonesian government's LCGC project have become important, with a market share of 22.1% (Fourin 2017: 72–75). All brands in the LCGC project are those of Japanese automotive MNCs. In addition, major brands in the MPV segment are Japanese, including Toyota (Kijang, Innova, and Avanza models), Isuzu (Panther model), Nissan (Serena model), Daihatsu (Xenia model), and Honda (Mobilio model). Indonesia is competitive in the production and export of these vehicles within the region. Moreover, it has gradually been catching up with Thailand using the advantage of its large domestic market, generated by its large population as its income rises, and is playing the role of a second hub in Southeast Asia after Thailand (see Chapter 6). With regard to parts production, Indonesia acts as the gasoline engine production base. Japanese automotive MNCs developed engine production in Indonesia due to the Indonesian government's requirement for the localisation of gasoline engine production for commercial vehicles by 1985 (Inoue 1990: 63–68). Subsequently Toyota, Mitsubishi, Isuzu, Daihatsu, Honda, and Nissan commenced the manufacturing of engines in Indonesia, exporting to other countries in the region.

Malaysia

In Malaysia, PVs are the most popular models, accounting for 67% (388,890 units) of total domestic sales (580,124 units) in 2016 (Fourin 2017: 94–95). Since the national car project started, the Malaysian government introduced various industrial policies for the protection of its national cars. Although Malaysia finally complied with WTO rules in 2004, the country still has grey-zone protectionist policies, which could be considered actionable under the WTO (see Chapter 7). Daihatsu is the leading producer, and partner of Perodua, the second national car, in Malaysia. However, Japanese automotive MNCs, other than Daihatsu, seem not to have a strong commitment in Malaysia, producing only for the domestic market. With regard to parts production, Japanese automotive MNCs generally manufacture resin moulding products and rubber products to take advantage of the country's rich natural resources and electronics-related components due to the presence of a highly developed Malaysian electronics industry. In Malaysia automotive parts production by Japanese automotive MNCs comprises wiper arms, steering gears, computers for engines, air-conditioning, etc. by Toyota; bumpers and plastic parts by Honda; and wipers, hoses, and steering gears by Mitsubishi. Items such as wheel housings and rear fenders produced in Malaysia are exported to other countries in the region (Katayama 2003: 88–89).

The Philippines

In the Philippines, vehicle assembly operations were small and inefficient for a long time. Surprisingly, even Ford, which was a leading producer in the country, withdrew from assembly in 2012. Due to its weak local supporting industry, the Philippines' automotive assembly industry depends heavily on imported components, which makes vehicle production costs higher than those in other countries in the region. According to Aldaba (2008: 22), total vehicle production cost in the Philippines is 1.4 times higher than that of Thailand for the same vehicle model. In this context, Japanese automotive MNCs in the Philippines cannot all utilise economies of scale in their automotive production. Under these circumstances, in 2015, the government introduced its CARS programme to target vehicle production of 500,000 units a year by 2022 (see Chapter 8). However, Mitsubishi and Toyota are the only participants in the project. The first participant, Mitsubishi, commenced their Mirage G4 model production in February 2017, aiming at a volume of 200,000 units over six years (Fourin 2017: 105). With regard to components production, the Philippines provides a competitive advantage for labour-intensive products in the automotive industry. The Philippines was the only country in the ASEAN-4 to employ foreign exchange trade balancing requirements for the automotive industry in order to reduce trade deficits after 1971 (Ofreneo 2008: 67). The first transmissions producer, Asian Transmission Corporation, was set up by Mitsubishi in 1973 as a result of these requirements. The firm has been playing a role as Mitsubishi's strategic transmission production base in Southeast Asia. In addition, Toyota, Honda, and Isuzu set up parts production firms in the Philippines in the 1990s. The Philippines has thus been established as a transmission (and wiring harness) production base for the Japanese automotive MNCs in Southeast Asia.

Vietnam

In Vietnam, the automotive industry was protected with high tariff barriers until 2018. Like the Philippines, the Vietnamese automotive industry has a weak supporting industry. After the liberalisation of the economy in the early 1990s, many foreign automotive producers established assembly operations. As a result, there are too many assemblers for a relatively small automotive market. One of the features in the Vietnamese automotive market is a relatively high proportion of imported CBUs, particularly from Korea. Thus, the Vietnamese automotive industry cannot provide economies of scale, and the industry is rather inefficient. The leading Japanese producer is Toyota. Nissan, Isuzu, Honda, Mitsubishi, and Suzuki each conduct relatively small assembly operations, while Mazda subcontracts a local firm, Thaco, under OEM arrangements. These small operations were still feasible behind high tariff barriers, and their continuing prospective difficulties led to the imposition of new (non-tariff) import barriers upon the start of Vietnam's participation in tariff-free intra-ASEAN trade in 2018 (see Chapter 9).

Local business strategies

In terms of economic efficiency, the Philippines and Vietnam (and perhaps Malaysia) are clearly not attractive locations for assembly operations, though both have established components exporting. Historically, and even recently, US automotive MNCs have repeatedly made investments – and then withdrawals – in Southeast Asia due to ASEAN countries' strict industrial policies, such as local content requirements, and to market slumps in the region. For example, in

Thailand, Ford and GM left in the 1970s and came back in the late 1990s; in the Philippines Ford and GM exited in the 1980s, and Ford did so again in 2012, transferring its production to Thailand. Why do Japanese automotive MNCs not produce in only one or two countries in Southeast Asia, utilising the full capacity and economies of scale to export to the rest of the region? In other words, why would a Japanese automotive MNC maintain an assembly operation in the Philippines, Vietnam, or Malaysia? First, there is a very distinctive difference in firm strategy (or management practice) between Japanese and US/European firms. The business behaviour of Japanese firms, in general, based on long-term relationships and trust, is fundamentally different from the typical market-oriented model of Anglo-American firms (Thoburn and Takashima 1992: ch.7). In the domestic market, Japanese firms are still based on the systems of life-time employment, seniority, and company unions (Abegglen 1958 and 2006). Japanese firms tend to adopt such systems in their affiliates abroad as much as they can, although degrees of difference exist in particular firms and countries (see Abo 1994 and 2015). In particular, Japanese firms emphasise job security and stable employment, and try to protect employees. Thus, lay-offs, or the closing down of a branch business, are considered as a last resort for Japanese MNCs (see Natsuda *et al.* 2020a). Second, Japanese MNCs prefer to establish JVs with local partners in order to create tight business linkages in the Asian market, while US firms have a strong preference for majority ownership. In this context, Japanese automotive MNCs have established more extensive business and political linkages with local economies, which encourage Japanese business activities to be favoured in the region (particularly in terms of market entry). Legewie (2000a) commented that Japanese automotive MNCs have made extensive use of informal networks, including the sometimes extra-legal accommodation of politicians and bureaucrats. Hence, Japanese MNCs are quite sensitive with regards to local employment issues and maintain their operations by forming relationships with local business partners, bureaucrats, and politicians.

Technology transfer at the firm level

The automotive industry requires the development of supporting industries. In order to support the operations of Japanese automotive MNCs, technology transfer plays an important role for local supporting firms. At a firm level, Japanese automotive MNCs have been playing an important part in the process of technology transfer through various channels. As we examined in Chapter 3, many Japanese automotive MNCs establish R&D centres in order to upgrade local technical capacity. Indeed, not only automotive assemblers but also Tier-1 suppliers such as Denso, Aisin, NSK, KYB, and Yazaki set up R&D centres in Thailand (Doner *et al.* 2013). Second, Japanese automotive MNCs provide various human resource development programmes. Two types of training – overseas and local – can be employed: for instance, staff members of PT Astra Daihatsu in Indonesia and Perodua in Malaysia are dispatched to Japan for management training programmes in Daihatsu. Similarly, Honda's

ASEAN staff are dispatched to Japan each year for skill development training. As an example of local training, Mitsubishi in the Philippines conducts training programmes, the so-called '*Monozukuri Dojo* (manufacturing school)' in body assembly, body painting, vehicle assembly, maintenance, and quality operations for all manufacturing employees in order to upgrade their skills and knowledge (JAMA 2016). This type of transfer is based on an intra-firm technology transfer from the main factories in Japan to local factories involving on-the-job training (OJT). A third type of technology transfer is based on inter-firm relations. Typically, Japanese assemblers organise their supply chain networks in Southeast Asia, like the Japanese vertical *keiretsu* system in Japan (Hatch and Yamamura 1996, Irawati 2012). Japanese assemblers provide regular technical training courses for their suppliers, even sending trainees to Japan. Typically, Japanese automotive MNCs give technical advice or guidance to local suppliers in order to meet assemblers' quality, cost, and delivery standards. Fourth, Japanese automotive MNCs have started linking industry and formal education programmes. For instance, in Thailand Chulalongkorn University commenced a bachelor's degree in its automotive engineering department in the early 1990s with Toyota's assistance. Similarly, Thammasat University set up automotive and design engineering courses, with help from some Japanese automotive firms, in 2005 (Intarakumnerd and Gerdsri 2014). In Indonesia, Toyota introduced a School-University-Industry link scheme, the so-called 'Toyota Technical Education Programme (T-TEP)' involving vocational schools and universities in order to develop local human resources in Indonesia (Irawati 2012). Furthermore, Hayashi (2001: 120–122) identified other types of technology transfers, such as licensing-based technology transfers, through spin-offs by local engineers from Japanese firms and through spin-offs by Japanese engineers who had worked for Japanese die-casting/moulding companies to local firms in Thailand.

Japanese automotive MNCs and the Japanese government

Another important actor in the region is the Japanese government. This government has supported the establishment of a supplier base for the automotive industry through government organisations because Japanese government officials took the view that the policy would reduce Japan's trade surplus with ASEAN countries and facilitate their economic development (Abegglen 1994). The Japanese government has been providing technical, financial, and human resource assistances through the Association for Oversea Technical Cooperation and Sustainable Partnerships (AOTS)[3] and the Japan External Trade Organization (JETRO), the Japan International Cooperation Agency (JICA), and the Japan Bank for International Cooperation (JBIC) (Natsuda 2008). In particular, the role of the Japanese government is to incorporate Japanese automotive MNCs' interests into the regional development of Southeast Asia by articulating the Japanese industrial system and the concept of a Japanese development model. These maintain the interests of the members within a three-party economic interdependence system: namely the Japanese government, ASEAN governments, and Japanese MNCs (see Natsuda 2009).

The Japanese government has also been keen on regional integration schemes, such as Asia-Pacific Economic Cooperation (APEC), AFTA and AEC. It has represented the interests of Japanese industry and negotiated with the ASEAN governments at a political level. Indeed, as noted briefly in Chapter 1, the ASEAN Economic Ministers (AEM) and the Ministry of International Trade and Industry (MITI) (now METI, the Ministry of Economy, Trade and Industry) of Japan set up the AEM–METI Economic and Industrial Cooperation Committee (AMEICC) in 1998.[4] Although under APEC there are many industry groups, including the automotive industry, the organisation strongly reflects American MNCs' interests. Consequently, the Japanese government organised AMEICC in order to assist Japanese automotive MNCs and the new ASEAN members of the CLMV countries in Southeast Asia (Interview, 27 November 2009). The institutional forum of government-business representatives was a Japanese initiative. In other words, the Japanese government has created extensive region-wide institutional networks. The automotive working group, under AMEICC, was designed to identify the problems and facilitate automotive regional development, such as the fostering of supporting industries and the promotion of regional automotive part complementation. At a multilateral level, therefore, the Japanese government (particularly METI) are able to co-ordinate Japanese interests across the region through an institutional forum.

Under the AMEICC, two kinds of working groups were organised (see Table 4.3). One were sector-specific working groups (the automotive, chemical, electronics, and textile and garment industries). The other were policy-oriented working groups (human resource development, statistics, SMEs and supporting industries, and the West–East corridor working groups). A striking aspect of these working groups is that their members are government officials and business representatives, and they have a similar structural orientation to the Japanese deliberation council system (Yoshimatsu 2003: 110). Formal institutional linkages,

Table 4.3 AMEICC Working Groups

Policy-Oriented Group	*Sector-Specific Group*
Human Resource Development-Working Group (HRD-WG)	Working Group on Automotive Industry (WG-AI)
Small Medium Enterprise / Supporting Industries / Related Industries Working Group (SME/SI/RI-WG)	Working Group on Chemical Industry (WG-CI)
West-East Corridor Development – Working Group (WEC-WG)	Working Group on Consumer Electronics Industry (WG-CEI)
Working Group on Statistics (WGS)	Working Group on Textile and Garment Industry (WG-TGI)

Source: Natsuda and Butler (2005: 334).

such as deliberation councils, provide information, consultation, and negotiation process for policymaking in Japan. The Japanese government, METI, in particular, takes the view that such a close government–industry relationship encourages more rapid industrial development than a *laissez-faire* economic system (Natsuda and Butler 2005). In this context, working groups under the AMEICC seem to be institutional linkages for high quality information flows, consultation, and coordination between the Japanese government, governments in Southeast Asia, and Japanese MNCs. Most importantly, Japanese MNCs play a pivotal role in AMEICC working groups as advisors in the drawing up of industrial policies for the ASEAN region.

In the automotive industry, the automotive working group under the AMEICC identified the problems of the industry in Southeast Asia and issued a report proposing that the automotive industry in each country be involved in the activities of the ASEAN Automotive Federation (AAF). In turn, the Japan Automotive Manufacturers Association (JAMA) should assist in such activities by establishing a representative office in the region (Yoshimatsu 2003: 111). Japanese automotive MNCs have been interested in the development of supporting industries and the construction of an intra-regional automotive parts trading networks within Southeast Asia;[5] the development of local supporting industries in Southeast Asia would be highly beneficial for such Japanese automotive MNCs, allowing them to procure components locally. Accordingly, the Japanese government, in association with JAMA and the Japan Auto Parts Industry Association (JAPIA), dispatched a number of Japanese technicians to assist local assemblers and parts suppliers, with the purpose of upgrading technological skills in the region (Hatch 2002). Indeed, the Japanese automotive industry has been attempting to harmonise technical and vehicle standards through the introduction of exhaust regulations, fuel specifications, and certification procedures for vehicle safety between Japan and Southeast Asia, implementing 45 projects and dispatching 22 experts to the AMEICC working groups (JAMA 2008). In this context, the Japanese government and business societies are establishing further industrial interdependence between the Japanese and Southeast Asian automotive industries.

In technology transfer and human resource development at the government level, the Association for Oversea Technical Cooperation and Sustainable Partnerships (AOTS) under METI has been operating as one of the most important organisations in Japan. AOTS aims to enhance the productivity in Japan's partner countries (many Asian countries) by providing a technical assistance program for Japanese affiliates and their links to local companies. At the same time, it has been promoting training programmes in Japan to workers who are employed by Japanese firms. In 2018, AOTS conducted 230 training programmes for 4,140 foreign participants in Japan and 23 overseas training programmes with 900 participants, and dispatched 340 Japanese experts to countries outside of Japan.[6] Furthermore, JAMA and JAPIA, in co-operation with the Japanese government, formed a project to dispatch engineers to assist automotive components' development by the local components producers in ASEAN. The Japanese government has been facilitating local components producers' technological development, which will, in turn, assist Japanese automotive producers.

At a bilateral level, the Japanese government provided knowledge of industrial development issues to individual countries. For example, after the AFC, a team from JICA conducted a study in Thailand, strongly influencing the establishment of the 'Master Plan for Supporting Industries', which was established by the Thai Ministry of Industry (Suehiro 1998: 160). Moreover, according to MITI/METI's guidance, the Thai government increased institutional capacity by creating institutions and financial management capacity to carry out SME development (Suehiro 2000). As an example from the automotive industry in Thailand, the Thai Automotive Institute (TAI) was established in 1998 in order to enhance the competitiveness of Thai automotive SMEs with the support of Japanese government–business co-operation. The institute has implemented five programmes: the supporting industry development programme, the 100% localisation support programme, the human resource development programme, the certificate development programme, and the testing and certification capability-building programme (Yoshimatsu 2003: 115). In order to conduct the supporting industry development programmes, experts from the Japanese government's organisations, such as JICA, JETRO and JODC, were dispatched to the local automotive supporting industry in Thailand. With regard to the 100% localisation support programme, the Thai Automotive Institute and three Japanese automotive MNCs – Toyota, Isuzu, and Honda – worked closely with one another to transfer the inspection of locally made parts and materials from Japan to Thailand and hereby reduce lead-times for production and production costs (Yoshimatsu 2003: 115–116).

Similarly, with regard to forming the Japan–Thailand Economic Partnership Agreement (JTEPA) in 2005, JICA, AOTS, JETRO, the Japanese Chamber of Commerce (JCC), and TAI jointly organised the Automotive Human Resource Development Programme (AHRDP) during the period 2006–2011,[7] aiming to upgrade the capability of the local automotive parts industry. Four Japanese firms participated in the programme and provided technical assistance to local supporting firms (Intarakumnerd *et al.* 2012). Under the programme, Phase 1 targeted the training of 302 master trainers, then these master trainers conducted training for over 40,000 people in local SMEs (see Table 4.4).

In Malaysia, the Japanese government set up the Malaysia-Japan Automotive Industry Cooperation (MAJAICO) agreement with the Malaysian government in order to provide industrial and technical assistance for the automotive and components industry for the transition to automotive liberalisation in Malaysia under the Malaysia-Japan Economic Partnership Agreement (MJEPA) in 2005. MAJAICO aimed to improve the global competitiveness of the Malaysian automotive industry, particularly targeting weak *bumiputra* vendors (suppliers), and commenced a comprehensive five-year scheme in order to assist the development of the Malaysian automotive industry, financed by Japanese ODA, in November 2006. The scheme consisted of ten programmes, including human resource development; technical upgrading, such as that for moulds and dies; and business development (see Table 4.5). Of these ten programmes, three were evaluated very favourably by the Malaysian government. The A1 programme, which was supported by Japanese technicians dispatched from Toyota and Daihatsu through JODC, was able to help Malaysian vendors to employ lean production systems, including ***kaizen*** activities (Muslimen *et al.* 2011). After training, local vendors made a presentation of the outcomes every half- or full year. The technical level of ***bumiputra*** vendors was much lower than that of the Japanese supply chain networks. However, through this programme, the level of some vendors came closer to the Japanese standard,[8] with some companies achieving a 50% reduction in total lead-time. Although MAJAICO was completed in 2011, the programme continued, supported by the MAI under MITI, targeting all vendors in Malaysia – initially the first-tier OEM suppliers and later the second-tier suppliers.[9]

The B programme, which aimed to train master trainers in automotive production, was also successful. A total of 149 Nissan technicians were dispatched to educate 33 local trainers in ADTEC, who, in turn, trained 1,922 local trainees in mechanical, electrical, and manufacturing technologies, and quality assurances. In practice, 155 modules were transferred to the Malaysian automotive industry.[10] Furthermore, the A3 programme of training for vehicle type approval, which is important for the control of imported vehicles, continued with Japanese support. MAJAICO has, to some extent, contributed to the development of the supporting industry in Malaysia by levelling up the technological capability and human resources of ***bumiputra*** vendors, and has clearly became a trigger for the Malaysian automotive industry to approach global competition.

Table 4.4 Automotive Human Resource Development Programme in Thailand

Firm	*Activity*	*Phase 1*	*Phase 2*
Toyota	Toyota Production System	24	1,483 (156 firms)
Nissan	Skill certificate	205	82 (216)*
Honda	Mould & die technology	26	1,482
Denso	Production technology	47	1,284

Source: Interview, March 2010.

Note: *Certificate was awarded to 82 people out of 216 participants.

Table 4.5 Overview of MAJAICO in Malaysia

No.	*Project*	*Activities*	*Malaysian Organisation*	*Japanese Organisation*
A1	Automotive Technical Assistance Programme	Dispatching Japanese experts to individual firms in Malaysia to teach lean production system	SMIDEC	JODC (Toyota and Daihatsu)
A2	Mould & Die Centre	Dispatching Japanese experts to SIRIM mould centre to enhance technical standards	SIRIM	JODC

No.	*Project*	*Activities*	*Malaysian Organisation*	*Japanese Organisation*
A3	Vehicle Type Approval	Dispatching Japanese experts to enhance model certification skill in MOT	MOT	METI
B	Automotive Skill Training Centre in Malaysia	To train master trainers for automotive production in ADTEC	MOHR (ADTEC)	JETRO (Nissan)
C	Automotive Skill Training Centre in Japan	Dispatching Malaysian technicians to production & quality control training in Japan	MOHR (ADTEC)	AOTS
D	Component & Parts Testing Centre	Dispatching Japanese experts to enhance the capacity of components testing centre	SIRIM	JICA
E	Business Development Programme	Sending business mission from Japan to Malaysia, vice versa	MACPMA	JETRO
F1	Cooperation in Automotive Market Information	To provide automotive market and technology related information	MIDA	JAMA
F2	Consultation on JV contract	Consultation with individual firm for JVs	MIDA	METI
F3	Cooperation in Exhibition	To organise Malaysian Automotive EXPO in Japan	MATRADE	JETRO

Source: Takehiro (2011) and Onozawa (2008).

Note: SMIDEC (Small and Medium Industries Development Corporation), SIRIM (Standard and Industrial Research Institute of Malaysia), MOT (Ministry of Transport), MOHR (Ministry of Human Resources), ADTEC (Advanced Technology Training Centre), MACPMA (Malaysian Automotive Component Parts Manufacturer Association), MIDA (Malaysian Investment Development Authority), and MATRADE (Malaysian External Trade Development Corporation).

ASEAN integration, Japanese automotive MNCs, and the Japanese government

The automotive industry has been acting as one of major drivers in deepening ASEAN regional integration. In the early years, ASEAN governments implemented various industrial co-operation and trade policies, but the initial co-operation schemes did not succeed due to conflicts between member countries. The first successful scheme was the BBC scheme in the late 1980s, followed by the AICO scheme and AFTA in the 1990s, and more recently by AEC. Japanese automotive MNCs have played a significant role in these regional integration policies. The BBC scheme in 1988 was initiated by Mitsubishi Motors as a result of negotiations with ASEAN governments, exclusively designed to enhance intra-firm trade between automotive MNCs within the region. The AICO scheme in the period of 1996–2010 was established as a result of negotiations between the Japanese automotive MNCs–government alliance and the ASEAN governments in order to span the transition period from the BBC scheme to

AFTA. Indeed, the Japanese automotive MNCs–government alliance has lobbied ASEAN governments to implement regional industrial schemes in favour of Japanese automotive industry in the region. We will now consider the various schemes in more detail.

Industrial cooperation schemes in ASEAN during the 1970s and 1980s

One of the first regional economic cooperation schemes in Southeast Asia was the ASEAN Industrial Project (AIP). It was agreed upon in 1976 in order to establish large industrial projects in each country by encouraging industrial co-operation within the region (Chatterjee 1990). AIP aimed to utilise raw materials, which were available in each country, to contribute to the creation of employment and food production, establishing them so as to obtain foreign currencies (Miki 2001: 179–180). There were a lot of conflicts of interest among the ASEAN countries in the allocation of industries. For instance, at the sixth AEM meeting in June 1978, there was strong friction between Singapore and Indonesia regarding the location of a diesel engine project. Indonesia asked Singapore to produce engines with more than 500 horse power because Indonesia, at that time, produced 40–120 horse power engines and had a plan to produce those with up to 500 horse power (Shimizu 1998: 52–54). Singapore finally gave up the diesel engine project as well as the AIP. In 1983, the ASEAN Industrial Joint Venture (AIJV) scheme was established in order to encourage the direct collaboration of manufacturers in at least two ASEAN countries by reducing import tariffs in the case of mutual parts delivery and by offering local content accreditation to these parts (Legewie 2000b: 213). In 1987, the scheme was amended to be open to foreign investors and require the agreement of more than two ASEAN countries out of the then six and a minimum of 51% local capital participation. However, it was held over due to powerful bureaucracy and prevailing rivalries between individual countries. Consequently, only three projects were carried out under the scheme (Sakurai 1997: 442).

The ASEAN Industrial Complementation (AIC) scheme was the first agreement to facilitate a complementation system within the region and proposed the development of an automotive industry in ASEAN. AIC aimed to encourage a structure of industrial specialisation in countries within the region so as to gain economies of scale as well as to expand intra-regional trade in industrial goods. It was agreed upon at the ASEAN foreign ministerial meeting in June 1981. The original idea of the ASEAN Industrial Complementation scheme was derived from the Ford and GM complementation strategy in Asia in the 1970s. The AIC was approved for two automotive package projects, which were applied for by the ASEAN Automotive Federation (AAF). The AAF proposed the 'ASEAN Automotive Complementation Scheme', which aimed to ensure automotive development within the region through the complementation of components from each country.[11] The AIC scheme aimed to produce made-in-ASEAN cars within the region, with the co-operation of ASEAN member countries. However, the scheme failed because foreign automotive producers (mainly) formed assembly bases in each country and did not co-operate with the AIC scheme (Shimizu 1998: 111). Moreover, due to the complexity of executing the scheme, it became impossible for ASEAN countries to co-operate with each other.

The brand to brand complementation (BBC) scheme in 1988

The BBC scheme originated from the AIC scheme. The failure of the AIC scheme opened a new opportunity for foreign automotive producers. Mitsubishi Motors, for instance, established production plants in Malaysia, Thailand, and the Philippines in response to local content regulations. At that time, they found difficulties in their operations in these countries due to the small size of the domestic markets. Mitsubishi built a plant to reduce investment costs by consolidating the production of particular parts in one country and then exporting them to plants in other countries. Mitsubishi assumed that regional complementation would enable them to reduce the cost of transmission components (by 10%) and door panels (by 5%) in comparison with imported components from Japan. It formed a plan of complementation within the ASEAN region: namely exporting pressed products, such as fuel tanks and floor panels, from Thailand to the Philippines; components for engines, such as gaskets and bearings, from Thailand to Malaysia; transmissions from the Philippines to Thailand; and door panels from Malaysia to Thailand (Kamo 1997: 72). Mitsubishi approached the Committee on Industry, Minerals and Energy in ASEAN, and submitted a proposal for a parts exchange scheme in 1982. The following year, a special meeting about the BBC scheme was organised by the Committee on Industry, Mineral and Energy, ASEAN Automotive Federation, and automotive producers. However, the plan was postponed for a time. In March 1987, Mitsubishi's affiliate in the Philippines, the Philippine Automotive Manufacturing Corporation, was requested to launch the BBC scheme by the Minister of Trade and Industry of the Philippines. At the same time, the Committee on Industry, Minerals and Energy realised that the AIC was unrealistic and requested that foreign producers, such as Mitsubishi, establish a parts complementation regime within the region. Mitsubishi was willing to do so because they had production plants across the region as well as previous experience in exporting transmissions with Mitsubishi's affiliate Asian Transmission Corporations in the Philippines to Mitsubishi's assembly plant in Thailand under the AIC regime. In the beginning of 1988, Mitsubishi negotiated with the governments of Thailand, Malaysia, and Indonesia; subsequently Malaysia and Thailand agreed with Mitsubishi's proposal, while Indonesia refused, claiming complete automotive production for its large domestic market (Shimizu 1998: 112–113).

Finally, the BBC scheme was adopted at the AEM meeting in October 1988. It was officially called the 'Memorandum of Understanding, Brand to Brand Complementation on the Automotive Industry under the Basic Agreement on ASEAN Industrial Complementation' and agreed upon the participation of Malaysia, Thailand, and the Philippines, signed by the six ASEAN countries. In

December 1988, Mitsubishi lodged an application for five items for the BBC scheme to the Committee on Industry, Minerals and Energy, and three of them were approved. The scheme aimed to allow for a 50% reduction in the import tariffs applied to an auto part exported by an assembly's subsidiaries based in one ASEAN country to another subsidiary in another ASEAN country (Yoshimatsu 2002a). After Mitsubishi, Toyota, Nissan, Honda, Volvo, DAF, and Mercedes Benz were also given approval to join the scheme (Legewie 2000b). In the early 1990s, the Indonesian government gradually shifted their interests to the BBC scheme because the government regarded the automotive industry as its main export industry after the oil industry. The executives of the Ministry of Industry of Indonesia negotiated with MITI (now METI) of Japan and Japanese automotive MNCs to increase automotive investment in Indonesia. In response to this request, MITI/METI proposed that the Indonesian government join the scheme and arrange the Japan–Indonesia policy talks. Eventually in 1994, the Indonesian government accepted Japan's request and announced that it would join the scheme (Yoshimatsu 1999: 507). In negotiations with the Thai government, the Japanese automotive MNCs and MITI/METI requested the provision of tariff privileges, which was not awarded under the BBC scheme in Thailand. In July 1994, MITI/METI organised the Japan–Thai policy forum and requested that the Thai government implement the scheme. As a result, the then Thai Vice-Prime Minister announced that the Thai government would provide tariff privileges under the BBC scheme in October 1994 (ibid.).

Establishment of the ASEAN Free Trade Area (AFTA) in 1992

In 1992, at the Fourth ASEAN Summit in Singapore, ASEAN officially announced that they would establish a free trade regime by 2008.[12] This ended up being established a lot earlier, in January 1993. The Common Effective Preferential Tariff (CEPT) scheme, established as the basis of AFTA, aimed at reducing existing tariff rates between members to 0–5% and eliminating quantitative restrictions and other non-tariff barriers. The original concept of CEPT was adopted at the ASEAN Economic Ministers Meeting in Bali in 1990, aiming to encourage intra-regional trade in the ASEAN region though the establishment of a common tariff system, which was set to less than 20%, and finally to 0% (Aoki 1997). AFTA was established in order to increase ASEAN's competitive advantage as a production base for the world market and enjoy economies of scale in production, encouraging foreign investment in the region, which would also stimulate the growth of supporting industries. Several motivations for the establishment of AFTA can be identified. First, the ASEAN governments realised the importance of a common market for the utilisation of economies of scale in accordance with the rapid industrialisation of the region. Second, a horizontal division of labour within the region, which had been spread by foreign MNCs, became a significant phenomenon. The high tariff structure in each country became an obstacle in the development of a horizontal division of labour (ibid.: 87). Third, ASEAN governments were concerned about the rise of China, which was becoming the largest destination of inward foreign investment in Asia (Miki

2001: 183). The ASEAN countries were keen on encouraging inward foreign investment in the region in order to compete with China. In relation to the automotive industry, there were difficulties with regard to AFTA. The ASEAN-4 countries initially registered automotive and automotive components on the Temporary Exclusion List (TEL).[13] However only three countries – Thailand, Indonesia, and the Philippines – transferred automotive and automotive components from the TEL to the Inclusion List (IL)[14] in 2000, and the tariffs were reduced to 0–5% by 2003. In contrast, Malaysia announced at the 31st AEM meeting in Singapore in September 1999 that tariff reductions on vehicles and automotive components would be rescheduled from 2003 to 2005 (Wakamatsu *et al.* 2001: 116). At the 32nd AEM meeting in Chiang Mai, Thailand, in October 2000, the Malaysian proposal was approved.

From BBC to the ASEAN industrial cooperation (AICO) scheme in 1996

After the establishment of AFTA, the members of ASEAN decided to abolish the BBC scheme at an informal ASEAN Economic Ministers Meeting in 1995. The ASEAN officials took the view that the AFTA/CEPT scheme, which involved a variety of industries, would replace the BBC scheme, which related only to the automotive industry. In response, Japanese automotive MNCs and their local affiliates argued to keep the BBC scheme. Moreover, the Japanese government and the Japan Automotive Manufacturers Association opposed abolition. JAMA, for instance, requested that, if the BBC scheme was abolished, an exceptional measure for the CEPT be introduced (Yoshimatsu 2002a: 132).

The BBC scheme provided a number of benefits to promote parts complementation within the region (see Shimizu 1998). However, there were still several criticisms of the scheme. First, it allowed only the automotive assembly industry to enjoy tariff reduction (leaving out the automotive components industry and other industries, such as electronics), and some local officials objected that the benefits were given only to foreign producers, not to local firms (Yoshimatsu 2002a: 131). The second issue for the BBC scheme was raised by automotive parts producers as it excluded them as well. Some large Japanese automotive part producers were keen on joining the scheme. Denso, the largest, had three factories in Southeast Asia.[15] It lobbied the ASEAN Secretariat and the member governments to be allowed to join in the BBC scheme. It received a positive reply from the ASEAN Secretariat and member countries to extend applications to the BBC scheme from automotive producers to automotive components producers (ibid.). Furthermore, the Japanese electronics industry was interested in the regional complementation scheme. As a result of the Japanese automotive industry's effort, the introduction of a new scheme was agreed upon in September 1995. In April 1996, BBC was replaced by an extended version called the ASEAN Industrial Cooperation (AICO) scheme at the AEM meeting in Singapore.

The scheme encouraged companies operating in different ASEAN countries to co-operate with each other in the manufacture of AICO-approved products. The AICO agreement required a minimum of two companies from two different countries, and approved products could obtain a preferential tariff rate of 0–5%, (a radical change from the previous tariff of 50% under the BBC scheme), local content accreditation, and other non-tariff incentives. The AICO scheme would be provided for any ASEAN-brand company which had a 30% or more ASEAN national equity (Fujita and Hill 1997: 317–318). Furthermore, it was applicable not only to the automotive industry but also to other industries, such as electronics. Applications for participation in the AICO scheme commenced in November 1996. The first applications were from Toyota, Denso, and Matsushita Electric (Panasonic) in December 1996. However, the number of applications was far smaller than expected. What is more, the processing and administration of the applications was slow and flawed. After the AICO scheme was agreed upon, the ASEAN countries, relevant companies, and industries negotiated its conditions. From the perspective of the ASEAN countries, the objectives of the AICO scheme were to facilitate industrial complementation, intra-regional trade, and inward investment. They viewed the scheme as a means to promote the interests of their local firms and economies, and imposed regulations in pursuit of these objectives. However, their policy orientation conflicted with the strategies of MNCs to enhance efficient inter-firm and intra-regional complementation (Yoshimatsu 2002a: 133). MNCs tried to take advantage of the scheme, but they had already established production bases in line with individual host government's requirements and could not meet those of AICO. Therefore, negotiations between Japanese MNCs-government and the ASEAN governments were started in order to facilitate and complement the scheme.

One of the largest negotiations occurred in relation to the restriction of national equity. As the scheme requested a minimum of 30% ASEAN national equity, firms with less than 30% had to increase their local equity shares. In Toshiba's operations, for instance, eight out of fourteen production plants were based in five ASEAN countries. Established in response to the local governments' preferential measures, which allowed a high foreign ownership share, Toshiba's plants could not meet the regulations of the AICO scheme due to the fact that each country had operations in different equity regulations (Noda 1999). Japanese MNCs and the Japanese government were opposed to the national equity regulation, claiming that it was counter to liberalisation; as a consequence it was listed on the waiver criteria. MNCs began to focus on the waiver criteria rather than the national equity regulations, as individual governments could approve a lower rate of national equity, thereby allowing the waiver criteria to overrule the national equity regulation (Fourin 2002: 11).

A number of problems could be identified in relation to the AICO scheme. One of the major problems was related to the industry policy differences among ASEAN countries. Both the Indonesian and Malaysian governments were, in general, reluctant to join the AICO scheme because they had already begun national car production. The second problem with the AICO scheme occurred in relation to trade imbalances between the ASEAN countries. The scheme was based on a bilateral trade structure, and the government officials, in general, viewed an increase in imports through the AICO scheme as an encroachment onto their home market by other countries (Yoshimatsu 2002a).

The AFC in 1997 led to a change in attitude toward the AICO scheme. Per capita income, intra-regional trade, inward investment, and manufacturing production in the ASEAN countries dramatically deteriorated due to the crisis, and the importance of regional co-operation was soon realised. After the Sixth ASEAN Summit in Hanoi in 1998, the ASEAN governments took a more open attitude toward the AICO scheme. The governments issued the 'Statement on Bold Measures', which allowed applicants a waiver of the AICO 30% national equity requirement during the period 1999–2000; as a result, meeting the application criteria has become easier (Shimizu 2011: 68–69). At the ASEAN Working Group on Industrial Cooperation (WGIC) Meeting, the Japan–ASEAN Auto Export Group Meeting, the ASEAN Secretariat Hearing, and the ASEAN Chamber of Commerce and Industry (ASEAN–CCI) Hearing, the Japanese government, in cooperation with Japanese automotive MNCs, discussed the AICO scheme with political and business leaders in ASEAN. Major automotive producers sent their delegates to the most important meetings of WGIC to deliver their opinions and suggestions about the AICO scheme. At the same time, the Japan Automobile Manufacturers Association lobbied the ASEAN governments in order to support the AICO scheme. For instance, JAMA and JAPIA organised the Japan-Indonesia Automotive Dialogue in 1998 in order to promote the AICO scheme in Indonesia. JAMA also established a close relationship with the ASEAN Automotive Federation and formed joint technological and management co-operation. Subsequently, the AAF encouraged the ASEAN Secretariat, ASEAN Chamber of Commerce and Industry, and local governments to accelerate AICO implementation (Yoshimatsu 2002a: 140).

As a result of the efforts made by Japanese automotive MNCs, as well as those by automotive associations and the ASEAN governments' recognition of the importance of regional co-operation, the application criteria and processes of the AICO scheme changed in 1999. These changes led to increased applications from 1999 to 2000. The AICO Scheme worked as a bridging agreement between BBC and the completion of tariff-free trade within ASEAN-6 countries under CEPT/AFTA in 2010. Table 4.6 shows the proportions of one Japanese MNC's intra-firm trade usage of these schemes in Southeast Asia. In 2003, the proportion of the AICO scheme was slightly higher than that of the CEPT/AFTA. After this period, the AICO scheme became less significant, accounting for only 2% by 2008. Eventually, its role was came to an end in 2010.

Table 4.6 Proportions of a Japanese Automotive MNC's Intra-Firm Trade Usage of Schemes in Southeast Asia, 2003–2009

Scheme	*2003 (%)*	*2004 (%)*	*2005 (%)*	*2006 (%)*	*2007 (%)*	*2008 (%)*	*2009 (%)*
AICO	43	28	11	12	4	2	2
CEPT .	44	38	44	49	54	70	72
Neither	12	34	45	39	42	27	26
Total	100	100	100	100	100	100	100

Source: Interview in March 2010.

Note: Percentages of firm's total intra-firm trade values.

ASEAN economic community (AEC)

In 2003, ASEAN decided to establish the ASEAN Economic Community (AEC) by 2020, but later, in 2007, it advanced the time to 2015 (Chia 2011).[16] The AEC aims to enhance the deepening of regional economic integration in Southeast Asia with four pillars: (i) a single market and production base, (ii) a highly competitive economic region, (iii) a region of equitable economic development, and (iv) a region fully integrated into the global economy (ASEAN Secretariat 2008: 6). Deepening regional economic integration is becoming increasingly important for ASEAN countries for three reasons. First, China has grown into a very attractive market, and the ASEAN region has become less attractive for MNCs. Second, the growing expansion of bilateralism and regionalism has created many new competitors for local firms in ASEAN as a result of the formation of regional trade agreements by ASEAN members with non-ASEAN member countries, including those in North America, Europe, and Asia. Third, ASEAN is playing an increasingly important role as the hub for FTA activities in East Asia (Austria 2012: 143–144).

Table 4.7 shows four pillars and core elements in the AEC Blueprint. A single market and production base targets a free flow of goods, services, investments, capital, and skilled labour. In addition, the agro-based, automotive, electronics, fisheries, rubber-based, textile and apparel, wood-based, air-transport, e-ASEAN/Information and communication technology, health care, logistics, and tourism industries are targeted as priority integration sectors. Making ASEAN into a highly competitive economic region can be achieved through competition policy, intellectual property rights, infrastructure development, avoidance of double taxation treaties, and e-commerce (Chia 2011). The development of SMEs is increasingly important for ensuring equitable economic development by enhancing local entrepreneurship, innovation, and employment creation. In addition, technical assistance and capacity building programmes for CLMV countries are another important core element in equitable economic

Table 4.7 Overview of the ASEAN Economic Community

Pillars	*Core Elements*
i Single Market and Production Base	Free flow of goods, services, investments, capital, and skilled labour, Priority integration sectors, Food, agriculture and forestry
ii Competitive Economic Region	Competition policy, Consumer protection, Intellectual property rights, Infrastructure development, Taxation, and E-commerce
iii Equitable Economic Development	SME development, and Initiative for ASEAN Integration
iv Integration into Global Economy	Coherent approach towards external economic relations, and enhanced participation in global supply chain networks

Source: ASEAN Secretariat (2008) and Chia (2013: 13).

development in the region (Chia 2013). Furthermore, integration into the global economy can be conducted through participation in global supply chain networks. AEC, however – unlike the European Economic Community, for example – does not have a common external tariff (that is, a common tariff against non-ASEAN countries).[17]

With regard to the automotive industry, AEC may influence regional countries and automotive producers and auto parts suppliers. First, the division between those countries which currently seem to be the winning countries, such as Thailand and Indonesia, and the losing countries, such as the CLMV countries, will become more apparent in terms of vehicle production. Losing countries have a relatively small domestic market and low local procurement ratio, and cannot utilise economies of scale. As part of the progress towards AEC, import tariffs on CBUs and parts were waived in 2010 for the ASEAN-6 and in 2018 for the CLMV countries. The automotive assembly industries in these countries will surely face harsh competition from their neighbouring countries, particularly Thailand. For instance, one of the leading Japanese assemblers assembled five models under high tariff barriers in Vietnam but expected to produce fewer models after the full implementation of AEC. In addition, imported CBU models were 20–30% cheaper than locally produced models in Vietnam (interview, 6 March 2015). In this context, it seems clear that the automotive assembly operations in Vietnam are less competitive in comparison with Thailand or Indonesia. It is worth noting that although tariff barriers were eliminated in the region, non-tariff barriers remain to protect their local industry. For instance, Vietnam strengthened inspections for all imported vehicles, requiring a new type of vehicle approval (particularly against Thailand) in early 2018 (see Chapter 9). In the case of Malaysia, excise tax is imposed, ranging from 75% to 200% on vehicles without local content. Moreover, it was announced that imported cars would be required to have a vehicle entry permit in 2017 (Automotive World 2018: 9). Second, with regard to vehicle producers, Japanese producers, such as Toyota and Honda, seem to have advantages due to their well-established regional production networks. Third, however, there might be new opportunities for the automotive parts industry in CLMV countries, and Vietnam in particular is already moving along that path. Like the Philippines, Vietnam has flourishing exports of automotive components and the automotive electrical component wiring harnesses (see Chapters 8 and 9). The labour-intensive auto parts industry in Thailand has been gradually relocating to CLMV countries due to Thailand's labour shortage, high labour costs, and the development of infrastructure in CLMV countries.[18] Moreover, even labour-intensive auto parts firms in Jakarta, Indonesia, are relocating their production activities to countries bordering Thailand (that is, Cambodia, Laos, and Myanmar) (Nakata 2015: 16). Particularly, Japanese automotive MNCs in Thailand have been establishing "Thai +1" production networks in the region. Under these networks, Thai operations coordinate their branch factories in CLMV countries (Ueki 2016). For instance, one of the leading Japanese auto parts suppliers, Minebea, established its first factory in Cambodia in 2011, increasingly expanding operations by procuring intermediate components from its factories in Thailand.[19] In this context, regional division of labour within ASEAN, particularly including CLMV countries, is becoming an important strategy for automotive MNCs.

In response to AEC, JAMA has been coordinating with Japan and the ASEAN automotive industry under the Working Group on the Automotive Industry of AMEICC. Mutual Recognition Arrangements (MRA), Standardisation of Rules of Origin (ROO), the early start-up of the ASEAN Single Window (ASW), road safety, and environmental issues became major points of discussion. JAMA and AAF made an agreement on a joint statement to strengthen their cooperative relationship. In addition, METI of Japan is introducing a comprehensive support programme for HR development within the ASEAN automotive industry (JAMA 2016).

Case study of Toyota's operations in Southeast Asia

In Southeast Asia, Toyota produced and sold nearly a million vehicles in 2016 (see Table 4.8). With regard to production, as Table 4.8 shows, Thailand is the most important country for Toyota, accounting for approximately 59% of the total vehicle output in the region, followed by Indonesia, Malaysia, the Philippines, and Vietnam in 2016. In terms of markets, Indonesia is the most important, accounting for 40.8% of the total sales in the region, followed by Thailand, the Philippines, Malaysia, Vietnam, Singapore, and Brunei in 2016.

Toyota established their first sales company in Southeast Asia in 1957. In response to the Thai Board of Investment's Industrial Investment Promotion Act in 1960 (later revised in 1962, with provision of various investment incentives), Toyota established its first CKD assembly operation in ASEAN, Toyota Motor Thailand (TMT), in co-operation with its local partner Bangkok Bank (which held a 50% equity) in 1962.[20] TMT was Toyota's second overseas factory after that in Brazil and commenced production with a capacity of 150 units a month in 1964. In 1970 Toyota's production capacity in Thailand increased to 600 units a month (Kuroiwa *et al.* 2016). In Thailand, Toyota produces seven models (Hilux, Fortuner, Corolla Altis, Vios, Yaris, Camry, Camry Hybrid,

Table 4.8 Toyota's Production and Sales in Southeast Asia, 2016

Country	*Production*	*Percent*	*Sales*	*Percent*
Thailand	555,907	58.9	245,087	26.1
Indonesia	218,720	23.2	382,610	40.8
Malaysia	56,454	6.0	65,110	6.9
Philippines	55,026	5.8	158,726	16.9
Vietnam	57,036	6.0	58,701	6.3
Singapore	–	–	24,468	2.6
Brunei	–	–	2,607	0.3
Total	943,143	100	937,311	100

Source: Adapted from Fourin (2017: 17, 166–168).
Note: Number of Vehicles.

and Hiace). Of the total production of 555,907 units in 2016, 318,658 units (or 57.2%) were exported to Europe (120,002 units or 37.7%), the Middle East (102,128 units or 32.0%), Central and South America (57,588 units or 18.1%), Oceania (57,504 units or 18.0%), Asia (55,281 units or 17.3%), North America (29,630 units or 9.3%), and Africa (4,525 units or 1.4%). In particular, the one-ton pick-up truck Hilux accounted for 217,480 units (or 68.2% of their total exports) (Fourin 2017: 174). In addition, Thailand is a major supplier of diesel engines in the region.

In Indonesia, PT Toyota Motor Manufacturing Indonesia was set up in order to assemble vehicles in 1970, and PT Toyota Astra Motor was established in co-operation with Astra International with the purpose of distributing vehicles in 1971. This was according to an Indonesian government decree of 1969, requiring that assembly operations and distribution operations be established by different entities. In Indonesia, Toyota produces six models (Fortuner, Innova, Vios, Yaris, Etios, and Sienta) with a total production of 218,720 units in 2016 (Fourin 2017: 173). It is worth noting that four models (Agyo, Rush, Calya, and Avanza) in Indonesia are OEM-supplied by PT Astra Daihatsu Motor (see Table 4.10). In addition, Indonesia is Toyota's major location for supplying gasoline engines to the region, exporting not only within ASEAN but also to India, Pakistan, South Africa, Egypt, Argentina, Venezuela, and Kazakhstan (Fourin 2017: 176).

In Malaysia, Champion Motors (the current Assembly Services) was established in 1968 to assemble Toyota vehicles. As of 2017, Assembly Services is wholly owned by UMW Toyota Motor – a joint venture between a local company, United Motor Works (UMW), holding 51% of its equity, and Toyota and Toyota Tsusho, holding 39% and 10%, respectively, in 1982 (Anazawa 2016). Assembly Services produces six models (Vios, Camry, Camry Hybrid, Innova, Hilux, and Hiace), based on CKD production in Malaysia, accounting for 56,454 units with approximately 3,000 employees in 2016. It is worth noting that UMW was also the largest equity holder, holding 38%, when Perodua was established.

In the Philippines, Toyota's initial partner was Delta Motors, which commenced production in 1962. A special model for the Philippine market, the Tamaraw, was introduced in 1976.[21] Due to political upheaval in the Philippines, Toyota withdrew from the country in 1984. The current operation in the country is conducted by Toyota Motor Philippines (TMP), established in association with Mitsui & Co and a local bank in 1988. Toyota produces only two models (Vios and Innova) based on CKD assembly in the Philippines, with total production of 55,026 vehicles in 2016. Toyota was planning to start producing a new model of the Vios under the Philippine's CARS programme in 2018, with a total production of 200,000 units over a period of six years (Fourin 2017: 163). Toyota also established Toyota Autoparts Philippines (TAP) in 1992, producing transmissions (Ofreneo 2008). TAP plays the role of transmissions supplier in the region, also exporting to other countries, such as South Africa and Japan.

In Vietnam, Toyota Motor Vietnam (TMV) was established in 1995 as a joint venture firm by Toyota (70%) with the state-owned enterprise Vietnam Engine and Agricultural Machinery (VEAM) Corporation (with 20%) and KUO Singapore (with 10%). TMV manufactures four models (Vios, Carolla Altis, Camry, and Innova), with a total of production of 57,036 vehicles in 2016 (see Table 4.8).[22] The local content ratio in foreign producers is rather low, heavily depending on imports of components from neighbouring countries. In this sense, Vietnam's position in Toyota's production networks in ASEAN seems to be becoming less significant under AEC. For instance, Fortuner production was replaced with an imported model from Indonesia in 2017. However, Chapter 9 does note some expansion plans by Toyota in the country.[23] The restructuring of their operation in Vietnam is expected as AEC progresses in the near future.

We can identify several features in Toyota's production strategies in Southeast Asia (Table 4.9). First, Thailand and Indonesia are their two important production locations for vehicle assembly, while the other countries (Malaysia, the Philippines, and Vietnam) depend on imports of CKD kits or CBUs (see Table 4.10). In this context, Thailand and Indonesia play a role as export platforms in the region. Second, co-operation with Daihatsu as an OEM supplier has been increasingly important, particularly in Toyota's Indonesian operation.

Table 4.9 Toyota's Operations in Southeast Asia, 2017

Country	*Company Name*	*Ownership*	*Operation*	*Main Models/ Components*	*Production Capacity*
Thailand	Toyota Motor Thailand (TMT) in 1962	Toyota 86.4%; Siam Cement 10%; Others 3.6%	Assembly	Hilux, Corolla Altis, Vios, Fortuner, Camry, Camry (Hybrid), Yaris	760,000 units
	Siam Toyota Manufacturing in 1987	Toyota 96%; Cement Thai holdings 4%	Parts production	Gasoline engines, Diesel engines (for IMV), Propeller shafts	1 million units (engines)
	Toyota Auto Works in 1988	TMT 37%; Toyota Auto Body 63%	Assembly	Hiace Commuter (CKD assembly)	20,000 units
	Toyota Daihatsu Engineering & Manufacturing in 2007	Toyota 100%	Regional Headquarter R&D	–	(2,550 employees)
Indonesia	PT Toyota Motor Manufacturing Indonesia in 1970	Toyota 95% Astra International 5%	Assembly & parts production	Innova, Fortuner, Etios Valco, Vios (Limo), Yaris, Sienta / gasoline engines, press parts, mould parts	250,000 units 411,000 units (engines)

Country	*Company Name*	*Ownership*	*Operation*	*Main Models/ Components*	*Production Capacity*
Malaysia	Assembly Services in 1968	UMW Toyota Motor 100%	Assembly	Vios, Camry, Camry (Hybrid), Innova, Hilux, Fortuner, Hiace	76,000 units
	Toyota Auto Body (Malaysia) in 2005	Toyota Auto Body 100%	Parts production	Bumpers, Instrument panels, Press parts	–
Philippines	Toyota Motor Philippines in 1988	Toyota 34% Mitsui & Co 15%; Metropolitan Bank 51%	Assembly	Vios, Innova	50,000 units
	Toyota Autoparts Philippines in 1990	Toyota Aisin	Parts production	Manual transmission (MT), Constant-velocity joint (CVJ)	MT:330,000 units CVJ:200,000 units
Vietnam	Toyota Motor Vietnam in 1995	Toyota 70%, VEAM 20%, KUO 10%	Assembly	Vios, Corolla Altis, Camry, Innova	46,000 units

Source: Adapted from Fourin (2017: 175–177).

Table 4.10 Toyota's Regional Division of Labour of Major Vehicle Production in Southeast Asia, 2017

Type	*Model*	*Thailand*	*Indonesia*	*Malaysia*	*Philippines*	*Vietnam*
PV	Agya/Wigo	*	(Daihatsu)	*	(Indonesia)	*
	Etios	*	○	*	*	*
	Yaris	○	○	*	(Indonesia)	(Thailand)
	Vios	○	○	CKD	CKD	CKD
	Corolla Altis	○	(Thailand)	(Thailand)	(Thailand)	CKD
	Camry	○	(Thailand)	CKD	(Thailand)	CKD
	Camry Hybrid	○	(Thailand)	CKD	*	*
SUV	Rush	*	(Daihatsu)	(Indonesia)	*	*
	Fortuner	○	○	CKD	(Indonesia)	(Indonesia)
MPV	Calya	*	(Daihatsu)	*	*	*
	Avanza	(Indonesia)	(Daihatsu)	(Indonesia)	(Indonesia)	*
	Innova	(Indonesia)	○	CKD	CKD	CKD
	Sienta	(Indonesia)	○	(Indonesia)	*	*
IMV	Hilux	○	(Thailand)	CKD	(Thailand)	(Thailand)
Van	Hiace	○	(Japan)	CKD	(Japan)	(Japan)

Source: Adapted from Fourin (2017: 169).

Note: ○ (local production), () (importing country or OEM supplier); *not sold.

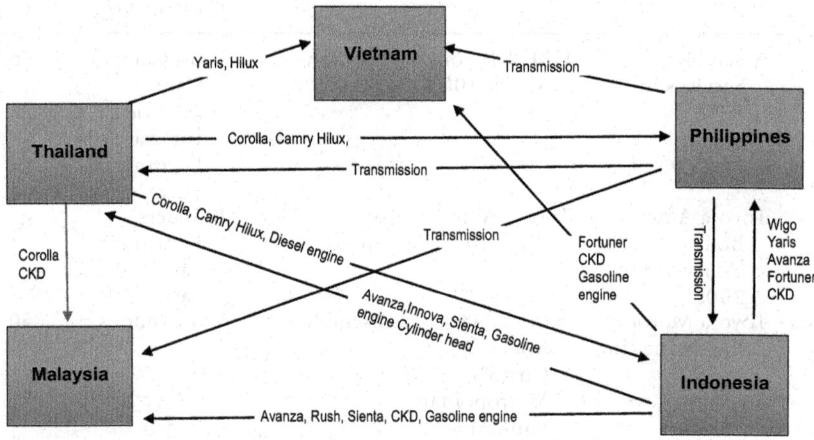

Figure 4.1 Toyota's Complementation Trade in Southeast Asia.
Source: Adapted from Fourin (2017: 172)

Toyota has expanded its regional complementation system in the ASEAN region. Before the BBC scheme was introduced, it had established assembly as well as components production bases in Thailand, Indonesia, and the Philippines in response to each government's industrial policy. However, the BBC scheme became a turning point in Toyota's regional production strategy. Toyota made a complementation plan in the region through BBC, AICO, and AFTA, and, most recently, through AEC. Table 4.10 shows Toyota's regional division of labour in their models in Southeast Asia, with Thailand and Indonesia representing the two strategic production locations. Thailand plays the role of a major production location for PVs and CVs, while Indonesia is a strategic production location for SUVs and MPVs. The production and sales strategies in the other three countries are mainly based on CKD assembly operations or imported CBUs. With regard to components, the Thai affiliate produces diesel engines, the Indonesian affiliate produces gasoline engines, and the affiliate in the Philippines manufactures transmissions, and they export to the other countries in the region (see Figure 4.1).

Conclusions

Japanese multinationals account for the bulk of both vehicle and component production within ASEAN and vehicle sales in the region. This chapter has reviewed the development of the operations of Japanese automotive MNCs in ASEAN and has shown the major role that the Japanese government and its agencies have played in promoting such developments in association with the companies and ASEAN governments. Economic integration within ASEAN has moved on from its early days when conflicting interests and views between member countries made for many frictions, restricting the planning of production between member countries so as to promote productive efficiency, particularly with regard to achieving economies of scale. The automotive industry has been at the forefront of establishing a more efficient division of labour between countries in Southeast Asia, both in terms of the location of production of particular models and the location of production of major components, such as transmissions. This has taken place, even against the background of the early years of import substituting industrialisation with high national tariff walls from the 1950s and 1960s, which led to automotive assembly being established in all countries of the ASEAN-4 – Thailand, Indonesia, Malaysia and the Philippines – and later in Vietnam. Successive agreements, such as the BBC scheme in 1988 (involving only the automotive industry) and the wider and more effective AIC scheme of 1996, have helped pave the way for the tariff-free trade achieved under AFTA, the ASEAN Free Trade Area, in 2010, even (from 2018) including the newer ASEAN members: Cambodia, Laos, Myanmar, and Vietnam. Cambodia, Laos, and Myanmar, bordering Thailand, have gradually been drawn into the regional production networks in which Thailand (and increasingly) Indonesia are central players. The maturing of AFTA into the ASEAN Economic Community, AEC, in 2015, has the potential to further strengthen the regional division of labour.

Notes

1 We are aware of the unusually large number of acronyms in this chapter. Readers are referred to the list of abbreviations at the start of this book, but from time to time in order to make the account easier to read we repeat in the text the full names of organisations and arrangements.
2 See Chapter 9 for a discussion of automotive industrial policy in Vietnam. We do not include it in the present table because policy changes in Vietnam have been undertaken in a very different (much later) timeframe than in the ASEAN-4.
3 Japan Overseas Development Corporation (JODC) and AOTS merged in to the Overseas Human Resource and Industry Development Association (HIDA) in 2012. HIDA was renamed as AOTS in 2017.
4 https://www.ameicc.org/activity/doc/document00042.pdf [accessed on 30 October 2018].
5 For instance, the Japanese Government and MNCs negotiated the ASEAN Industrial Cooperation (AICO) scheme, a low tariff automotive parts trading scheme set up in conjunction with AFTA and the ASEAN governments. Refer to Yoshimatsu (2002a) for more details.
6 AOTS' website: https://www.aots.jp/hida/en/about/pdf/guide_to_aots_en_1807.pdf [accessed on 29 October 2018].
7 JICA's website: https://www.jica.go.jp/thailand/english/activities/coop02.html [accessed on 29 October 2018].
8 Interview with Commercial Attache at the Japanese Embassy in Malaysia on 23 February 2012.
9 Interview with the Deputy Secretary General in MITI, Malaysia on 28 February 2012.
10 Interview with Senior Director at JETRO Kuala Lumpur on 1 March 2012.
11 The first project involved 80–135 horse power diesel engines, accelerators for motorbikes, and wheel rims from Indonesia; domestic vehicle body panels, transmissions, and rear accelerators from the Philippines; commercial vehicle body panels, brake drums, and shock absorbers for heavy vehicles from Thailand; spokes, chains, seat

belts, and crown wheels from Malaysia; and universal joints, oil seals, and V belts from Singapore. The second project involved steering systems from Indonesia, rear accelerators for heavy vehicles from the Philippines, carburettors from Thailand, head lights from Malaysia, and fuel jet pumps from Singapore (Kamo 1997).

12 All members of the ASEAN 6 agreed to a deadline of 2008 for reducing tariffs to 0–5% in 1992. However the deadline was moved forward to the year 2005, and later amended to 2003 at the AEM meeting in September, 1994 in Thailand, which was agreed upon to shorten the time frame for the realisation of AFTA, from 15 to 10 years, finishing by 1 January 2003 instead of 2008. Furthermore, at the Fifth ASEAN Summit in December 1995, the deadline for certain items were brought forward to the year 2000 (Fourin 2002: 14). In fact, tariff-free trade among the ASEAN-6 was not completed until 2010.

13 TEL: all items on the list are temporarily excluded, however, these items on the list were to be transferred to IL by 2000.

14 IL: tariffs of all items on the list would be reduced to 0–5% by 2003. Late comers in ASEAN, Vietnam and Laos joined in 2006, while Myanmar and Cambodia joined in 2008, and 2010 respectively.

15 Denso Thailand, which produced alternators and starter motors; Denso Indonesia, which manufactured compressors and spark plugs; and Denso Malaysia, which produced various electronics parts (Fourin 2002: 96).

16 2018–2020 for CLMV countries, though in the event, it was 2018.

17 And nor did AFTA, which had CEPT, the Common *Effective* (not *External*) Preferential Tariff. In 2010, AFTA was renamed as ATIGA, the ASEAN Trade in Goods Agreement, although intra-ASEAN tariffs could still be applied by the newer members of AFTA – Vietnam, Cambodia, Myanmar, and Laos – until 2018. These intra-ASEAN tariff-free trade arrangements were subsumed under AEC in 2015, although many commentators continued to refer to AFTA. One of AEC's tasks, as Table 4.7 implies, is to help remove ***non-tariff*** barriers to intra-ASEAN trade (see https://www.mti.gov.sg/-/media/MTI/improving-trade/multilateral-and-regional-forums/AEC/MTI-AEC-2015-Handbook.PDF [accessed on 24 September 2019].

18 See also Chapter 9.

19 See Minebea's website: http://www.minebeamitsumi.com/news/press/2010/1185738_5963.html and http://www.minebeamitsumi.com/corp/company/factories/cambodia/1186630_6294.html [accessed on 5 November 2018].

20 See Toyota's website: https://www.toyota.co.jp/jpn/company/history/75years/text/taking_on_the_automotive_business/chapter2/section9/item4_a.html [accessed on 11 November 2018].

21 https://www.toyota-global.com/company/history_of_toyota/75years/text/entering_the_automotive_business/chapter2/section5/item6.html [accessed on 11 November 2018].

22 There seems to be some doubt about this production figure in the sense that Table 4.9 gives Toyota's production capacity (from the same source) as 46,000 units. Toyota Vietnam's own homepage (see Chapter 9) gives a capacity of 30,000 units (though this is only based on two shifts a day operation)

23 See *Hanoi Times* (22 June 2018), http://www.hanoitimes.vn/economy/industry/2018/06/81e0c8d5/toyota-vietnam-unveils-reasons-for-plant-expansion-plan/ [accessed on 25 September 2019].

5 Thailand

Introduction

This chapter examines the development of the Thai automotive industry in historical perspective, paying special attention to the role of industrial policy in the country's automotive industrialisation. Since the abolition of local content requirements (LCRs) in 2000, now outlawed under World Trade Organization (WTO) rules, the Thai government has been successfully adjusting to the new environment by shifting its policy orientation towards using effective fiscal policy with selective state intervention. Unlike neighbouring Malaysia, which created national champion *firms* in the automotive industry (see Chapter 7), Thailand does not have a national brand producer, but it has developed its industry using foreign assemblers, mainly from Japan. Thai automotive industrial policy has focused on selecting national *product champions* (picking a winning type of vehicle); and by setting lower excise tax rates on them, the government helps to create a particular market demand by consumers. At the same time, the government has provided tax concessions, such as low corporate tax, for attracting investors in national product champion production. Consequently, Thailand has joined the major vehicle producers of the world and has become the most important vehicle exporter in the ASEAN region. We explore the transition from the import-substituting industrialisation (ISI) policies and LCRs of the 1960–1990 period to the export expansion after the 1997 Asian financial crisis (AFC), and then to the WTO-compliant policies of the 2000s. The next section overviews the Thai automotive industry. The second main section examines the development of the Thai automotive industry over the period 1960–2018. The third main section addresses challenges to the Thai automotive industry, and is followed by the chapter's Conclusions.

Overview of the automotive industry in Thailand

Debates on automotive industrialisation in Thailand

There is already a small and useful literature on Thailand's automotive industrialisation, but opinions differ on the role of industrial policy. Wad (2009: 175 and 183) emphasises that policy must be set against the more powerful 'drivers of change' in the motor industry in the forms of the strategies and capabilities of the lead firms in the automotive global value chain (GVC) and local firms' responses to them, all in the context of developments in the global automotive economy and national political economy. He concludes that industrial policy did not play a decisive role in the growth of Thailand as an exporter of vehicles. Similarly, Busser (2008: 42) says that '... the Thai government and Thai enterprises have little means to influence the strategies and operations of Japanese firms in Thailand', which dominate the industry. In contrast, Hassler (2009: 2244) concludes that the development of the Thai automotive industry 'has clearly been influenced by the institutional power of the state'. Rock (2001) argued, more generally, that in the period of the early import-substituting industrialisation strategy in the 1960s through to the more recent export-led industrialisation, Thai industrial policies with selective government intervention in collaboration with foreign direct investment (FDI) were effective and successful. Our own research suggests that Thai automotive industrialisation policies have been effective in influencing not only domestic consumers' purchases of locally produced vehicles but also Japanese automotive MNCs into making Thailand their most important export base in Southeast Asia.

The differences in emphasis between the commentators on Thai industrial policies seem sharper when applied to the specific issue of LCRs. Wad (2009: 190) and Athukorala and Kohpaiboon (2010: 13) seem to view the abolition of LCRs as a wholly positive aspect of economic liberalisation. Hassler (2009: 2236–2237), conversely, argues that LCRs in the 1990s were a key part of a regulatory framework that significantly increased the territorial embeddedness of the motor industry in Thailand in the 1990s. He also notes that for automotive exporters from Thailand (from 2004), *de facto* LCRs continued under AFTA in the form of rules of origin to qualify for preferential access to the markets of other ASEAN countries.

Thailand in the global automotive industry

In the last two decades, the geographical location of vehicle production has been shifting from developed to developing countries, both in a search for lower production costs and in response to rising (particularly Asian) demand relative to the saturated car markets of Europe and North America (Athukorala and Kohpaiboon 2010: 11–12). Thailand, taking advantage of these trends, also improved its position from the world's 19th largest producer in 2000 to the 11th, accounting for 2.2 million vehicles, in 2018 (OICA website). During this period, the production volume in Thailand increased over five-fold, overtaking several developed countries such as the UK and Italy. During this period of expansion, Thailand's ability to attract inward FDI by having one of the largest domestic markets for vehicles in Southeast Asia worked in its favour, the industry being subject to large economies of scale both in vehicle and (often even more so) in some auto parts production (Yoshimatsu 2002a: 130–132).

Production and sales of the Thai automotive industry

In Thailand, there are 18 automotive assemblers, producing 2.2 million vehicles, with over a million units of domestic sales (approximately 48% of the total production) and over 1.14 million units of exports in 2018 (Fourin 2019: 27). Table 5.1 shows production volume by automotive assembler in 2018. Toyota is the leading producer in the country, accounting for 596,533 vehicles (or 27.5% of total vehicle production in Thailand), followed by Mitsubishi (385,192 and 17.8%), Auto Alliance Thailand (AAT) – a joint venture firm between Mazda and Ford (267,229 and 12.1%), Isuzu (259,652 and 11.9%), and Honda (246,068 and 11.4%). These can be compared to a probable minimum efficient scale for vehicle production of about 200,000 units per year at the plant level (Yoshimatsu 2002a: 132).[1] In this context, some assemblers in Thailand do not achieve economies of scale (discussed later). Commercial vehicles (CVs), particularly pickup trucks, are the main products in Thailand, accounting for 57.7% of the total production in 2018 (see Table 5.2). Thailand is one of the largest markets in the world for one-tonne pick-up trucks.

Figure 5.1 shows sales volume by automotive assembler in Thailand in 2017. Of total domestic sales in Thailand, Toyota accounted for 27.5%, followed by Isuzu (18.4%), Honda (14.7%), Mitsubishi (8.0%), and Nissan (6.9%). Although Mitsubishi is the second largest producer in the country, their local sales share is rather low; Mitsubishi uses Thailand more as an export platform in the region, as does Ford.

Table 5.1 Production Volume and Share by Automotive Assembler in Thailand, 2018

No.	*Assemblers*	*Production*	*Percent*
1	Toyota	596,533	27.5
2	Mitsubishi	385,192	17.8
3	AAT	262,229	12.1
	Mazda	(137,892)	(6.4)
	Ford	(124,337)	(5.7)
4	Isuzu	257,652	11.9
5	Honda	246,068	11.4
6	Nissan	163,588	7.6
7	GM	60,489	2.8
8	Suzuki	60,266	2.8
9	Ford	58,294	2.7
10	SAIC-CP (MG)	28,595	1.3
11	Mercedes-Benz	15,387	0.7
12	BMW	15,303	0.7
13	Hino	10,381	0.5
14	UD Trucks	5,010	0.2
15	Scania	707	(0.03)
Total	–	2,167,694	100

Source: Adapted from Fourin (2019: 33–34).

Note: Number of vehicles.

Table 5.2 Types of Vehicle Production in Thailand, 2018

Type	*Production*	*Percent*
PVs	877,015	40.5
CVs	1,290,679	59.6
(1 tonne pick-up)	(1,250,483)	(57.7)
Total	2,167,694	100

Source: Adapted from Fourin (2019: 32).
Note: Number of vehicles, PVs (passenger vehicles), CVs (commercial vehicles).

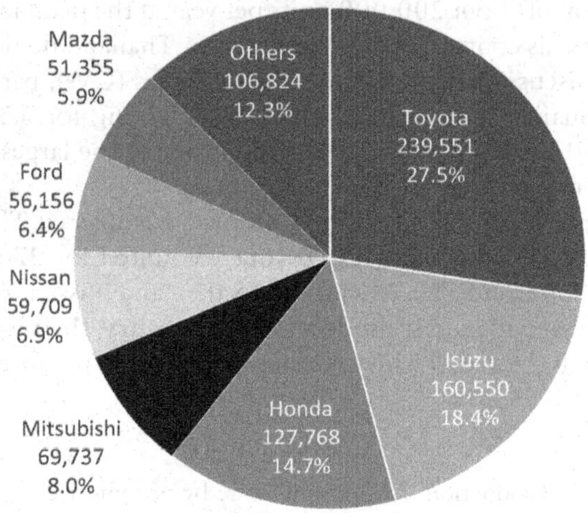

Figure 5.1 Sales Volume and Market Share by Automotive Brand in Thailand, 2017.
Source: Adapted from Fourin (2018: 319).
Note: Total 871,650 vehicles.

Structure of the Thai automotive industry

Figure 5.2 shows the structure of the Thai automotive industry. There are 462 Tier-1 firms and 1,137 Tier-2 firms in Thailand in 2017. Of 462 Tier-1 firms, 31% are classified as foreign capital firms, 23% are local capital firms, and 46% are JV firms (of which foreign-majority firms account for 27 percentage points, local-majority firms 16, and 50/50 firms are 3). Of 1,137 Tier-2 firms, 31% are classified as foreign capital firms, 42% are local capital firms, and 27% are JV firms (of which foreign-majority firms are 12 percentage points and local-majority firms are 15 percentage points). The Thai Automotive Industry Association (TAIA) estimated that the automotive industry generates approximately 525,000 direct jobs in Thailand, with automotive assemblers employing approximately 100,000 workers, Tier-1 firms 250,000 workers, and Tier-2 firms 175,000 (Fourin 2017: 35). In addition, employment is created by car distribution networks and after sales services. The automotive industry is one of the most important industrial

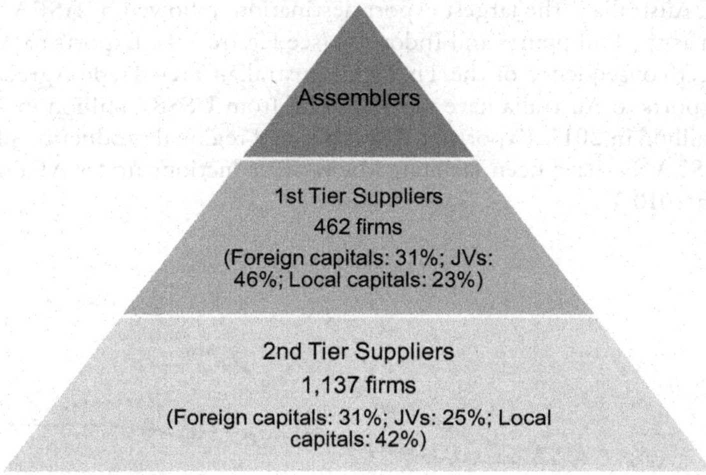

Figure 5.2 Structure of the Thai Automotive Industry, 2017.
Source: Adapted from Fourin (2017: 36).

employers in the country. Some studies claim that the Thai automotive industry depends on foreign firms, particularly in comparison with its Northeast Asian counterparts (e.g. Doner and Wad 2014). However, compared with Central and Eastern European countries, the role of Tier-1 local firms in Thailand is far more significant in the automotive value chain (see Natsuda *et al.* 2020b).

Thailand in the regional automotive economy[2]

Thailand's position in the regional economy of Asia has been overwhelmingly influenced by the activities of Japanese motor assemblers and large suppliers in the automotive GVC. Since the 1980s, Japanese automotive MNCs have become increasingly international in their operations. Their overseas investment – along with that of their Japanese component suppliers – was given a strong stimulus by the sharp appreciation of the yen exchange rate in the late 1980s after the Plaza Agreement of 1985, and the resulting 'high yen' (*endaka*) crisis for Japanese exporters; and by labour shortages and high wages in Japan. Whilst some Japanese major vehicle investments have been made in North America and Europe in order to circumvent import barriers and avoid trade frictions, much of the activity of Japanese automotive MNCs has been regional, focussed on Asia, making use of various Asian countries within regional production networks.

The CBU exports of the Thai automotive industry amounted to 1,126,000 vehicles (and 56.6%) of the total of 1,988,000 vehicle production in 2017 (JETRO 2018a: 16). Figure 5.3 shows the export trends of the Thai automotive industry over the period 1998–2017 in terms of value. The exports of the automotive industry (category HS87) have grown 21.6-fold, from US$ 1.3 billion to 28.5 billion during this period. Illustrating the importance of the regional economy, Australia is the largest export destination, followed by ASEAN countries such as the Philippines and Indonesia (see Figure 5.4). Exports to Australia are a direct consequence of the Thailand–Australian Free Trade Agreement of 2005. Exports to Australia have risen 32-fold, from US$87 million in 2004 to US$2.8 billion in 2017. Exports to ASEAN – and regional production planning within ASEAN – have been facilitated by tariff reductions under AFTA, down to zero in 2010.[3]

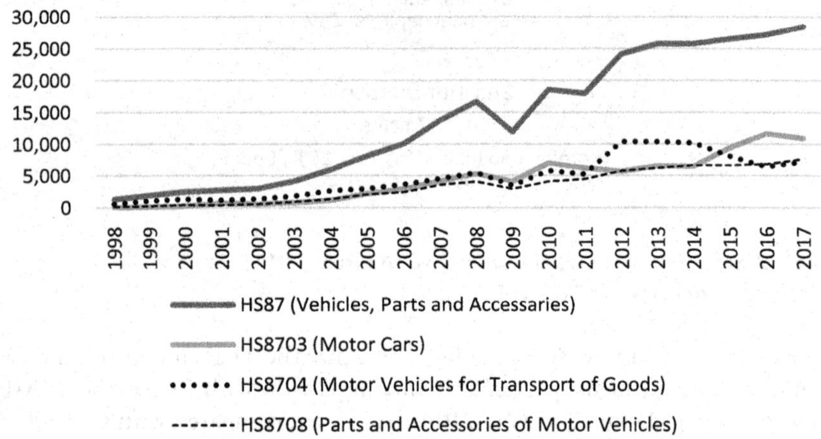

Figure 5.3 Automotive Exports of Thailand, 1998–2017.
Source: Global Trade Atlas (database).
Note: US$ Million.

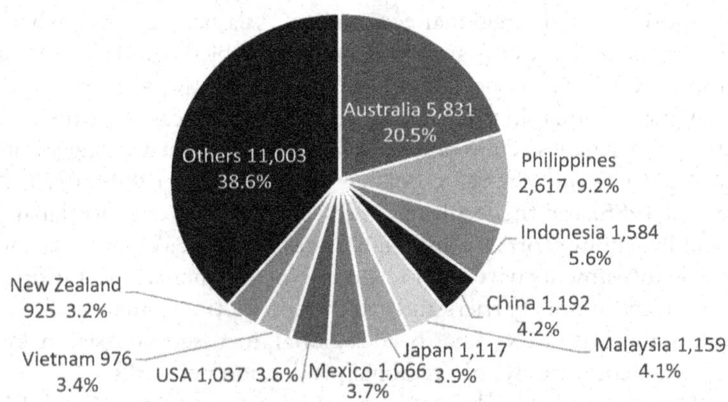

Figure 5.4 HS87 (Vehicles, Parts, and Accessories), Top Ten Export Destinations of Thailand, 2017.
Source: Global Trade Atlas (database).
Note: US$ Million (shown above the percentages).

The most remarkable growth has come from the export of PVs. The export under the category HS8703 increased 168-fold, from merely US$66 million in 1998 to over US$10.8 billion in 2017. Figure 5.5 shows the top 10 export destinations of PVs from Thailand in 2017. Australia is the largest export destination (accounting for approximately US$2.8 billion), followed by the Philippines, Mexico, Saudi Arabia, China, Indonesia, New Zealand, Russia, and UAE in 2017.

With regard to CVs, the export (of HS8704) increased 11-fold, from US$652 million in 1998 to over US$7.3 billion in 2017 (see Figure 5.3). Figure 5.6 indicates the top 10 destinations of CVs. As for PVs, Australia is the largest destination (accounting for US$2.7 billion), followed by New Zealand, Vietnam, the Philippines, Malaysia, Chile, UK, Indonesia, Saudi Arabia, and Italy in 2017.

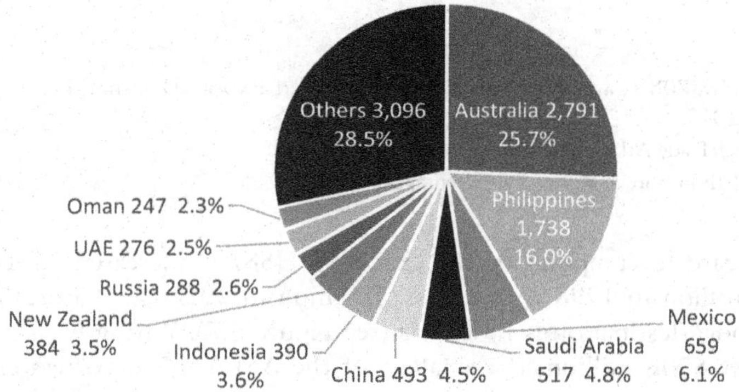

Figure 5.5 HS8703 (Motor Cars), Top Ten Export Destinations of Thailand, 2017.
Source: Global Trade Atlas (database).
Note: US$ Million (shown above the percentages).

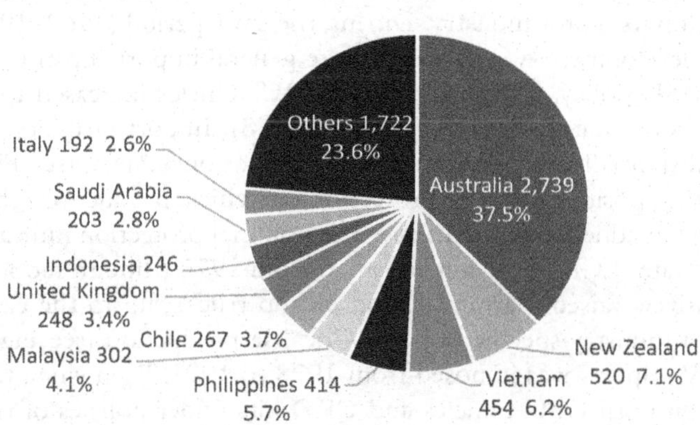

Figure 5.6 HS8704 (Motor Vehicles for Transport of Goods), Top Ten Export Destinations of Thailand, 2017.
Source: Global Trade Atlas (database).
Note: US$ Million (shown above the percentages).

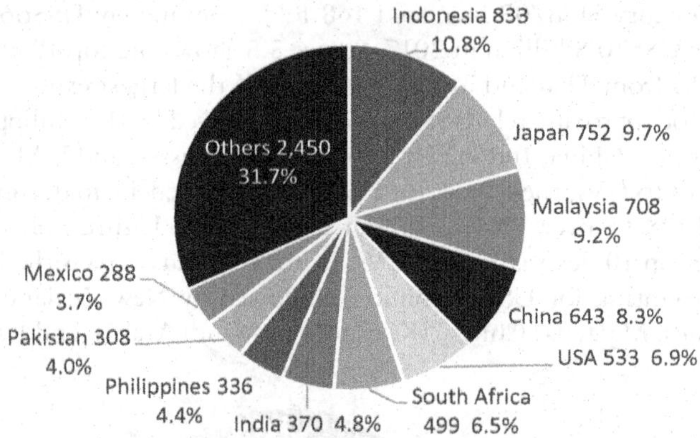

Figure 5.7 HS8708 (Parts and Accessories), Top Ten Export Destinations of Thailand, 2017.

Source: Global Trade Atlas (database).

Note: US$ Million (shown above the percentages).

With regard to components, the export of HS8708 increased 33-fold, from US$652 million in 1998 to over US7.7 billion in 2017 (see Figure 5.3). The largest export destination is Indonesia (see Figure 5.7). Wiring harness exports are another $508 million, the smallest of the ASEAN-5 exporters except for Malaysia.

Development of the automotive industry in Thailand

Figures 5.8–5.11 offer summaries of the main policy measures used by Thailand to develop its motor industry. During the early period (1960–1970), when automotive development was part of a more general import-substituting industrialisation (ISI) policy, import tariffs on CBU vehicles increased to over 50% for CVs, and even higher for PVs (see Figure 5.8). Import tariffs on CKD kits increased substantially too, though not as much as on vehicles (see Figure 5.9), thus generating positive effective protection on vehicle production (that is, protection on value-added) over and above the nominal protection indicated by the CBUs' tariff rate. LCRs were implemented from 1975 (though mooted earlier) and progressively raised, particularly on pickup trucks, up to the early 1990s, as part of an industry-specific policy to localise production (see Figure 5.10). A ban on PV imports was imposed from 1978 to 1991. Even when tariffs were cut sharply on both CBU vehicles and CKD kits under policies of trade liberalisation in the 1990s, LCRs were maintained (though subject to some local criticism). With the end of LCRs in 2000, tariffs were retained on both cars and pick-up trucks, with lower rates on CKD kits, much lower than the levels of the 1980s. LCRs, to a considerable extent, succeeded in raising local content, but since 2000, the policy has shifted to strongly supplementing trade

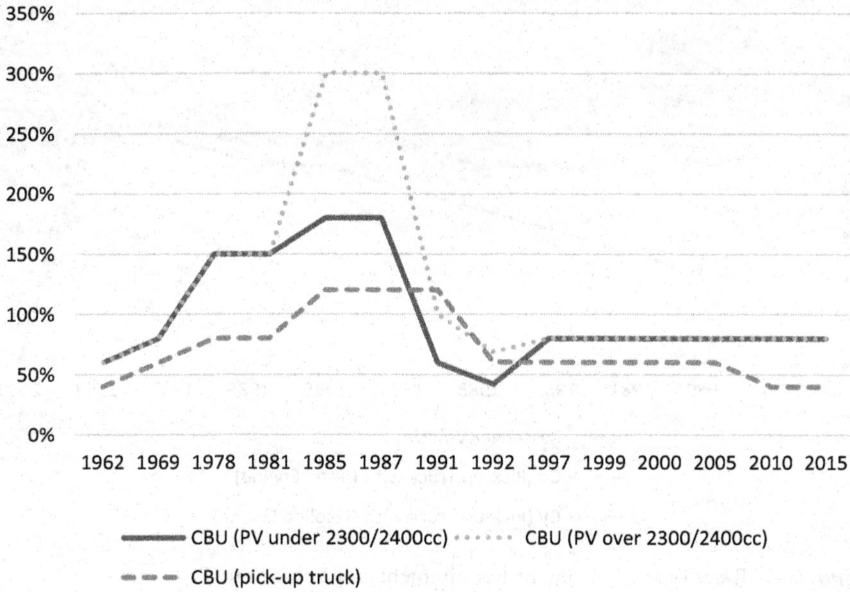

Figure 5.8 Tariffs on CBU Vehicles in Thailand, 1962–2015.
Source: Adapted from Komura (2000), Fourin (2000, 2002, 2008, 2011, and 2015).
Note: Vehicle categories changed from 2300 cc to 2400 cc in 1992 and later in 2005 into four categories such as under 2000 cc; 2001 cc-2500 cc; 2501 cc-3000 cc; and over 3000 cc.

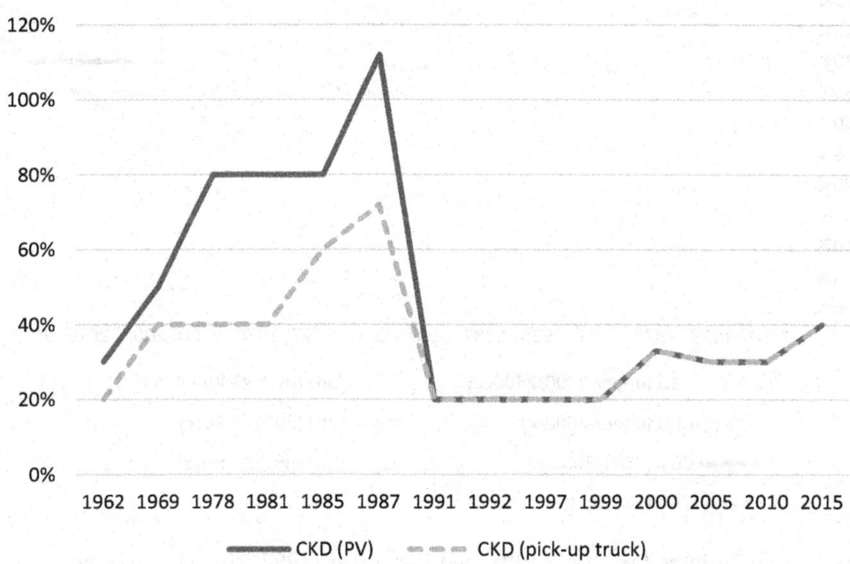

Figure 5.9 Tariffs on CKD Vehicles in Thailand, 1962–2015.
Source: Adapted from Komura (2000), Fourin (2000, 2002, 2008, 2011, and 2015).

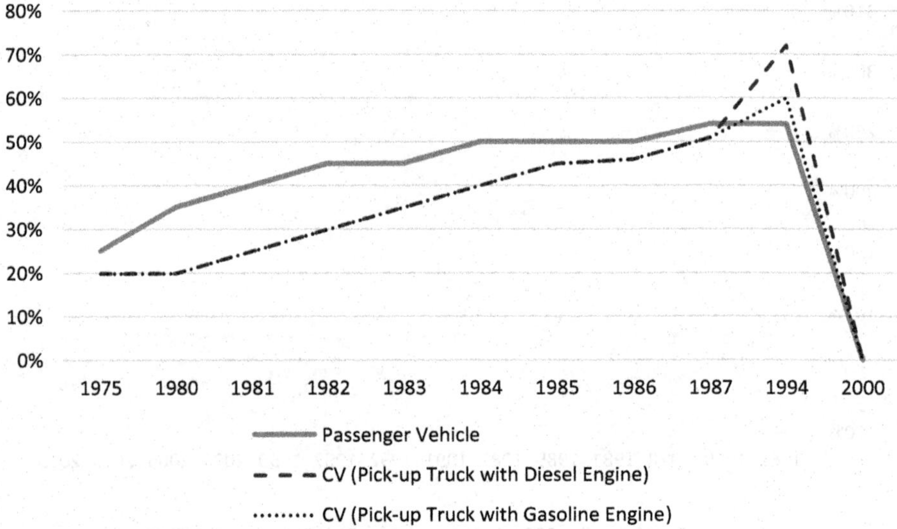

Figure 5.10 Rates of Local Content Requirements for Vehicles in Thailand.
Source: Adapted from Higashi (2000), Terdudomtham (2004) and Fourin (2000 and 2002).
Note: CV (commercial vehicle).

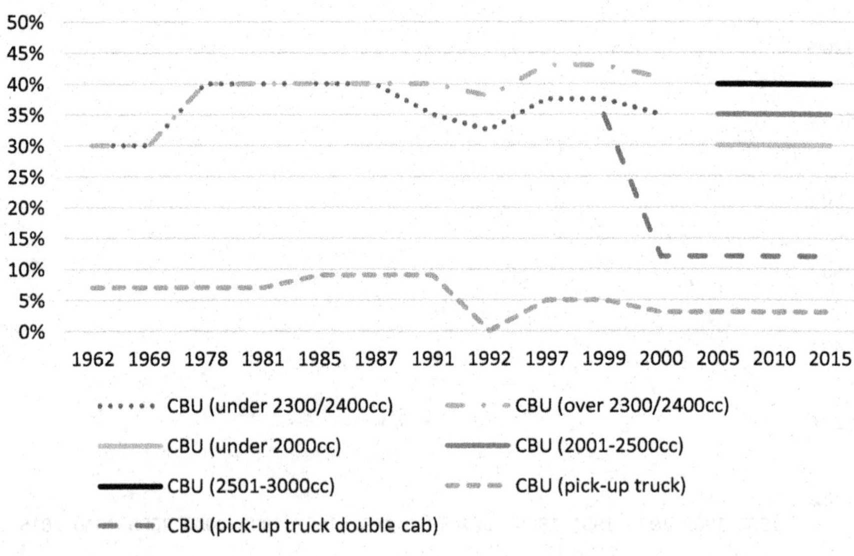

Figure 5.11 Business Tax (1962–1991) and Excise Tax (1992–2015) in Thailand.
Source: Adapted from Komura (2000), Fourin (2000, 2002, 2008, 2011, and 2015).
Note: CBU (pickup truck double cab) in 1999 is between 35% and 48%.

policy with tax policy (see Figure 5.11), with a view to promoting particular types of vehicle as national product champions. We now examine these policies in five phases: import-substitution period (1960–1970), localisation period (1971–1977), strengthening localisation period (1978–1990), liberalisation period (1991–1999), and the WTO-compliant period (2000–present).

Initial policies of import substitution (1960–1970)

Up to 1960, the automotive industry in Thailand was based on the repair business, with CBU vehicles all being imported. The country's first industrial policy, covering the automotive industry but not exclusive to it, was introduced by the Board of Investment (BOI) in the form of the 'Industrial Investment Promotion Act' in 1960, later revised in 1962. This plan provided incentives for investors such as temporary corporate tax exemptions, tariff reductions and exemptions on imports of inputs and machinery, reduction in export tax, and deregulation of land ownership and of invitation of technical experts (Adachi 1987). In response to this ISI policy, the first Thai automobile company, Thai Motor Industry (a JV between Ford UK and Anglo Thai Motor), was established in 1961 in order to conduct local assembly operations for the importation of CKD kits (TAI 2008). Tariff rates on imported CKDs were set at 30% for PVs, 20% for CVs, while CBUs duties were 60% and 40%, respectively, in 1962, and subsequently increased (see Figures 5.8 and 5.9, and Higashi 2000).

By 1969, six major foreign automobile companies had established JVs with Thai capital. During this period, the number of vehicles produced in Thailand increased from a mere 525 in 1961 to over 10,000 for the first time in 1965. However, the domestic sales of domestically manufactured vehicles accounted for only 18.5% of total domestic vehicle sales in 1969 (see Figure 5.12).

Localisation policy and LCRs (1971–1977)

The Ministry of Industry of Thailand (MOI) established the Automotive Development Committee in 1969 and tried to facilitate the localisation of parts production by providing special tax incentives for the production of particular parts such as tyres, batteries, radiators, and leaf springs (TAI 2008). The Federation of Thai Industries (FTI) criticised the tax policies and incentives, and the failure of the Committee to develop a long-term industrial development strategy. It particularly emphasised the heavy dependence on assembly operations using imported CKD kits that created critical balance of trade and payment deficits by the late 1960s for this domestic-market-oriented industry (Doner 1991).

In response to these problems, the government introduced Thailand's first specific industrial policy for the automotive industry in 1971. The new policy consisted of three measures:

- to set limits on the number of models and series in order to better achieve economies of scale,

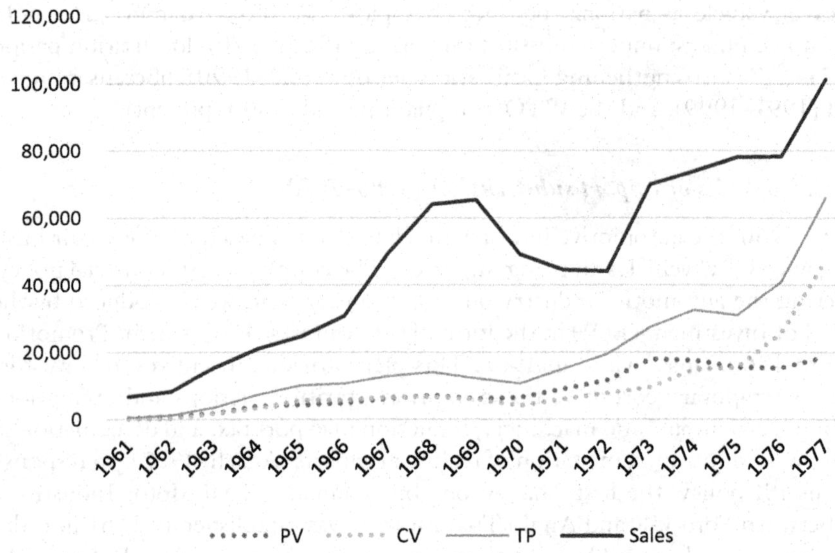

Figure 5.12 Production and Sales of Vehicles in Thailand, 1961–1977.
Source: Adapted from Higashi (2000: 146).
Note: Number of vehicles, PV (passenger vehicle), CV (commercial vehicle), TP (total production).

- to impose LCR of 25%,[4] which would become effective in 1973, and
- to require, as conditions for new market entry, over 0.2 million baht for investment (except for land) and production capacity of 30 units per day (Adachi 1987, Kaosa-ard 1993).

However, due to political change and pressure from new automotive assembly companies, the government dropped the limitations on the number of models, series and production capacity, and the new entry restrictions (Higashi 2000). In terms of the likely economic efficiency of new import-substituting production in an industry characterised by large economies of scale, these revisions can hardly be seen as desirable changes. LCRs came to be implemented only from 1975 (see Figure 5.10).

Following these policy changes, an additional eight automotive assemblers entered the Thai market in the period 1972–1977, including Bangchan General Assembly (GM) in 1972 and Ford Motor Thailand in 1974. Multinational components producers, particularly from Japan (such as Denso), established JVs in Thailand in order to supply locally produced components to assemblers to correspond to the LCRs (Terdudomtham 2004).

While the local content (LC) level increased close to 25%, automobile prices remained high, and quality in general was low in the industry (Doner 1991). However, during the period 1971 to 1977, domestic vehicle production rose more than four-fold, from 15,014 units in 1971 to 65,874 units in 1977, and accounted for 65% of total vehicle sales in 1977 (see Figure 5.12); however, trade deficits in the automotive industry increasingly worsened (Kaosa-ard 1993: 14).

Strengthening localisation capacity (1978–1990)

Further localisation policies appear to have been driven primarily by a desire to reduce trade deficits. Firstly, the Ministry of Commerce imposed an import ban on CBU PVs in January 1978, and at the same time, the Ministry of Finance increased the tariff rates on CBUs and CKD kits (Abbot 2003, Higashi 2000). More importantly, a more explicit localisation policy for the automotive industry was introduced in 1978 after extensive negotiations among government officers, FTI, assemblers, and Thai parts firms. Local parts manufacturers became a powerful lobby and established the Thai Automotive Parts Manufacturer's Association (TAPMA) in 1972 (Doner 1991, Higashi 2000).[5] As a result of the strong influence from TAPMA, MOI implemented the following two localisation measurements in 1978:

- an additional LCR for passenger cars was revised from 25% to 35% in the first two years, then to increase by 5% every year until 1983, eventually reaching 50% (see Figure 5.10), and LCR for CVs with windshields was revised from 20% to 45% (Higashi 2000, Kaosa-ard 1993); and
- to force assemblers to localise specific parts production, it introduced a mandatory deletion scheme, targeting specific parts, such as brake drums and exhaust systems, which were deemed able to be produced locally (Doner 1991).

These measures stimulated local assemblers to increase investment in components production (Busser 2008). The policy also resulted in a division among the automotive assemblers in the market. Large assemblers such as Toyota and Nissan were able to increase their LC ratios. By contrast, smaller assemblers such as Hillman and Simca failed to meet the LCRs (which were harder to meet for PVs than for CVs) and were eventually eliminated from the market in the late 1970s (Doner 1991), thus helping to reduce the multiplicity of models and sub-optimal production runs often associated in the automotive industry with import substitution in protected markets. In addition, two American giant automotive producers – Ford and GM – also withdrew from the Thai market due to sales slumps in 1976 and 1977, respectively (Adachi 1987).

In 1984, the LCRs reached 50% for PVs and 45% for CVs, which were eventually increased to 54% for PVs and 51% for CVs in 1987. Furthermore, MOI began to regulate the series and models of domestically assembled PVs by limiting to 42 series, and two models for each series, in 1984 (Higashi 1995 and 2000). In 1986, the Thai government specified locally manufactured components for PVs and also decided to commence localisation of diesel engines. The government in 1989 mandated assemblers to use locally made diesel engines for their pickup trucks production. This aimed to set an initial 20% localisation rate for engine

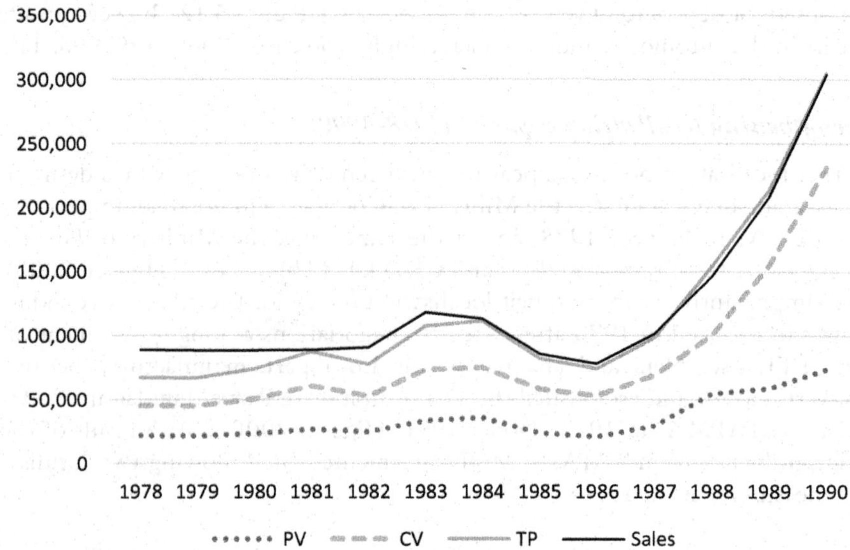

Figure 5.13 Production and Sales of Vehicles in Thailand, 1978–1990.
Source: Adapted from Higashi (2000: 146) and Fourin (2011: 189).
Note: Number of vehicles, PV (passenger vehicle), CV (commercial vehicle), TP (total production).

parts, which eventually increased to 60% for BOI projects and 80% for MOI projects by 1995 (Ueda 2007: 98).[6] Vehicle production in Thailand increased slowly from the late 1970, and reached over 100,000 units for the first time in 1983 (see Figure 5.13). While the local sales exceeded local production until 1987, vehicle production has overtaken sales since 1988. It grew rapidly in the late 1980s, reaching over 150,000 units in 1988, to over 200,000 units in 1989, and finally to over 300,000 units in 1990.

Liberalisation, exporting, and the 1997 Asian financial crisis (1991–1999)

Up to the end of the 1980s, Thailand's automotive sales had depended mainly on the growth of the domestic market. Vehicle exports started in 1987, followed by the exports of some components (Abdulsomad 1999). Rapid economic growth in Thailand in the late 1980s saw a rapid increase in vehicle demand, and exports too increased somewhat[7] in the context of a general Thai export boom from 1986 to 1996 (that is, up to the 1997 AFC) (Lauridsen 2004: 570–572). Domestic vehicle production exceeded domestic sales for the first time in 1988 (see Figures 5.13 and 5.14), but Thai automotive production growth could not been seen as export-driven. During this time, imports of CBU PVs under 2300 cc remained banned, PVs over 2300 cc had a 300% tariff, and tariffs on CKD PV kits were 112% (Kaosa-ard 1993).

The beginning of liberalisation

A turning point in Thailand's automotive industrialisation policies was associated with the establishment of the Anand Panyarachun government after a military coup in February 1991. The new government for the first time introduced liberalisation policies in the automotive industry, lifting the ban on imports of CBUs and substantially reducing tariffs on both CBUs and CKDs (see Figures 5.8 and 5.9). Investments for new establishments of assembly plants for PVs were approved. Foreign ownership in the automotive assembly industry was deregulated, allowing 100% foreign ownership in place of the earlier limitation to up to a maximum of 49% (enacted in 1979), provided they exported 60% of their total production. In 1994, the government also introduced a tax exemption measurement for export activities (Fourin 2000: 35, Yoshimatsu 2002b: 130).

These liberalisation policies had several purposes, one of which was to lower domestic automotive prices and increase domestic competition in part by attracting inward FDI from non-Japanese automotive assemblers. During this time, all assemblers, except for Thai Swedish Assembly (with Volvo affiliation), were associated with Japanese capital and enjoyed oligopolistic advantages in the market. Indeed, the vice minister of MOI, Vira Susangkarahan, criticised the LCR policy on the grounds that it did not facilitate the growth of automotive industry in Thailand, but just created higher automotive prices. In short, it was argued that the automotive industry had received a lot of protection, while consumers received no benefits – LCRs generating apparently 'bad' backward linkage effects.[8] The Japanese-affiliated assemblers were viewed as receiving excessive rents under a virtual cartel with government protection (Ikemoto 1994: 173). Nevertheless, other measures were put in place, which were relied on to increase competition and reduce excess profits. LCRs were actually *raised* in 1994 (see Figure 5.8), but, finally, in 1996, the government announced their abolition by July 1998 (Fourin 2000: 35, Terdudomtham 2004: 39–40). That is, LCRs were to be abolished prior to the WTO target date, though eventually the abolition was delayed until 2000.

These liberalisation policies appeared to succeed in attracting more inward FDI: the American big three assemblers – Ford, Chrysler, and GM – decided to establish their own assembly plants in Thailand as regional hubs in Asia (Abbot 2003). Auto Alliance (a JV between Ford and Mazda) and GM relocated into the newly developed Eastern Seaboard Industrial Estate. Japanese producers, such as Toyota and Honda, decided to expand their production capacity in the suburbs of Bangkok by establishing new plants. In addition, American components suppliers such as Dana, Visteon, and Delphi also followed the American assemblers in Thailand (Terdudomtham 2004).

Impacts of the 1997 Asian financial crisis

The Thai automotive industry had developed rapidly with the liberalisation policies since 1991, but with the AFC in 1997, the number of vehicles sold in

Thailand decreased rapidly (see Figure 5.14). As a result, 600 local firms either went bankrupt or were taken over by foreign firms. A total of 20,000 jobs were lost in the industry in the period 1997–1999 (Abbot 2003: 143).

The AFC, however, proved to be a major turning point for exports. In response to the domestic sales slump, and aided by the substantial depreciation of the Thai baht during the crisis, automotive producers shifted to increasing exports well beyond the modest levels achieved by the early 1990s (see Figure 5.14). The baht depreciation also potentially helped domestic parts suppliers by increasing the cost of imported components.

In addition, foreign assemblers increased their equity share in their JVs and assisted their parts suppliers by providing various kinds of financial support (UNCTAD 2001). The Thai government changed the investment regulations in 1997, allowing foreign-majority ownership in joint ventures in order to encourage foreign investment. At the same time, it introduced new tax policies to reduce the budget deficit, increasing VAT and adding 5% excise tax on vehicles (see Figure 5.11). The Thai government sharply increased tariffs on CBU vehicles (see Figures 5.8 and 5.9), which resulted in a large reduction of imports into the Thai market, from 16,000 units in 1997 to 2,549 units in 1998 (Fourin 2000: 42). Also, in order to enhance institutional (policy) and research capacity in the automotive industry, the MOI established the Thailand Automotive Institute (TAI) in 1998.

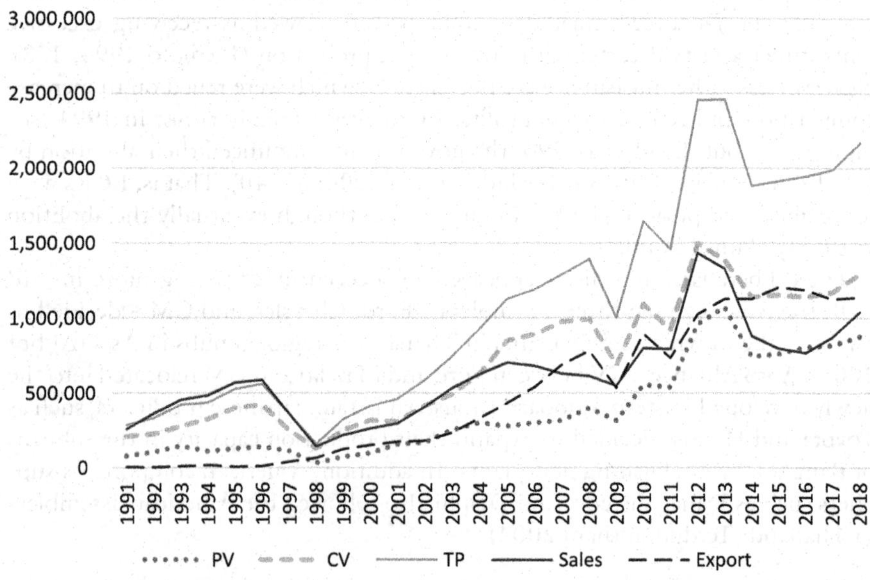

Figure 5.14 Production, Sales, and Exports of Vehicles in Thailand, 1991–2018

Note: Number of vehicles, PV (passenger vehicle), CV (commercial vehicle), TP (total production)

Source: Adapted from Fourin (2017: 35) and Fourin (2019: 27)

In 1997, the government announced the postponement of the abolition of LCRs to January 2000. At the culmination of its LC policy, LCRs were 72% for pickup trucks with diesel engines, and 54% for PVs in 1994 (see Figure 5.10). Before the abolition, some vehicle models were able to meet these requirements. In the case of, Toyota, for example, their strategic PV in the ASEAN market, the Soluna model, and their most popular pickup truck, the Hilux model, had achieved over 70% local content in 1999 (Fourin 2000: 34).[9]

Creating international competitiveness and 'product champions' with WTO-compliant policy making (after 2000)

Since 2000, when the Thai government lifted LCRs in response to the WTO's requirements, Thailand has not shifted its policy orientation simply to *laissez-faire*; rather, it has started using discretionary powers that are still compatible with the WTO rules. To be precise, the Thai government started employing a selective industrial policy of *picking* a winner *type* of vehicle, or *product champion*, and linking this with effective fiscal policy and some local production incentives. In order to do this, the Thai government modified the excise tax rates (e.g. decreasing for double-cab pick-up trucks[10] from 35–48% to 12%, for the 1st Eco-cars from 30% to 17%, and for the 2nd Eco-cars to 12–14%) for consumers on the one hand, while providing corporate tax exemption in order to attract foreign investors on the other hand.

In the aftermath of the AFC, the Thai government began to employ various fiscal policies in 2000 to foster the industry:

- increasing the tariff rate on CKDs from 20% to 33%, thus both increasing protection for vehicle parts production and decreasing effective protection for assemblers, and
- reducing excise tax on double-cab pick-up trucks from 35–48% to 12%, on other pickup trucks down to 3–5%, and on passenger vehicles (less than 2400 cc) from 37.5% to 35% (Fourin 2000: 369).

Excise tax was reduced in order to alleviate the burden on consumers of increased import tariffs on CKD parts. With its tax policy, the Thai government deliberately strengthened the market demand for pickup trucks, particularly double-cab pick-up trucks. Corporate tax exemption was provided for a period of 3–8 years[11] for foreign investment projects worth over 10 billion baht. At the same time, tax reduction was provided for imported machinery and materials.

The 1st Automotive Master Plan (2002–2006)

The 1st Automotive Master Plan was implemented under the new populist government of Thaksin Shinawatra (2001–2006). This plan is sometimes referred to as the 'Detroit of Asia' plan (Busser 2008). It aimed for Thailand to act as a regional hub for automotive exports in Southeast Asia by targeting 2.5 million units of CBU vehicle production, and to become one of the top ten automotive producers in the world by 2016.[12] In addition, the Thai government introduced selective industrial policy by picking product champions, linking with various fiscal policies. In January 2002, the BOI introduced a 'New Automotive Investment Policy', targeting both pickup truck production and related components industries as its first product champion. The scheme provided exemption of import tariffs on machinery and three years corporate tax exemption for related component producers in the case of comprehensive projects worth over 10 billion baht, including suppliers (Fourin 2002: 214–215). Furthermore, the BOI also aimed at functional upgrading of the industrial structure by providing various tax incentives for the establishment of R&D and regional operating headquarter (ROH) functions.

In response to the government policies, Toyota, for example, decided to relocate its global pickup truck production base from Japan to Thailand, accessing Thailand's large pickup truck market, commencing with its Innovative International Multipurpose Vehicle (IMV) project in 2002. It aimed to use Thailand as a global production base for its Hilux-level small-size, multipurpose vehicles, exporting CBUs to over 90 countries and CKD parts to nine countries in 2004 (Shimokawa 2010: 254–256). In parallel to this, Toyota chose Thailand, not only as a production base but also as a product development base for the IMV project. In 2005, Toyota established R&D in Thailand, its first R&D centre outside of North America and Europe (Staples 2008: 209). Furthermore, it also relocated most of its regional operating functions from Singapore to Thailand by establishing Toyota Motor Asia Pacific Engineering & Manufacturing (TMAP-EM)[13] in 2007. Similarly, Isuzu relocated its entire pick-up truck (D-MAX) production from Japan to Thailand in 2002, and started exporting to over 130 countries in 2003. It eventually also relocated its entire R&D function for pickup trucks to Thailand in 2010.[14] Auto Alliance also started exporting pickup trucks (SUV Everest) to over 50 countries in 2005. Honda established an R&D centre to develop local parts procurement and vehicles by investing 2.4 billion baht in 2005 (Fourin 2006: 120). As a result of the automotive producers' expansion of production capacity in Thailand, over 70 Japanese automotive parts suppliers invested in 2005, of which four companies, one being NSK, established R&D centres in Thailand (ibid.:176). In the first half of the decade of the 2000s, Thai vehicle production and export grew rapidly by nearly 2.8-fold, from 411,721 units of production in 2000 to over 1.1 million units in 2005, and from 152,836 units of export in 2000 to 434,902 units in 2005 (see Figure 5.14). Indeed, Thailand became the 14th largest vehicle producer in the world in 2005 (OICA website). The growth of the Thai automotive industry continued until the collapse of Lehman Brothers affected the Thai market in 2009.

The 2nd Automotive Master Plan (2007–2011)

The 2nd Master Plan aimed to expand the export capacity and the development of local supporting industry through the introduction of Eco-cars (Fourin 2017: 38). The Thai government has taken the view that the automotive demand will shift from pickup trucks to passenger vehicles in the long term, as the size of the middle class in the country grows. The Thai government policy has been to encourage this trend (Fourin 2011). In order to develop the industry further, the government's first product champion, the pickup truck, by itself is not enough. As a result, the Thai government has also targeted the development of small, economical, ecological passenger vehicle production. To attract additional FDI from automotive producers, it introduced the 'Eco Car' project as the second product champion in 2007 (see Table 5.3). One of the most important features of this project is to use both excise and corporate tax policies effectively linked to localisation of the automotive components industry, particularly facilitating the growth of local industrial capacity of engine production. Under this scheme, the Thai government selected which technology should be localised and encouraged local production by offering several tax incentives. Following the view of Dunkley (1997), this kind of policy could be considered to be a *positive* application of the WTO's TRIMs requirements. Moreover, the Thai government tactically introduced a market stimulation policy, based on excise tax. While under 2000 cc engine vehicles were subject to 30% excise tax, Eco-cars' excise tax was reduced to 17%. In this context, consumers were able to buy Eco-cars more cheaply compared to the other models.

In response to the announcement of the Eco-car project, initially seven companies – five Japanese producers, namely, Nissan, Honda, Suzuki, Mitsubishi, and Toyota, and two others, namely, Volkswagen and Tata Motors – showed their interest and obtained approval from BOI. However, eventually, only the Japanese producers decided to engage in the project (Table 5.4).[15] For instance, Nissan decided to create a new regional division of labour between Japan and Thailand for relatively small and inexpensive automobile production by employing the Eco-car scheme. Nissan closed its production lines for the March (Micra) model in Japan and relocated the capacity to Thailand, aiming to export a 'Thai-Made March' to the Japanese market.[16] Nissan commenced their first Eco-car production in March 2010, accounting for 59,441 units in production and 42,328 units in export (mostly to the Japanese market) in the same year (Fourin 2011) and continued to increase the production, accounting for 144,019 units in 2012 (Fourin 2015).

As a result of the Thai government's industrial policy, many component suppliers have also made substantial investments in Thailand. Investment in automotive components accounted for 104 cases and over 33 billion baht (on an approval basis) in 2010, of which approximately 60% in both numbers and value were from Japan (Fourin 2011: 212–213). In addition, Ford, for instance, decided to relocate its Focus model's production from the Philippines in order to take advantage of the highly developed automotive clusters in Thailand. The BOI estimates that Thailand has over 2,300 parts suppliers, in comparison with Malaysia with 700 suppliers and Indonesia with 500 suppliers.[17] In the case of one interviewed Japanese automotive MNC, it sourced its components from 203 Tier-1 suppliers under OEM contracts, and 95% of these suppliers were located in Thailand (see Table 5.5). The average local procurement ratio in 2010 was slightly less than 90% within Thailand and over 90% when all content from the ASEAN region was included.[18]

Table 5.3 Overview of the 1st and 2nd Eco-Car Projects in Thailand

		1st Eco-Car *Application period: June–November 2007*	*2nd Eco-Car* *Application period: August 2013–March 2014*
Requirements	**Investment**	Over 5 billion baht (except for land and operating capital)	Over 6.5 billion baht (participants in 1st Eco-car project – over 5 billion baht)
	Commencement	From 2010	By the end of 2019
	Production Volume	Over 100,000 units of production after 5 years the project commences	Over 100,000 units of production after 4 years the project commences
	Engine size	Gasoline engine - under 1300 cc Diesel engine - under 1400 cc	Gasoline engine – under 1300 cc Diesel engine –- under 1500 cc
	Mileage	Over 20 km/L	Over 23.3 km/L
	Environmental standard	Meeting Euro 4 exhaust gas standard	Meeting Euro 5 exhaust gas standard
	Safety standard	Meeting UN-ECE regulation articles 94 and 95	Meeting UN-ECE regulation articles 94 and 95, ABS/ESC: UN-ECE R13H
	Local production requirement	Local production requirements for vehicles and engines and for four out of five component items (cylinder head, cylinder block, crankshaft, camshaft, connecting rod). Additional requirement for local machine work for three items (cylinder head, cylinder block, crankshaft)	(Considered the same as the 1st Eco-car project)
Benefits	**Excise tax**	17% (the rate of under 2000 cc and 220 hp engine vehicle is normally 30%)	14% / 12% (E85 fuel)
	Corporate tax	Maximum of 8 years tax exemption for Eco-car project, but the amount of tax exemption should not exceed investment amounts	6–8 years tax exemption
	Import duty (machinery)	Import tariff exemption for all production equipment and machineries	Same as the 1st Eco-car project
	Import duty (intermediate goods)	Maximum of 90% of tariff exemption for input materials for 2 years	Same as the 1st Eco-car project

Source: Fourin (2017: 40).

Table 5.4 Participants in the Eco-Car Project in Thailand

(a) 1st Eco-Car Project

Company	*Investment (Billion Baht)*	*Production (Units)*	*Starting Year*	*Note*
Nissan	5.51	120,000	2010	March/Micra model (1200 cc) majority is for export to Japan, local procurement ratio of 90%
Honda	6.7	120,000	2011	Brio model (1200 cc), 50% for domestic market and 50% for export
Suzuki	9.5	138,000	2012	Swift model (1200 cc), 26,000 units for domestic market, the rest are for export
Mitsubishi	16	150,000	2012	Global Small model (1000–1200 cc) export to ASEAN countries and Japan
Toyota	6.64	100,000	2012	Vios/Yaris model, 50% for export to ASEAN countries

Source: Fourin (2011:191).

(b) 2nd Eco-Car Project

Company	*Investment (Billion Baht)*	*Production (Units)*	*Starting Year*	*Note*
Nissan	8.66	123,000	2018	Next March (Micra) model
Honda	8.16	100,000	–	–
Suzuki	8.44	100,000	2017	Next Swift model
Mitsubishi	11.54	220,000	2016	Mirage model
Toyota	10.41	100,000	–	Next Vios and Yaris models, (Daihatsu is leading the development)
Mazda	12.64	158,000	2015	Mazda 2, new establishment of engine factory
Ford	18.18	180,000	–	–
SAIC	7.61	110,000	–	–

Source: Fourin (2017: 40).

Table 5.5 Procurement by a Japanese MNC in Thailand, 2010

Type of Firm	*Number*	*Percent*
Japanese firms (including JVs) in Thailand	129	64
Local (Thai) firms	51	25
US and European firms (including JVs) in Thailand	12	5
Imports: from 10 countries (11 affiliates)	11	5
Total	203	100

Source: Interview in March 2010.

The 3rd Automotive Master Plan (2012–2016)

The 3rd Master Plan aimed at the sustainable development of the automotive industry through the establishment of a production hub for global ecological vehicles and higher value supply chain networks (Fourin 2017: 38). Thanks to Thailand's proactive effort to encourage the Eco-car project after the 2008 Lehman shock (Doner and Wad 2014), the production of the Thai automotive industry jumped from just below 1 million vehicles in 2009 to 1.7 million in 2010, becoming the 12th largest producer in the world. In the following year of 2011, however, the Thai automotive industry was damaged by floods and decreased production. Nevertheless, in 2012–2013, the industry recorded the highest production (over 2.45 million vehicles) and sales (1.3–1.4 million vehicles) in its history, and finally joined the world's top 10 producers (see Figure 5.14). This rapid growth was achieved by the Yingluck government's 'First-Time Car Buyer Program' in 2011 by targeting low-middle-income people to own their first car with discounted prices (through a tax refund of 10% of the maximum vehicle purchase price for cars with engines below 1500 cc) and stimulate economic growth (Attavanich 2017). In short, the programme was to stimulate potential future demands. Production dropped after this period; but it stabilised at approximately 1.9 million units until 2017 and increased to over 2.1 million units in 2018. Moreover, in order to boost vehicle production again, the Yingluck government (2011–2014) introduced the 2nd Eco-car project in 2013, with a slight upgrading of environmental standards and lowering of excise tax (see Table 5.3). Correspondingly, the five initial Eco-car producers plus three newcomers (Mazda, Ford, and China's SAIC) participated in the project (see Table 5.4), and the production of the 2nd Eco-car was required to commence by the end of 2019. In this context, the presence of non-Japanese firms in Thailand as well as in the ASEAN region will surely increase in the near future.

Electric vehicle action plan (2016–2036)

Although the Thai automotive industry holds a strong competitive advantage in the production of power-train related components for gasoline and diesel engine vehicles, the local supporting industry related to electric vehicles (EVs) is relatively limited (Fourin 2017: 39). In response to future sustainable automotive development, the National Energy Policy Council of Thailand approved the 'EV Action Plan (2016–2036)' in 2016, aiming to achieve 1.2 million units of EV production, including plug-in hybrid electric vehicles (PHEVs), and 690 charging stands in the domestic market by 2036 (ibid.:42).

Furthermore, in February 2017, the BOI announced a new industrial policy, 'the National Competitiveness Enhancement Act for Targeted Industries', by targeting ten potential sectors including the automotive and auto parts industries, waiving corporate income taxes for up to 15 years and subsiding investment expenses to the total of 10 billion baht (US$286 million) for R&D and innovation. These incentives are in addition to the existing incentives such as exemption from import duties, and non-tax benefits such as visas for foreign experts.[19] In the first half of 2017, the targeted sectors attracted the total investment value of 291 billion baht (approximately US$8.77 billion). Among all sectors, the automotive and auto parts sectors attracted the largest value in application, accounting for 31 billion baht.[20]

Soft industrial policy

Technology transfer and human resource development

Technology transfer and human resource (HR) development are important factors in the development and upgrading of the automotive industry. As we saw in Chapter 4, Japanese automotive MNCs in concert with Japanese government organisations such as AOTS, JICA, and JETRO have created extensive technology transfer and human resource development programmes in cooperation with ASEAN governments. In Thailand, this has involved enhancing the establishment of TAI and various technology transfer and HR development programmes related to TAI. Besides this, Intarakumnerd and Gerdsri (2014) identified two linkages related to interactive learning in the industry, namely, assemblers-suppliers and firms-universities (research institutes), which have been playing a crucial role in Thai automotive development. In relation to assembler-supplier linkages, automotive MNCs have been transferring technology to local suppliers through information sharing, licencing, spin-offs of engineers, and so forth (Hayashi 2001). In Thailand, inter-firm technology transfer changed from simple 'operational technology' to a higher level of 'process engineering technology', and then to 'product engineering capabilities'. This technological upgrading led automotive MNCs to establish R&D centres or regional hubs of strategic vehicle production in Thailand (Intarakumnerd and Gerdsri 2014, Lee *et al.* 2019: 12).

More importantly, local human resource development has been facilitated through industry-university linkage in Thailand. Two types of industry-university linkage can be identified. The first type is curriculum development. Thailand's leading Chulalongkorn University has consolidated a strong partnership with Toyota. The university introduced the first automotive engineering degree programme in the country. Toyota assisted the university not only to set up up-to-date equipment but also to help in drafting curriculums and providing instructors in the field of automotive manufacturing with required insightful knowledge and practical experience. By the same token, other universities and automotive MNCs jointly developed similar programmes in Thailand. These linkages enabled the Thai automotive industry to upgrade from production engineering skills to acquire knowledge and skills for design and development (ibid.). The second type is characterised by a joint project and programme. For instance, King Mongkut's Institute of Technology Ladkrabang (KMITL) participates in the Student Formula Competition (to design racing cars) with financial support from automotive and related firms such as Suzuki and Cobra. Benefits from such a relation are generated not only for the university but also for firms. In the case of Suzuki, KMITL's project allowed the company to modify the Suzuki engine so as to be able to operate with 100% ethanol at low temperatures (Intarakumnerd *et al.* 2012). Another example is the Sirindhorn International Thai-German Graduate School of Engineering (TGGS) under KMITL. TGGS offers a joint masters degree programme in automotive engineering in association with Germany's RWTH Aachen University, by providing internships, faculty research, and consulting projects in close relationship with the automotive industry (Intarakumnerd and Gerdsri 2014).

Clustering

Clustering in the Thai automotive industry has already been alluded to. As an industrial policy, it was highlighted during the Thaksin years (2001–2006). Firms in clusters group together to derive competitive advantages from external economies and from joint action between firms (Schmitz and Nadvi 1999). The cluster policy explicitly was linked with the well-known work of Michael Porter (1990) on competitiveness, and indeed with Porter himself as a consultant in Thailand. The automotive industry in Thailand was chosen as one of five key sectors for action. There are some doubts, however, about how effectively the policy was pursued (Lauridsen 2009: 415), and sometimes there was confusion because the government was also using clusters for rural development policy.[21]

Clustering, though, long predated Thaksin's policies, in practice if not necessarily in name. As Lecler (2002) has shown, automotive clusters had developed based on a policy of using industrial estates to attract investment, and there were already small clusters in and around Bangkok in the early 1970s. Japanese auto parts manufacturers tended to locate their factories near those of their customers. Existing clusters, indeed, tended to induce more clustering (Lecler 2002: 802–803). By 1997, there were 215 auto parts investment projects in Thailand, compared to only 62 in Malaysia.

By the late 1980s, agglomeration *dis*economies, such as traffic congestion, rising land prices, and labour shortages, pushed companies towards industrial zones set up by the government in new areas, in particular those on the eastern seaboard south of Bangkok and areas further out to the north of Bangkok. Major Japanese assemblers located new plants in these new areas to supplement their existing production in estates near Bangkok. They were also influenced by the good port facilities on the eastern seaboard as companies turned increasingly to exports after 1997, and Thailand grew as their regional production centre for the automotive industry. Similar considerations applied to new US and European motor investment.

Encouragement to clustering survived the demise of the Thaksin Shinawatra government. Interviewed in September 2012, the Thai Board of Investment indicated its interest in targeting the automotive industry (and two other sectors: electronics and machinery) for clustering. It wished to attract both auto assemblers and parts suppliers with incentives (such as tax exemptions for imported materials and machinery), and wanted them normally to be located near the assembler, especially in areas away from Bangkok. The BOI's Unit for Industrial Linkage Development (BUILD) programme, set up in 1992, still attempts to bring prospective suppliers and industrial customers together and encourages firms to use the ASEAN Supporting Industry Database (ASDIC). There is now an 'automotive belt' stretching from north of Bangkok down through the eastern seaboard (Techakanont 2008: 24).

Upgrading within the automotive GVC?

The Thai automotive industry clearly has been 'upgraded' in the sense that it has attracted not only major automotive assemblers but also large Tier-1 suppliers, mainly, though not exclusively, from Japan, and has moved progressively through the industrial upgrading stages: shifting from (1) repairing of CBU vehicles, to (2) assembly of imported CKD kits, (3) localisation of components production of lower value-added parts with low LC ratio, (4) localisation of components production of higher value-added parts with high LC ratio, (5) localisation of R&D, and (6) R&D for product development and design and regional headquarters functions (see Table 2.2 in Chapter 2). The automotive industry now has a deep economic structure with several tiers of suppliers and continuingly high local content, encouraged by policy, even though explicit LCRs have gone.[22] Thailand is by no means alone in having a motor industry dominated by foreign firms – witness the case of the United Kingdom – and the country still gains from the employment, foreign exchange, and tax revenue they provide, and from spillovers to domestic firms. But upgrading in the normal way as used in the GVC literature (that is, of products, processes, and functions by firms, either individually or in clusters) is hardly relevant to foreign firms assemblers like Toyota or Tier-1 suppliers like Denso, which already represent global best practice. Whilst some foreign firms might operate inefficiently in the context of a protected domestic market on the basis of cheap Thai labour – particularly if there is a multiplicity of models, each produced on a small scale – it is hard to argue this where major firms are competitive (direct or indirect) exporters. Some exporters have achieved greater economies of scale by product specialisation, like those making the one-tonne pickup trucks and Eco-cars strongly encouraged by Thai tax policy. Hassler (2009: 2238–2240) has argued this specialisation also has been associated with a deeper structure of the domestically based suppliers. This greater efficiency – which can be regarded as upgrading by those foreign firms – has been partly achieved using of labour-saving robotics, in the face of labour shortages and the need for higher quality (Lee *et al.* 2019).

The idea of upgrading within the GVC is mainly relevant, then, to the domestic Thai firms that operate in the industry as suppliers. Busser (2008) has argued that little upgrading has taken place among domestic Thai suppliers. More recently, Pollio and Rubini (2019: 6–8), while noting that the automotive industry in the early to mid-2000s was generating 12% of GDP, 10% of manufacturing employment, and 12% of manufacturing exports, argued that the dependence on foreign automotive assemblers had not led to domestic development in terms of promoting higher-tech production by local suppliers. Such suppliers, despite substantial Thai representation among first-tier firms, were mainly confined to non-core products such as seating, rather than core ones such as engines or transmissions. In this sense, the wider development impacts of the Thai automotive industry were seen as limited.

Worries were expressed by our interviewed exporting assemblers about Thai suppliers' ability to supply products on time and of consistent quality. Where there was no Japanese supplier available, and component imports were made too expensive by high transport costs or continuing tariff protection against imports from non-AFTA sources,[23] attempts were made to upgrade Thai suppliers. In this sense – and in these circumstances – Japanese assemblers have been 'drivers' of upgrading. However, when more Japanese suppliers entered Thailand as assemblers expanded exports, Thai Tier-1 suppliers were pushed down to lower tiers or out of business.

Lauridsen (2004 and 2009), in instructive studies of Thai policy towards supplier development, argues that attempts directly to increase local sourcing by foreign investors in the 1990s and early 2000s – and, in practice, to promote the development of Thai small and medium enterprises – were ineffective because of problems of implementation and lack of political support. They also changed somewhat with changes of government; successive governments each wanting their own new policies (such as Thaksin on clusters). With regard to the BUILD programme mentioned earlier, Lauridsen notes that, having been focussed originally on developing Thai small-scale suppliers, it moved in the mid-1990s more towards trying to bring Japanese component suppliers into Thailand to service the existing Japanese assemblers (Lauridsen 2004: 575 and 580). By contrast, in the view of Intarakumnerd *et al.* (2012) and Intarakumnerd and Tachakanont (2016), Thai local firms have been upgrading their technical capability based on links with MNCs and the national system of innovation.

However, according to Busser (2008: 39), Japanese assemblers have discouraged suppliers from developing new products or designs, requiring the use of their own supplied designs. A more optimistic view is provided by Ueda (2007 and 2009). In her case study of two prominent Tier-1 suppliers of Thai origin, she traces their beginnings in the repair business, and their expansion into OEM (original equipment manufacturer) in the 1970s as LCRs were introduced. Showing that they have been heavily dependent on Japanese technology transferred from the customers, she notes that the transfer is as yet far from complete (Ueda 2009: 35–36). Among our own Thai interviewees – one large first-tier joint-venture firm with activities overseas as well as in Thailand, and two Tier-2 suppliers – there was quite a positive view of the help provided by Japanese customers, though always on the basis of supplied designs. Notwithstanding this, only 25% of Toyota's suppliers in Thailand were purely local Thai (Table 5.5). To take the counter-example of Czechia, the largest automotive producing country in Central and Eastern Europe, where we have also worked, this ratio is still much higher than in Czechia. In the case of one of the major Japanese assemblers, of the total of 240 suppliers, 88 suppliers are located in Czechia (1 purely local, 31 Japanese, 56 non-Japanese/local capital) and 152 suppliers are located in other EU countries (23 Japanese and 129 non-Japanese capitals) in 2016 (Interview, 20 September 2016). Indeed, almost all local parts suppliers in Czechia are Tier-2 suppliers (see Natsuda *et al.* 2020b, Pavlinek and Janak 2007). Thus, the role of the local automotive industry in Thailand is far more significant than that of Czechia. Indeed, as we saw in Chapter 3, a number of Thai local firms have upgraded themselves into being MNCs in recent years.

Challenges to the Thai automotive industry

Although the Thai automotive industry has successfully developed in the last few decades, the industry faces five main issues. The first challenge is factory capacity utilisation. Automotive MNCs have expanded their production capacity; nonetheless, the factory capacity utilisation in many firms is not high in Thailand.[24] In 2018, the nine largest producers in the country produced 2,090,311 units (see Table 5.1) out of 3.08 million units of total production capacity (see Table 3.5 in Chapter 3). In this regard, the average factory operating ratio was approximately 68% in the top nine producers. Nevertheless, in two out of nine firms, the average factory operating ratio was below 50%.

The second challenge can be associated with the first problem. Local market demand decreased following policies of excessive market stimulation. One the one hand, there is no doubt that the Thai government introduced effective industrial policies and enhanced the development of the automotive industry. One the other hand, the *First-Time Car Buyer Program* in 2011 seems to have been excessive in creating temporary/artificial market demand, followed by fall in demand. It is obvious that the programme stimulated short-term demand, generating sales of over 1.4 million vehicles in 2012 and 1.3 million in 2013 (see Figure 5.14). However, local vehicle sales after this period continually decreased, to 0.76 million in 2016, and subsequently some firms have been facing low capacity utilisation. In this context, it is questionable whether short-run market stimulation policies are useful or not in terms of mid-term development. It is also important to note that vehicle sales are estimated at over 0.9 million in 2018 due to some repurchase demands after the programme (JETRO 2018a: 15).

The third challenge is political. Despite the fact that the Thai political economy has been chaotic after the collapse of the populist Thaksin government in 2006, Thai automotive industrial policy seems to have been consistent in terms of its development perspective. As we saw, the Thaksin administration's 'Detroit of Asia' plan, and its *product champion* programme under the AMP, have been maintained not only by the Thaksin-influenced Yingluck administrations (2011–2014) but also by the Abhisit government (2008–2011) and even under the current military government of Prayuth (following the coup in 2014 and victory in the national election in 2019). There is no doubt that Thai automotive industrial policies have been stable except for the aforementioned *First-Time Car Buyer Program.* However, political instability must be seen as a potential risk to the Thai automotive industry.

The fourth challenge is possible future competition from Indonesia where the automotive industry has been growing rapidly. Indonesia has been expanding its export capacity in the last decade. Despite the fact that many automotive MNCs have created a regional division of labour of production models according to market demands in Southeast Asia (e.g. see Table 4.10 in chapter 4), there are still some overlapping areas in the production of particular models between Thailand and Indonesia. As the supporting industry and the technological capability of the Indonesian automotive industry grow in the future, some such models might shift to Indonesia due to its lower labour costs, larger population, and growing domestic market.

The fifth challenge is related to unavoidable natural disasters – flooding. In October and November 2011, Bangkok and its surrounding provinces faced a serious flooding problem which affected the automotive industry. In particular, factories in Ayutthaya (where Honda and their main suppliers are located) were badly flooded in October 2011. In the case of Honda, it took 174 days to resume operations; factories of Toyota and Nissan were not flooded, but their production was shut down due to lack of components (Toyota for 42 days and Nissan for 29 days) (Haraguchi and Lall 2013: 10–11). Consequently, the total Thai production of vehicles dropped by 12.9% in 2011, accounting for 1.46 million in comparison with 1.65 million units in the previous year (see Figure 5.14). This problem has acted as one of the main drivers for the 'Thai + one' strategy of Japanese automotive multinationals in recent years (see Chapter 4).

One further issue which can be seen as something of a challenge to domestic Thai auto parts producers – though a factor making for greater efficiency from the point of view of assemblers – is the emerging division of labour between Thailand and the CLMV countries – Cambodia, Laos, Myanmar, and Vietnam. This has particularly involved the first three of these countries, which have a common border with Thailand, more than Vietnam, which does not.[25] The challenge for Vietnam of having vehicle parts production develop more in the other CLMV countries is discussed in Chapter 9.

Conclusions

This chapter has traced the development of industrial policy towards the Thai automotive industry over the past six decades. The industry, encouraged as part of a general policy of import substitution, initially developed in the 1960s as an assembly activity based on the import of CKD kits, with heavy effective protection. Oriented to the domestic market, with a multiplicity of models, the industry's high import content and resulting balance of payment deficits were seen as a problem to be solved by the localisation of auto parts production. Local content requirements became a central part of the first auto industry-specific policies introduced in the early 1970s, although proposals to limit the number of models of vehicle were withdrawn after industry opposition. Localisation of component supply was achieved, especially by Japanese-owned assemblers, both by encouraging their component suppliers to locate in Thailand and by encouraging lower tiers of domestic Thai suppliers where no Japanese supplier was available.

Although the Thai economy has one of the largest domestic vehicle markets in the ASEAN region, exports are important to an industry subject to large economies of scale both in finished vehicles and in some major auto parts. The Thai government policy moved towards strengthening of export capacity in the 1980s, and exports started in 1987. Exports, both of vehicles and parts, continued into the 1990s. They were encouraged by exporting conditions imposed on FDI, but their main stimulus came with the temporary collapse of the domestic market following the 1997 Asian financial crisis and the large accompanying devaluation of the Thai baht.

Whilst the import substitution policy had achieved a rapid expansion of Thai automotive production, and even some exports by the end of the 1980s, the world trend towards liberalisation caused a major policy shift with the change of government in 1991. The ban on imports of passenger vehicles was removed and tariffs reduced, while ownership rules in relation to export requirements were relaxed. However, LCRs, which had been strengthened in the 1980s, were retained throughout the liberalisation of the 1990s until 2000 – the WTO target date for their removal. One particular issue driving liberalisation was the belief that continued protection and LCRs had allowed an apparent cartel of (particularly) Japanese vehicle assemblers to keep domestic prices and profits high to the detriment of consumers. However, while these high prices and profits were tackled by measures to promote new entry and more competition, LCRs were actually increased. In this sense, LCRs were made to work more effectively.

A success of the liberalisation years, especially after 1997, has been the expansion of exports both of vehicles and parts, driven in part by the collapse of the domestic market during the 1997 financial crisis. This also owes much to Thai industrial policy being attractive to foreign investors, particularly Japanese, but also to Americans, who then have been willing to choose Thailand as their main regional base to develop both regional exports and parts sourcing. There has been sufficient 'critical mass' in various industrial clusters to attract component supplier inward investment. What is also interesting, though, is that this attractiveness – and the associated export expansion – has been compatible with maintaining tariff protection against many extra-ASEAN imports, and with quite a directive industrial policy, including the *product champions* scheme. Nominal tariff protection on auto assembly, though, has been progressively reduced over the years, and effective protection (that is, protection on value-added) on auto assembly has also been reduced by the increase in tariff protection given to component makers against imports from non-AFTA sources.

Given the successful direct (and indirect) export performance of the Thai motor industry, it is hard to imagine that tariff protection is now truly necessary for survival, although it does give some scope for cross-subsidisation of export sales from domestic market profits.

Developments after 2000 suggest that the Thai government has been able to maintain considerable policy space to foster the auto industry. In a similar vein, Noble *et al.* (2005) have argued in the case of China that WTO accession and the country's pledging to WTO rules tended to discipline policy towards the auto industry rather than making it ineffective.[26] Although the LCR policy has sometimes been criticised, and its abolition treated as an inducement to automotive development in Thailand, it was administered pragmatically in response to industry suggestions, and did indeed succeed in providing a basis for further localisations that took places subsequently. It is hard to argue that continuing high local content – the legacy of past LCRs – represents a 'bad' backward linkage, given the successes of Thailand's component suppliers as indirect (and sometimes direct) exporters. Later industrialising countries, however, if they abide by current WTO rules on TRIMs, would not be able to follow Thailand and base the initial deepening of their industrial structure on the use of LCRs. Although as we have shown, they would be able to use other incentives: the ladder would have been kicked away (in Chang's 2002 parlance) only partially. Although writers such as Lauridsen (2004 and 2009), and more recently Pollio and Rubini (2019), have argued that the expansion of the Thai automotive industry has not done enough to develop Thai domestic producers, this view is not shared by all commentators on the industry, and we have noted that a number of Thai auto parts firms have been able to grow into multinational enterprises. Also, technology transfer and human resource development more generally have been promoted by various 'soft' policies by the government, industry, and universities, and various automotive MNCs, from the 2000s, have transferred to Thailand some more sophisticated activities beyond assembly (Lee *et al.* 2019: 12).

Notes

1 Economies of scale are associated with the minimum efficient size of *plant.* This can vary according to the degree of vertical integration, though that now is usually very low, with perhaps 30% of the value of a car represented by assembly. MES usually is thought to vary from about 40,000 vehicles a year (for little beyond assembly) to 200,000–300,000 (for a more integrated operation), and is considerably larger for some components like engines. The minimum size of *firm* is much larger than that of an assembly plant because of the economies of scope needed for the massive R&D costs of developing new models. Nolan (2012: 25) puts it as high as 5 million vehicles a year for a global mass market assembler (see Thoburn and Natsuda 2018, note 4, which cites more references on this topic).

2 On Thailand in the regional automotive economy, see also Wad (2009). We have discussed these issues with major motor assemblers in interviews in Thailand and Singapore. Thoburn and Natsuda (2018) discuss intra-regional trade in relation to Indonesia and the Philippines, but some information on Thailand is also included.

3 And for the less developed (CLMV) countries – Cambodia, Laos, Myanmar, and Vietnam - progressively to zero over the period 2015 to 2018 under the AEC.
4 LCR was further revised to 20% for CVs with windshields (effective in 1975) in 1974 (Higashi 2000).
5 FTI was under the strong influence of assemblers, particular Japanese corporations, which were opposed to localisation policies. By contrast, TAPMA was formed by local automotive parts suppliers, who supported localisation policies (Higashi 2000).
6 Toyota, Nissan, and Isuzu started projects under BOI, and Mitsubishi was under MOI.
7 This was despite the apparent anti-export bias generated by tariff protection of the domestic market. Exporting strengthens economies of scale and avoids saturation of the domestic market, and there can be cross-subsidization of exports using(protected) domestic market profits. It is a typical 'East Asian' pattern (Chang 2002), expanding exports, while keeping the domestic market protected.
8 See Thoburn (1973) on 'good' vs 'bad' linkage effects.
9 This ratio includes 9% of ASEAN content. Note, though, that LC figures achieved are sometimes in terms of the *number* of locally sourced components, rather than their value. We thank Rajah Rasiah for this point.
10 Single-cab pickup trucks retained the lowest rate of 3%.
11 Depending on the location of investment – Zone 1 (Bangkok and the surrounding 5 provinces) for 3 years, Zone 2 (12 provinces outside of Zone 1) for 5 years, and Zone 3 (except for Zones 1 and 2) for 8 years.
12 Interview with the President of TAIA on 23 August 2011.
13 The current Toyota Daihatsu Engineering and Manufacturing (TDEM).
14 Isuzu's website: www.isuzu.co.jp/press/2010/3_26pup.html [accessed on 8 December 2018].
15 According to the president of TAIA, VW does not own well-established supplier networks in Thailand in comparison with Japanese competitors, and so it was difficult to meet the Eco-car's requirements. TATA produced only LNG engine vehicles, so they also could not meet the requirements.
16 According to the president of TAIA (also vice president of Nissan), the major reason for the relocation was the concern about the continuous appreciation of the Japanese yen after the global financial crisis.
17 Interview with deputy secretary general at BOI on 15 February 2011.
18 Interview in March 2010.
19 See *The Nation* (15 February 2017): http://www.nationmultimedia.com/news/business/EconomyAndTourism/30306346, [accessed on 10 December 2018]; *Global Legal Monitor*: http://www.loc.gov/law/foreign-news/article/thailand-new-law-on-competitiveness-in-targeted-industries/ [accessed on 10 December 2018].
20 BOI's website: http://www.boi.go.th/upload/content/2017-08-10%20PR103-O59%20BOI%20Board%20half%20year_82386.pdf [accessed on 10 December 2018].
21 Rural development clusters in Thailand were based on sub-districts, or *tambons*; hence, the famous one-*tambon*-one-product (OTOP) idea (Lauridsen 2009: 415), based on the earlier one-village-one-product movement in Japan (Natsuda *et al.* 2012).
22 Except, as noted earlier, the local content requirements for exports to other ASEAN countries under AFTA and the AEC.
23 But note that not all non-AFTA sources are subject to protection. Witness the free trade agreement with Australia, as already indicated, and the Japan-Thailand Economic Partnership Agreement, signed 2007, that included the progressive elimination of tariffs on vehicles and their components.
24 Calculated from Table 3.5 and Table 5.1, Toyota (85.2%), Mitsubishi (93.0%), Mazda (98.5%), Ford (63.0%), Isuzu (55.3%), Honda (58.6%), Nissan (44.0%), GM (33.6%), and Suzuki (60.3%).

25 Remember that our comments here refer only to the motor *vehicle* and parts industry. A study of intra-industry trade, including *motorcycles* and parts, between Thailand and Vietnam by Techakanont (2012), found stronger evidence of intra-industry trade. Reference forward to Figures 9.7 and 9.8 in our Chapter 9 shows that only 9.1% of Vietnam's exports of vehicle auto parts were to Thailand (whereas 33.8% went to Japan, Vietnam's largest export market for this category), and for wiring harnesses the figure was a mere 1.7%, while 65.7% went to Japan.

26 However, they do focus mainly on ownership requirements and intellectual property rights, and have almost nothing to say on LC or export requirements.

6 Indonesia

Introduction

This chapter examines the development of the Indonesian automotive industry in historical perspective, paying attention to the role of industrial policy in Indonesia's automotive industrialisation. Having started vehicle assembly as long ago as the 1920s, Indonesia's vehicle production reached over 1 million units for the first time in 2012, accounting for over 1.3 million units in 2018, and ranked as the 17th largest vehicle producer in the world (OICA website). Indonesia has some interesting features in contrast to its ASEAN neighbours. Like Malaysia, it tried to develop a national car, but without Malaysia's 'success' in keeping the main national car in production. While Malaysia sailed close to the wind of flouting the WTO rules, and got away with it, Indonesia's attempt to establish a national car in the 1990s was so blatantly anti-competitive that it suffered effective protests under WTO dispute procedures from the home countries of rival vehicle producers (Hale 2001). Similarly, Thailand has continued effectively to promote increased local content, though local content requirements (LCRs) are banned under the WTO's Trade-Related Investment Measures (TRIMs) rules (see Chapter 5). It has done so by using fiscal measures that were sufficiently WTO-compliant to avoid protest (Natsuda and Thoburn 2014). In contrast, Indonesia's LCRs were strongly attacked under the conditionality imposed on loans from the International Monetary Fund (IMF) after the 1997 Asian financial crisis (AFC). In more recent years, the Indonesia government has been pursuing a Thai-style product champion strategy by introducing the low-cost green car (LCGC) (Natsuda *et al.* 2015a).

In Indonesia, state capacity generally has been viewed as low, with extensive cronyism and poor governance, often characterised by the acronym of KKN (the Indonesian words for corruption, collusion, and nepotism); this is thought to have weakened Indonesia's ability to implement effective industrial policies for the automotive industry (Hill 1996, MacIntyre 1994). In this context, Aswicahyono *et al.* (2000) explained that the Indonesian automotive industry failed to develop. However, Indonesia is now at an interesting stage of development. As Basri (2012: 30–33) notes, the country is enjoying a 'demographic dividend', with its young middle class generating a growing demand for consumer goods like cars, an optimistic view that our interviewees in the Indonesian motor industry appear to share. Industrialisation thus looks more promising than in the recent past, which has been characterised by some de-industrialisation compared to the pre-AFC period under President Suharto (Tadjoeddin and Chowdhury 2019).[1] Indeed, the rapid development of automotive exports in the 2000s and 2010s is one of the successes of the post-1997 AFC period. Our next section provides an overview of the Indonesian automotive industry. Then the following main section investigates the development of the Indonesian automotive industry over the period 1928–2018, with an emphasis on the past 20 years, including discussion of industrial policy with regard to the LCGC programme. A further section examines challenges for the industry within the automotive GVC, and the last section concludes.

Overview of the Indonesian automotive industry

Automotive production and sales trends

In Southeast Asia, Thailand, Indonesia, and Malaysia expanded their global share and the volume of production between 2000 and 2018. In the case of Indonesia, vehicle production increased 4.6-fold, much faster than neighbouring Malaysia, which had a similar production volume in 2000. Figure 6.1 indicates the total number of vehicles produced, sold, and exported in Indonesia in the period 1976–2018. Production expanded to over 325,000 units in 1994, and reached its first peak of 389,279 units in 1997. However, the Asian financial crisis caused a serious market slump, and subsequently the production decreased to only 58,000 units in 1998. Although Indonesia's vehicle production has expanded steadily in the first half of 2000s, reaching over 500,000 units in 2005, vehicle demand decreased sharply by 40% in 2006 in comparison with the previous year, due to increases in fuel prices (which doubled) and in interest rates (Fourin 2008: 208). Since this event, the market demand has expanded rapidly (except for 2009 due to the Lehman shock) and finally reached over 1 million units in 2012. The second highest production volume in the Indonesian history accounted for nearly 1.3 million vehicles in 2014. In general, Indonesia's automotive sales exceeded domestic production until 2013, when the sales volume of 1.23 million units was the highest in its history. However, due to a slight slowdown in Indonesia's GDP growth rate, from 5.6% in 2013 to 4.9% in 2015 (*World Development Indicators*, online), caused by the depreciation of rupiah, a rising inflation rate, and the stagnation of domestic infrastructure investment, domestic sales decreased to 1.01 million units in 2015 (Fourin 2017: 68, JETRO 2016: 23). Under these circumstances, US producers Ford and GM decided to leave Indonesia in 2015. In 2016 and 2017, domestic demand slightly recovered, to 1.06 million units, subsequently facilitating increases in domestic production. In 2018, Indonesia recorded the highest production volume of over 1.3 million units. Although Indonesia has been facing a sales slump since 2013, domestic sales have stayed at over a million units and constitute the largest

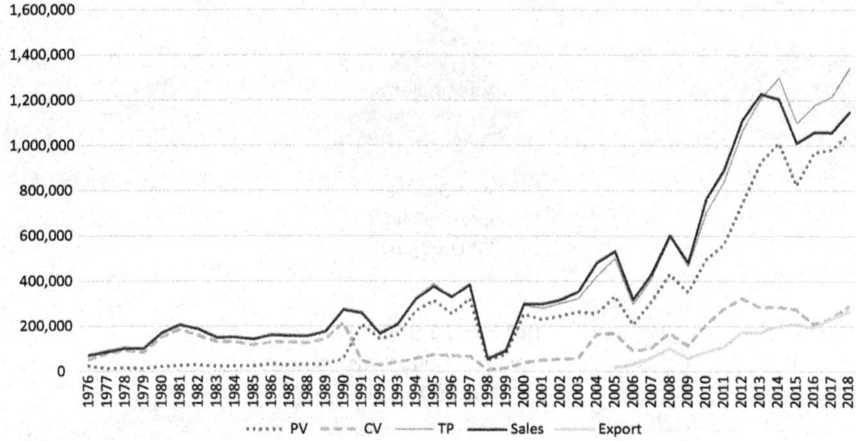

Figure 6.1 Production, Sales, and Exports of Vehicles in Indonesia, 1976–2018.
Source: Adapted from Fourin (1994, 1999, 2011, 2017, and 2019) and JETRO (2015 and 2018a).
Note: Number of vehicles, PV (passenger vehicle), CV (commercial vehicle), TP (total production), Indonesian government changed categories of PVs and CVs in 2004, 1991–2010 based on new criteria, and 1976–1990 based on old criteria.

automotive market in Southeast Asia. The Indonesian automotive industry produced 1,343,714 units (1,055,774 passenger vehicles and 287,940 commercial vehicles), sold 1,151,291 units, and exported 264,553 units in 2018 (Fourin 2019: 40). As Figure 6.1 shows, by the late 2010s, total vehicles production exceeded total sales, indicating positive *net* exports.

In Indonesia, multi-purpose vehicles (MPVs), like Toyota's Kijang (the current Innova) model, historically have been the most popular category of vehicle. Indeed, MPVs accounted for 40% (431,294 units) of domestic market sales, while pickup trucks accounted for merely 1.3% (14,027 units) in 2016 (Fourin 2017: 72). The 7-seater MPVs are particularly popular in Indonesia due to (1) the typically large family size, and (2) the height of the vehicle body (much higher than sedans), which is very useful in the poor road conditions of Indonesia and in floods. More recently, the demand for LCGCs has been increasing rapidly, from 51,180 units in 2013 to 234,554 units in 2017 (a market share of 22%). In contrast, the sales of sedan cars, which still incur relatively high luxury taxes of between 30% and 125% (see Table 6.1), have sharply decreased by 73%, from 34,193 units in 2013 to 9,139 units in 2017 (JETRO 2018a: 22).

The structure of the Indonesian automotive industry

In Indonesia, there were 20 assembly plants, approximately 550 Tier-1 parts suppliers and 1,000 Tiers-2 and 3 suppliers in 2015 (Figure 6.2). It is estimated that the Indonesian automotive industry generates a total employment of

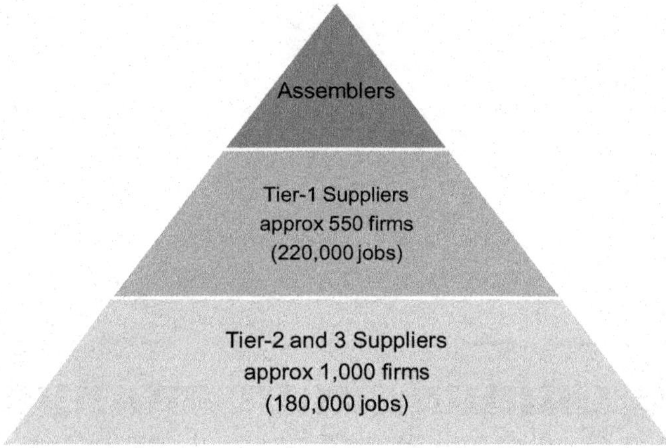

Figure 6.2 Structure of the Indonesian Automotive Industry, 2015.
Source: Adapted from Fourin (2015: 89).

approximately 445,000 people, divided between assemblers (45,000 workers), Tier-1 suppliers (220,000 workers) and Tiers-2 and 3 suppliers (180,000 workers). The additional 884,000 employment consists of workers in authorised outlets including sales service and workshops (380,000 workers) and non-authorised outlets (504,000 workers). In total, over 1.3 million jobs are estimated to have been created by the automotive industry in Indonesia in 2015 (Fourin 2015: 89). The Indonesian Automotive Parts and Components Industries Association (GIAMM) had 161 member firms: 95 joint venture (JV) firms and 66 local firms in 2012. Of the 95 JV firms, 69 were Japanese. According to GIAMM, Indonesia's auto parts industry is under Japanese *keiretsu* (business group) control, which has advantages in terms of long-term business relationships based on trust, guarantees of technical support, and flexibility of production and quantity, although cost reduction pressure is high.[2] However, our interviews with several automotive assemblers in Indonesia found that parts-sourcing practice in Indonesia is somewhat different from the traditional *keiretsu* system in Japan, employing a more open system of procuring not restricted to single *keiretsu* networks.

A unique feature of the Indonesian automotive industry is the division of labour between MNCs and local capital firms. According to an Indonesian government decree of 1969 (see later section), and still operative, assembly operations on the one hand, and distribution operations on the other, must be organised by different entities. Foreign automotive assemblers have been in charge of product development, production management, and business administration, and local firms have been in charge of distribution and sales operations (Nomura 2003: 25). Furthermore, large Indonesian business groups such as Astra International and Indomobil have been formed to control sales and distribution operations with various foreign assembly firms. For example, for Toyota's PT. Toyota Motor Manufacturing Indonesia[3] was established in order to assemble vehicles in 1970. In parallel with this, PT. Toyota Astra Motor was established (with 51% of capital from Astra International and 49% from Toyota Motor) in 1971 in order to conduct distribution and sales operations in Indonesia. In addition, Toyota's partner, Astra International, also conducts sales and distribution operations for Daihatsu, Isuzu, Nissan Diesel, BMW, and for Honda for 2-wheelers only. Similarly, the Indomobil group has operations with Suzuki, Mazda, Nissan, Hino, and Volvo.

In Indonesia, a handful of motor producers, predominantly Japanese, dominate the market. The top two vehicle producers accounted for the bulk of output, and the top six producers accounted for approximately 90% in both production and domestic sales (see Figures 6.3 and 6.4). Daihatsu is the leading producer in the country, accounting for 40.7% (546,541 units) in production in 2018. In terms of sales, Toyota is the leading company, followed by Honda, Daihatsu, Suzuki, and Mitsubishi. Daihatsu is the leading producer, but the third automotive brand in the country in terms of sales – it supplies five models (Avanza, Agya, Calya, Rush, and Town Ace) to Toyota under OEM contracts, with production of 345,151 units, accounting for 63% of its total production in 2018. Indeed, Toyota has been increasingly strengthening collaboration with its affiliate Daihatsu in Southeast Asia. Hence, the Toyota group (Toyota, Daihatsu, and Hino) alone accounted for 57.8% of production in 2018 and 54.4% of domestic sales in 2017 in Indonesia.

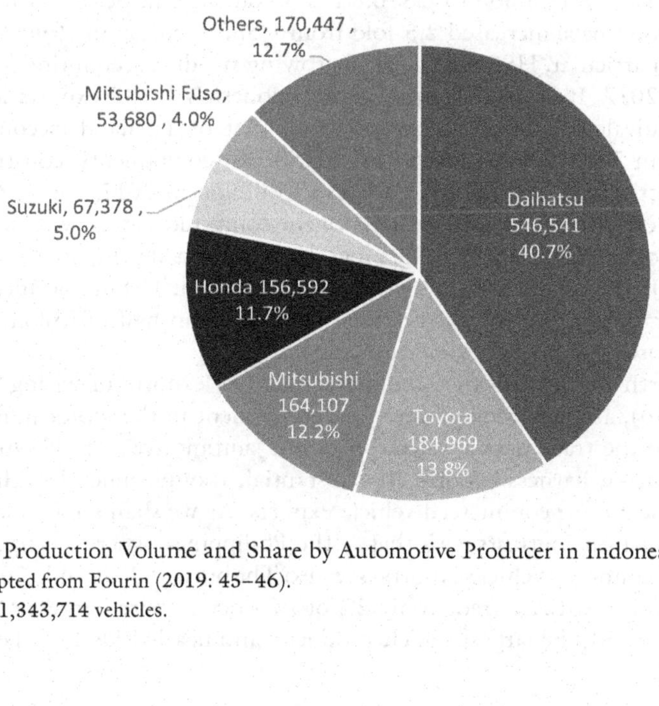

Figure 6.3 Production Volume and Share by Automotive Producer in Indonesia, 2018.
Source: Adapted from Fourin (2019: 45–46).
Note: Total 1,343,714 vehicles.

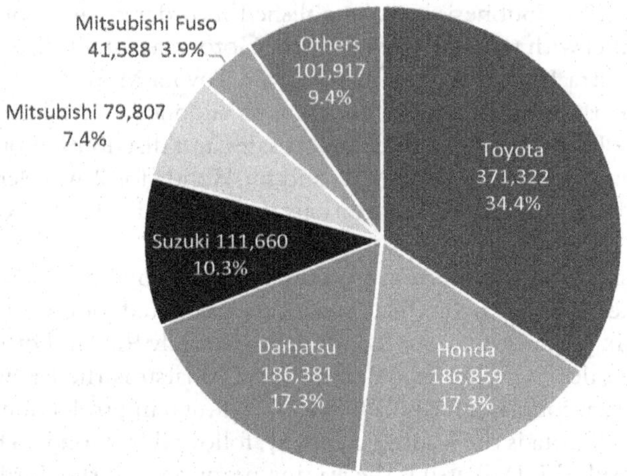

Figure 6.4 Sales Volume and Share by Automotive Brand in Indonesia, 2017.
Source: Adapted from Fourin (2018: 324).
Note: Total 1,079,534 vehicles.

Indonesia's automotive trade

Figure 6.5 shows trends in Indonesian automotive trade over the period 1996–2017 in terms of value. In HS87, its imports were much larger than its exports until 2014. This trend reversed after 2015. The exports of HS87 have grown 24-fold, from US$283 million to US$6.8 billion during this period, while the imports of HS87 have increased 2.5-fold from US$2.7 billion in 1996 to US$6.8 billion. In particular, HS8703 has been growing steadily, accounting for US$3.1 billion in 2017. It is worth noting that Indonesia's HS87 exports accounted for the equivalent of approximately 24% of that of Thailand (accounting for US$28.5) in 2017. On the import side, HS8708 (components) constituted the highest proportion, accounting for US$3.16 billion in 2017. Figure 6.6 shows the top 10 export destinations in 2017 for the composite category vehicles, parts, and accessories (HS87); the Philippines is the largest destination, followed by Thailand, Japan, Saudi Arabia, Vietnam, and Malaysia. The importance of intra-ASEAN trade is indicated by the fact that more than half of Indonesia's total HS87 exports go to other ASEAN members.

It is worth noting too that Indonesia also has exports of wiring harnesses (HS854430), an increasingly important component in the motor industry, but classified in the trade data as 'electronic', not 'automotive'. At US$908 million in 2017, wiring harness exports are substantial, though much less than Indonesia's passenger or commercial vehicle exports. As we shall see in a later chapter, this situation contrasts with that of the Philippines, where wiring harnesses dwarf that country's vehicle exports (see also Thoburn and Natsuda 2018). With regard to intra-ASEAN trade, only 2% of Indonesia's wire harness exports are sold to Thailand, the largest vehicle producer, and nearly 85% go to Japan.[4]

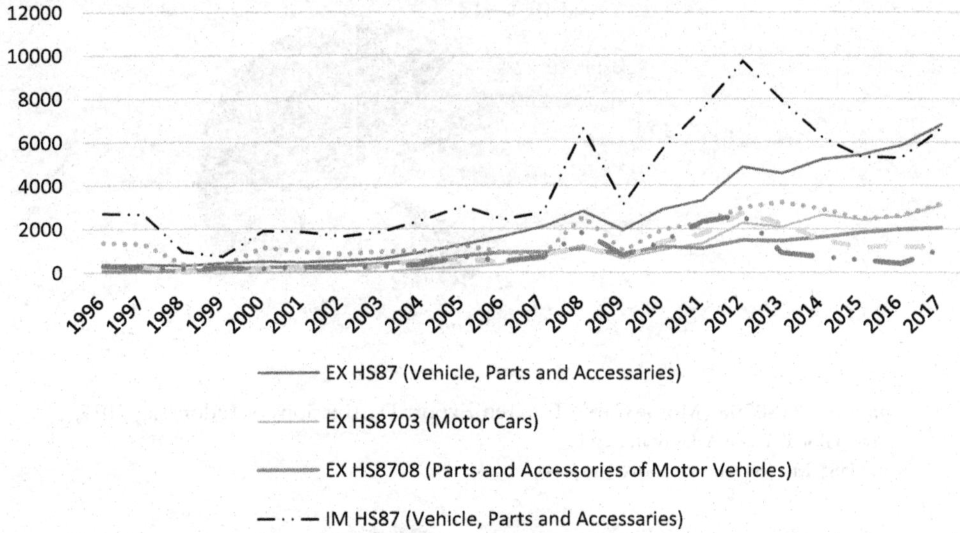

Figure 6.5 Automotive Exports of Indonesia, 1996–2017.
Source: Global Trade Atlas (database).
Note: US$ Million, EX (export), IM (import).

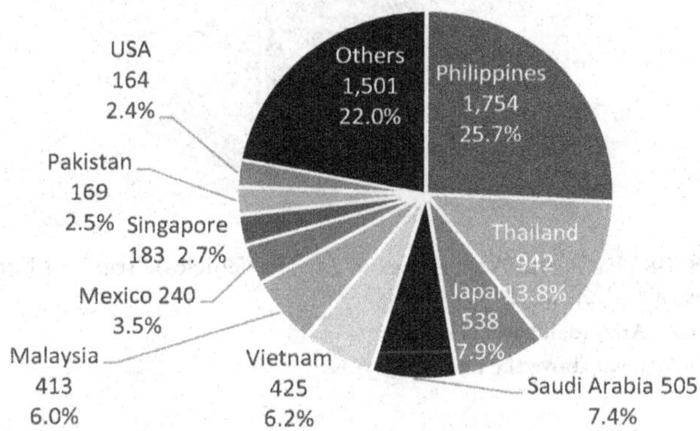

Figure 6.6 HS87 (Vehicles, Parts, and Accessories), Top Ten Export Destinations of Indonesia, 2017.
Source: Global Trade Atlas (database).
Note: US$ Million (shown above the percentages).

The most remarkable growth has come from the export of PVs. The export under the category HS8703 increased 111-fold, from merely US$28 million in 1996 to over US$3.1 billion in 2017. Figure 6.7 shows the top 10 export destinations of PVs from Indonesia in 2017. The Philippines is the largest export destination (accounting for approximately US$1.2 billion), followed by Saudi Arabia, Vietnam, Thailand, Japan, and UAE in 2017. In terms of the number

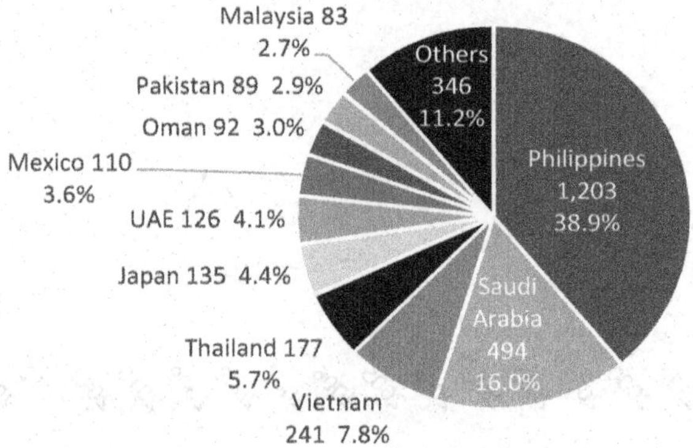

Figure 6.7 HS8703 (Motor Cars), Top Ten Export Destinations of Indonesia, 2017.
Source: Global Trade Atlas (database).
Note: US$ Million (shown above the percentages).

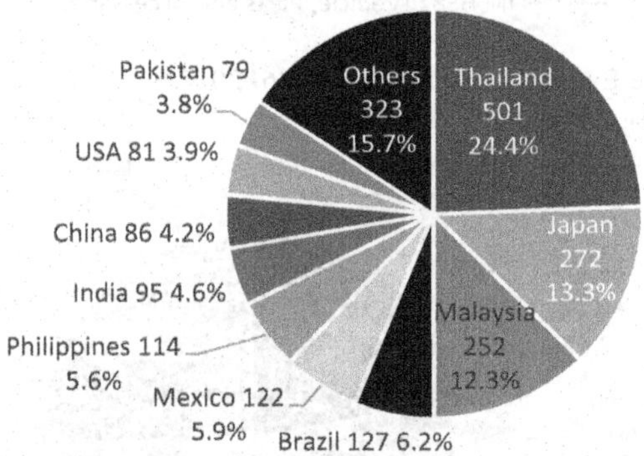

Figure 6.8 HS8708 (Parts and Accessories of Motor Vehicles), Top Ten Export Destinations of Indonesia, 2017.
Source: Global Trade Atlas (database).
Note: US$ Million (shown above the percentages).

of vehicles, the export increased rapidly by 13-fold, from merely 17,805 units in 2005 to 231,169 units in 2017 (see Figure 6.1). The export of CBUs (completely built-up vehicles) is mainly conducted by two firms: Toyota and Daihatsu. Toyota exported three models (Fortuner, Innova, and Vios), totalling 116,971 units. Daihatsu exported three models under Toyota's OEM: Avanza and Wigo for the Philippines, and Town Ace to Japan, totalling 80,667 units in 2017 (JETRO 2018a: 21).

With regard to components, the export of HS8708 increased 38-fold, from US$59 million in 1996 to over US$2 billion in 2017 (see Figure 6.5). The largest export destination is Thailand (accounting for US$501 million), followed by Japan, Malaysia, Brazil, Mexico, and the Philippines (see Figure 6.8).

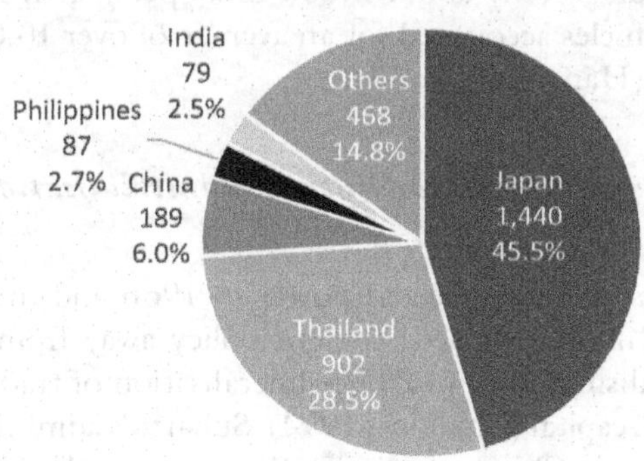

Figure 6.9 HS8708 (Parts and Accessories of Motor Vehicles), Top Five Import Sources in Indonesia, 2017.

Source: Global Trade Atlas (database).

Note: US$ Million (shown above the percentages).

More importantly, the import of HS8708 is much larger than its export, accounting for US$3.16 billion (see Figure 6.9). The import of components in Indonesia heavily depends on Japan and Thailand. The importance of Thailand, and to a lesser extent the Philippines, in these statistics shows how Indonesia has become integrated into an ASEAN automotive production network.

Development of the Indonesian automotive industry

Background: early stages (1928–1968)

Indonesia has the longest history of automotive production in Southeast Asia. The first automotive assembly plant was established by GM, with a production capacity of 6,000 vehicles a year in 1928. In GM's overseas operations, its Indonesian assembly plant was established as the third plant in Asia, after Japan and India, and earlier than Mexico and Brazil (Sato 1992). However, this was automotive assembly in a rather notional sense. Automobiles were imported in two-unit packs, mainly because this was cheaper than shipping CBU vehicles. It was not until after the Second World War that CKD (completely knocked down) kits were imported (Witoelar 1983: 18).

After independence in 1949, Indonesia's development policies emphasised two features: (1) development of a strong indigenous (*pribumi*) business class and (2) economic development through industrialisation, which strongly influenced the automotive industry (Chalmers 1994: 18). The GM plant was nationalised and merged into the state-owned Gaya Motors under the Sukarno administration's Benteng programme, which aimed to create a national automotive industry (Hale 2001). GM withdrew from Indonesia in 1954 (Sato 1992). Although automotive industrialisation commenced early in Indonesia, the Indonesian automotive industry failed to develop throughout the 1960s, with an average rate of vehicle production of only about 2,000 units per year from 1963 to 1968, while imports of vehicles accounted for an average of over 10,000 units per year in the same period (Hansen 1971: 38).

Localisation through import-substituting industrialisation (1969–1992)

When Major-General Suharto seized power in 1966 and introduced his New Order, he shifted Indonesia's development policy away from Sukarno's vision of Indonesian socialism and towards the liberalisation of trade and investment, linking with foreign capital (Chalmers 1994). Suharto's administration was heavily dependent on ethnic Chinese business. For instance, the Indonesian Chinese Liem group, built on clove and flour milling supply to the military, linking to Suharto, diversified its business to the assembly of Japanese vehicles (the current Indomobil group). Similarly, the Astra group entered the automotive assembly business in 1968 under the New Order, taking over Gaya Motors (the former GM plant), which had become a financial burden for the government at that time, and later linked up with Japanese automotive producers including Toyota (Doner 1991: 128).

The Indonesian government imposed an array of localisation policies in the automotive sector under import-substituting industrialisation (ISI) in order to upgrade the local industrial structure. This was done in two stages. The first stage aimed to shift from the importation of CBU vehicles towards local assembly, gradually banning the import of CBUs progressively over different regions of Indonesia, from the period starting 1969 until a complete all-country ban was enforced by 1974 (Sato 1992: 340–341). In the second stage, the Indonesian government aimed to achieve higher local content ratios (localisation of components production) in the assembly of vehicles by introducing a mandatory deletion programme (MDP) for CVs, replacing imported components with locally produced ones in 1976 (Degree No. 307). Initially, paint, tyres, and batteries were targeted in 1977. The MDP was later extended to higher value-added components including engines, transmissions, brakes, and axles, and covering a wider range of components by 1984 (Aswicahyono *et al.* 2000: 215). However, the plan was temporary frozen due to low market demand caused by the second oil shock in 1978, and it was revised somewhat in 1979 (Doner 1991: 152). During this period, Indonesian automotive production increased from only 75,570 units in 1976, to 108,667 units in 1978, but then decreased to 98,555 units in 1979 (see Figure 6.1).

The localisation policy for components production resulted in an interesting split in the automotive industry in the 1980s. Local business groups linked with Japanese automotive producers came gradually to support the policy, because these groups had invested heavily on components production to meet the LC requirements. By contrast, local business groups linked to US and European producers faced difficulty in meeting the requirements (Chalmers 1994). Of the eight automotive producers establishing plants for engine production by 1990, seven were Japanese assemblers (Toyota, Mitsubishi, Daihatsu, Suzuki, Isuzu, Hino, and Honda) and only one firm, Mercedes-Benz, was from Europe (Inoue 1990: 72–73). During this period, automotive production hovered around 200,000 units. It accounted for 212,674 units in 1981, decreased to 156,192 units in 1988, and then increased to 271,712 units in 1990 (see Figure 6.1).

New protectionist policy, the national car, and the WTO dispute (1993–1998)

Indonesia's automotive policies in the 1990s became controversial, containing various elements contrary to the rules of the WTO, newly established in 1995. These included (1) a new incentive system providing incentives according to the degree of localisation, and (2) a national car plan supported by highly discriminatory measures. In June 1993, the Indonesian government introduced a new automotive policy deregulation package consisting of (1) ending the ban of import of CBU vehicles and (2) reducing tariffs and luxury tax on imported components based on types of vehicle and local content level. The policy aimed to encourage the localisation of automotive production by allowing assemblers to access more favourable tax rates according to their localisation efforts in Indonesia. The old MDP system forced assemblers to localise their production without much choice in the matter, while the new incentive system enabled assemblers to select parts to be localised according to their own firm strategy. In this regard, it was a more market-oriented system, though still in fact heavily regulated (Aswicahyono *et al.* 2000).

While the previously mentioned measures contradicted the spirit rather than the letter of WTO rules, in 1996, the Indonesian government announced a very ambitious – and in WTO terms much more contentious – automotive development plan. This was the *Program Mobil Nasional*, which aimed to establish the production of a national car (like Malaysia's national car, Proton). The scheme allowed the national producer access to a three-year exemption of import duty and luxury taxes, which were estimated at 40% of vehicle costs, if they would meet the following three criteria: (1) be 100% national capital, (2) use an original brand, and (3) and have a local content ratio of 60% by the end of a three-year time period[5] (Nomura 1996: 81). In February 1996, President Suharto designated the *Timor Putra National* (TPN) company, owned by his son, Hutomo Mandala Putra (widely known as Tommy), as the sole producer of the national car, *Timor* (Hale 2001). Subsequently, in order to access international technology and marketing skills, and despite the 100% national capital stipulation, PT. Kia-Timor Motors (KTM) was established jointly by Kia Motors from Korea, TPN, and Indauda (which was also local capital), holding 30%, 35%, and 35% of the equity, respectively (Fourin 1996: 80). Kia used the name *Timor* for the brand of car but did not participate in the equity in TPN. Timor was treated as the Indonesian national car by the Indonesian government (Nomura 1996).

Although KTM targeted 50,000 units of production in 1997 and 100,000 units in 1998, the Indonesian government allowed KTM to import Kia's CBU vehicles under Timor's brand name for one year, exporting Indonesian workers and Indonesian components to Kia in Korea (Fourin 1999: 94–95). Indeed, 39,715 vehicles were imported from Kia in Korea over the period June 1996 to July 1997, and sold under special provisions of import duty and luxury taxes exemption (Hale 2001: 632). As a result of these exemptions, the price of the Timor S515 model (which was the same as Kia's Sephia model, a 4-door sedan with a 1500 cc engine) was almost half the price of Toyota's similar model, the Corolla (Nomura 2003: 47).[6]

In response to this, the EU, Japan, and the USA brought a case to the Dispute Settlement Panel in the WTO. In July 1998, the panel judged that the incentive system, introduced in 1993, violated the TRIMs rule. The national car project also contravened the SCMs (the Agreement on Subsidies and Countervailing Measures) rule (ibid.: 54–55). The panel ordered the Indonesian government to abolish the incentive system by July 1999. Furthermore, the Indonesian government requested TPN to repay the import tariff and luxury tax exemptions of US$326 million (Fourin 1999: 92). However, TPN did not have sufficient resources to repay and declared bankruptcy in March 2001.

In the 1990s, Indonesia's vehicle production reached over 300,000 units for the first time in 1994, and continued to increase until 1997 (with the first peak of 389,279 units of production). However, the production dramatically dropped to only 58,079 units in 1998 as a result of the AFC in 1997 (see Figure 6.1).

Under the post-WTO regime

The Liberalisation Era (1999–2012)

The Asian financial crisis, which hit Indonesia hard, resulted in some reform of the automotive industry. The industry became a target of structural adjustment required by the IMF,[7] and the Indonesian government was forced to introduce liberalisation policies, including a reduction of import tariffs, elimination of the incentive system, and an assurance of Indonesia's commitment to the WTO rules (Hale 2001, Nomura 2003). As a result, Indonesia, liberalising the industry in accordance with the WTO rules for the first time, issued the *1999 Automotive Policy Package*, which abolished the incentive system and introduced a new import duty system based on types, engine sizes, and weight of vehicles in July 1999 (see Table 6.1). As the tariffs on CBUs were consistently higher than on CKDs, the effective rate of protection (that is, protection on value added) on vehicle assembly was greater than the nominal tariffs on CBUs suggest.

Although vehicle production increased steadily in the post-liberalisation period, the Indonesian government could not implement strategic automotive development policies due to the political instability prior to the fall of Suharto in 1998. The first policy in the post-liberalisation period was related to the LC issue, since such LCs were low.[8] In order to achieve higher LC ratios, the Indonesian government introduced the innovative IKD (incompletely knocked down) system in 2006.[9] The government targeted subcomponents, which were

Table 6.1 Import Duty and Luxury Tax Rates in Indonesia, 1999–2016

			Import Duty (MFN)												*Luxury Tax*		
			CBU					*CKD*				*IKD*					
Category		*Remarks*	*1999*	*2006*	*2007*	*2010*	*2015*	*1999*	*2006*	*2008*	*2011*	*2007*	*2010*	*2011*	*1999*	*2004*	*2015*
PVs	Sedan	CC≤1.5 (G/D)	65	60	55	50	40	35	25	15	10	15	10	7.5	30	30	30
		1.5<CC≤3.0 (G)/2.5(D)	70	60	55	50	40	45	30	15	10	0	0	0	40	40	40
		CC>3.0(G) / 2.5 (D)	80	60	55	50	40	50	40	15	10	0	0	0	50	75	125
	LCGC	0.98≤CC≤1.2(G), CC≤1.5 (D)	–	–	–	–	–	–	–	–	–	–	–	–	–	–	0
	4x2	CC≤1.5 (G/D)	45	45	45	45	40	25	20	15	10	15	10	7.5	10	10	10
		1.5<CC≤ 2.5(G/D)	45	45	45	45	40	25	20	15	10	15	10	7.5	20	20	20
		2.5<CC≤ 3.0(G)	45	45	45	45	40	25	20	15	10	15	10	7.5	20	40	40
		CC>3.0(G) / 2.5 (D)	45	45	45	45	40	25	20	15	10	15	10	7.5	30	75	125
	4x4	CC≤1.5 (G/D)	45	45	45	45	40	25	20	15	10	0	0	0	30	30	30
		1.5<CC≤3.0 (G)/2.5(D)	45	45	45	45	40	25	20	15	10	0	0	0	40	40	40
		CC>3.0(G) / 2.5 (D)	45	45	45	45	40	25	20	15	10	0	0	0	50	75	125
CVs	Bus	GVW5–24t	40	40	40	40	40	25	20	15	10	5	5	0	10	10	0
		GVW>24t	5	10	10	10	10	0	5	5	5	5	5	0	10	10	0
	Pickup / Truck	GVW<5t	40	45	45	45	40	25	20	15	10	15	10	7.5	10	0	n.a
		GVW5–24t	40	40	40	40	40	25	20	15	10	5	5	0	10	0	n.a
		GVW>24t	5	10	10	10	10	0	5	5	5	5	5	0	10	0	n.a
	Double Cabin	GVW<5t	40	45	45	45	40	25	20	15	10	15	10	7.5	10	20	20

Source: Fourin (2002, 2004, 2008, and 2015) and GAIKINDO document.
Note: Unit (%); G (gasoline engine), D (diesel engine), n.a. (not available), GVW (gross vehicle weight), KD (incompletely knock down).

not produced locally in Indonesia, as IKD parts, by providing lower tariff rates than CKD parts. The IKD system aims to encourage imports of subcomponents rather than CKD parts as a whole, thus encouraging the assembly of CKD parts locally (e.g. importing engine parts and assembling engines locally, rather than importing complete engines). Thus, by effectively setting duty rates, the IKD system encouraged foreign assemblers and parts producers to transfer production knowledge and know-how through foreign investment into assembly technologies including tools and equipment. In short, within the 'policy space' still consistent with the WTO rules, the Indonesian government has targeted the upgrading of the industry from CBU import to CKD import for vehicle assembly, and then on to IKD import for local CKD assembly, which requires more capital in each industrial upgrading.

In the first half of 2000s, vehicle production gradually recovered from the AFC, reaching over 400,000 units in 2004 and the second peak of 500,710 units in 2005. However, vehicle production decreased sharply by 40% in 2006, due to increases in fuel prices (which doubled) and interest rates. After that, production recovered and developed rapidly, reaching over 600,000 units in 2008, over 700,00 units in 2010, over 870,000 in 2011, and, finally, over 1 million units in 2012 (see Figure 6.1).

New industrial policy: the low cost green car project (2013–present)

In 2009, the government announced a new auto industrialisation policy, which targeted the development of new categories of vehicle – small and environmentally friendly. There are several relevant issues. Firstly, as the size of the middle class in the country is growing in Indonesia, market demand has started to shift from motorcycles to cars.[10] Secondly, the government's fuel subsidy was becoming a significant problem. Indonesia, which used to be an oil exporter, has become an oil-importing country since 2003. A large proportion of the domestic fuel price is subsidised by the government.[11] In order to reduce the subsidy cost – which is politically difficult to do by directly cutting the subsidy – improvement in the fuel consumption of vehicles has become very important.[12] Thirdly, despite the incentives of the IKD system, the Indonesian automotive industry continued to have a weak local supporting industry.

As noted earlier in this chapter, and in response to these issues, the Indonesian government has targeted the development of small, affordable, economical, ecological PV production, the so-called Low Cost Green Car (LCGC). The project was expected to expand the market demand, create economies of scale, and thus reduce components costs and eventually the vehicle costs. The Indonesian government aimed to stimulate market demand by exempting the LCGCs from luxury tax (see Table 6.2). The LCGCs are affordable, with a price estimated at US$8,000–9,000. In parallel to this, the Indonesian government also aims to develop a low-carbon emission (LCE) programme by attracting investment in electric vehicles (EVs), hybrid electric vehicles (HEVs), and alternative-fuel cars such as biofuel and compressed natural gas (CNG). These

Table 6.2 LCGC and LCE Programmes in Indonesia

	LCGC Programme	*LCE Programme*
Year	August 2013	August 2013
Aim	(1) Expansion of the middle-class market (2) Industrial development of local contents (3) Reduction of fuel subsidy	Mitigation of global warming
Vehicle type	Passenger vehicle (except for sedans and station wagons) -Gasoline engine: 980 cc to 1200 cc -Diesel engine: up to 1500 cc	Sedan, Station Wagon, 4 × 2, 4 × 4, Double cabins and bus -advanced gasoline and diesel engine, flexible-fuels, compressed natural gas, liquefied gas, bio, hybrid, and electric vehicles
Mileage	20 km/L or more	20 km/L or more
Incentive (luxury tax exemption)	Exemption of luxury tax (normally 10%)	Mileage: 20–28 km/L – 25%, above 28 km/L – 50% of exemption of luxury tax (tax is imposed on 25–75% of sales prices) Electric vehicle: Exemption of luxury tax

Source: GIAMM (Interview, 20 February 2013) and Fourin (2017: 66).

plans were passed in the Parliament in February 2013, and finally approved by the president in May 2013.

Indonesia's new policies are somewhat similar to Thailand's 'Detroit of Asia' and 'Eco Car' projects, which have enabled Thailand to enjoy rapid auto industrialisation since 2000 (see Natsuda and Thoburn 2013 and 2014). Both countries use fiscal policy to target particular types of vehicles to be developed, and conform to the WTO rules. However, some differences can be identified with regard to Thailand. Firstly, Thai policies aimed not only to stimulate the market demand by reducing excise tax on particular types of vehicles, but also to help foreign investors by providing various special tax exemption incentives for automotive assemblers (which were also designed to cover their parts suppliers). By contrast, Indonesia did not offer special incentives in the automotive sector, which was not even included in its five strategic industries.[13] On this point, for instance, at a public seminar, the president of PT. Toyota Motor Manufacturing, Indonesia, strongly stressed the importance of the introduction of special incentives to encourage Tier-2 and 3 suppliers' investments.[14] Secondly, Thai policies are targeted at localising higher value-added components such as engine parts by imposing local production requirements in exchange for tax incentives. By contrast, Indonesia does not directly target localisation activities, although the IKD system is a move in this direction. Thai policies are more systematically organised to attract FDI and link with upgrading of local production activities. Furthermore, the Board of Investment (BOI) of Thailand established a special unit for industrial linkage, the 'Unit for Industrial Linkage Development (BUILD)', coordinating industrial linkage between assemblers and local industry.[15] By contrast, in Indonesia, executive officers of the auto parts industry pointed to the lack of effective government policy in localisation, human resource development, and technology transfer within the country.[16]

Although incentives in Indonesia are not as attractive as those in Thailand, five Japanese automotive producers in Indonesia (Toyota, Daihatsu, Nissan, Suzuki, and Honda) commenced LCGC projects. For instance, Toyota in association with Daihatsu announced their first LCGC models in September 2012, even before the official approval of the project. Toyota's Agya started to be produced by Daihatsu under an OEM arrangement in 2013. In addition, Daihatsu commenced the production of the same model as 'Ayla' under the Daihatsu brand. The Agya-Ayla model was designed for Indonesia's local road conditions and new market needs, which aimed to introduce small city vehicles and shift from motorcycles to PVs.[17] Nissan also launched its strategic model/brand in emerging economies – 'Datsun' – which was produced only in Russia, India, and Indonesia in 2014. LCGCs have expanded from small PVs to MPVs. In 2017, five vehicle producers introduced eight LCGC models in Indonesia, accounting for 249,834 units of production and 234,554 units of sales in Indonesia (Fourin 2017: 67, JETRO 2018a: 22).

The LCGC programme has attracted FDI not only from assemblers but also from their parts suppliers. Prior to the LCGC programme, automotive FDI jumped to 94 projects in 2011, worth US$637 million, and to 103 projects, worth US$1,465 million in 2012 (see Figure 6.10). Of these figures, parts and accessories investments accounted for 66.9% and 79.2% in value of the total

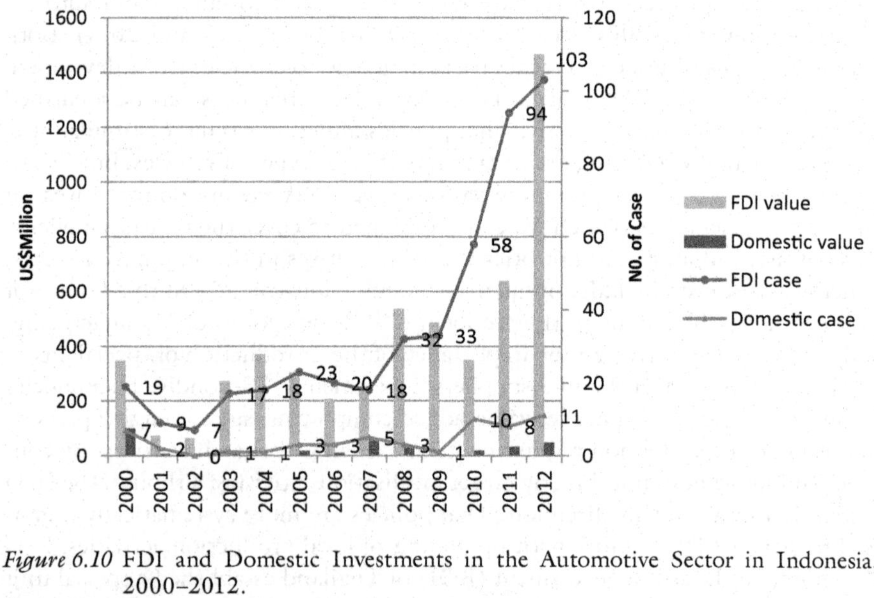

Figure 6.10 FDI and Domestic Investments in the Automotive Sector in Indonesia, 2000–2012.

Source: Data Supplied by BKPM in 2013.

Note: Realisation basis.

investments of the automotive sector in 2011 and 2012, respectively. With regards to the origins of FDI, Japan accounted for the bulk – 65.2% in terms of projects (227 projects), and 74.4% (US$2,901 million) in terms of the total value of FDI over the period 2000–2011.

The LCGC programme has brought some positive influences on the Indonesian automotive industry. Firstly, it increased the output of vehicles in Indonesia by over 200,000 units. Indonesian vehicle production reached over 1.2 million units in 2013, and nearly 1.3 million units in 2014 (see Figure 6.1). Secondly, the automotive parts industry has been growing through LCGC production. As a result of massive investments from automotive parts firms, localisation of the automotive industry has been accelerating. Indeed, the LC ratio of LCGCs seems to be higher than that of traditional models in Indonesia. The LC ratio of LCGCs is estimated at 80–95% (Fourin 2017: 64) in comparison with 71–76% in the case of the most popular vehicle models of Toyota in Indonesia (GAIKINDO 2010: 26–27). In this context, localisation of the automotive industry has been encouraged by the programme. Thirdly, Indonesia's export capacity has been also expanded by the programme. To be precise, Daihatsu's LCGC, Ayla (or the Agya model in the case of Toyota), started to be exported to the Philippines as the Wigo model, with sales of 18,430 units under Toyota's OEM in 2016 (Fourin 2017: 110, JETRO 2018a: 21). On the other hand, the programme influenced non-LCGC assemblers negatively. For instance, Ford entirely withdrew from the Indonesian market (both in terms of its production and its sales operations) in 2015, because it failed to target its model according to Indonesian market demands. By the same token, GM also withdrew from Indonesia in the same year (see Chapter 3). Thus, although the LCGC programme has been, to some extent, successful for the Indonesian automotive industry, there is no significant impact on the low-carbon emission programme. It can be explained by the immaturity of technological capability and industrial policy in the Indonesian automotive industry. In comparison with Thailand, the Indonesian automotive industry seems to lack a comprehensive industrial policy, particularly soft industrial policy, for upgrading local technological capability; however, compared to the Philippines, Indonesia's automotive policy has been more effective (Thoburn and Natsuda 2018)

Challenges to the Indonesian automotive industry

The role of local parts suppliers

Although the Indonesian automotive industry is growing, there are still several reasons for concern. Firstly, in comparison with the trend of FDI, domestic investment in the automotive and parts industries has been extremely low (see Figure 6.10). For example, local investment accounted for merely 11 projects, worth US$48.6 million (an amount equivalent to only 3.3% of automotive FDI), in 2012. Within the automotive GVC, despite there being some possible transfers of technology, especially by Japanese firms, the upgrading opportunities of local parts-supplying firms may be hindered by competition from incoming foreign firms, especially in terms of moving to higher tiers in the subcontracting system. This issue is confirmed by our interviews with executive officers of the local parts industry in Indonesia. It is also a problem that was apparent back in the 1970s when Witoela's study (1983) noted that much of the manufacture of 'original equipment' auto components had been captured by local conglomerates linked to foreign assemblers, leaving indigenous suppliers only the replacement market. It is also pointed out in a more recent study by Aswicahyono and Kartika (2010: 69–70) that some unpublicised requirements in Japanese automotive production networks forced some local Indonesian parts suppliers to shift to after-market activities.

Our interviews with major Japanese automotive assemblers in Indonesia found that each automotive producer has approximately 100 Tier-1 suppliers in Indonesia: Nissan has 100 Tier-1 suppliers (most of them Japanese JVs), Toyota has 80 Tier-1 suppliers (approximately 80% were Japanese JVs and 20% were local firms), and Mitsubishi (P.T. Krama Yudha Tiga Motors) has 125 Tier-1 suppliers (60% Japanese JVs and 40% local firms, but purely local firms were estimated at 10–15%). In the case of neighbouring Thailand, although such a strong tendency towards foreign domination exists, there are some indigenous suppliers which have been growing globally (or regionally) at the same time. For instance, the parts-maker Thai Summit started making foreign investments in Malaysia, Vietnam, Indonesia, China, and India, to supply its components to Japanese as well as other assemblers (Fourin 2012: 220–221).

Clusters and the absence of soft industrial policy

As mentioned earlier, the Indonesian automotive industry lacks effective soft industrial policy in relation to localisation, human resource development, and technology transfer within the country.[18] In Indonesia, the cluster networks are not fully supported by the government, depending instead on the actions of Japanese automotive MNCs (Irawati 2010 and 2012). In the Indonesian automotive clusters, two type of linkages – vertical and horizontal – can be identified. The former is characterised by a Japanese hierarchical (*keiretsu*) network between assemblers and Tier-1 suppliers and between Tier-1 and Tiers-2 and 3 suppliers. The latter is based on links between suppliers and, more importantly, between university and industry (see Aminullah and Adnan 2012, Irawati 2012, Purwaningrum *et al.* 2012). In terms of vertical linkages, Japanese automotive firms generate employment and business opportunities for the local automotive components industry in Indonesia. More importantly, from the perspective of industrial upgrading in the GVC, Japanese automotive assemblers provide HR development and knowledge transfer through their supplier development programmes. While the horizontal linkages between universities and industry are extremely limited in Indonesia (Purwanigrum *et al.* 2012), according to Aminullah and Adnan (2012), sources of knowledge in process innovation, organisational innovation, and management innovation typically come from internal sources, while production innovation comes from external sources such as firm competition and transfer of product technology from assemblers to suppliers. In addition, universities and public research institutions (PRIs) play an important role in external sources of innovation.

Although the Indonesian government facilitates innovation activities among PRIs, industry, and universities, with the provision of grants to finance R&D, the role of universities and PRIs is extremely limited as external resources of innovation, due to the absence of effective government soft industrial policy. In terms of the relationship between the automotive industry and universities, the industry assists universities with the provision of equipment and machinery used in university laboratories only as part of corporate social responsibility (CSR). With regard to innovation activities, there is no relationship between PRIs and automotive firms in Indonesia (ibid.). In the view of Irawati and Charles (2010), although vertical knowledge linkages have been effective for upgrading the Indonesian automotive industry, it is not known if the linkages will continue to be effective for the next stage of development in the Indonesian automotive industry, because it is doubtful that Japanese automotive MNCs will want to encourage local Indonesian firms to upgrade their position in production networks to become independent automotive firms. In this context, the role of horizontal knowledge networks will be increasingly important for the Indonesian automotive industry in the future.

Conclusions

The Indonesian automotive industry has been growing rapidly and seems to have taken off in recent years as the country's per capita incomes have risen. Until the late 1990s, the development of the industry was slow. At that time, capital accumulation in the industry was inhibited by political-bureaucratic problems. The Indonesian government introduced an array of localisation requirement policies in order to upgrade the local industrial structure, but these policies were not strongly effective. After the liberalisation forced by the IMF and the WTO, the Indonesian automotive industry has developed steadily, finally producing over a million vehicles in 2012. However, issues such as increased political stability may well have been more important drivers of expansion than simple liberalisation or particular policies, though such policies have become more influential as the investment climate has improved and become 'good enough', and the impact of policies on the attraction of automotive FDI from Japan has been especially important. The growth trend is expected to continue with future domestic market growth – which assemblers seem to regard as at least as important as policies, provided policies are 'good enough' – and also partly due to Indonesia's new auto industrial policy in the form of the LCGC project. The LCGC development seems to be strongly supported by the Japanese vehicle assemblers.

In terms of policies, leaving aside for the moment Indonesia's very brief and abortive attempt to set up production of a national car in the 1990s, there are clear comparisons with Malaysia. Malaysia's attempts to aid national car production, particularly that of Proton, have greatly skewed policy away from the promotion of other automotive activities. This has had a strong negative effect on the perception of Japanese automotive investment whose decisions have been to do not much more than servicing the already well-filled Malaysian domestic market (Natsuda *et al.* 2013, Otsuka and Natsuda 2016, Segawa *et al.* 2014). In the light of the problems Malaysia has faced in keeping its national car, Proton – and the network of indigenous suppliers to Proton – in business, Indonesia's failure with its national car appears as a blessing in disguise,[19] freeing the country to focus on the foreign-based automotive development that also has characterised Thailand.

Indeed, the policies followed by Indonesia have been notably similar, in many respects, to those of Thailand. Both countries banned the import of complete vehicles (CBUs) for long periods – from 1978 to 1991 in Thailand in the case of passenger cars, and from 1974 to 1993 in Indonesia. Both countries used heavy protection by tariffs on CBUs after the bans were lifted: around 50 to 70% in Thailand from the mid-1990s onwards (Natsuda and Thoburn 2013), and broadly similar levels in Indonesia over the same period (Table 6.1).[20] Both countries imposed lower, but generally not negligible, tariffs on CKDs, thus raising the effective rate of tariff protection on CBUs beyond the nominal rate. Both countries used local content requirements and mandatory deletion policies to raise local content prior to their prohibition by the WTO in the 2000s.

Both countries undertook a degree of trade liberalisation in the 1990s. Indonesia's policies to enhance its motor industry came later than Thailand's policies, mainly after the fall of Suharto in 1998. Both countries removed explicit local content requirements in the 2000s under WTO-TRIMs. Thailand skilfully used excise duty provisions to encourage its *product champions* – first the pick-up truck, then the Eco-car (Natsuda and Thoburn 2013 and 2014). Indonesia, though, has also gained from its focus on MPVs and on light commercial vehicles for private use whose economies of scale are less than those of sedans. Indonesia is encouraging investment in its LCGCs by exempting it from luxury tax, but not, and importantly as we have indicated, direct investment incentives as in Thailand (Natsuda and Thoburn 2014).

It is sometimes argued that Indonesia suffers from shortages of human capital and from other supply-side constraints (Basri 2012: 40) and that it has had a high-cost economy, for example, in the cost of industrial real estate compared to Thailand (Witoelar 1983: 55). Furthermore, lack of effective soft industrial policy such as human resource development is a bottleneck for the economy (Aminullah and Adnan 2012). While this helps explain the slow development of an indigenous sector of local component manufactures in Indonesia compared to Thailand, it needs to be emphasised that Thailand's success in the motor industry is overwhelmingly one of attracting inward direct investment, principally from Japan, rather than the development of indigenous firms. However, some indigenous suppliers of components have developed. Although Thailand's extensive components industry also has a heavy foreign presence, 23% of Tier-1 firms are purely local capital and an additional 19% of firms are local-majority, or

50/50 local/foreign capital firms including some local capital global automotive suppliers (see Chapters 3 and 5).

We have chronicled not only the recent rapid rises in Indonesian vehicle output but also the rapid rise in FDI in further production capacity, particularly in auto components and particularly from Japan. The expansion of the assemblers' foreign suppliers in Indonesia offers scope for local producers to upgrade to some extent, though simultaneously closing much of the top tier of parts production to them. Major Japanese motor manufacturers we have interviewed appear optimistic about Indonesia's potential as a producer. The main recent driver of the automotive industrialisation in Indonesia derives from its market potential – the largest population in Southeast Asia combined with growing income per capita – and its steady economic growth rate. It successfully enables Indonesia to attract investments in the automotive sector without providing more attractive incentives. After having been frustrated in the past by WTO rules in relation to developing its national car, it has been able to find enough policy space to foster its LCGC project without violating WTO rules; however, further help towards local suppliers might require more ingenuity beyond the already useful IKD system. Indonesia's strategic geographical position, which offers direct export possibilities to Australia and the Middle East, could well be one of the drivers in the future.[21]

Notes

1 At the start of Suharto's New Order in 1966, Hill (2000: 155) notes that after the depredations of the previous Sukarno years, Indonesia was initially one of the least industrialised among the world's *large* developing countries. Later in the post-Sukarno era, under President Suharto, industrialisation attempts enjoyed considerably more success, although they included some unsuccessful tries in the 1980s, to leapfrog into high-technology sectors like aircraft (Tadjoeddin and Chowdhury 2019). The 1980s and early 1990s also saw the successful development of light manufacturing exports (Thoburn 2001), but this has slowed as wages have risen (Basri 2012: 41).

2 Interview, 20 February 2013.

3 With 95% of capital from Toyota Motor and 5% from Astra International in 2013 (Interview, 25 February 2013).

4 These are 2018 figures. In the same year, Thailand imported only 7% of its total wiring harness imports from Indonesia, but nearly 27% from the Philippines (followed very closely by those from Cambodia, and then Vietnam). Thailand's own wiring harness exports were equivalent to little more than half of those of Indonesia (and less than a third of those of the Philippines). Thailand, in any case, was only a very minor net exporter of wiring harnesses (its imports were equivalent in value to three-quarters of its exports). Figures from https://comtrade.un.org/db/ [accessed on 29 January 2020].

5 To achieve LC of 20% in the end of first year, 40% in the end of the second year, and 60% in the end of the third year.

6 The sales price of S515 was 37.75 million Indonesian rupiah (IDR) in comparison with the Corolla, priced at IDR 76.35 million (Nomura 2003: 43).

7 Basri (2012: 38) notes that the IMF package also captured most of the World Bank agenda for trade deregulation.

8 LC ratios in Indonesia are based on the calculation of the total value of four types of CKD parts (engines, transmissions, axles, and chassis and bodies).

9 Information from interviews with GAIKINDO (on 27 February 2013) and Ministry of Industry, Jakarta (on 5 March 2013).

10 For instance, as of 2012, a total of 35 million motorcycle users were expected to shift to cars in the future (Presentation document of BKPM in March 2012).

11 According to JETRO in Jakarta, the oil price after the subsidy accounted for IDR 4,500 per litre in comparison with a pre-subsidised price of IDR 9,800 in February 2013, a 54% subsidy by the Indonesian government (Interview, 22 February 2013).

12 The fuel subsidy also became one of the most important policies and political campaigns before the national election in 2019. See https://asia.nikkei.com/Politics/Indonesia-s-Widodo-backtracks-on-fuel-aid-as-elections-near [accessed on 2 February 2019].

13 Five industries are eligible for tax holidays (Interview with BKPM, Investment Coordinating Board, 20 February 2013).

14 JETRO seminar in Jakarta on 4 March 2013.

15 Interview with the Director of BUILD on 4 September 2012.

16 Interview, 20 February 2013.

17 Interview with the president of PT. Toyota Motor Manufacturing Indonesia on 4 March 2013.

18 Interview, 20 February 2013.

19 However, there were some press reports in the mid-2010s that Indonesia's then new president might like to try again (Natsuda *et al.* 2015b). The idea of producing an Indonesian national car (*mobnas*) still does not seem to have died totally. The *Jakarta Post* (25 March 2019) carried an article which expressed scepticism about the idea of *mobnas*, thinking that the market was already crowded and that it would be suicidal for Indonesia to try to introduce a new model to compete against established foreign-brand vehicles. This would be especially so if the vehicle were given preferences over foreign brand vehicles, and especially in a situation where electric vehicles may eventually replace petrol (gasoline) ones. Interesting, Indonesian efforts towards a national car are compared unfavourably to the activities of the Vingroup's attempt to produce Vietnam's first national brand car (see our Chapter 9 on the VinFast motor company), see https://www.thejakartapost.com/academia/2019/03/25/car-making-is-not-for-everyone.html [accessed on 29 January 2020].

20 On non-AFTA imports. Import duties were reduced to between zero and 5% on imports from AFTA members from 2003 to 2004.

21 Interview with a major Japanese motor assembler in Indonesia on 7 March 2013.

7 Malaysia

Introduction

During the 1960s and 1970s, many developing countries established automotive assembly industries as part of import-substituting industrialisation (ISI) programmes, offering heavy protection against imports in order to attract inward foreign investment and to facilitate the establishment of domestic industries supplying components. As moves towards trade liberalisation gathered pace in the 1990s under the influence of the 'Washington consensus' set of ultra-free-market economic policies, these industries have been making a transition to an environment of intense international competition. In the automotive industry, the most that many developing countries can expect is to have major multinational assemblers use their country as an export base for particular models, or as a source of regional supply for particular components.

Malaysia, in contrast, has had different ambitions. The realisation of its dream of producing a national car has been a source of pride – so much so that the first national car, the Proton,[1] found a place of honour on the back of the Malaysian 100 ringgit (RM) note. To date, Malaysia is the only country in Southeast Asia where national automotive producers account for high shares of domestic sales (approximately 48% in 2016), having displaced the previously dominant multinational automotive producers. This is partly because the Malaysian government has been protecting its domestic automotive market by introducing various hard industrial policies.

With the intensification of globalisation under the World Trade Organization (WTO), the signing of AFTA and later the AEC agreements, and a number of bilateral free trade agreements, the Malaysian government has in recent years been facing increasingly strong pressure to liberalise its automotive industry (Alavi and Hasan 2001, Natsuda *et al.* 2013, Rasiah 2005, Segawa *et al.* 2014). The WTO's Trade-related Investment Measures (TRIMs) and also its Subsidies and Countervailing Measure (SCMs) requirements have been of some importance in limiting the developing countries' policies towards the automotive industries since 2000 (Natsuda and Thoburn 2014). In the case of Malaysia, the government used TRIMs-unfriendly policies such as local content requirements (LCRs), which are no longer admissible. This chapter examines the development of the Malaysian automotive industry by exploring Malaysia's automotive industrial policy in some depth. The next section gives an overview of the Malaysian automotive industry. The following section investigates Malaysian automotive development since 1960, and policies over this period. Then a further section examines challenges to the Malaysian automotive industry in the liberalisation era. The last section concludes.

Overview of the Malaysian automotive industry

Debates on automotive industrialisation in Malaysia

Malaysian industrialisation was initiated alongside the country's New Economic Policy (NEP) in 1971, which resulted from the inter-ethnic conflict of 1969 (Segawa *et al.* 2014). The NEP aimed to alleviate poverty, redistribute wealth within the country, and eliminate the identification of 'race' (in Malaysian parlance) with economic function. The Malaysian government targeted the development of the manufacturing sector by forming links with local *bumiputra* (indigenous people, mainly Malays) under the NEP in order to improve their economic situation (Lall 1995, Rasiah and Shari 2001). From the 1980s in particular, the Malaysian government began actively diversifying into heavy industries such as steel, motorcycle, and automotive, along with strong state intervention, establishing various state-owned joint venture enterprises between the Heavy Industry Corporation of Malaysia (HICOM) and multinational corporations (Anazawa 2006, Lall 1995). The automotive industry in Malaysia has been developed as an archetypal driver of such a heavy industrialisation. The Malaysian government has promoted the development of local automotive assemblers and their supporting industry and is the first and only country in Southeast Asia (and among other Islamic nations) to produce national cars (Rosli 2006). The Malaysian automotive industry has been very politicised. Proton was developed in line with NEP in order to enhance the economic position of *bumiputra* over a 30-year period (Anazawa 2006, Segawa *et al.* 2014, Tham 2004, Torii 1991a). On the one hand, the Malaysian government's intervention helped to develop local automotive assemblers and the associated components industry, particularly *bumiputra* suppliers. On the other hand, state protection effectively reduced competitive pressure on local producers (Yoshimatsu 2000). For instance, Rasiah's empirical study (2009) suggested that Malaysia's industrial policy towards automotive parts companies had not been effective in upgrading their technological capabilities due to the lack of external competition. Rosli and Kari's study (2008) also indicated that even among Proton's vendors, local suppliers performed worse than foreign suppliers. Wad and Govindaraju (2011) argued that the Malaysian automotive industry failed in the areas of industrial upgrading and international competitiveness due to low technological and marketing capability. Abdulsomad (1999) stressed that the Malaysian government has been handicapped by having to develop the National Car Project (NCP) within the constraints of its *bumiputra* policy. More recently, Otsuka and Natsuda (2016) empirically showed that

Malaysian industrial policies – to protect the national car producers from international competition and to favour bumiputra firms – seem to have an adverse impact on productivity in the industry. Natsuda and Thoburn (2014) also revealed that the Malaysian automotive industry, which still has various direct and indirect state interventions flavoured with strong industrial nationalism, has been facing serious challenges in response to liberalisation pressures from the WTO, and under AFTA and the AEC. Doner and Wad (2014) have shown how the pro-Proton coalition has weakened due to a reluctance to bail out government-linked enterprises in the context of regional trade liberalisation.

Production, sales, and structure of the Malaysian automotive industry

Among the ASEAN countries, Malaysia is the third largest vehicle producer, producing 564,800 units in 2018. It was ranked 23rd among the producers of the world, in comparison with Thailand (11th) and Indonesia (17th) in 2018 (OICA website). There are 27 assembly firms and approximately 641 suppliers (*vendors*). Of the 641 vendors, over 200 firms can be categorised as Tier-1 suppliers. It was estimated that 70% of suppliers were local or had local-majority ownership, while 30% were foreign or had foreign-majority ownership in 2012.[2] With regard to employment, 27 assemblers, 641 parts suppliers, and 53,001 firms of after service sectors have created over 700,000 jobs in the country (Fourin 2017: 89).

The volume of production reached its first peak of approximately 450,000 vehicles before the Asian financial crisis (AFC) in 1997, but it rapidly dropped to 164,125 in 1998. The production recovered by early 2000, reaching its second peak of 567,715 vehicles in 2010 and its highest peak of 614,664 in 2015 (see Figure 7.1). However, production decreased to below 500,000 vehicles in 2017, with a domestic sales slump caused by the introduction of GST (goods and services tax) in 2015, low price of oil, and depreciation of the ringgit (Fourin 2017: 84). The largest producer in the country, Perodua[3] – a partly nationally owned company (about which more later) – accounted for 237,037 vehicles and a 42% production share, ahead of Honda with 108,531 and 19.2%, and Proton with 54,103 vehicles and 9.6% production in 2018 (see Figure 7.2). Proton was the leading producer of the country for a long time. However, its production volume has continued to decline since 2010, and it has dropped to being the third producer in the country (see Figure 7.1).

In Malaysia, domestic sales have been larger than domestic production since 2007: in 2017, net imports accounted for 76,996 units (JETRO 2018a: 18–19). There are two important characteristics of the Malaysian automotive market. Firstly, demand for passenger vehicles (PVs), particularly sedans, is very high, accounting for approximately 89% (and 514,679 units out of 576,635 units) of the market share in 2017 (ibid.). This is very different from Malaysia's neighbouring countries of Thailand and Indonesia. In fact, Malaysia has the biggest sedan market in the ASEAN region. Secondly, Malaysian automotive demand

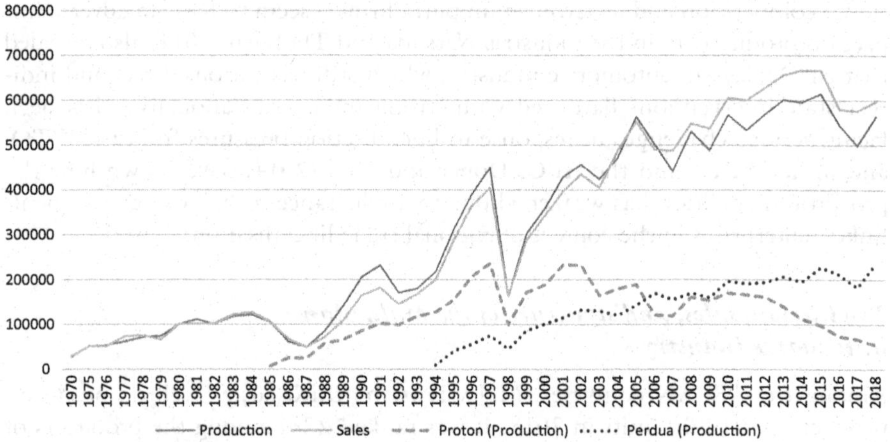

Figure 7.1 Production and Sales of Vehicles in Malaysia, 1970–2018.
Source: Adapted from Fourin (1991, 1996, 1999, 2002, 2004, 2011, 2017, and 2019).
Note: Number of vehicles.

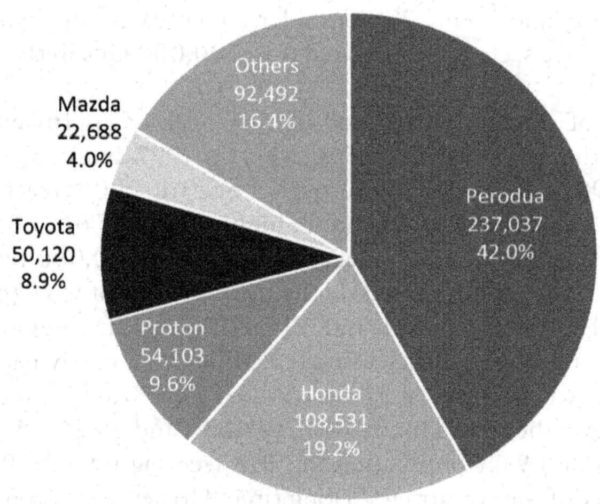

Figure 7.2 Production Volume and Share by Automotive Producer in Malaysia, 2018.
Source: Adapted from Fourin (2019: 56–57).
Note: Total 580,124 vehicles.

has reached an early stage of maturity. In 2015, Malaysia's motorisation ratio of 439 was much higher than that of Thailand (228), Singapore (145), and Indonesia (87) (see Table 3.1 in Chapter 3). In this regard, it is difficult to expect much further rapid growth in the automotive demand in the Malaysian market in the near future.

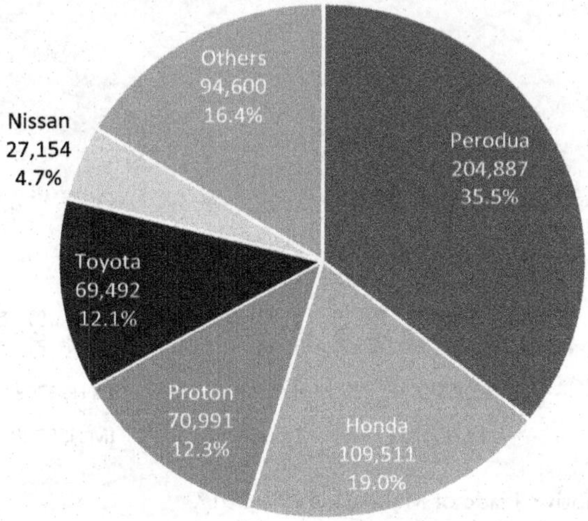

Figure 7.3 Sales and Market Share by Automotive Brand in Malaysia, 2017.
Source: Adapted from Fourin (2018: 329–330).
Note: Total 576,635 vehicles.

With regard to market share, Perodua accounted for 35.5%, followed by Honda with 19% and Proton with 12.3% in 2017 (see Figure 7.3). In addition, the other Malaysian national automotive firm Industri Otomotif Komersial Malaysia (Inokom) sold merely 4,100 units (0.7%) in 2017 (Fourin 2018: 329–330).

Malaysian automotive trade

Figure 7.4 shows Malaysia's trade trends in the period 1997–2017. Firstly, Malaysia has had automotive trade deficits since 1997. In HS87, Malaysian trade deficits accounted for US$3,762 million in 2017, with its export of US$1,717 million and import of US$5,479 million. Indeed, Malaysia's automotive exports are quite small: it exported only US$242 million worth of CBUs (HS8703) and US$783 million worth of auto parts (HS8708) in 2017.

With regard to PVs, the import position has not changed much since 1997. Indeed, import value (HS8703) in 1997 was slightly larger than in 2017. The largest source of imports is Germany (accounting for US$675 million), followed by Japan (US$568 million), Thailand, Indonesia, and the UK. Although the neighbouring countries of Thailand and Indonesia are ranked among the top five countries from which Malaysia imports, the share of these countries is relatively limited (accounting for only 8.7%) in import of PVs into Malaysia (see Figure 7.5). With regard to components, the import of HS8708 increased 6.5-fold from US$372 million in 1997 to over US$2,332 million in 2017 (see Figure 7.4). The largest source of imports is Thailand (US$827 million), followed by

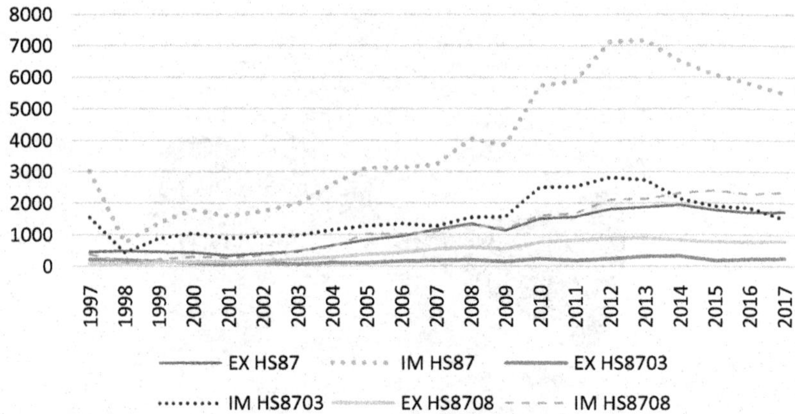

Figure 7.4 Automotive Trade of Malaysia, 1997–2017.
Source: Global Trade Atlas (database).
Note: US$ Million, EX (export), IM (import).

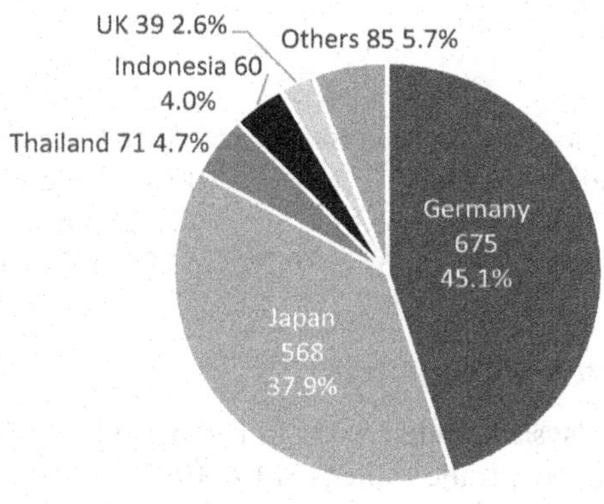

Figure 7.5 HS8703 (Motor Cars), Top Five Import Sources in Malaysia, 2017.
Source: Global Trade Atlas (database).
Note: US$ Million (shown above the percentages).

Japan, China, Germany, and Indonesia (see Figure 7.6). Thailand has been playing an important role as a parts supplier for the Malaysian automotive industry. Finally, with regard to trade in wiring harnesses (HS 854430) – an important (electrical) component not included under automotive components (HS 8708) – Malaysia is a very small player. Its exports are equivalent to only 11% of those of Thailand, 6% of those of Indonesia, and less than 4% of those of the Philippines. It has small net imports, with almost equal supplies coming from Germany, Thailand, and China.[4]

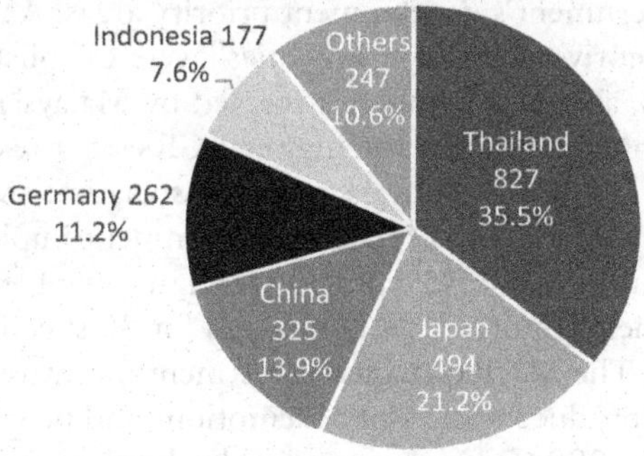

Figure 7.6 HS8708 (Parts and Accessories of Motor Vehicles), Top Five Import Sources in Malaysia, 2017.

Source: Global Trade Atlas (database).

Note: US$ Million (shown above the percentages).

Development of the Malaysian automotive industry

The development of the Malaysian automotive industry can be classified into three periods: import substitution (1967–1982), state-led development (1983–2003), and post-2000 WTO regime (2004–the present). We examine the historical development of the Malaysian automotive industry, based on these three periods, in more detail.

Import substitution period (1967–1982)

After Malaysia gained its independence from the UK in 1957, the Malaysian government introduced a policy to promote an integrated automotive industry under its import substitution programme. However, the Malaysian government needed to revise this policy when Singapore gained independence from Malaysia in 1965 (Jayasankaran 1993, Jomo 1994). In 1966, the government had begun to impose import duties on all completely built-up (CBU) vehicles; also, under the so-called 'Approved Permits (AP)' system (Torii 1991a), all distributors and dealers required import licenses. In 1967, the Malaysian government introduced its manufacturing licensing (ML) system and granted the first assembly licenses to six plants[5] in order to enhance the development of the domestic automotive components industry, which was hoped to facilitate overall industrial development through its multiplier effects (Abdulsomad 1999, Jayasankaran 1993). After the six companies received approval, the Malaysian government restricted the establishment of new assembly plants, except for Tan Chong Motor Assemblies in 1974, which received special permission due to its enhancement of local-owned assembly capacity. In order to promote *bumiputras'* participation in the automotive industry, the government shifted their approval criteria in 1976, basing it on (1) having a relatively high level of local indigenous capital and (2) building the plant in the government's development priority areas. As a consequence, an additional five automotive assembly companies[6] were established (Torii 1991b).

In the mid-1970s, six parts manufactures, led by Malaysian Sheet Glass, began to lobby government officials for higher LCRs; as a result, the Malaysian Automotive Component Parts Manufacturers Association (MACPMA) was established in 1978. In 1980, the Malaysian government implemented a mandatory deletion programme (MDP), requiring foreign assemblers to delete certain components from their imported CKD kits and for 30 specified components to be produced locally. The MDP provided investment incentives and tariff protection for component producers and duty exemptions and penalties for assemblers (Doner 1991, Tham 2004). Consequently, the local content levels increased from only 8% in 1979, to 18% in 1982, reaching 30% in 1986 (Jayasankaran 1993: 273–274).

Although the Malaysian government had been increasing the LC level since the 1970s, the automotive industry still contributed little to Malaysian industrialisation in the early 1980s (Jomo 1994). At the time, the Malaysian automotive industry exhibited a high cost structure. For instance, the cost of locally assembled CBUs was over 50% higher than imported ones. This high cost structure was the result of the failure of Japanese assemblers to reduce the price charged by local producers of parts deleted from CKD packs and also the result of extensive market fragmentation, with many models being assembled for a relatively small market (Doner 1991). Moreover, the Malaysian government failed to implement clear and concise long-range policies. On the one hand, the government tried to rationalise the industry, and on the other hand, the government tried to support *bumiputra* economic development by allowing an increase in assembly plants (Jayasankaran 1993). In the period from 1970 to the early 1980s, the total production of vehicles grew over threefold, from approximately 28,000 units in 1970 to over 100,000 units for the first time in 1980 (see Figure 7.1).

State-led development period (1983–2003)

In the early 1980s, the Malaysian government promoted a second stage of ISI with strong state intervention in order to further enhance *bumiputra* participation in heavy industries. The government founded the state-owned enterprise (SOE), Heavy Industry Corporation of Malaysia (HICOM) in 1980, and established various joint venture SOEs between HICOM and foreign capital that included the steel, motorcycle, and automotive sectors (Anazawa 2006).

In October 1982, Prime Minister Mahathir announced the first National Car Project under HICOM in the automotive sector. In May of the following year, Proton was established as a joint venture between HICOM (with 70% of initial capital of RM 150 billion) and Mitsubishi Motors and Mitsubishi Corporation (with 15% stake each); it planned to produce the Malaysian-made vehicle known as the 'Saga' for the domestic market in 1985 (Jomo 1994, Tham 2004).[7] The NCP was expected not only to rationalise the automotive industry through the introduction of a national car but also to foster supporting industries; encourage the upgrading of technology and technical skills; supply an affordable, original automobile in the market; and enhance *bumiputra* participation in the industry (Anazawa 2006, Jomo 1993, Torii 1991a). Moreover, as the production of a vehicle is considered to require 20,000–30,000 components, this could provide opportunities to *bumiputra* entrepreneurs as suppliers to the industry.

The production of Proton's Saga commenced with an output capacity of 8,000 vehicles a year in July 1985, with a target to produce 84,400 in 1988, and eventually 120,000 by 1995. According to the Industrial Master Plan (IMP) (1986–1995), the market share of Saga was expected to increase from 6.4% in 1985 to 50.3% in 1987 (Torii 1991b: 279–280). However, when production commenced, Proton suffered due to the collapse of local demand as a result of the worst economic recession in 1985 and 1986 since Independence, and also due to the higher prices of imported components from Japan as a result of the appreciation of the yen following the Plaza Accord in 1985 (Abdulsomad 1999). Consequently, the total sales of vehicles in Malaysia dropped from 127,090 in 1984 to 106,988 in 1985 (see Figure 7.1). This trend had become even worse by 1987, with just 54,340 vehicles sold, the lowest figure since 1970 (Fourin 1994: 186). Similarly, the total domestic sales of Proton was 7,047 vehicles (a 6.5% market share) in 1985, 23,890 (30.3%) in 1986, and 24,970 (44.2%) in 1987 (Fourin 1991: 178). As a result, Proton recorded continuous losses from 1985 until 1988, but in 1989, it eventually achieved for the first time a pre-tax profit of RM 32.6 million on a turnover of RM 820 million (Abdulsomad 1999: 279). After this, Proton became the most popular vehicle in Malaysia, accounting for a market share around 50% until 2002. Furthermore, Proton commenced its first export to Bangladesh in 1986, and later to diversified markets including the UK, which was the largest, accounting for 21,000 vehicles and 23% of total sales in 1994 (ibid.).

In the 1990s, the Malaysian government actively pursued its state-led automotive development policies by diversifying segments of the industry. In 1991, Prime Minister Mahathir revealed a second NCP for small cars. Under this policy, Perodua was established as a joint venture between Toyota's affiliated Daihatsu Motors and Malaysian firms in 1993,[8] and it commenced the production of its 'Kancil' model (which was based on Daihatsu's Mira) in 1994, with an engine capacity of 660 cc. There was an initial concern to develop a new market segment for small cars, which had never existed in Malaysia before. However, Perodua was able to utilise Proton's vendor networks, which enabled both firms to reduce the cost of parts procurement by using economies of scale (Anazawa 2006: 303). By the same token, the Malaysian Truck and Bus (MTB) was established by a joint venture between HICOM and Isuzu Motors in 1994, and it commenced truck and bus production in 1997. Also, Inokom was established between Hyundai Motors and Malaysian firms, and it commenced small truck production in 1997.

In November 1996, the Malaysian government announced its Second Industrial Master Plan (IMP2, 1996–2005), and the automotive industry was placed first out of the eight strategic industries, aiming (1) to enhance efficiency and strengthen the competitiveness of the industry, (2) to develop an offshore market, (3) to expand the market segments of national cars (as aforementioned), (4) to strengthen production technology, R&D, and marketing capacity, and (5) to strengthen the components industry (Fourin 1999: 112). In particular, with regard to the development of technology and R&D, the Malaysian government became increasingly concerned about Mitsubishi's reluctance to participate in technology transfers and about its high licensing fees (Jomo 1994). Thus, Proton was eager to become more self-sufficient, shifting away from its heavy dependence on Mitsubishi. In 1995, Proton entered into a technical licensing agreement with the French producer, Citroen, to acquire the technology for Proton to produce the 'Tiara' model (based on the Citroen AX), which commenced production in April 1996 (Fourin 1996). More importantly, just prior to the introduction of IMP2, Proton took over 64% of the equity in the British Lotus International Group in October 1996,[9] in order to give Proton access to better engineering technology and R&D capacity (Fourin 1999). Consequently, Proton was able to develop its own platform for the 'Waja' model in 1998, and finally an engine in 2003. Furthermore, Proton developed the new Campro (Camshaft Profile) engine technology in association with Lotus, and introduced its 'Gen-2' model by using their own platform and engine, which achieved 90% of local content ratio in 2004 (Fourin 2004).

In the late 1980s, Malaysian automotive market demand recovered from the recession, and the volume of production increased to over 200,000 vehicles in 1990. By 1995, it accounted for over 300,000, reaching its first peak of 449,765 in 1997. After the AFC, the production volume dropped rapidly. However, it had recovered by the early 2000s, accounting for over 450,000 vehicles in 2002. Proton's production commenced with 7,047 vehicles in 1985, and expanded rapidly after this, achieving its highest peak of 235,936 in 1997. The production volume recovered after the crisis, accounting for over 200,000 vehicles in 2001 and 2002. By the same token, Perodua commenced its first production with 10,184 vehicles in 1994; it continued to expand the capacity, accounting for over 130,000 in 2003 (see Figure 7.1).

Preferential tax and license policies

The Malaysian government introduced a series of discriminatory and protective policies in order to assist the growth of Proton. The Malaysian automotive industry – particularly its national producers (see later in the chapter) – was protected from foreign competition by establishing tariff and non-tariff barriers. Malaysian import tariffs on CBU PVs in nominal terms have been high. For instance, Malaysia had import tariffs of 140–300% on CBU PVs in 1997 (see Appendix 7.1), in comparison with neighbouring Thailand, which imposed 80% for CBU PVs in the same year (Natsuda and Thoburn 2013). In addition, the effective rate of protection for the transport and equipment sector indicated a very high figure of 252% in 1987 (Alavi 1996: 174).

With regards to procurement of components for assemblers, there was favourable treatment for national car producers. CKD kits attracted a 40% import duty, while Proton was exempted from this obligation until the early 1990s (Torii 1991b: 280–281). In July 1992, this rate was set at only 13% for Proton (and later Perodua), but remained at the 40% level for other producers until December 2003 (see Appendix 7.2).

Non-tariff barriers consisted of import quotas under the Approved Permit (AP) system in 1966, manufacturing licensing (ML) in 1967, and discriminatory allocation of incentives. AP was used to limit imports of CBU vehicles during the early stage of the policy, and it later extended to CKD kits (Rosli and Kari 2008). Discriminatory incentives were set for national car producers. For example, Proton and Perodua were given a 50% discount on excise duties until December 2003 (see Appendix 7.3). Furthermore, low interest rates and subsidised automobile loans were provided for public servants exclusively for the purchase of Proton vehicles (Anazawa 2006). Consequently, there were many criticisms from foreign vehicle manufacturers relating to the price differences between national car producers and others.

Vendor development and local content strategy

As we have noted, the National Car Policy was expected not only to strengthen the automotive industry through the introduction of national cars but also to foster supporting industries and encourage the upgrading of technology and technical skills. The Vendor Development Programme (VDP) was introduced in order to create greater industrial linkages between small and medium-sized enterprises (SMEs) and large firms. In 1988, Proton was selected as the first VDP company to develop SMEs as its suppliers. New start-up *bumiputra* firms were encouraged to join the scheme, and subsequently the number of vendors increased rapidly after the commencement of the scheme, from 17 firms in 1985, to 134 in 1994 and to 186 in 1999. Eighty percent of these were registered with the Proton Vendor Association and supplied more than 3,000 locally produced components (Rosli and Kari 2008: 108). Under VDP, Proton conducted a travelling guidance programme for individual vendors to enhance their productivity and technological skills, while also facilitating a 'match-making' type of technical cooperation between Mitsubishi's Japanese suppliers and their other vendors in the late 1980s and early 1990s. Proton employed a single sourcing system[10] to enable vendors to achieve economies of scale (Anazawa 2006). At the same time, the Ministry of International Trade and Industry of Malaysia (MITI) provided a total of RM22 million in subsidies to Proton during the 1986–1995 period in order to expand *bumiputra* participation in high-technology component manufacturing and supporting industries, such as forging, electroplating, tool-making, and machining (Abdulsomad 1999: 292). Under this component scheme, Proton selected potential SMEs that had initial capital of less than RM2.5 million, a minimum *bumiputra* equity of 70%, and a *bumiputra* in the work force of more than 55%. The selected SMEs were qualified to apply for a maximum of RM1 million government grant (Yoshimatsu 2000: 187–188). Grants were awarded on an annual basis.

Several further factors lay behind the implementation of this scheme. Firstly, due to the appreciation of yen from 1985, as already mentioned, imported components from Japan had become expensive. Secondly, in order to meet the General System of Preference (GSP) criteria for exporting to the UK market, the local content ratio needed to exceed 60% (Anazawa 1998). In consequence, the Malaysian government followed its earlier mandatory deletion programme with a new Local Material Content Policy, started in 1992, that required progressive annual increases in LC by type of vehicle (see Table 7.1). Proton was able to achieve 67% local content based on the GSP scheme in 1995 (Abdulsomad 1999: 290).

The Second Industrial Master Plan (1996–2005) also aimed to develop industrial clusters in the automobile industry so that vendors can enjoy the advantages of collective efficiency.[11] In 1996, the collaborative industrial estate project, 'Proton City', commenced between the government and Proton in order to locate their vendors around Proton's second assembly plant in Tanjung Malim, in the northern state of Perak. This project was temporarily suspended after the 1997 AFC, but it was finally completed in 2002 (Fourin 2002: 255).

The Vendor Development Programme has placed a heavy burden on Proton, resulting in higher cost and poorer-quality products (EIU 2005: 17). Not only has Proton needed to upgrade its own capabilities in order to compete, with inadequate help from foreign partners, but it has had to take on more of the governance of its own supply chain than do other, more powerful assemblers. As we have seen, increasingly in the automotive GVC, assemblers have devolved design and the manufacture of complete sub-assemblies down to multinational Tier-1 suppliers, who, in turn, have taken on the governance of their lower-tier subcontractors. In this sense, Proton could be expected to find it more difficult than a major assembler such as Toyota to conform with LC requirements while not comprising on efficiency.[12] Although some major Tier-1 firms are in Malaysia, such as Denso from Japan and Bosch from Germany, the presence of such firms is less than in Thailand.[13] Referring to Table 7.3, it is interesting that both Perodua and, more especially, Toyota, have lower local content than Proton.[14] Nevertheless, former Prime Minister Mahathir viewed Proton's higher prices

Table 7.1 Local Content Requirements in Malaysia

Type of Vehicle	*1992*	*1993*	*1994*	*1995*	*1996*	*2002–2004*
PVs: less than 1850 cc	30.0%	40.0%	50.0%	55.0%	60.0%	Abolition
PVs: 1851–2850 cc	20.0%	30.0%	35.0%	40.0%	45.0%	
PVs: over 2850 cc	Mandatory deletion items only					
CVs: less than 2,500 GVW						
CVs: over 2,500 GVW						

Source: Tham (2004: 55).

Note: GVW (gross vehicle weight).

Table 7.2 Vendor Associations in Malaysia, 2011

Vendor Association	*Estimated Number of Member Firms*
Proton Vendor Association (PVA)	150–200*
Perodua (KVP: Klub Vendor Perodua)	105
Toyota Suppliers Club	65

Source: Data supplied by MACPMA in 2012.

Note: There are many overlapping firms among associations. *150 firms are PVA official members and a further 50 are suppliers but not members.

and poor quality as playing an acceptable role in the building up of Malaysia's automotive engineering capability (EIU 2005: 17). Proton's domestic component suppliers have also come under threat from trade liberalisation, both from AFTA and from Malaysia's FTA with Japan. Although this liberalisation, in principle, could allow Proton to become more cost-efficient by sourcing more effectively within the region, we think this is unlikely. More likely is the continuation of the industrial linkage programme (ILP, discussed later) to protect (especially *bumiputra*) the domestic vendors. As of 2017, there were 641 vendors (from Tier-1 to Tier-3 suppliers) in Malaysia. The three major assemblers organised their own supply chain networks in Malaysia in 2011 (see Table 7.2).

Under the post-2000 WTO regime

Liberalisation period (2004–present)

The regional context of the Malaysian automotive industry changed considerably in the 2000s, with the establishment of greater free trade under AFTA. The automotive industry faced difficulties when dealing with AFTA. The ASEAN-4 countries initially registered automotive and automotive components on the Temporary Exclusion List (TEL).[15] However only three countries, Thailand, Indonesia, and the Philippines, transferred automobiles and automobile components from the TEL to the Inclusion List in 2000, which aimed to reduce the tariffs to 0–5% by 2003, and finally to 0% by the end of 2010. In contrast, Malaysia announced that tariff reductions on automobiles and components would be rescheduled from 2003 to 2005 (Wakamatsu *et al.* 2001: 116). In fact, the Malaysian automotive industry was deemed to suffer less damage than others, but Thailand, Indonesia, and the Philippines selected the liberalisation approach, while Malaysia chose to continue protecting its local automotive industry (Tham 2004: 64).

The Malaysian government responded to its liberalisation obligations, under AFTA, by setting lower automotive tariffs and, under WTO, by abolishing LC requirements and the mandatory deletion programme in January 2004[16] (see Table 7.1 and Appendix 7.1 and 7.2). However, other policies were introduced so as to maintain *de facto* protection, partly as a result of many political pressures (Suffian 2020). While all the tariffs on CBU vehicles and CKD kits were reduced,[17] the government, at the same time, started imposing a 60–100% excise tax (depending on categories, see Appendix 7.3), and later it tactically linked tax refunds according to the level of local content achieved. Shortly after, in January 2005, the Malaysian government revised the tax structures by reducing tariffs for CBUs and CKDs, while at the same time increased excise duties. However, in March 2006, when the tariffs on CBUs under the CEPT were further reduced to 5%, the excise tax was also slightly *reduced* (to 75%) with the announcement of the National Automotive Policy (NAP) under the IMP 3 (2006–2020).

These countervailing measures, however, seem not to have been effective in helping Proton to develop. While Malaysian automotive production slightly expanded in the 2000s, reaching over 500,000 vehicles in 2005 for the first time, and 614,664 in 2015, Proton's production rapidly decreased by approximately 60%, from 233,297 vehicles in 2001 to 97,602 in 2015 (see Figure 7.1), and its production share dramatically dropped from 54.4% to 15.9% over the same period. In contrast, Perodua increased its presence, accounting for 228,482 vehicles (37.2% of the country's production). Since 2006, the position of Proton and Perodua has reversed, with Perodua becoming the largest producer in Malaysia.

National automotive policy: 2006, 2009, and 2014

In 2006, the NAP was introduced in order to promote the competitiveness of the Malaysian automotive industry and facilitate its integration into the global automotive GVC.[18] One of the most significant elements of this policy was to advocate a strategic partnership between Proton and the global automotive producers that would allow the national car producer to enhance its competitiveness, long-term viability, and access to the latest technology such as R&D activities, thus enabling Malaysia to play the role of regional hub for the industry by increasing exports (MITI 2009). In addition, the NAP was further revised in October 2009, in response to the global environment changes, particularly in relation to attracting investments in high-technology sectors such as electric and hybrid vehicle production (MIDA 2010). This time, the NAP 2009 seemed to be more realistic than idealistic. The Malaysian government's ambition of producing a national car subsided somewhat, primarily due to the various problems associated with Proton, which required both external assistance and links with the global market. In addition, potentially higher future-demand segments of the automotive sector (such as electric and hybrid) were seen as needing to be developed, not by national but by foreign assemblers. The NAP 2009 was further revised in 2014, aiming (1) to encourage competitiveness and sustainable domestic automotive industry, (2) to increase sustainable value-added activities in the industry, (3) to create the regional hub in energy-efficient vehicles (EEVs), (4) to facilitate export capacity, (5) to promote *bumiputra* participation in the automotive value chain, (6) to enhance the ecosystem in the domestic automotive industry, and (7) to offer safer and better-quality products at competitive price (MAA website).[19] In particular, the Malaysian government is aiming to develop EEVs with the provision of special incentives (based on a case by case negotiation with the government). Unlike Thailand and Indonesia, the Malaysian EEV project targets not only small PVs but also large PVs, SUVs, and MPVs. Perodua's Axia model was approved as the first EEV model in 2014, followed by Proton's Ertiga model, Honda's HR-V model, Toyota's Innova and Fortuner models by 2017. In 2016, EEVs accounted for 42.8% of the total production. NAP 2014 aims to increase the ratio to 85% by 2020 and 100% by 2025 (Fourin 2017: 88–89). Furthermore, in the Malaysian government forecast, vehicle production was expected to increase to 1.35 million units with exports of 250,000 units, and creating additional 150,000 employment by 2020 (MAA website).[20] However, these targets seem to be very far from the reality.

Challenges to the Malaysian automotive industry

Cluster and soft industrial policies

As noted earlier, the Malaysian government encouraged the automotive cluster project, 'Proton City', under IMP2 (1996–2005). Furthermore, under IMP3 (2006–2020), automotive clusters were planned to be established in Tanjung Malim (in Perak state), Gurun (in Kedah), and Pekan (in Pahang), where assemblers, suppliers, and distribution networks have been established (Kikuchi 2007). Although industrial clusters are encouraged by policy in Malaysia, there are several issues. The Malaysian automotive supplier networks have been facing difficulties in two ways. *Bumiputra* suppliers under NCPs, particularly Proton, are facing technological problems (Segawa *et al.* 2014), while the suppliers working for foreign assemblers seem to suffer from a lack of utilisation of economies of scale due to the low LC ratios in foreign models (see Natsuda and Thoburn 2014).

With regard to HR development and R&D policies, Wan (2001) referred to the fact that Malaysian automotive firms found it difficult to undertake education and training of their workforces due to extensive job hopping and limited budgets. Furthermore, Chandran *et al.* (2009) revealed that skills development in the Malaysian universities, in general, is limited due to the mismatch in the curriculum and the lack of industrial exposure among graduates. Moreover, Chandran *et al.* (2014) identified the mismatch between universities and industries in R&D collaboration. In Malaysia, science, technology, and education policies target universities in order to encourage the linkages with industry, but there is no strong emphasis on initiative from the industrial side. In the Malaysian automotive industry, such issues in soft industrial policy need to be addressed if there is to be further upgrading.

Protectionist policies

The Malaysian government also introduced various new measures under the NAP. Firstly, the Automotive Development Fund (ADF)[21] was established in order to rationalise and restructure supporting industries by providing low interest loans to vendors. These loans were to allow the merger and acquisition of weaker vendors affected by the reduction of the CKD tariff (Onozawa 2008). In particular, Proton, which had a number of weak suppliers, would be able to undertake the inevitable reorganisation of its supply chain network. More controversially, the Malaysian government introduced a new industrial policy, the Industrial Adjustment Fund (IAF), which is linked with LC under the NAP. This has enabled assemblers to receive incentives such as interest-free loans and grants based on scale and industry linkage, subject to a sustainable level of overall capacity. In addition, further consideration would be provided to firms that promote sustainable and competitive *bumiputra* participation (MACPMA 2008: 8). The Malaysian government also linked the existing Industrial Linkage Programme (ILP) with local content, which allows assemblers to access a refund of excise duty according to the level of locally added value[22] (METI 2011: 90–91). These industrial policies are very contentious. It is true that there is no discrimination between national and foreign assemblers in terms of receiving the benefits,[23] so the policies do not directly contravene the TRIMs and GATS rules under the WTO. However, it is clear that national car producers get a lot of advantages from them. For instance, national car producers are more likely to access the excise tax refund scheme, which enables them to set lower selling prices[24] in their dealerships (see Table 7.3 for estimated LC ratios). Such incentives remain under NAP 2014.[25] The Malaysian government also introduced various new programmes under MAI, the Malaysia Automotive Institute, including a Lean Production System programme in collaboration with Proton and Perodua, the Automotive Supplier Excellence Programme (ASEP)[26] to develop world-class automotive suppliers, and the Dealers Entrepreneurship Enhancement Programme (DEEP)[27] to develop capability of dealers under NAP 2014.

Two licence systems, which do not conform to WTO rules, still exist in the Malaysian automotive sector.[28] With the introduction of the NAP, the Malaysian government initially announced that the AP system would be phased out by 2010 and 2015, but after the revision of the NAP in 2009 and 2014, the abolition of the AP system was postponed twice. Open AP for used vehicles, which was due to be abolished by December 2015, was retained under NAP 2014. In addition, it charges RM10,000 for every permit given after 2010, using this income to assist *bumiputra* entrepreneurs. By the same token, Franchise

Table 7.3 Estimated Local Contents of Major Assemblers and Models in Malaysia, 2012

Company	*Models*	*Estimated LC Ratio (%)*	*Main Country Source of Components Import*
Proton	Saga, Wira	90	Japan and France
Perodua	Myvi	60–70	Japan and Indonesia
Toyota	Vios	50	Japan and Thailand
Honda	Jazz	40–50	Thailand
Nissan	Sunny	40–50	Japan

Source: Data supplied by MAA in 2012.

AP (which deals with a particular producer's new vehicles) would continue until December 2020 (Fourin 2017, METI 2011, MITI 2009). The Malaysian government also froze any new issuing of MLs. However, by introducing the NAP, the government opened up some segments of vehicle production, such as luxury vehicles with engine capacity of over 1800 cc and a price of over RM 150,000, pickup trucks and commercial vehicles, and hybrid and electric vehicles, which were based on no equity conditions (MACPMA 2008, MIDA 2010 and 2018, MITI 2009). Despite this, the Malaysian government still protects vehicles with small engine size, which is not a problem for already existing automotive producers such as Toyota and Nissan, but might be a problem for newly advancing automotive producers.[29]

Proton

Even though Malaysian automotive production steadily increased until 2015, Proton has faced various problems. One of the most significant of these was Proton's weak product development and marketing capacity, which have not been able to deliver what consumers want.[30] Although Proton released their new, original vehicle, the Gen-2 model, in 2004, it failed to capture consumer demand, selling only 20,066 vehicles in 2004, 40,173 in 2005, and 4,248 in 2010 (Fourin 2011: 72). Similarly, Proton also failed to promote successfully the other models, Waja and Savvy, in the domestic market. Furthermore, Proton's export strategy was not successful. Targeting the UK market, where Proton sold relatively well in the 1990s, became problematic due to the low quality and the decline in reputation as a result of additional costs of servicing, despite the pricing of the vehicles at below production costs (Wad and Govindaraju 2011: 166). In fact, 21,000 vehicles were sold in the UK in 1994, but this dramatically declined to a mere 767 in 2010 (Fourin 2011: 74). Since 2006, Proton has shifted its strategy to developing ASEAN markets, which enables it to use the CEPT scheme. Thailand has become the largest off-shore market for Proton, buying 5,264 vehicles out of Malaysia's total Proton export of 11,869 in 2010 (ibid.), though these export sales are minimal when compared to Thailand's own vehicle exports.

As a result of its failures in both the domestic and foreign markets, capacity utilisation in Proton's two assembly plants, with a total potential output of 350,000 vehicles, has been low – estimated to be less than 50% since 2006 (in particular, only 19.2% in 2016). The lack of opportunities to produce at full volume, as well as the small volume of each model, has increased production costs. Consequently, Proton recorded a loss of RM587 million in 2007 and RM339 million in 2009. In order to reduce production costs, Proton, by using the ADF scheme, began rationalising production management by employing more effective use of JIT production (inventory control) and enhancing quality by discarding vendors who were uncompetitive technologically. This resulted in a decrease in supplier numbers, from 291 firms in 2005 to 228 in 2008. As a consequence, the defect product rate was improved by 58% in the Tanjung Malim plant in 2007 (Fourin 2008: 62).

Proton has recognised the importance of foreign cooperation for access to technology and marketing since its inception. However, its original partner, Mitsubishi, as a result of its financial problems in Japan and diminishing sales within Malaysia, sold their equity holdings in Proton in January 2004. Consequently, in October that same year, Proton began negotiations with Volkswagen with a view of forming a strategic partnership in place of Mitsubishi Motors. This partnership would have enabled Proton to access Volkswagen's technology, while Volkswagen would have been able to utilise Proton's spare production capacity and export to other ASEAN countries under AFTA, where Japanese firms currently dominate. In the negotiations, the main obstacle was the issue of management control: the initial proposal for Volkswagen's equity share was 49%, but the Malaysian government believed that Volkswagen would take over the management of the company in the long term (Fourin 2008: 66). Eventually, negotiations broke down due to Malaysia's industrial nationalism, which could not allow a foreign producer to take over a national flagship company (Athukorala and Kohpaiboon 2010, Fourin 2008, Nizamuddin 2008). Similarly, negotiations with Peugeot, Citroen, and General Motors also failed in 2007. As a consequence, Proton decided to return to Mitsubishi Motors for technical cooperation in December 2008, and released the Inspira model in 2010.[31]

As a result of Proton's continuous losses, its Malaysian biggest shareholder, the sovereign wealth fund Khazanah Nasional, sold all of its shares on January 2012 to a large Malaysian conglomerate, DRB-Hicom, for RM1.29 billion (US$410 million). It is apparent that the selection of DRB-Hicom's bid was influenced by the government's desire to keep the company in Malaysian hands (Nehru 2012). Although the ownership changed, the sales of Proton still have been declining every year, from 115,770 units in 2012 to only 65,302 units in 2016. In 2014, the Iriz model, equipped with its own platform and engine, was introduced, but the sales did not perform well due to the weak product development and marketing capacities of the company. With such poor performance of Proton, DRB-Hicom eventually sold their 49.9% of the equity of Proton to the Chinese automotive producer Geely in 2017. Proton is aiming to utlise Geely's capital and product development capacity particularly with regard to Geely's control of the Swedish car maker Volvo (Fourin 2017: 262–264). Proton also aims to be engaged in the world's largest automotive market in China under the partnership, by signing a JV agreement in China in August 2018.[32]

In an instructive contrast to Proton, the second national car producer, Perodua, had its Japanese partners, Daihatsu and Mitsui Corp, taking over 51% of equity in 2001. The company then came under Japanese management control, utilising Japanese technology and global networks. It has been increasing its production and market shares, and even exporting vehicles under Daihatsu's brand. In this regard, Perodua seems to play the role of a production and export base for Daihatsu Motor.

In comparison, Malaysia's real problem with Proton is its inability to cultivate markets with its own capacity. Malaysian automotive policy still has a lot of protectionist elements. These policies are, in general, not for Perodua or other automotive producers, but only for Proton. In an interview with one of the executives of the Malaysian automotive sector, it was remarked that Proton is a political creation and a political problem, and the reality is that local suppliers cannot win in competition with foreign suppliers in such an environment.

Significantly, the stumbling block in negotiations with prospective foreign partners for Proton, like Volkswagen, was the Malaysian government's reluctance to cede majority ownership to the foreign partners. With majority foreign ownership as in Perodua, the allocation of Malaysian production to service regional and potentially global markets is under the brand of the foreign partner – in which case the car may no longer be perceived as a truly national one. The majority foreign ownership too may well involve the foreign partner choosing component suppliers only on the basis of competitiveness, with less regard to their *bumiputra* status. In this context, although Geely is holding a minority ownership, the Proton-Geely alliance might be able to upgrade Proton's competitiveness in the Malaysian automotive industry.

Conclusions

This chapter has traced the development of Malaysia's automotive industrial policy over the past six decades. Encouraged as part of a general policy of import substitution, the industry initially developed in the 1960s and 1970s as an assembly activity based on the import of CKD kits while controlling the market though the ML and AP systems. An increased local content ratio was achieved through a mandatory deletion programme for replacing imported components.

The Malaysian government actively employed a state-led auto development policy in the 1980s and 1990s by establishing national car producers, namely Proton and Perodua. During this time, the Malaysian government provided various discriminatory and protective industrial policies in order to foster the development of the national car producers, especially Proton. The Malaysian policy measurements included the provision of favourable tariff rates and excise duties for national car producers. In addition, the Malaysian government encouraged many *bumiputra* entrepreneurs into the automotive industry through the Vendor Development Programme in order to rapidly expand the supporting sector, with provision of subsidies to Proton in particular.

However, such strong industrial policy measures in Malaysia needed to be changed after its accession to AFTA and intensified globalisation in the 2000s. The Malaysian government implemented its first liberalisation policy in the automotive sector by lowering tariffs and by abolishing local content requirements and discriminatory measures for national car producers, later introducing the National Automotive Policy in 2006. However, the Malaysian government still has controversial policies, such as the IAF and ILP links, with local content and non-tariff barriers, such as the ML and AP systems.

Proton has lost its market competitiveness. In contrast, the second national car company, Perodua, has increased its production, sales, and exports under Japanese management control. The Malaysian government has little choice but to employ controversial industrial policies in order to protect Proton and its related *bumiputra* businesses. In this regard, it is apparent that the Malaysian automotive policies are distorted mainly because of Proton.

Unlike Malaysia, neighbouring Thailand and Indonesia have employed a more industry-wide automotive policy that focusses on selecting national *product champions,* which identifies winning *types* of vehicle. As a result, the automotive industries in Thailand and Indonesia have been rapidly developing by means of attracting foreign investment. In conclusion, there is a lesson for other developing countries: policies should be oriented towards the industry as a whole, not tailored towards particular firms. In another words, picking a government-owned national champion *firm* is no longer an effective strategy within the current global environment.

Notes

1 *Perusahaan Otomobil National* - National Automobile Enterprise, in Malay.
2 Interview with Head of Strategic Research Division of MAI on 28 February 2012.
3 *Perusahaan Otomobil Kedua* - Second Automobile Enterprise.
4 2018 figures from COMTRADE.
5 Six assembly companies: Swedish Motor Assemblies, Oriental Assemblers, Kelang Pembena Kereta-Kereta, Cycle & Carriage Bintang, Assembly Services, and Associate Motor Industry, produced 319 passenger vehicles (PVs) and 947 commercial vehicles (CVs) in 1967 (Torii 1991a).
6 Five companies: Sarawak Motor Industries, Kinabalu Motor Assembly, Automotive Manufactures, Tatab Industries, and B.G. Motors.
7 See Jomo (1993: 266–268) for Mitsubishi Motors' regional strategy.
8 Of the RM140 million of total initial investment capital, UMW Holding held 38% of the stake, Med-Bumikar MARA had 20%, Permodala National 10%, Daihatsu 20%, Daihatsu Malaysia 5%, and Mitsui Corporation hold 7% (Fourin 1994: 192).
9 Proton's ownership of equity increased to 80% in 1998 and 100% in 2002.
10 A particular component is supplied by only a single firm.
11 Competitive advantage in clusters derives from external economies and joint action (Schmitz and Nadvi 1999).
12 See Lauridsen (2008, vol. 2: 643–662) for a discussion of such conflicts in the case of supplier development in Thailand.
13 See ASEAN (2014: 11) for a list of the top 20 OEM auto parts makers in ASEAN. Interestingly, ASEAN (2017: 17–18) indicates that none from a long list of Japanese automotive parts and components industries within ASEAN was expanding in Malaysia in 2016–2017, and only one non-Japanese firm was expanding. Yet 25 out of the 35 Japanese firms, and 6 of the 10 non-Japanese firms were expanding in Thailand.
14 Note though that LC figures are normally for the *direct* import content, and indirect imports (sub-components for components assembled locally) are not taken account of.
15 TEL: all items on the list were temporarily excluded; however, these items on the list must be transferred to Inclusion List by 2000 (Fourin 2002: 14).
16 Some mandatory deletion items were abolished in 2002.
17 For example, CBU PVs with less than 1800 cc engine from 140% to 80% for non-ASEAN countries and 70% under CEPT.
18 The NAP consisted of the following six objectives: (1) to promote a competitiveness of the automotive sector, in particular national car manufacturers, (2) to become a regional hub of the automotive industry, (3) to enhance value added and local capabilities in the industry, (4) to promote export-oriented Malaysian manufacturers as

well as component and parts vendors, (5) to promote *bumiputra* participation in the industry, and (6) to safeguard the interests of consumers in terms of value for money, safety, and quality of product and services (MACPMA 2008).

19 http://www.maa.org.my/pdf/nap_2014_policy.pdf [accessed on 8 February 2019].

20 http://www.maa.org.my/pdf/nap_2014_policy.pdf [accessed on 8 February 2019].

21 The eligibility of the scheme is for the member firms of the Proton Vendor Association, the Perodua Vendor Association or the MACPMA, and firms are entitled to access a maximum of RM 10 million.

22 Local added value = ex-factory value – input material value (= local procurement costs + labor costs + direct expenditure + profit). The scheme requires over 30% of LAV for less than 2500 cc engine cars and 25% for over 2500 cc (METI 2011).

23 To be precise, extra consideration is based on race (indigenous) background, not nationality.

24 Dealer prices include vehicle price, excise tax, and sales tax.

25 https://themalaysianreserve.com/2017/11/02/incentives-local-vendors-automotive-policy-stay/ [accessed on 8 February 2019].

26 http://mai.org.my/v5test/index.php?option=com_content&view=article&id=13&Itemid=160&lang=en [accessed on 8 February 2019].

27 http://mai.org.my/dealers-entrepreneurship-enhancement-program-deep/ [accessed on 8 February 2019].

28 Actually, Malaysia is an original WTO member. During the trade review with the WTO, the Malaysian government explained the special circumstance of the Malaysian automotive sector, including the *bumiputra* policy, and the WTO understood the situation (Interview with the Deputy Secretary General in MITI of Malaysia on 28 February 2012).

29 Interview with Commercial Attaché at the Japanese Embassy in Malaysia on 23 February 2012.

30 Interview with Vice President of MACPMA on 21 February 2012.

31 Technical cooperation (TC) with Mitsubishi Motors did not involve equity participation. Mitsubishi Motors played a complementary role with Proton, the latter of which can produce only 1300 and 1600 cc engines with its own technology. TC includes (1) joint development of engines, (2) Proton's platform production for Mitsubishi Motors, (3) unification of components between Mitsubishi Motors and Proton, and (4) electric and hybrid vehicle technology. See Mitsubishi Motors' website: http://www.mitsubishi-motors.com/publish/pressrelease_jp/corporate/2011/news/detailb915.html [accessed on 11 February 2019].

32 https://www.straitstimes.com/asia/se-asia/malaysias-proton-in-jv-with-geely-to-assemble-and-sell-cars-in-china [accessed on 11 February 2019].

Appendices

Appendix 7.1 Tariffs on CBU PVs in Malaysia, 1997–2017

PVs: CBUs Engine Size	*Before 1997.Oct (%)*	*1997 Oct (%)*	*2004 Jan (%)*	*2005 Jan (%)*	*2006 Mar (%)*	*2011–2017 May (%)*
Less than 1800 cc	140	140	80	50	30	30
1800 cc–1999 cc	170	170	100	50	30	30
2000 cc–2499 cc	170	200	120	50	30	30
2500 cc–2999 cc	200	250	160	50	30	30
Over 3000 cc	200	300	200	20	30	30
ASEAN: Less than 1800 cc	–	–	70	20	5	0
ASEAN: 1800 cc–1999 cc	–	–	90	20	5	0
ASEAN: 2000 cc–2499 cc	–	–	110	20	5	0
ASEAN: 2500 cc–2999 cc	–	–	150	20	5	0
ASEAN: Over 3000 cc	–	–	190	20	5	0

Source: Fourin (2002, 2004, 2006, and 2017) and MAA.

Appendix 7.2 Tariffs on CKD PVs in Malaysia, 1997–2017

PVs: CKDs Engine size	*Before 1997 Oct (%)*	*1997 Oct (%)*	*2004 Jan (%)*	*2005 Jan (%)*	*2006–2017 May (%)*
National (Proton etc)	13	13	–	–	–
Less than 1800 cc	42	42	35	10	10
1800 cc–1999 cc	42	42	35	10	10
2000 cc–2499 cc	42	60	35	10	10
2500 cc–2999 cc	42	70	35	10	10
Over 3000 cc	42	80	35	10	10
AEAN: Less than 1800 cc			25	0	0
ASEAN: 1800 cc–1999 cc			25	0	0
ASEAN: 2000 cc–2499 cc			25	0	0
ASEAN: 2500 cc–2999 cc			25	0	0
ASEAN: Over 3000 cc			25	0	0

Source: Fourin (2002, 2004, 2006, and 2017).

Appendix 7.3 Excise Duty on PVs in Malaysia, 1997–2017

PVs	*1997. Oct*		*2004 Jan (%)*	*2005 Jan (%)*	*2006 Mar (%)*	*2017 May (%)*
	Non-national (%)	*National (%)*				
OMV: Less than RM 7,000	25	12.5	–	–	–	
OMV: RM 7,000–9,999	30	15.0	–	–	–	–
OMV: RM 10,000–12,999	35	17.5	–	–	–	–
OMV: RM 13,000–19,999	50	25.0	–	–	–	–
OMV: RM 20,000–24,999	60	30.0	–	–	–	–
OMV: Over RM 25,000	65	32.5	–	–	–	–
CBU/CKD: Less than 1800 cc	–	–	90	60	75	75
CBU/CKD: 1800 cc–1999 cc	–	–	120	70	80	80
CBU/CKD: 2000 cc–2499 cc	–	–	150	80	90	90
CBU/CKD: 2500 cc–2999 cc	–	–	200	90	105	105
CBU/CKD: Over 3000 cc	–	–	250	100	125	105

Source: Fourin (2002, 2004, 2006, and 2017).

Note: OMV (open market value); consumers need to pay additional sales tax of 10%.

8 The Philippines

Introduction

This chapter examines the development of the Philippines' automotive industry in historical perspective, paying attention to the role of industrial policy in the country's automotive industrialisation. In the past, the Philippines introduced a series of automotive development policies including the Progressive Car Manufacturing Programme (PCMP) in 1973 and the Car Development Programme (CDP) in 1987, using various performance requirement policies for assemblers, which now would violate the current World Trade Organization (WTO) rules. The Philippines government also was later obliged under World Bank conditionality to liberalise its automotive industry by reducing tariffs and abolishing import bans on vehicles, and later by removing foreign exchange (balancing) requirements in 2001 (as the result of negotiation with the United States). Local content requirements (LCRs) were abolished under the WTO in 2003. The industry declined throughout the 2000s.

Despite the lack of success of industrial policies in the Philippines in terms of automotive assembly, certain types of automotive component production, particularly transmissions, which were established under earlier local content provisions and foreign exchange requirement policies, have become internationally competitive and serve as export platforms within Southeast Asia. The Philippines' other main component export, wiring harnesses (an electrical item), however, possibly owes more to the country's abundance of low-cost but educated labour than to policies *per se*.

In 2015, the Philippines introduced a new industrial policy, the Comprehensive Automotive Resurgence Strategy (CARS) programme. It hopes to develop the automotive industry further by 2022, with an intended domestic output of over 500,000 vehicles. Certainly, the Philippines' economy is expected to grow in the future, but the CARS programme faces various challenges such as low LC ratios, competition from imported second-hand vehicles, and from cars imported under free trade agreements (FTAs). This chapter is organised as follows: the next section sets out an overview of the automotive industry in the Philippines. The following section looks at the development of the country's automotive industry since the 1960s. The next section examines competitiveness and challenges to the automotive industry in the Philippines and the final section offers some conclusions.

Overview of the automotive industry in the Philippines

Automotive production, sales, and structure

The Philippines has a long history of vehicle production. In the mid-1970s both vehicle production and sales were almost equal to those of Malaysia, though both were only at about 50,000 units. Vehicle production in the Philippines (51,265 units) was larger than that of Thailand (30,981) in 1975 (Fourin 1994). There was no significant difference among these 'ASEAN-4' countries except for Thailand's relatively large net vehicle imports up to the 1980s. In the 1990s, before the Asian financial crisis (AFC) of 1997, both vehicle production and sales had increased rapidly in these three countries, while the growth of the Philippines was much slower.

Most recently, Thailand and Indonesia have become major vehicle-producing countries. Thailand employed a series of automotive industrial policies (by selecting *product champions*) and successfully boosted the growth of the industry as an exporter of pickup trucks and compact passenger vehicles (PVs), namely, Eco-cars (Natsuda and Thoburn 2013 and 2014). In Indonesia, the automotive industry has developed along with the expansion of its large domestic market, and more recently by employing industrial policies targeting environmentally friendly vehicles, the so-called low-cost green cars (LCGCs) (Natsuda *et al.* 2015a, Thoburn and Natsuda 2017 and 2018). In contrast to these countries, the Malaysian government launched national car projects – Proton and Perodua – in the 1980s and 1990s, employing strongly discriminatory policies against foreign assemblers and parts suppliers, which have continued to some extent under the post-2000 WTO policy regime, though with limited success (Natsuda *et al.* 2013, Natsuda and Thoburn 2014). Even the newly producing country in the region, Vietnam, has already overtaken the Philippines in production (see Chapter 9).

Figure 8.1 indicates the total number of vehicles produced and sold in the Philippines over the period 1975–2018. Unlike Thailand, Malaysia, and Indonesia, in the Philippines, vehicle production has never surpassed sales of vehicles: the Philippines always has been a net importer of vehicles. The Philippines' vehicle production developed, albeit slowly, in the 1970s. The industry subsequently was damaged by political upheaval and economic crisis in the early 1980s,[1] and production dropped to the lowest ever in 1987. Vehicle production started growing from the late 1980s to the mid-1990s and reached a peak in 1996. However, the AFC caused a serious market slump. Production dramatically declined in 1998, and it never again reached its pre-AFC level except briefly in 2017. The large (44%) fall in vehicle output between 2017 and 2018 is attributed by CAMPI's president to TRAIN, the Tax Reform for Acceleration and Inclusion law, implemented at the beginning in 2018, which raised excise tax on vehicles and

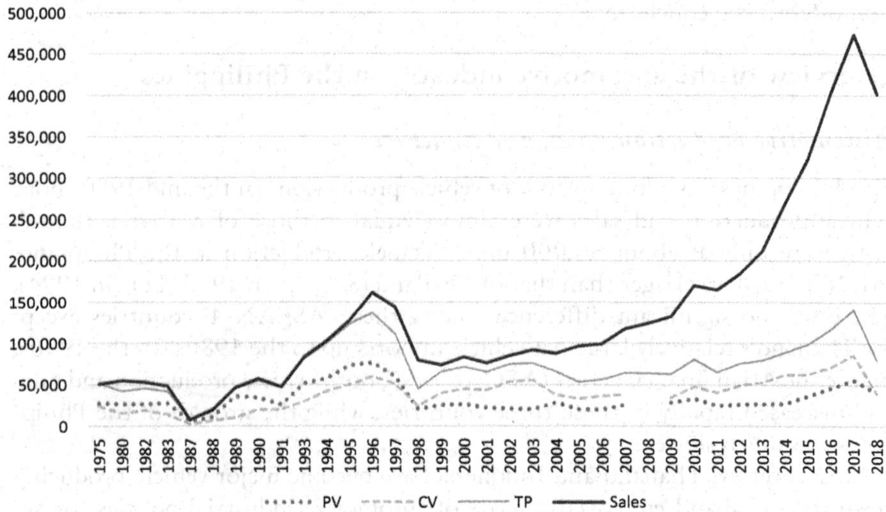

Figure 8.1 Production and Sales of Vehicles in the Philippines, 1975–2018.
Source: Adapted from Fourin (1993, 2008, 2017, 2019).
Note: Number of vehicles, PV (passenger vehicle), CV (commercial vehicle), TP (total production).

caused prices to increase.[2] Both production and sales in the Philippines had almost similar volumes and trends until the mid-1990s. However, sales of vehicles have surpassed production since 1996, as net imports have risen. Particularly after the progressive full implementation of the ASEAN Free Trade Area (AFTA) over the period 2004–2010, vehicle sales grew approximately four-fold over the period 2006–2018, but production (79,763 vehicles) in 2018 was only 20% of domestic sales (401,809), indicating substantial net imports. Among the four well-established major automotive-producing nations in the ASEAN region, the Philippines' automotive industry has a relatively small number of assemblers: 11 firms and 256 parts suppliers. Employment in the industry is also the smallest among the four countries, accounting for 66,800 workers.[3]

According to the Chamber of Automotive Manufactures of the Philippines (CAMPI), Toyota accounted for 47% of locally produced vehicles in the Philippines in 2014.[4] Among the approximately 90 Tier-1 parts suppliers,[5] foreign control was clear: 60% were joint ventures, 30% foreign, and only 10% purely local, though virtually all of the 175 Tiers-2 and 3 suppliers were local firms in 2015. Major multinationals parts suppliers operating in the Philippines – as of the mid-2010s – included Denso and Hitachi Automotive Systems from Japan; Bosch, Continental, and ZF Friedrichshafen from Germany; and Lear and Cummins from the USA (ASEAN 2014: 157, ASEAN 2017: 56).

Out of the total sales of 473,943 vehicles in 2017, Toyota accounted for a market share of 38.5%, followed by Mitsubishi, Hyundai, and Ford (see Figure 8.2).

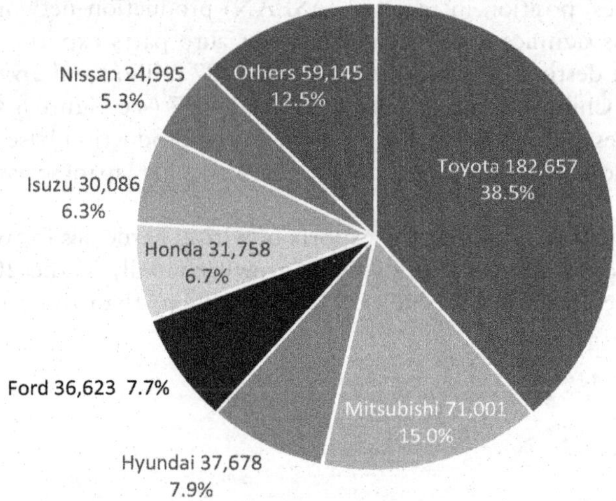

Figure 8.2 Sales Volume and Market Share by Automotive Brand in the Philippines, 2017.
Source: Adapted from Fourin (2018: 332).
Note: Total 473,943 vehicles.

The Philippines is the only country in the ASEAN-4 where non-Japanese automotive producers such as Hyundai and Ford are ranked in the top five brand vehicles in terms of market share. Hyundai has no production in the Philippines, but its sales presence has grown in recent years. Indeed, Hyundai has been increasing its market share in lower-income ASEAN countries such as Vietnam and Cambodia, selling small PVs. In the case of Ford, it had long committed itself to the Philippines as its strategic production location in Southeast Asia, but withdrew from the country in 2012, and has been expanding production capacity in Thailand.

Automotive trade in the Philippines

Figure 8.3 shows trends of the automotive trade in the Philippines over the period 1997–2017. The Philippines' automotive trade deficits have been growing rapidly since 2009 (see Figure 8.3). In 2017, these deficits accounted for US$7,200 million with exports of US$1,168 million and imports of US$8,368 million in HS87 (vehicles, parts, and accessories). In particular, the import of PVs (HS8303) has increased in value and nearly doubled from US$2,217 million in 2015 to US$4,389 million in 2017. Surprisingly, the Philippines had a trade surplus between 2004 and 2008 in HS87. This surplus was made through auto parts (HS8708) exports. In fact, the Philippines created export capacity in automotive components due to its localisation policy and foreign exchange controls in the 1970s. However, the export of auto parts decreased by 48%, from US$2,052 million in 2008 to US$1,072 million in 2017. In this context, the Philippines' position in regional (ASEAN) production networks has been becoming less significant in recent years. For auto parts exports, Japan is the largest export destination, accounting for US$287 million and 26.8%, followed by Thailand, China, Germany, and the USA in 2017 (see Figure 8.4). However, the Philippines still has been playing a role in the production base of transmission in the global automotive production networks for Japanese assemblers (see Table 8.1).

It is important to note that the exports of wiring harnesses for vehicles, classified separately as electrical items, were growing rapidly in the 2010s, and in 2017, they were greater in value (US$2,034 million) than those of the whole

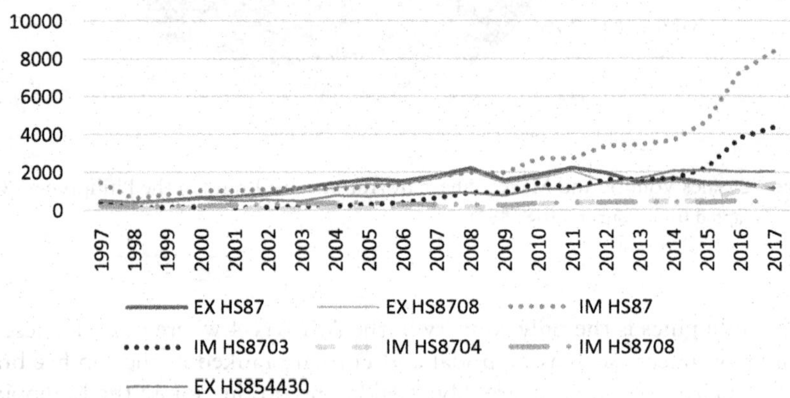

Figure 8.3 Automotive Trade of the Philippines, 1997–2017.
Source: Global Trade Atlas (database).
Note: US$ Million, EX (Export), IM (Import).

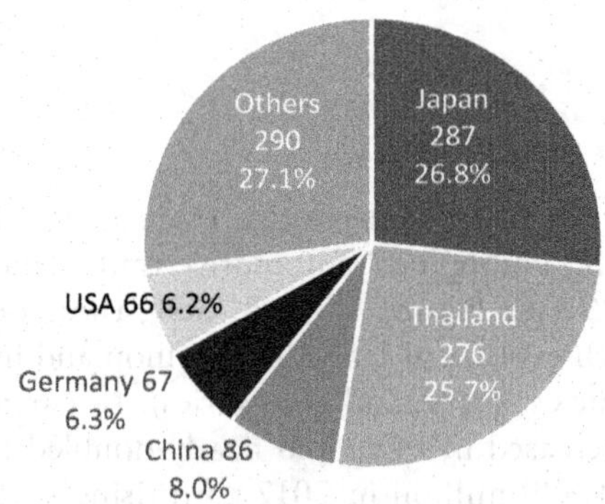

Figure 8.4 HS8708 (Parts and Accessories of Motor Vehicles), Top Five Export Destinations of the Philippines, 2017.
Source: Global Trade Atlas (database).
Note: US$ Million (shown above the percentages).

automotive industry of US$1,168 million of HS87. Indeed, the Philippines plays a role as a strategic export platform for wiring harness products for Japan and North America. Automotive wiring harness (HS854430) accounted for 91.7% of the total wiring harness export (HS8544) in the Philippines, exporting to Japan (US$926 million), the USA (US$546 million), Canada (US$274 million), Thailand (US$96 million), and Korea (US$53 million) in 2017.

With regard to the origins of imports in the Philippine automotive industry (HS87), the neighbouring countries of Thailand and Indonesia accounted for the majority (58.4%) in value, followed by Japan, China, and Korea (see Figure 8.5). With regard to PVs (HS8703), Thailand and Indonesia accounted for 75.3% of imports in the Philippines, followed by Japan, Korea, and Germany in 2017 (see Figure 8.6).

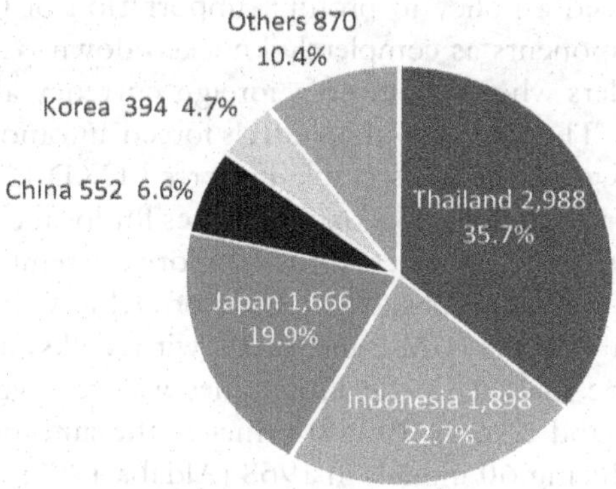

Figure 8.5 HS87 (Vehicles, Parts, and Accessories), Top Five Import Sources in the Philippines, 2017.
Source: Global Trade Atlas (database).
Note: US$ Million (shown above the percentages).

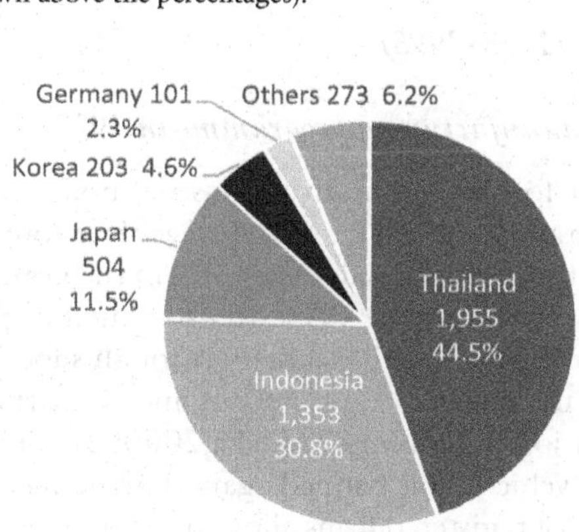

Figure 8.6 HS8703 (Motor Cars), Top Five Import Sources in the Philippines, 2017.
Source: Global Trade Atlas (database).
Note: US$ Million (shown above the percentages).

Development of the automotive industry in the Philippines

The development of the Philippines' automotive industry can be classified into four periods: import substitution (1951–1972), localisation (1973–1995), liberalisation (1996–2002), and the period under the post-WTO regime (2003–present).

Import substitution period (1951–1972)

The early development of the automotive industry up to 1950 was based on the importation of completely built-up (CBU) vehicles mainly from the United States. Due to the depletion of foreign exchange reserves, the government of the Philippines introduced a policy to prohibit importation of CBU vehicles. The importation of components as completely knocked down (CKD) kits was only allowed for assemblers who were given a foreign currency allocation (Quimba and Rosellon 2012). The import ban on CBUs forced automotive manufacturers to establish their own plants to assemble imported CKD kits (Ofreneo 2016). Simultaneously, it provided business opportunities for local entrepreneurs in the Philippines to diversify their business into automotive assembly by forming joint ventures with foreign producers such as those of Delta with Toyota, Francisco Motor with General Motors (GM), and DMG with Volkswagen (VW) (Doner 1991). Although the market in the Philippines was relatively small and fragmented with a demand of only 10,000 vehicles, the automotive industry had 29 assemblers, producing 60 models in 1968 (Aldaba 1997: 3). The import ban and foreign exchange controls were eventually abolished and replaced with high tariffs (over 100%) under the Diosdado Macapagal administration in the 1960s (Ofreneo 2008: 9).

Localisation period (1973–1995)

The progressive car manufacturing programme in 1973

The Philippines' first formal automotive industrial policy, the Progressive Car Manufacturing Programme (PCMP), aimed to achieve foreign currency saving by manufacturing automotive parts domestically, in the hope of raising LC from 10% in 1973 to 60% by the end of 1976. It also aimed to promote local small and medium-sized enterprise (SMEs) activity through subcontracting and technology transfer, and to facilitate exports of automotive parts in a regional automotive complementation programme (Aldaba 2000: 2). Under the scheme, the importation of CBU vehicles was banned again. Furthermore, to rationalise the industry, the number of registered firms allowed to import CKD kits was limited to only five assemblers: Delta Motors (Toyota), Ford and PAMCOR (Mitsubishi), Franciso (GM), and DMG (Nissan) (Aldaba 1997: 4, Ofreneo 2008: 68).

Additionally, a Progressive Truck Manufacturing Programme (PTMP) for commercial vehicle production and a Progressive Manufacture of Automotive Diesel Engines (PMADE) for the localisation of truck engine production were introduced in 1977.

Probably the most important aspect of the PCMP was that it created the foundation of the current auto parts export capacity of the Philippines. The programme forced the participants to make investments in the production of their own components. Mitsubishi established the Asia Transmission Corporation (ATC), Toyota established an engine plant, Nissan invested in a press-forming facility to manufacture engine parts, Ford established Ford Ensite for car body stamping, and GM invested in engine transmission production. The number of parts suppliers increased from 32 firms in 1974 to more than 200 in the late 1970s (Ofreneo 2008: 68–69). However, the PCMP turned out to be a disappointment in terms of overall localisation progress as well as rationalisation of the industry (Doner 1991). Despite the development of some component production, the local content of total vehicle production was low due to a lack of local supporting industries such as steel mills and plastics (Aldaba 1997: 4).

The PCMP was ended as a result of political upheaval followed by economic crisis in the early 1980s, and vehicles sales slumped from 48,954 units in 1983 to 4,335 in 1986 (Fourin 1993: 204). At the time, automotive assemblers, all highly dependent on imported components, could not access foreign exchange due to the government's foreign exchange ban introduced in 1983. Consequently, assemblers such as Ford, GM, and Toyota withdrew from the programme, and only two assemblers, Mitsubishi and Nissan, remained in the country. The number of components suppliers decreased from 220 firms in 1978 to 40 firms in 1984 (Aldaba 1997: 4–5). The inconsistency of government policy was also a major problem. Under the PCMP, Renault and Mercedes were allowed to import CBU vehicles without establishing an assembly plant. Worse, some CBUs were even imported tax-free under the Marcos administration. DMG (Nissan's local partner) was taken over by one of Marcos' associates (Ofreneo 2008).

The car development programme in 1987

To revitalise the automotive industry in the Philippines, the Aquino government replaced the PCMP with the Car Development Programme (CDP). The CDP aimed to develop PVs of less than 2800 cc to increase the local content of assembled vehicles, earn and save foreign exchange, create employment, and develop local supporting industry (Quimba and Rosellon 2012). The CDP continued to ban import of CBU vehicles. Secondly, it limited participation to only three assemblers: Mitsubishi, Nissan, and Toyota (Toyota withdrew from the market in 1985, but came back in 1988). Thirdly, and importantly, it imposed on assemblers the requirement to earn, from revenues derived from exports, 50% of their foreign exchange needs for their CKD imports. Fourthly, it imposed minimum LCRs, which increased annually (Aldaba 2000: 3, Fourin 1994: 206).

To encourage the production of commercial vehicles (CVs), the government also introduced a Commercial Vehicle Development Programme (CVDP), replacing the PTMP, in 1987. The CVDP aimed to facilitate locally produced CVs such as the Asian Utility Vehicle (AUV),[6] light commercial vehicles (LCVs), trucks, and replacement parts and components (Aldaba 2000: 3). The CVDP also employed LCRs by type of vehicle (see Appendix 8.1). Like CDP, the CVDP banned vehicle imports (Aldaba 2000). In addition, AUVs were exempted from excise tax until 2003 (Aldaba 2000: 11, Ofreneo 2008: 74), an interesting comparison with Thailand which retained tax preferences for its product champion vehicles.

CDC revision: the people's car programme of 1990 and the luxury car programme of 1992

The government targeted the development of small PVs with gasoline engines of less than 1200 cc, the so-called 'People's Cars', by amending the CDP in 1990. Under this scheme, the government imposed three requirements: firstly, a price ceiling, progressively increased up to the mid-1990s; secondly, LCRs of 35% in 1991, finally raised to 51% in 1993; and, thirdly, once again, automotive producers had to earn part of the foreign exchange (at least 50% in this case) for their own import requirements by exporting automotive or non-automotive products. Furthermore, participants in the scheme were required to invest at least 200 million peso in production of their main components (Aldaba 2008: 3). Under the PCP, seven assemblers were registered. Although most were not profitable under the PCP scheme due to the price ceiling, they became eligible after one year of operation to operate under the main CDC, which had no price ceiling. This added another five assemblers to the main programme, and further fragmented an already small market with more models (Aldaba 1997: 6).

The government of the Philippines tried to develop luxury PVs with engine sizes of above 2800 cc by amending the CDP in 1992, allowing Volvo and Mercedes Benz to enter the market. In addition, the CDP was again revised for the entry of new assemblers under the ASEAN Industrial Joint Venture (AIJV) Scheme, which allowed Malaysia's Proton to enter the Philippines market in 1994. However, the programme was undermined as a result of investment liberalisation, which was part of the government's subsequent compliance with a structural adjustment programme (SAP) of the World Bank (Ofreneo 2008: 71). Under the SAP, tariffs in the automotive industry were forced to be cut from 70% in 1981, 50% in 1982, to 40% in 1993. Tariffs on CKDs were much lower: 30% in the 1980s, 20% in 1993–1994, 10% in 1995, and 3% in 1996–1997. These tariffs on CBUs and CKDs were among the lowest in the ASEAN-4 countries (ibid.: 72), although the lower tariffs on CKDs compared to CBUs meant that the effective rates of protection (protection on value-added) on CBUs were higher than the nominal tariffs indicated.

Liberalisation period (1996–2002)

Moves to liberalisation: deregulation of the automotive industry in 1996

In 1996, a first liberalisation deregulated the importation of all types of PVs and CVs and also removed restrictions on the number of models (Aldaba 1997 and 2000). On the one hand, the Philippines pursued liberalisation in terms of the entry of new models into the country, which was deemed to be of benefit to consumers. On the other hand, the government strengthened performance requirement policies for vehicle assemblers, aiming to localise the automotive industry by gradual increments of foreign exchange requirements and LCRs by 2000 (see Appendix 8.2). For vehicle assemblers, these were strong contradictions in government policy. Assemblers had to commit to localisation of vehicle production in response to the government's performance requirements; yet imported CBUs were expected to increase in importance in the market, working against localisation.

Not long after the liberalisation policy was introduced, the industry faced the Asian financial crisis of 1997–1998. Vehicle sales halved between 1996 and 1998, and production fell by two-thirds (see Figure 8.1). The tariff on PV CKD kits was increased from 7% in 1998 to 10% in 1999 (see Appendix 8.3). However, this rate was still much lower than that of other ASEAN countries, which was in the 33–80% range. Consequently, imported CKD kits were used for assembling in the Philippines, instead of locally produced components (Ofreneo 2008: 73). The World Bank-driven liberalisation policy thus appears to have hindered localisation.

Under the post-2000 WTO regime (2003–present)

Liberalisation and the automotive export programme of 2003

As mentioned, the government of the Philippines employed various performance requirements such as for LCs and foreign exchange as a core set of automotive industrial policies. However, these performance requirement policies clearly violated the WTO's TRIMS rule, due to be implemented from the year 2000, and actually phased out by the Philippines by 2003 (Fourin 2004, Ofreneo 2007, Quimba and Rosellon 2012).

To enhance the industry's competitiveness, the government introduced an Automotive Export Programme (AEP) in October 2003 (effective for five years), granting the incentive of a reduced tariff rate on any CBU vehicles that the exporting assembler imported into the Philippines (Aldaba 2007: 6–7). However, participation was very low, with no assembler except for Ford. Vehicle production decreased by over 12,000 units in the period 2003–2009. Ford itself exported four models to Thailand and Indonesia under the programme (Rosellon and Medalla 2012). In fact, as was noted earlier, Ford eventually closed down its production and withdrew from the Philippines in 2012, relocating to Thailand. One of the main reasons for the failure of this programme was that the policy could not successfully attract Japanese automotive foreign direct investment (FDI) in competition with Thailand. At that time, Thailand, under its 'Detroit of Asia' plan, was aiming to enhance the export capacity of the Thai automotive industry, principally by giving incentives to producers and consumers of the *product champion* vehicle, the one-ton pickup truck. After this, Japanese automotive assemblers as well as parts suppliers made massive investments in Thailand, which led the country to become a regional export platform as well as a major world automotive producer (Natsuda and Thoburn 2013).

In parallel to the AEP, the automotive excise tax system was revised, shifting from the size of engine displacement to vehicle price in October 2003, with the rate progressively increasing (see Appendix 8.4). However, policies again were introduced which discouraged domestic automotive production. There were two problems. Firstly, the lowest category of small compact cars was set at a low 2% of excise tax based on the idea of affordability for the country's rising middle class. However, these vehicles were not assembled locally but imported from other ASEAN countries, particularly Thailand (Ofreneo 2008: 73–74). Secondly, excise tax was imposed on AUVs for the first time from September 2003, as they had been previously exempted. These models had enjoyed fiscal incentives, accounted for a high market share until the early 2000s, and had relatively high LCs (Ofreneo 2008). Following the excise tax imposition, AUV models, which accounted for 42% of the market in 2002, decreased in share to about 27% after 2004. Consequently, one Japanese assembler scrapped its 200,000 vehicle production plan in the Philippines, which had aimed at using AUVs as its strategic export model (Fourin 2006: 339).

The comprehensive automotive resurgence strategy (CARS) programme of 2015

Industrial policy in the automotive sector in the decade after AEP in 2003 was noticeably absent in the Philippines. During the period 2003–2014, import penetration greatly increased: although sales of vehicles nearly tripled, production increased by only 14%. Indeed, vehicle production in 2014 was still more than 50,000 units lower than the peak of 1996. To revive the industry, the government of the Philippines cooperated with the private sector from 2012 to develop a 'Philippines Automotive Manufacturing Industry Roadmap' (Llanto and Ortiz 2015). In 2015, the so-called Comprehensive Automotive Resurgence Strategy (CARS) was approved. The objective is to increase competitiveness through facilitating increased production volumes, further localisation of the component industry, and generating employment. The programme aims to encourage new investments in bulky components and large plastic parts (Gutierrez 2015). It also expected to generate 20,000 jobs in direct employment, for vehicle production of 506,000 units[7] (350,000 for domestic and 156,000 for export) by 2022.

The market share of locally manufactured vehicles was hoped to increase to 70% by 2022 (Llanto and Ortiz 2015, Ofreneo 2016).

The CARS programme is limited to the manufacture of three models with body shell assembly and large plastic assembly. It has fiscal incentive support in two categories: ***fixed incentive support*** to facilitate parts and components production, covering capital expenditure for tooling, equipment, and training costs; and ***production incentive support*** to encourage vehicle production, with eligibility criteria including production of at least 100,000 vehicles and the manufacture of major components in large plastic parts assemblies. Incentives are paid through a tax payment certificate that can be used to settle tax liabilities including income tax, value-added tax (VAT), and excise and customs duties.[8] There is also ***industry-wide non-fiscal policy support*** to develop the domestic market through regulatory reforms and improvement of the policy environment for automotive manufacturing, such as streamlining registration processes and business-matching activities among investors and local parts suppliers (Llanto and Ortiz 2015).

In the Philippines, incentives are given to producers through tax concessions, but not to consumers. In comparison to Thailand and Indonesia – which used excise or luxury tax concessions to promote purchases of favoured kinds of vehicle[9] – the Philippines lacks a demand-side strategy. In other words, there is no market signal for consumers under the CARS programme. The difference between the Philippines and others appears to spring from weak state capacity in the Philippines. A high-ranking official in the Department of Trade and Industry (DTI) explained that, unlike Thailand, it is extremely difficult to revise excise tax in the Philippines, which requires approval from the national congress, namely, a 'Republic Act' provision. Instead, the DTI is trying to use Executive Orders, as under the CARS programme, to enhance the industry, unlike Thailand, which has decentralised more authority to ministries.[10]

The CARS programme seems to be based on the expectation of continuous market growth in the Philippines in the future. Figure 8.7 indicates GDP per capita and GDP growth rate in the Philippines in the period of 2000–2023. Our interviewees in Southeast Asia suggest that motorisation starts when GDP per capita reaches US$3,000, which allows the middle class to be able to purchase cars (Natsuda *et al.* 2015a). The IMF expected GDP per capita in the Philippines to grow to over US$3,000 by 2018, which it did,[11] and US$4,000 by 2022.

In response to the CARS programme, some Japanese automotive producers have shown quite strong interest. Mitsubishi views the Philippines as a core strategic location after Thailand and Indonesia, expanding production capacity there (Kurasawa 2014), because the Philippines is the only country in Southeast Asia where Mitsubishi thinks it can maintain a top-three market share. Prior to the CARS programme in 2015, Mitsubishi acquired Ford's former factory of 50,000 vehicles production capacity (Fourin 2015: 139). In February 2016, Mitsubishi formally announced their participation in CARS, investing in a new

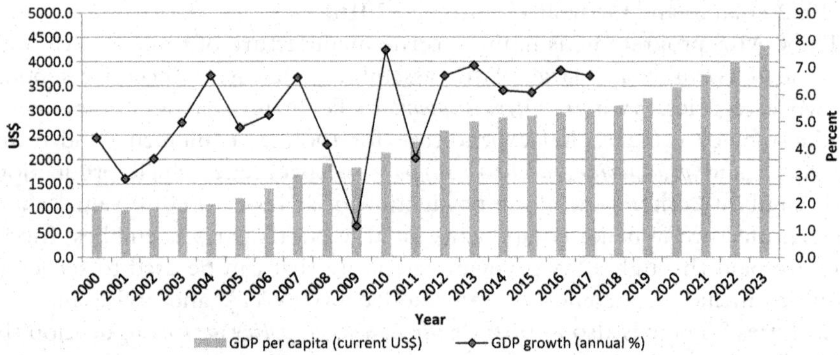

Figure 8.7 GDP per Capita and GDP growth rate in the Philippines, 2000–2023.
Source: World Development Indicators (online) and World Economic Outlook (online).
Note: IMF's forecast IMF's forecast for the period 2018–2023.

press factory and producing small PVs (Mirage models) in the Philippines in 2017 (Fourin 2017:107). Similarly, Toyota planned to produce its Vios model in 2018, by replacing imported components from Thailand with local production in the Philippines, to increase LC ratios (Fourin 2015: 138–139 and 2017: 107–108). Though these two producers responded to the programme, an additional 400,000 vehicle production is necessary to achieve its target by 2022. One of the uncertainties derives from the fact that unlike Thailand and Indonesia, there are no clear market policy signals to consumers, indicating the type of vehicle to be promoted locally with tax incentives.

Among Japanese automotive component manufacturers, it was reported that Furukawa Denki was setting up a new plant for automotive coils in the Philippines in 2016 (ASEAN 2017: 17) and expanding in 2018, and Murata Manufacturing was constructing a second plant for electronic components in 2018 (ASEAN 2018: 42).

Challenges to the Philippines' automotive industry

Automotive components

Foreign exchange and LCR policies forced automotive assemblers to establish exports of certain auto components, which continued after these policies were abandoned in 2001 and 2003, respectively, under the WTO. These activities consolidated the components industry into regional production networks under regional free trade agreements (FTAs) such as the Brand-to-Brand Scheme (BBC) in 1988, the ASEAN Industrial Cooperation (AICO) scheme in 1996, AFTA, and since 2015, AEC. Such networks involve a regional division of labour, with specialisation on particular components using economies of scale in each country.

During the 1970s, when participants in PCMP were required to manufacture components not only for the domestic market but also for export to acquire foreign currencies, the Philippines provided labour competitiveness in terms of a combination of labour cost, manual dexterity, and technical skills. A feature has been the production of transmissions. After Mitsubishi established Asian Transmission in 1973, other firms such as Toyota, Honda, and Isuzu followed to produce and export transmissions in the Philippines, particularly under the AICO, aiming to create regional parts complementarity in the 1990s. Japanese manufacturers believed that workers in the Philippines were suitable in terms of manual dexterity and technical skills to assemble the numerous tiny gear parts (such as seals, springs, shafts, interlock assemblies) that make up a gear box (Ofreneo 2016). These assemblers established parts manufacturing for export to other ASEAN countries, as well as to Japan and elsewhere, separately from assembly operation (see Table 8.1).

The Philippines has been growing as a production base for wiring harnesses, although most exports are to outside of Southeast Asia, with Japan and North America taking the bulk of them.[12] There are at least 15 firms that produce wiring harness, including the major exporters Yazaki-Torres and International Electric Wiring Systems. Six of the 15 are ranked among the largest 10 exporters of automotive parts in the country (Sturgeon *et al.* 2016). Wiring harness is characterised by labour-intensive and skill-intensive production, requiring dexterity and technical skills, with workers who are mostly high school graduates with postsecondary technical skills training (Ofreneo 2016).

Now in the Philippines, 11 assemblers and 265 parts suppliers manufacture approximately 330 components. At least 123 firms are located in the Philippine Economic Zone Authority, exporting at least 70% of their products. Of these, the largest 15 exporting firms account for 80% of total automotive export revenue in the Philippines (Sturgeon *et al.* 2016: 29). However, the components industry overall in the Philippines generally still remains underdeveloped and has failed to diversify. The Philippines' industrial structure has remained hollow or missing in the middle, characterised by weak linkages between SMEs and large firms (Aldaba 2013). Despite the success of foreign exchange requirement

Table 8.1 Assemblers' Parts Production Firms in the Philippines

Firm	*Establishment Year*	*Components and Production Capacity*	*Main Export Destination*
Asian Transmission	1973	MT: 540,000 units Engine: 30,000 units	ASEAN countries, Japan and Taiwan
Toyota Auto Parts	1992	MT: 330,000 units CVJ: 200,000 units	Asian Countries and South Africa
Honda Parts	1992	MT: 140,000 units	ASEAN countries
Isuzu Auto Parts	1996	MT: 248,000 units	n.a.

Source: Fourin (2015: 147).

Note: MT (manual transmission), CVJ (constant velocity joint), n.a (not available).

policies in developing production and export of key components, vehicle import penetration and export performance represent failures to develop the industry, particularly compared to Thailand and Indonesia (see Figure 8.3).

Local content and vehicle costs

Government policy since the early days of automotive development up to the early 2000s had attempted to increase LC by the use of LCRs. Yet although the Philippines has expanded its export capacity of some automotive parts, the LC ratios in locally produced vehicles are still very low. For instance, the LC ratio of Toyota's Vios (which was the largest production model in the Philippines in 2014) is estimated at an average of 23% (Fourin 2015: 138). Aldaba (2008) analyses the comparative cost structure of vehicle production between Thailand and the Philippines, asserting that the total vehicle production cost with a 23% of LC ratio in the Philippines is 1.4 times higher than that of Thailand with a 67% LC ratio, with the implication that a higher LC ratio reduces costs. In terms of assembly cost, it was 1.75 times higher in the Philippines than in Thailand in the early to mid-2000s (Aldaba 2008: 22). According to CAMPI, it is estimated that locally produced vehicles in the Philippines are approximately US$1,800–2,000 more expensive than imported vehicles from Thailand of the same model.[13] The CARS programme may enhance local parts production of bulky components and large plastic parts. Nonetheless, it is still uncertain to what extent the locally made parts will be used in the local assembly of vehicles. An executive interviewed in the industry thinks that some bulky parts, along with wiring harness and transmissions production, will survive in the Philippines, but the rest of components production might be eliminated in competition with other ASEAN countries under AEC.[14]

Importation of second-hand vehicles

A significant challenge – and policy implementation failure – for the Philippines' automotive industry is the importation of second-hand vehicles from Japan and Korea. In general, used car imports have been banned in the Philippines. However, this did not apply to free ports, which were allowed to operate as separate custom territories ensuring free flow of goods and capital. In the case of the Subic Bay Freeport (one of the largest in the Philippines), approximately 70 firms were channelling second-hand cars into the country (Aldaba 2008: 4–5).

In 2002, the importation of all types of used cars and components was prohibited, except some which were allowed to be imported under certain special conditions (Llanto and Ortiz 2015). However, this could not be enforced due to a temporary restraining order in March 2003, as second-hand vehicle importers were able to obtain court injunctions because of their powerful political patrons (Ofreneo 2016). Finally, the Supreme Court ruled to prohibit the import of second-hand vehicles except for the Subic Bay Freeport (but on condition that vehicles could not be taken into other areas in the country) (Aldaba

2008, Nomura 2007). Though second-hand imported vehicles are banned in most regions, the ban is not fully implemented. A high-ranking official in the Department of Trade and Industry estimated 20% of registered vehicles (about 3.5 million vehicles in 2014) in the Philippines had been illegally imported.[15]

Free trade agreements

Another challenge for the Philippines is in relation with FTAs, since it is less competitive than its main rivals, Thailand and Indonesia. In the ASEAN-4 countries, Japanese-brand vehicles accounted for over 80% of the market in 2016 (87% including Malaysia's Perodua).[16] Most of the major Japanese assemblers in Southeast Asia produce their vehicles to sell within the region (and also export to the rest of the world in the case of Thailand),[17] and a regional division of labour to achieve economies of scale in vehicle production has been established within the ASEAN region. The location of CBU production in each country is planned within the region according to the local market demand (such as Thailand's for one-ton pickup trucks) and local conditions including government policies. As we examined in Chapter 4 (see Table 4.10), Toyota specialises in particular models to produce in each country and exchanges their products between countries as intra-firm trade. For example, Toyota in association with Daihatsu started exporting their Indonesian LCGCs to the Philippines in 2014.[18]

In addition to Japanese producers, a large volume of investment has been planned by non-Japanese assemblers, namely, GM, Ford, and VW in Thailand and Indonesia in recent years.[19] In Thailand, Ford and GM were planning to produce Eco-cars by 2019; VW is also planning to establish a new factory. In Indonesia, GM was planning to produce 150,000 compact cars a year in 2017. Similarly, VW was also planning to manufacture 100,000 vehicles from 2017. These firms do not own production bases in the Philippines and may export to the Philippines under AEC to compete with local vehicles. In this sense, the strong influence of multinational assemblers has not been channelled sufficiently towards the Philippines by the country's automotive policies.

The ASEAN-Korea Free Trade Area (AKFTA) poses another challenge. Under AKFTA, tariffs on vehicles from Korea set at 20% in 2015 were reduced to 5% in 2016.[20] Korean producers have only small assembly operations in Southeast Asia, depending instead on vehicle exports from Korea.[21] As mentioned earlier, the Philippines is the only country in which Hyundai has a significant market share in the ASEAN-4. Imported vehicles under AKFTA will thus be a threat unless the CARS policy can attract Korean automotive investment into the Philippines.

Conclusions

The Philippines has to conduct its automotive policies within the regional context in ASEAN of automotive global value chains and production networks governed mainly by Japanese assemblers, who, in turn, influence the activities of their multinational Tier-1 suppliers. Policy needs to influence the decisions of these assemblers. In this chapter, we have focussed on 'hard' industrial policies such as ISI and LCRs, rather than 'soft' policies such as support for innovation (UNDP 2013: 67). Investigation of the role of soft policies in the Philippines would require further research, but our findings on hard policies impact have highlighted, we think, some interesting issues.

Broadly speaking – Malaysia's national car policy aside – the Philippines has followed similar industrial policies as that of its main ASEAN rivals, Thailand, Indonesia, and Malaysia: that is, ISI conducted initially with import bans, then with tariffs, all backed by LCRs, and followed in the 1990s by some liberalisation (though more so in the Philippines than in other ASEAN-4 countries). There have been differences, however. In particular, the Philippines' use of foreign exchange requirements, not much used elsewhere in the ASEAN automotive industry, has induced multinational assemblers in the country to set up domestic component production for export, like transmissions, to earn their necessary foreign exchange.

Wiring harnesses exports, though, seem to have depended more on their inherent labour-intensive production, making use of the Philippines' abundant educated labour, than on policies like LCRs.[22] This export success has continued despite the ending of such policies under WTO-TRIMs, reflecting that labour-intensive component exports are not 'comparative-advantage-defying' in Lin's sense (Lin and Chang 2009). On the other hand, unlike Thailand, and now increasingly Indonesia, the Philippines has not promoted ***product champion*** types of vehicles such as Thailand's one-ton pickup truck or Indonesia's low-cost green car, nor has it tried to encourage the domestic sales of such vehicles by using preferential tax concessions; when it had a chance to do so with its Asian Utility Vehicle, it chose instead to tax it more heavily, thus failing to take advantage of the remaining 'policy space' under the post-2000 WTO. Unlike other ASEAN countries, particularly Thailand, the Philippines' lesser success in using the standard policies is due to combinations of political instability, contradictions between different policies, weak state capacity for enforcing implementation (especially on second-hand car imports), and some trade liberalisation urged by the World Bank. It was put to us by several industry sources in the Philippines that the country liberalised its trade regime prematurely, and certainly the Philippines' automotive tariffs in the 1990s and early 2000s were lower than those in other ASEAN countries. Yet no substantial growth in imports occurred until the intra-ASEAN tariff under AFTA was dropped to 5% in 2004 (and then to zero in 2010) (Thoburn and Natsuda 2018).

Japanese automotive assemblers interviewed elsewhere in the ASEAN region have indicated that market size and growth are more important to their investment decisions in a country than preferential policies, although they may reduce their activities in the face of unfavourable policies, as in Malaysia. The Philippines' economy may well continue to grow, consolidating a take-off into motorisation. However, its total market will still be much smaller than Indonesia's or Thailand's, with less scope for local economies of scale, and it is uncertain how far its local demand for vehicles will be met by local production. This is due in part to the absence of demand-side market signals and policy to stimulate local consumption of particular domestic vehicles. Furthermore, there are still challenges from the Philippines' continued apparent inability to control imported second-hand vehicle sales and from vehicles likely to be imported under free trade agreements in the future; the substantial fall in vehicle production between 2017 and 2018 is not a hopeful sign.

Notes

1 The collapse of the Marcos government seriously damaged the industry (see Doner 1991: chapter 7).
2 See https://www.carmudi.com.ph/journal/local-vehicle-production-suffers-44-reduction-in-2018/ [accessed on 20 February 2020].
3 Interview with the president of CAMPI on 6 February 2015.
4 Interview with the president of CAMPI on 6 February 2015.
5 However, Ofreneo (2016) identifies 124 suppliers as Tier-1. See our Chapter 3.
6 An originally Philippine-designed (or similarly designed) LCV with a higher local content than normal LCVs.
7 Many newspapers indicate 600,000 vehicles (without export target). For example, http://business.inquirer.net/192860/palace-oks-road-map-for-automotive-industry [accessed on 15 February 2019].
8 http://industry.gov.ph/cars-program/ [accessed on 15 February 2019].
9 For example, in Thailand, excise tax on double-cab pickup trucks was cut after 2000 from 35–48% to 12%, and on other pickup trucks reduced to 3–5%, to cut prices to consumers. Assemblers of such vehicles could import machinery free of import duty, and their major components suppliers got corporation tax holidays. See Natsuda and Thoburn (2013: 416 and 428–430) on Thailand, and Natsuda *et al.* (2015a) on Indonesia.
10 Interview, 13 February 2015.
11 The Philippines' GDP per capita was $3,103 in 2018 (*World Development Indicators* online).
12 In 2016, ASEAN was the export destination of only 6.4% of the Philippines' exports of wiring harnesses (HS854430), while 40% was sold to Japan and 45% to North America (See Table 3.11 and Thoburn and Natsuda 2018).
13 Interview with the president of CAMPI on 6 February 2015.
14 Interview, 10 February 2015.
15 Interview, 13 February 2015.
16 See Table 3.3 in Chapter 3.
17 Thailand exports product champion pickup trucks and Eco-cars.
18 Toyota's website: http://www2.toyota.co.jp/en/news/14/02/0203 [accessed on 15 February 2019].
19 *Nikkei Shinbun* (3 February 2015), http://www.nikkei.com/article/DGXLZO827 19990S5A200C1FFE000 [accessed on 15 February 2019].
20 http://akfta.asean.org [accessed on 15 February 2019].
21 See Chapter 3.
22 An interviewee in the Philippines indicated that if the Philippines automotive industry purchased all its wiring harness requirements locally, it would only absorb about 5% of the country's wiring harness output.

Appendices

Appendix 8.1 Local Content Requirements under CVDP in the Philippines, 1988–1990

Commercial Vehicle Category	*1988 (%)*	*1989 (%)*	*1990 (%)*
Category I: AUVs up to 3,000 kg gross vehicle weight (GVW)	43.10	51.21	54.86
Category II: LCVs up to 3,000 kg GVW	35.62	41.69	44.42
Category III: Vehicles from 3,001 kg to 6,000 kg GVW	16.83	20.33	21.90
Category IV: Vehicles from 6,001 kg to 18,000 kg GVW	16.50	19.91	21.44
a) 6,001 kg to 9,000 kg GVW	17.00	20.64	22.24
b) 9,001 kg to 12,000 kg GVW	10.69	12.65	13.53
c) 12,001 kg to 15,000 kg GVW	10.87	12.87	13.77
d) 15,001 kg to 18,000 kg GVW			

Source: Aldaba (2000: 3–4).

Appendix 8.2 Local Content and Foreign Exchange Requirements in the Philippines, 1997–2000

Category	*LC Requirement (%)*	*Foreign Exchange Requirement*				*Requirement for New Entrant*
		1997 (%)	*1998 (%)*	*1999 (%)*	*2000 (%)*	
PV I	≧40	7.5	7.5	15.0	15.0	Min of US$10 million investment for component production
PV II	≧40	45.0	50.0	50.0	55.0	
PV II	–	75.0	75.0	75.0	75.0	
CV I	≧45	7.5	7.5	15.0	15.0	Min of US$8 million investment for component production
CV II	≧45	7.5	7.5	15.0	15.0	
CV III	≧21.9	5.0	5.0	5.0	5.0	
CV IV	≧21.9	5.0	5.0	5.0	5.0	
CV V	10.87–16.5	5.0	5.0	5.0	5.0	

Source: Fourin (1999: 133).

Note: PV (passenger vehicle), CV (commercial vehicle); category I–IV are same as Table 1; PV1: with engine of 1200 cc or below and with a price determined by the BOI; PV2: with engine from over 1200 cc to 2190 cc; PV3: with engine of over 2190 cc; CV V: Over 18,000 kg GVW.

Appendix 8.3 Tariff, Excise Tax, and VAT Structure for CKD and CBUs in the Philippines in 1999

Type of Vehicle			*CKD*			*CBU*		
			Tariff	*Excise*	*VAT*	*Tariff*	*Excise*	*VAT*
PV	Gasoline	ED≦1600 cc	7%	15%	10%	40%	15%	10%
		1600 cc <ED≦2000 cc	in 1998	35%			35%	
		2000 cc <ED≦2700 cc	10%	50%			50%	
		2,700 cc≦ED	in 1999	100%			100%	
	Diesel	ED≦1800 cc	7%	15%	10%	40%	15%	10%
		1800 cc <ED≦2300 cc	in 1998	35%			35%	
		2300 cc <ED≦3000 cc	10%	50%			50%	
		3000 cc≦ED	in 1999	100%			100%	
C	Van	Up to 9 passenger	(PV)	(PV)	10%	40%	(PV)	10%
V		Over 10 passengers	3%	0%		20%	0%	
	Trucks	Gasoline engine	3%	0%	10%	40%	0%	10%
		Diesel engine				20%		
	Bus	GVW≦18t	3%	0%	10%	20%	0%	10%
		18t <GVW				20%		
	4WD	Up to 9 passenger	(PV)	(PV)	10%	40%	(PV)	10%
		Over 10 passengers	3%			20%	0%	
	SPV	Ambulance etc.	3%	0%	–	10%	0%	10%

Source: Fourin (1999: 133).

Note: ED (engine displacement); PV: same as PV rates.

Appendix 8.4 Excise Tax System in the Philippines, 2003–2017

Vehicle Price (Peso)	*Excise Tax (Peso)*
Up to 60,0000	2%
600,001 – 1,100,000	12,000 + (vehicle price – 600,000) × 20%
1,100,001–2,100,000	112,000 + (vehicle price – 1,100,000) × 40%
Above 2,100,000	512,000 + (vehicle price – 2,100,000) × 60%

Source: Fourin (2008: 236, 2017: 106).

9 Vietnam

Introduction[1]

Within ASEAN, Vietnam is a late starter as a vehicle producer. Although there was state production of military vehicles in the country from the 1950s, the modern automotive[2] industry dates only from the early 1990s (Hansen 2016), some 30–40 years behind the other ASEAN vehicle producers. Vietnam's total vehicle production by 2015 (171,753 units), however, had exceeded that of the 1995 production of the long-established producer – The Philippines (98,768 units) – though Vietnam's production at that time was still only 9% of that of Thailand, and in 2018 it is only 11% (236,000 compared to nearly 2.2 million units) (OICA website).

Like the automotive industries of the ASEAN-4 – with the only partial exception of Malaysia – automotive development in Vietnam has been heavily dependent on inward foreign investment, mainly, though not exclusively, from Japan. Following the introduction of Vietnam's *doi moi* programme of extensive economic reforms in 1986,[3] and the country's subsequent opening to foreign investment, a substantial number of foreign automotive assemblers invested in Vietnam in the early and mid-1990s, including Mazda, Kia, Toyota, Suzuki, Daihatsu, Daimler-Chrysler, Isuzu, and Ford (Kobayashi 2017: 10).

Although Vietnam experienced quite rapid growth in vehicle production in the 2010s, albeit from a low base, its motor vehicle industry remained quite heavily protected from import competition by tariffs, giving multinational assemblers an incentive to continue domestic production to circumvent the protection. Within ASEAN, and unlike the ASEAN-4 automotive producers, Vietnam's protection continued until the start of 2018, under a special derogation[4] from the other countries' move to free trade in 2010 under AFTA.[5] In any case, as we have shown in earlier chapters, the ASEAN-4 already also had made moves towards trade liberalisation in the 1990s.

In the mid- to late 2010s, then, the Vietnamese vehicle industry was vulnerable, mainly carrying out assembly with low local content, and with domestic vehicle costs being about 20% higher than those of similar imported models.[6] It was thought likely that a number of the then 20 assemblers would leave the country and supply the Vietnamese market by exports instead, for example, from Thailand.[7] More encouragingly, Vietnam had already started to develop exporting some components, although very labour-intensive ones, like wiring harnesses, bur it also had some vulnerability to relocation to other lower-wage countries in the ASEAN region, namely Cambodia, Laos, or Myanmar.

This chapter now looks first at the structure of the Vietnamese vehicle industry in terms of production, sales, and market share, and at trade structure and recent developments in foreign trade. It then traces the development of the industry, though more briefly than in earlier country chapters because of Vietnam's shorter period of automotive development. Next, it considers the various challenges the industry faces, and finally it offers conclusions and comparisons, where some material on automotive developments in Myanmar, Laos, and Cambodia is briefly introduced.

Overview of the automotive industry in Vietnam

Automotive production and sales

The production and sales figures illustrated in Figure 9.1 show a strongly rising trend in both since the mid-2000s until 2016 when expectations of falling vehicle prices, resulting from expected free trade in 2018 under the AEC, started to affect sales and production. The consistent excess of sales over production indicates continuing net imports. Figure 9.2 indicates the importance of Japanese brands in total vehicle sales, though with strong minority positions for the Korean brand Kia and for the US brand Ford.

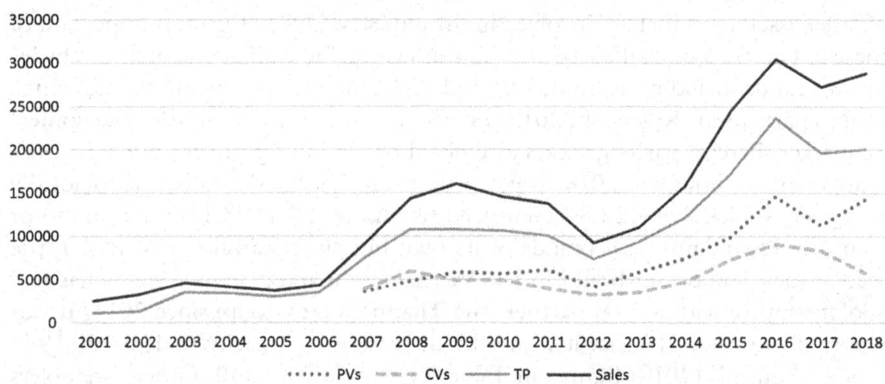

Figure 9.1 Production and Sales of Vehicles in Vietnam, 2001–2018.

Source: From Fourin (2017and 2019).

Note: PV (passenger vehicle), CV (commercial vehicle), and TP (total production).

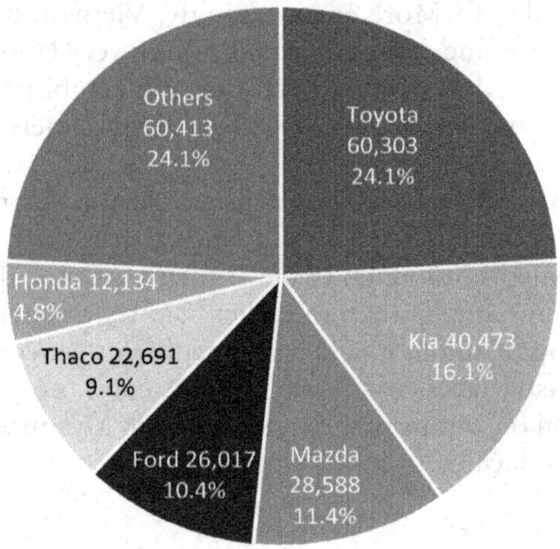

Figure 9.2 Sales Volume and Market Share by Automotive Brand in Vietnam, 2017.
Source: Fourin (2018).
Note: Total 250,619 vehicles (VAMA members only).

Automotive structure

Table 9.1 shows the production capacities of major assemblers in Vietnam.

As of 2015, our interviews suggested, there were 20 assemblers in Vietnam,[8] and this is also the figure given by Kobayashi (2017: 16). According to the current list of 17 member companies in the Vietnam Automobile Manufacturers' Association (VAMA),[9] there are, in addition to the brands listed in Table 9.1, a number of other assemblers that are involved in the industry. One of the most important of these is Thaco, in central Vietnam – and shown in Table 9.1 – assembling vehicles under brands including Kia, Mazda, and PSA, and also producing a small range of auto parts itself (Kobayashi 2017: 14–15). According to Kobayashi, the domestic market share of passenger cars assembled by Thaco slightly exceeded Toyota's share in 2014, though in 2018, Toyota's share of what VAMA calls 'sales of locally assembled vehicles' was 22.8% compared to Thaco's 20.4%.[10] The Korean motor company Hyundai – with brands of its own but closely affiliated with Kia, the second most important brand in the Vietnamese market (Figure 9.2) – has had a joint venture with a local partner (the Thanh Cong Group) since 2011. It was reported in early 2019 that it would be increasing its capacity to 100,000,[11, 12] though Fourin's (2019) figures in Table 9.1 cite only 82,000. Other assemblers include VEAM, the Vietnam Engine and Agricultural Machinery Corporation, involved in truck assembly,[13] Daewoo Bus (despite its name, assembling passenger cars), Hino Motors Vietnam, a Toyota affiliate assembling trucks,[14] Vina (assembling Mitsubishi vehicles, see ASEAN 2014: 181), and Samco Vietnam which distributes a variety of makes and assembles some vehicles.[15]

Table 9.1 Production Capacities of Major Assemblers in Vietnam, 2019

Assembler	*Capacity*	*Notes*
VinFast	280,000	Producing GM models by using VinFast brand name under GM license; took over GM plant in Vietnam in 2019
Thaco	120,000	Truck (50,000), bus (25,000), passenger vehicles (40,000), special vehicles (5,000) including subcontracting for Hyundai, Kia, Foton, Peugeot, and Mitsubishi Fuso
Hyundai	83,000	JV with Thanh Cong
Toyota	51,000	Established in 1995
Mazda	50,000	Established Thaco Mazda factory in March 2018
Ford	14,000	Established in 1995
Honda	10,000	Established in 1995
Isuzu	9,400	Established in 1995
Transinco	8,000	Bus assembler
Nissan	6,500	Started the operation in 2013
Mitsubishi	5,000	Former Vina Star Motors
Suzuki	5,000	Started the operation in 1996
Hino	4,000	Established in 1996
SAMCO	4,000	Bus assembler, established in 2004
Mercedes	3,500	Started the operation in 1996
Total	652,400	

Source: Fourin (2019: 72–73); Mazda additional information from https://tuoitrenews.vn/news/business/20180326/japans-mazda-opens-largest-southeast-asia-factory-in-vietnam/44747.html, Hyundai from https://www.vir.com.vn/vietnamese-automobile-manufacturers-growing-up-to-the-task-57655.html, Thaco from http://www.thacogroup.vn/en/business-activities/Automobiles-mechanics/ [all accessed on 16 January 2020].

Note: Vehicles per annum.

A range of secondary sources (e.g. Schröder 2017), as well as our interviewees, have stressed the limited range of automotive component suppliers operating in Vietnam, resulting in low local content figures. The low LC, in turn, is a reason why imported cars are said to cost some 20% less than domestically assembled models.

A number of major mega-suppliers do operate in Vietnam, however. Of the top 20 global automotive parts manufacturers shown in ASEAN (2014: 157), ten were listed as being active in the country: Bosch (from Germany, producing belts for continuously variable transmissions – see ASEAN 2014: 32), Denso (Japan, affiliated to Toyota), Yazaki (Japan), ZF Friedrichshaften (Germany), Lear (USA), BASF (Germany), Sumitomo Wiring Systems (Japan), Toyota Boshoku (Japan), Hitachi Automotive Systems (Japan), and Cummins (USA). As of 2013, Bridgestone announced they were increasing their capacity to produce tyres in Vietnam (ASEAN 2014: 84). In addition, ASEAN (2017: 17) notes that the Japanese auto parts and components suppliers Shin Etsu Chemicals and Toyoda Gosei (making airbag parts) had expansion plans in Vietnam. EU automotive component manufacturers in Vietnam also included Thyssenkrupp from Germany and the tyre company Michelin from France (ASEAN 2017: 56).

As we shall note in our discussion of Vietnam's trade data, these large supplier firms are not necessarily supplying components primarily to meet the needs of the domestic vehicle industry in Vietnam. Thus, Yazaki and Sumitomo Wiring Systems are engaged in the production of wiring harnesses, Vietnam's most important automotive export (broadly defined),[16] and similar comments relate to the production of airbags and transmissions.

Toyota is said to have the highest local content (37%) of any assembler in Vietnam, compared to a national average in 2018 of 7–10%, even though the government was said to have aimed for 40% LC by 2005 and 60% by 2010 (for vehicles with fewer than nine seats) (*Vietnam Economic News*, 11 January 2018[17]). Toyota has 18 (Tier-1) suppliers, including Denso supplying system control components, Yazaki supplying wiring harnesses and the Thai international firm Summit supplying seat sets.[18]

A major weakness of the Vietnamese automotive supply industry is the lack of second- and third-tier suppliers. A study of the automotive supply industry by Schröder (2017) – broadly defined by him to include producers of motorcycle components – notes how automobile component suppliers and motorcycle component suppliers are often closely related. Of a sub-sample of 141 suppliers, 69 supplied only motorcycle parts, 51 supplied both the automobile and motorcycle industries, and only 21 worked for the automobile industry alone. More confusingly, another 284 sampled component supplier firms could not be so classified as they also produced parts for the electronics and white goods sector. Quite strikingly – albeit aggregating automobile and motorcycle component suppliers – there were more Tier-1 suppliers than either Tier-2 or Tier-3; and in a further attempt to classify 188 otherwise unclassifiable firms, there were more Tier-1/Tier-2 firms than those in lower tiers, although there were still 104 firms left unclassifiable (Schröder 2017: 41–44). Given the predominance of motorcycle component suppliers in the statistics, it seems likely that the pyramid structure of suppliers typical of the ASEAN-4 vehicle producers – with increasing numbers of suppliers as one descends to lower tiers (see, for example, Figure 5.2 for Thailand and Figure 6.2 for Indonesia) –does not characterise Vietnam, where Tier-2 and Tier-3 suppliers, particularly local ones, are scarce.

Automotive trade in Vietnam[19]

As is clear from Figure 9.3, Vietnam's exports of passenger vehicles (HS8703) are negligible (as also is true for the vehicles for the transport of goods, HS8704). The country's main automotive export – that is excluding motorcycles and cycles – is that of automotive components (HS8708).[20] Figure 9.3 shows how overall automotive imports (HS87) increased steeply in the early 2010s and then tailed off down to 2017. Imports of passenger vehicles (HS8703) continued to increase, though not sharply, but the decrease in overall HS87 imports is mirrored by the decrease in imported automotive components (HS8708).

Interestingly, for HS 8708 in the early 2010s, automotive component exports (at around US$1 billion) were as large in imports, though subsequently a trade gap opened noticeably. Component exports are quite specialised, with transmissions and safety airbags accounting for over half of total component exports.[21]

Sources for the total imports of HS87 are shown in Figure 9.4, where Thailand is the biggest source, but Thailand and Indonesia together only supply about a third of Vietnam's HS87 imports. For passenger cars (HS 8703), though, Thailand and Indonesia – the ASEAN-4's main vehicle producers – supply nearly 60% of the total, indicating the growth of intra-ASEAN trade as Vietnam gradually cut its tariffs under AFTA/ATIGA/AEC. Exports of passenger cars by Vietnam (not shown) are negligible.[22] For HS8708, automotive components (Figure 9.6), Thailand is a much less important supplier than for cars, with around two-thirds coming from Korea, Japan, and China. Similarly, as a destination for Vietnam's

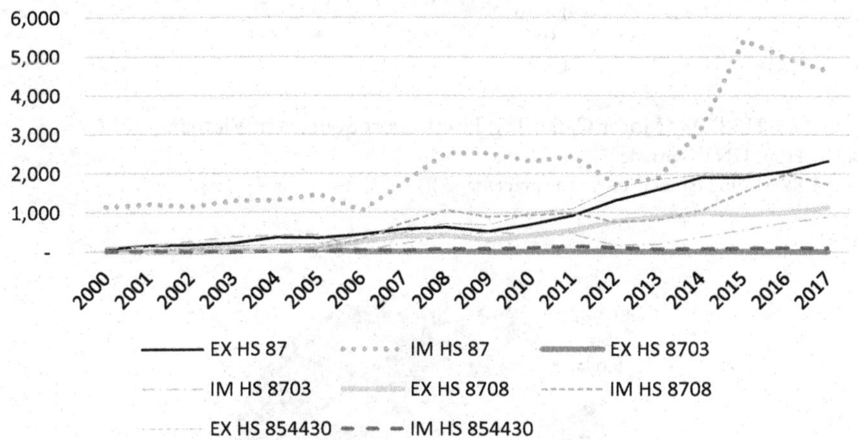

Figure 9.3 Automotive Trade of Vietnam, 2000–2017.
Source: from UN Comtrade.
Note: US$ Million.

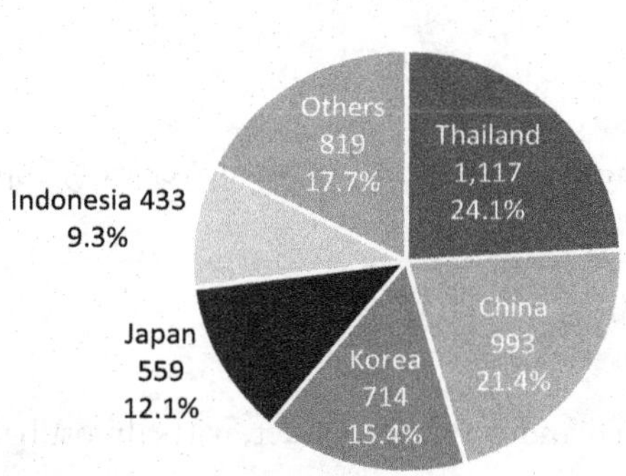

Figure 9.4 HS87 (Vehicles, Parts, and Accessories), Top Five Import Sources in Vietnam, 2017.
Source: From UN Comtrade.
Note: US$ Million (shown above the percentages).

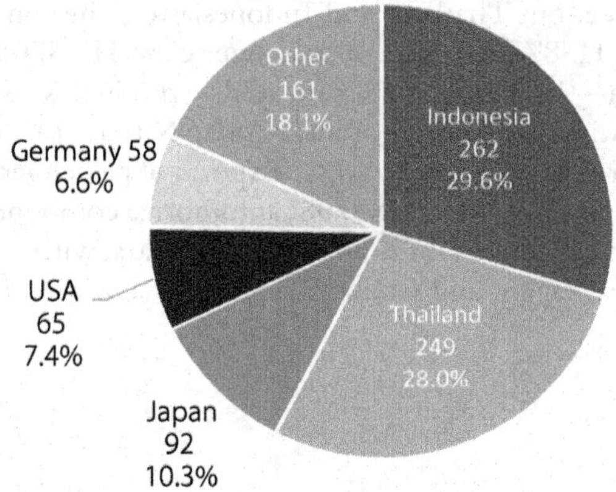

Figure 9.5 HS8703 (Motor Cars), Top Five Import Sources in Vietnam, 2017.
Source: From UN Comtrade.
Note: US$ Million (shown above the percentages).

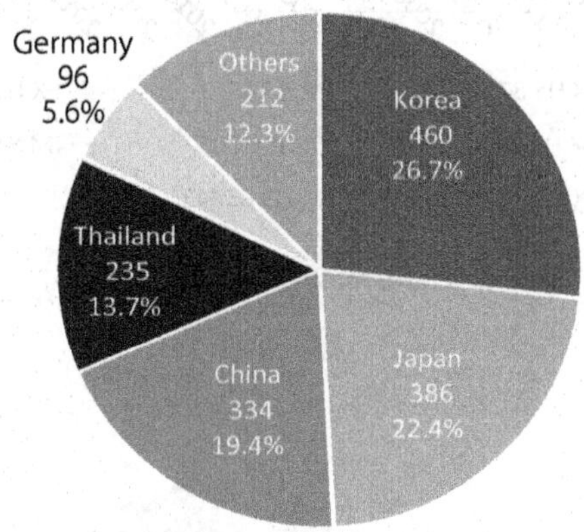

Figure 9.6 HS8708 (Parts and Accessories of Motor Vehicles), Top Five Import Sources in Vietnam, 2017.
Source: From UN Comtrade.
Note: US$ Million (shown above the percentages).

HS 8708 exports, Thailand is a small market, with almost half of the total going to Japan and China.

The export destinations for wiring harnesses (HS 854430) are shown in Figure 9.8, two-thirds of which are sent to Japan, and indeed Japan and North America combined take some 90% of Vietnam's exports of this product.[23] Exports of wiring harnesses, an important component not included in the

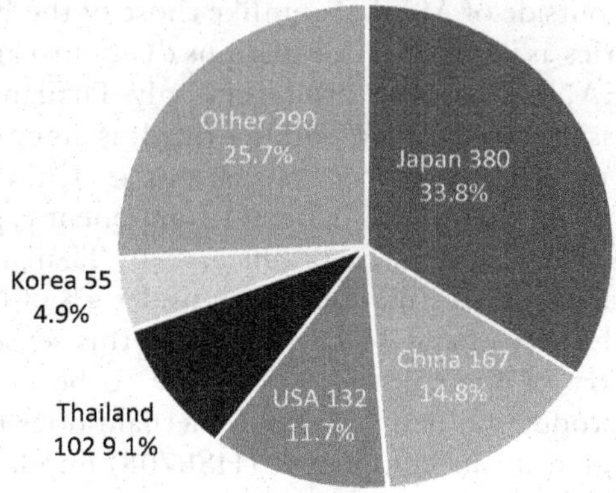

Figure 9.7 HS8708 (Parts and Accessories of Motor Vehicles), Top Five Export Destinations of Vietnam, 2017.

Source: From UN Comtrade.

Note: US$ Million (shown above the percentages).

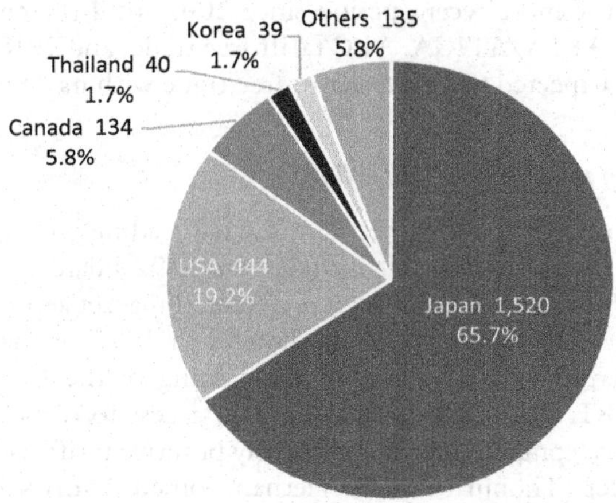

Figure 9.8 HS854430 (Wiring harnesses), Top Five Export Destinations of Vietnam, 2017.

Source: From UN Comtrade.

Note: US$ Million (shown above the percentages).

normal automotive component categories (HS 8708), currently around US$2 billion, were as large as total HS87 imports in the early 2010s, though subsequently they did not increase as fast as total HS87 imports. Interestingly, the pattern of substantial exports of wiring harnesses and transmissions, with negligible exports of motor vehicles, mirrors the trade of the Philippines. It also mirrors the pattern of exports of wiring harnesses, which is mainly to outside of ASEAN. However, Vietnam's exports of transmissions are also mainly directed to outside of ASEAN – unlike those of the Philippines, which has ASEAN countries as important destinations (Thoburn and Natsuda 2018: 524). Among ASEAN automotive producers only Thailand (taking 16% of Vietnam's transmission exports, and ranking third) is among the top ten destinations, whereas the top two export destinations are China (41%) and Japan (27%). Similarly, for the next most important component export, airbags (HS 870895), among ASEAN automotive producers only Thailand was among the top ten Vietnamese export destinations, with under 4% of the total, whereas 58% were exported to Japan and 14% to Korea. In this sense, the automotive components industry of Vietnam does not seem to be much connected to ASEAN regional production networks, and Vietnam does not depend much on the ASEAN region for its component (HS8708) imports (Figure 9.6) or exports (Figure 9.7) either.

Development of the automotive industry in Vietnam

The development of the Vietnamese automotive (vehicle) industry can be conveniently divided into three stages: the period prior to the country's joining the WTO in 2007, the more recent period since 2007 until the end of Vietnam's derogation from AFTA/ATIGA/AEC tariff-free trade, and 2018 onwards when the country was expected to be subject to free trade with its ASEAN partners.

Prior to joining the WTO (1990–2006)

This is the period during which Vietnam started trading with industrial countries outside of the Soviet bloc. It includes the 1992 bilateral agreement with the European Union to allow Vietnam preferential market access on GSP (Generalized System of Preferences) terms; the end in 1994 of the US trade and investment embargo on Vietnam; and the signing of the US Bilateral Trade Agreement (USBTA) of 2001, giving Vietnam access to the US market on *de facto* WTO terms, compared to the previously punitive tariffs faced by Vietnam in the US market (Thoburn 2007). Vietnam joined ASEAN (and AFTA) in 1995, applied in 2005 to join the WTO, and did so in 2007.

The early to mid-1990s, when, as noted earlier, there was a substantial inflow of inward investment from foreign vehicle producers, was also a period when the domestic private sector was extremely small and highly restricted in its activities.[24] In these circumstances, inward automotive foreign investment not only was able to link Vietnam to automotive GVCs, but it also substituted – like other inward foreign investments – for an almost absent domestic private sector in an economy in which most industrial activity was run by state enterprises at various levels. State enterprises, however, did develop local bus and truck production, so foreign investment was most needed for cars.

The absence of a domestic private sector was an early limitation for the car industry in Vietnam as it is typically a highly outsourced activity where, as we have seen in earlier chapters, assemblies and components are bought in by assemblers from tiers of supplying companies, including very small firms in the third tier.[25] Thus, in the early stages, most components would be imported, or they would have to be produced by assemblers in-house or by persuading their overseas suppliers to establish production in Vietnam.

As we have shown in earlier chapters, the 1990s was a decade in which considerable trade liberalisation took place in the ASEAN countries, including in relation to the automotive industry. Yet this was a time when tariffs on vehicle imports in Vietnam remained higher in relation to its ASEAN neighbours; and as in the ASEAN-4 in earlier decades, Vietnamese vehicle production in the 1990s developed under general policies of import substitution. There was a difference, though, that Vietnam was still in the process of reforming its trade regime from its earlier command economy, which had relied little on import tariffs as a policy tool.[26]

A study by Timothy Sturgeon (1998), based on fieldwork in Vietnam in 1998 immediately as the effects of the 1997 Asian financial crisis (AFC) were being felt, chronicles the early development of the industry. In 1991, Auto Hoa Bing, a company with a history of manufacturing military vehicles, formed the first joint venture – the Vietnam Motors Corporation (VMC) – with companies from the Philippines and Japan, and became an assembler of Kia (Korea), Mazda (Japan), BMW (Germany), and Subaru (Japan) vehicles; then in 1992, Mekong Corporation, a joint venture with capital from Korea, started to assemble Mitsubishi (Japan) and some Fiat (Italy) vehicles. Additional licences for assembly were given to joint ventures involving Mitsubishi, Daewoo (Korea), and Daimler Benz (Germany) vehicles. Surprisingly, in Sturgeon's opinion, a further eight joint ventures were then licenced by the end of 1997, involving companies including Toyota, Daihatsu, Isuzu, and Ford. By 1998, there were 11 assemblers (including the two licensed assemblers – VMC and Mekong – of other companies' brands).

Even in 1997, just before the AFC, there was severe excess capacity. Of the total sales of 21,000 vehicles, only 5,000 were locally produced – a volume shared among the 11 assemblers! In 1998, sales halved, leaving the industry with even more severe excess capacity. At that time, virtually all vehicle production was from imported CKD kits, and only three foreign auto parts makers were in the country. Sturgeon (1998: 8) notes that because of low plant and equipment utilisation, assembly costs were significantly higher than in the assemblers' home countries. A Toyota Corolla sold for US$26,000 in Vietnam compared to only US$14,000 in the USA. Khai Nguyen (2003: 182) notes that against a pre-Asian financial crisis (1997) domestic demand which they estimate at 15,000 vehicles, assemblers in Vietnam had a combined capacity variously estimated at between 75,000 and 150,000 units a year. Under the serious impacts of falling demand after the AFC, VMC, the second largest assembler, failed, and Chrysler also left Vietnam. As Van Arkadie and Mallon (2003: 214) observe, the rush of international assemblers trying to gain a foothold in a developing country is nothing new, and it was a mistake repeated in Vietnam.

According to Kobayashi (2017: 15), 'It was only after the 1990s that the automobile industry was designated as an industry to be fostered in Viet Nam'. Later, a master plan for the automotive industry was approved by the government in 2004, and the industry was officially designated as a 'spearhead industry' in 2007 (Hansen 2016: 556).

Some details of Vietnam's very complicated trade and incentive system to attract foreign investors into the automotive industry from the early 1990s to the early 2000s are given in Nguyen Bich Thuy (2008), using a variety of Vietnamese sources. Foreign automakers were required to form joint ventures with local partners (normally state-connected companies), whose contribution would be in the form of land and buildings. These JVs were then supported by a variety of fiscal measures including time-limited income tax exemptions and, later, preferential rates and value-added exemptions. Taxes were imposed differentially to favour locally produced vehicles in comparison to imported one. Tariffs too were imposed differentially, with higher rates on CBU vehicles than on CKD kits, thus raising vehicle production's effective rate of protection, although some high tariffs also were imposed on components produced locally. These incentives were contained in individual investment agreements between incoming foreign firms and the Ministry of Planning and Investment. Such agreements also contained commitments to increase local content to 5% by the fifth year of operation, and 30% by the tenth year. From 2004, some reductions in incentives were made, both in terms of tax remissions and in ending of the VAT differential in favour of locally assembled vehicles. Also, tariffs would be raised somewhat on CKD kits. Subsequently, a change was made that tariffs would no longer be imposed on CKD kits *per se*, but at different rates on components divided up into 100 individual groups of parts (Nguyen Bich Thuy 2008: 10–11).

Not only were the incentives offered to the car industry complicated, but they were very changeable and sometimes inconsistent, particularly though not exclusively in the run-up to WTO membership. Over the period 2005–2007, value-added tax and excise special tax were introduced and twice amended. The tax on vehicles was changed eight times, and on components four times (Hansen 2016: 558, citing a Ministry of Industry and Trade source). From 2003 to 2005, as part of plans to apply to join the WTO, excise tax on domestically assembled small cars increased from 5–24% to 50%, while that on imported small cars was cut from 100% to 50%. Hansen (2016: 558) regards this as an attempt to reduce import protection, but it also had the effect of increasing the already very high prices of cars in the Vietnamese domestic market. These prices, as Ohno and Mai The Cuong (2004: 14–18) document, were already among the highest in late 2003 in the Asian region, more than double those in Thailand's domestic market (in terms of US dollars) for a basic 1500 cc sedan.[27]

A useful set of estimates of tariff protection in these pre-WTO years has been made by Athukorala (2006) for 2003,[28] a year when he says there were no quotas on vehicle imports. He gives a figure of 68.75% as the nominal rate of protection (based on average tariffs for the sector)[29] for the input-output category 'motor vehicles' as a whole, and an effective rate of protection of 79.22%.The excess of the ERP over the NRP is smaller than one might expect in the automotive industry, and this results (partly) from protection also given to component production, the weighted average tariff on components being 26.75%. Nevertheless, the ERP for motor vehicles was higher than most other sectors, and much higher than the average for Vietnam's traded goods sector as a whole of 24.87%. The sector also had the highest average tariffs (NRP) of any of the 85 sectors for which protection was calculated, except for the two sectors 'liquor (excluding beer)', and 'beer'![30]

Vietnam after joining the WTO (2007–2017)

Policy inconsistency continued into the WTO period. The import duty on CBUs, which had been cut four times in 2007 – from 100% to 60% – was increased again in 2008, from 60%, to 70% to 83%, the maximum allowed under the ASEAN CEPT tariff at the time (Hansen 2016: 558). This tariff commitment on CBU imports of 83% was the highest among the country's tariff commitments (Truong and Nguyen 2011: 276).

By the time Vietnam joined the WTO in 2007, it had already committed itself under AFTA to reducing all its tariffs on imports from its ASEAN neighbours, progressively from 50% in 2015, to 40% in 2016, 30% in 2017, and finally to zero at the start of 2018.[31] Vietnam's trade with ASEAN, particularly in terms of vehicle imports, had grown in importance during the 2000s and 2010s. With regard to the country's overall automotive imports (HS87), in 2000, only Thailand among the ASEAN vehicle producers was in the top five suppliers, accounting for 16% of Vietnam's total HS87 imports.[32] By 2017, among the ASEAN vehicle suppliers, Thailand had become the biggest supplier of HS87 imports into Vietnam (with a 24% share), and Indonesia the fifth (with 9%) (Figure 9.4). For passenger vehicles specifically (HS8703, which excludes buses), only one 'other Asian *nes*' was in the top five suppliers in 2000 (5th, with only a 1% share). By 2017, the top two suppliers were Indonesia (30% share) and Thailand (28%), leading Japan, USA, and Germany, which had much smaller shares (Figure 9.5). WTO membership involved various rules outlawing the use of Local Content Requirements and other 'TRIMs'. Membership also required 'national treatment' for foreign investors, outlawing imposing on them different rates of tax compared to domestic producers.

Vietnam's prime minister approved an 'Automobile Industry Development Strategy by 2025' in July 2014.[33] Under the strategy, the Vietnamese government targeted (1) small and economical PVs, (2) small CVs, (3) buses, and (4) special vehicles, aiming at 228,000 units of production by 2020, 466,000 units by 2025, and 1.53 million units by 2035. With regard to LC ratios, it targeted 35% by 2020 and 65% by 2035 (Fourin 2017: 117–118). In spite of this strategy (and targets), no detailed industrial policy has been implemented in Vietnam (ibid.). In this context, the strategy has merely indicated a broad vision for Vietnamese automotive development.

AEC free trade[34] *(2018–present)*

When Vietnam cut its automotive tariffs to zero in 2018, it was expected that there would be a surge in imports of vehicles, with accompanying decrease in vehicle prices in the Vietnamese domestic market and consequently adverse effects on local assemblers. Some consumers appear to have delayed purchases until 2018 in anticipation of the price falls to be caused by the tariff cuts. Even though heavy discounting was taking place, the overall volume of cars sold in Vietnam was marginally down even in the first six months of 2017 – by 1% on a year-on-year basis (*Nikkei Asian Review*, 8 August 2017).[35]

In fact, the Vietnamese government responded to the potential threat to the domestic automotive industry by imposing a complicated set of non-tariff barriers under the so-called Decree 116[36] (*Automotive World* 2018: 26–27). This decree, in force from the start of 2018, required Vehicle Type Approval (VTA) certification, which involved vehicles needing quality certification from the country in which they were made, and each batch of imports being inspected.

In consequence of the Decree 116 restrictions, it was reported in the press that vehicle exports to Vietnam from Thailand, one of the country's most important suppliers, had declined by 80% from January to June 2018 on a year-on-year basis (*Nikkei Asian Review*, 27 January 2019),[37] although it seems possible that over the whole of 2018 such exports more than doubled.[38] Exports of HS8703 by Indonesia, however, Vietnam's largest source of car imports in 2017 (see Figure 9.5), only increased from US$241 million in 2017 to US$273 in 2018,[39] despite the fall in the intra-ASEAN tariff from 30% to zero.

As an indication of the positive impact on the local vehicle assembly industry of the restrictions on imports, it was reported that 'sales of locally assembled vehicles' increased 5.8% over the whole of 2018.[40] Despite this small general rise in sales, one casualty of the problems of 2018 has been General Motors' production in Vietnam. GM was reported to be selling its plant to the local conglomerate VinGroup, whose automotive arm VinFast was said to be planning to launch in June 2019 three vehicle models of its own (*Nikkei Asian Review*, 27 January 2019).[41] Inaugurated, as planned, on 14 June 2019, with Vietnam's prime minister present, VinFast was the country's first Vietnamese-brand automotive factory.[42] Its phase I design capacity was for 250,000 vehicles, planning to increase to 500,000 cars, including petrol-driven and electric vehicles.[43] VinFast has partnerships with a number of overseas companies including Bosch, Siemens, and Torino Design.[44] The factory complex is more vertically integrated than is usual in the industry, including a stamping workshop; a welding workshop; and body shell, paint shop, engine shop, and auxiliary workshops, together with the assembly workshop, connected and automated with ABB robots, with Siemens, and SAP intelligent manufacturing operating systems.[45] VinFast has appeared at the Paris Motor Show, the first Vietnamese automotive brand to do so.[46]

Challenges to Vietnam's automotive industry

Motorisation

Our interviews in Southeast Asia have suggested that Japanese manufacturers, as a crude rule of thumb, expect *motorisation* – the widespread use of motor vehicles – to begin in a country when it reaches a per capita income of about US$3,000 per year. Vietnam was expected to reach that figure in around 2020, its per capita income having grown rapidly since the mid-2000s (see Figure 9.9), and indeed since *doi moi* (Thoburn 2007 and 2013). Of course, the extent of motorisation also depends on income distribution, and particularly on the development of an urban middle class.

Motorisation is influenced too by population size as well as by per capita income, in view of the economies of scale needed for automotive production, which usually would depend on efficient development for the domestic market before exports could be grown. With a population of 97 million in 2018,[47] Vietnam thus seems to offer great market potential, especially as at present Vietnam has one of the lowest figures for vehicle in use per person (23 in 2015) in the Asian region. Its usage is only a quarter of that of Indonesia (87) and exceeds only those of India (22), Pakistan (17), and Bangladesh (4) (figures from OICA).

Motorisation will also be influenced by the quality of a country's infrastructure, including its road network, availability of public transport, and urban parking facilities. Government tax policy too affects the size of the domestic market and the demand for particular types of vehicles. We turn to these issues in the next subsection.

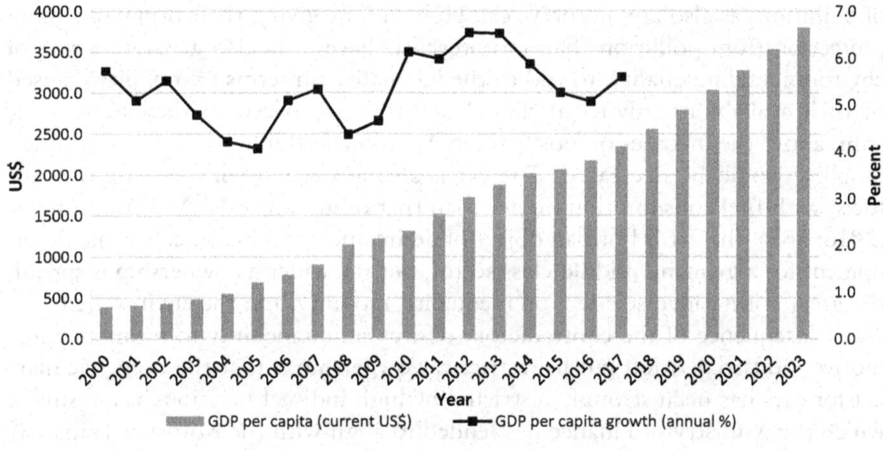

Figure 9.9 GDP per Capita and GDP Growth Rate in Vietnam, 2000–2023.

Source: World Bank World Development Indicators (online) and IMF World Economic Outlook (online).

Note: IMF's forecast for the period of 2018–2023.

Policy conflicts

We have seen already in the Philippines chapter how conflicts between the Ministry of Finance and the Ministry of Industry hampered the development of the country's Asian Utility Vehicle. The issue was whether the AUV should have been subject to low excise taxes to promote its sales so as to develop it as a Thai-style product champion, or subject to higher taxes to generate government revenue from a vehicle already selling well. Such conflicts are even more in evidence in Vietnam and have been widely commented on.[48] At first sight, such disputes might seem simply to reflect inter-ministerial rivalry and different priorities, but in Vietnam, as Hansen (2016 and 2017) has strongly argued, they reflect fundamental dilemmas about the use of automotive development as a driver of industrialisation. On the one hand, automotive development is seen as a way of moving the pattern of economic growth away from traditional labour-intensive industries like garments and footwear, towards activities which require higher technology and more skilled labour. Because it can be initiated by foreign investment by assemblers, it also offers great scope for backward linkages into the rest of the economy to promote local industrial development. Linking to global value chains via foreign investors is a potential source both of technology and export markets, and of access to imported inputs of high quality via regional production networks. This is a view taken by the Vietnamese Ministry of Industry and Trade.

On the other hand, however, the Vietnamese Ministry of Transport is worried that unrestricted growth in vehicle ownership would actually restrict mobility – compared to motorcycles and in the absence of adequate public transport – in Vietnam's densely populated urban areas. Motor vehicles also are major sources of pollution (as also are motorcycles). However, by giving their occupants more protection from pollution than motorcyclists have, cars also generate a sort of environmental inequality, to add to the inequality (in terms of mobility) caused by their availability only to an elite class if they are priced (as they are in Vietnam) above the incomes of most people. Yet if ownership were wider, everyone's mobility would be decreased. The car is also associated with the use of fossil fuels, with fuel consumption higher than that of motorcycles. As Hansen notes (2016: 555), the car is both an object of desire and a symbol of economic development for a growing middle-class sector, but the wider its ownership is spread, the greater is its adverse effect on inequality, mobility, and the environment.

A consequence of the contradictory desires simultaneously to promote automotive industrialisation but to restrict car ownership is that the domestic market for cars has been strongly restricted by high indirect taxation, as a result of which the Ministry of Finance has tended to align with the Ministry Transport (Hansen 2016: 559). Ohno and Mai The Cuong (2004: 17) have referred to the vicious circle of a small market and high prices resulting in low efficiency and high costs in the automotive industry, which, in turn, perpetuated the small market. This repression of the domestic market still was a complaint of international assemblers interviewed in Hanoi in 2015.[49] [50]

Automotive components, local content, and vehicle costs

In the early years of the industry in the late 1990s, Vietnamese policy was that vehicle assembly should have 5% local content after five years of operation, and that LC should be 30% after ten years. These LC requirements were stated only very generally, without particular parts being specified and without reference either to what automotive assembly was already in operation or in terms of the ASEAN perspective of major producers of parts (Sturgeon 1998: 32–33). There appears to have been no attempt to use the sort of mandatory deletion policies common in other ASEAN automotive producers. MD policies would have been permitted to Vietnam until it moved towards WTO membership even after their prohibition to WTO members under TRIMs from the early 2000s.

Even today, LCs are low in Vietnam. The average – said to be the lowest in ASEAN – is between 7% and 10%. The highest is 37% achieved by Toyota (with its Vios model, a four-door subcompact car), with 33 suppliers,[51] including five Vietnamese vendors, providing more than 400 products.

It is widely accepted that higher local content is important in reducing vehicles costs, as local production of components saves considerable transport costs (see, for example, Cheewatrakoolpong *et al.* 2013: 24), but scale is important too. With production in 2017 of less than 250,000 units (see Figure 9.1), and production split between at least ten major OEM producers (as well as a number of minor assemblers), the hopes of reaching an efficient scale of perhaps 50,000–100,000 (or more) units annually are limited.[52] Two strategies can be identified among Vietnamese automotive assemblers. Toyota and Honda stopped assembling certain models (Toyota's Fortuner and Honda's Civic) in Vietnam in 2017, replacing with imports from Indonesia and Thailand, respectively. Other groups such as Thaco, Mitsubishi Fuso, Nissan, and Mercedes-Benz have been expanding their production capacity (Fourin 2017: 127). The capacity even of the largest and most successful multinational producer, Toyota, has only recently increased from 30,000–35,000 vehicles per year to around 50,000. Low volumes also deter investment by new Tier-1 suppliers and expansion by the existing ones, and such suppliers are important in providing markets and help to lower-tier suppliers. Even for lower-tier suppliers, the demand generated by the scale of vehicle production is important. In the supply of many automotive components, capital intensity may be higher than in assembly, and the required equipment is likely to be indivisible and thus subject to minimum efficient scale requirements (Ohno and Nguyen Anh Nam 2006: 5–6).

However, some expansions of vehicle capacity have been announced among major producers. Mazda, in association with Thaco, was reported to be planning to increase its capacity from 25,000 to 100,000 units (Schröder 2017: 39). As noted earlier, VinFast, the automotive arm of the VinGroup, is planning a major expansion of output with its home-grown brand,[53] and Toyota was planning in 2018 to expand its capacity towards producing eventually 90,000 vehicles a year.[54]

We have noted earlier that some firms were supplying both motorcycle and automobile parts, and this raises the issue of how far component suppliers working for Vietnam's successful motorcycle industry could be converted to supplying the automotive sector. Schröder's (2017) study stresses the lower technical sophistication of motorcycle parts production. The suppliers of such parts often would need substantial upgrading in terms of technology, and in adherence to quality and delivery requirements, to be accepted as suppliers by major multinational vehicle assemblers or Tier-1 mega-suppliers. Even so, acceptance as accredited components suppliers is a lengthy process, in which suppliers would also need to gain ISO-style quality and environmental accreditation. One hopeful sign is that of the two most important local motorcycle manufacturers – Honda and Yamaha – Honda is also established in Vietnam as an automotive producer and thus has an incentive to upgrade its motorcycle parts suppliers to produce automobile parts.

The Vietnamese government has been reported as aiming to increase local content in local production of vehicles from around 10% to 35% to 40% by 2020, possibly using incentives via subsidies for firms reaching this target (*Nikkei Asian Review*, 27 January 2019). Some expansion of LC is already taking place. Thus, VinFast, which has taken over General Motors' former plant, is planning further local content, localising the pressing and welding of auto body parts (*Vietnam Economic News*, 11 January 2018).[55]

Importation of second-hand vehicles

Unlike the Philippines, importation of second-hand vehicles appears not to be a very serious problem in Vietnam, despite the lifting of an import ban in 2006 (PWC 2007: 4). Legally imported vehicles have been priced out of the market by the tax and import duties systems, both before and after the WTO, according to interviewees, and we have not heard of reports of extensive illegal exports.

Free-trade agreements and the AEC[56]

In addition to its large tariff reduction commitments made progressively under AFTA/ATIGA/AEC, Vietnam had a number of free-trade agreements, mostly bilateral but some as an ASEAN member. As of 2018, the WTO's tariff data base[57] listed import duty rates imposed by Vietnam under the following FTAs.[58]

- ASEAN-Japan free-trade agreement
- ASEAN-Australia-New Zealand free-trade area
- Free-trade agreement with China
- Free-trade agreement with India
- Free-trade agreement with (Republic of) Korea
- Viet Nam-Japan free-trade agreement
- Viet Nam-Chile free-trade agreement
- Viet Nam-Korea, Republic of free-trade agreement
- Viet Nam-Eurasian Economic Union (EAEU) free-trade agreement

Clearly, these FTAs may well involve vehicles coming in at lower than MFN duties, and therefore more import competition for the Vietnamese motor industry beyond that generated by ASEAN competitors. This competition can be either in the form of influencing the decisions of foreign producers in Vietnam to bring in more vehicles from their home country or from another production site (such as Thailand), or more 'direct' competition from brands not produced in Vietnam. Ascertaining the details of FTAs is by no means straightforward, since there is so much variation of tariffs even within narrowly defined product categories.[59] Some available information is available from interviews and secondary sources, however. Interviews suggested that the ASEAN-China agreement excluded CBU vehicles because of objections from Thailand, although automotive components carried only a low import duty. Schröder's study gives more details of the Vietnam-Korea FTA, suggesting that Vietnamese tariffs on some automotive items, particularly components, were not high, and selected automotive components' import duties into Vietnam would be reduced to zero by 2018 (and all import duties on components would be phased out over a 5–15-year period) (Schröder 2017: 12).

Tariffs cuts under Vietnam's various FTAs were announced in ten draft decrees effective from 2018. Besides those under the AEC, and for other products under other FTAs, there were tariff cuts to zero, affecting the automotive industry on vehicle parts under the Vietnam-Japan Economic Partnership Agreement, and on 'automobile, and spare parts' to apply under the Vietnam-Eurasian Economic Union FTA. Also, there would be tariff cuts towards zero by 2022 in ASEAN's FTAs with Korea, Japan, India, Australia, New Zealand, and Chile.[60]

Import statistics presented in diagrams earlier in this chapter suggest that competition in passenger cars was not significant in 2017 as a result of FTAs (except for the AEC itself), with only Japan among FTA partners (with a 10% share) being in the top five import sources; but for automotive components, overall, Korea, Japan, and China were the top three suppliers, with Thailand in the fourth place, and for Vietnam's exports of components, Japan, China, and Korea were the first, second, and fifth more important destinations, respectively.

Conclusions and comparisons

We have traced the history and policies of Vietnam towards its motor industry. The industry's apparent lack of success so far, especially in terms of the local content of production, in relation to its main ASEAN rivals – particularly Thailand and Indonesia – has been shown partly to be the result of inconsistent policies. It is also the result of genuine policy dilemmas between promoting automotive industrialisation as a driver of development, on the one hand, and recognising its negative externalities in the Vietnamese context in terms of impacts on mobility when infrastructure and public transport are so little developed[61] as well of the issue common to other countries of its environmental impacts, on the other hand.

Vietnam's participation from 2018 in intra-ASEAN tariff-free trade under the AEC has so far not resulted in the feared difficulties of large numbers of assemblers quitting the country – and expanding in other ASEAN locations such as Thailand. This seems to have been largely prevented (apart from the case of General Motors) by the non-tariff barriers to increased imports set up by the Vietnamese government since 2018, at least for the present. But the danger remains.

Despite the difficulties caused by inconsistent and opaque policies, much commented on in our interviews with assemblers, we have noted that some expansions of capacity by major assemblers are underway. Also, JETRO's survey of business conditions facing Japanese-affiliated firms in Asia and Oceania – conducted in October and November 2018 – reported that in the motor vehicles and motorcycles sector, 78% of respondents forecast there would be profits in 2018, and 76% said they expected to expand (JETRO 2018b: 10 and 22). These are optimistic figures, although the sample was small (51 respondents) and the aggregation of motor vehicles and motorcycles could be dominated by motorcycle firms' responses.

We have seen that Vietnam's exports of motor vehicles are negligible, but it has substantial exports of automotive components and of wiring harnesses.[62] Unlike the Philippines or Indonesia, its automotive components are not directed much to ASEAN (Thoburn and Natsuda 2018: 524), suggesting it is not yet much involved in ASEAN regional production networks (nor for component imports), although some of its free-trade agreements may be affecting its trade flows.

As well as Vietnam facing competition from its well-established ASEAN automotive competitors, particularly Thailand and Indonesia, there arc signs of some shifts in foreign automotive investment to the other lower-income countries in the ASEAN 'CLMV' group – Cambodia, the Lao PDR, and Myanmar.[63] Apart from Vietnam, none of the CLMV countries appears in OICA's list of vehicle producers (OICA website). However, Nissan, in partnership with the originally Malaysian motor firm Tan Cheong, is assembling vehicles in Myanmar[64] joined by Suzuki, Kia, and Ford, driven by a new set of import restrictions imposed by Myanmar despite ASEAN's move to tariff-free trade in 2018.[65] In addition, Chinese Chery and Indian TATA Motors own assembly plants along with local capital (Fourin 2015: 190). Among major component makers, United Motor Works, headquartered in Thailand, was reported as planning expansion in Myanmar in 2018 (ASEAN 2018: 42).

In Cambodia, there is vehicle assembly with plants producing Korean Hyundai vehicles near the Thai border, and Chinese and Ford vehicles are also assembled. Near the Thai border, there also is production of wiring harnesses by the two major producers Yazaki and Sumitomo (Kobayashi and Jin 2013: 45–46). About three-quarters of Cambodia's wiring harness exports of $104 million were to Thailand, and almost all the remaining were to Japan. [66]

The Japanese Minebea company, manufacturing components,[67] was relocated from Thailand to Cambodia under their 'Thai +1' strategy in 2011. In addition, the Toyota-affiliated Japanese mega-supplier Denso has been in operation in Cambodia since 2013, making automotive and motorcycle parts,[68] and in

2016, it opened a plant there to produce magnetos and oil filters for export to Denso's subsidiary in Thailand. There is also a Japanese-Thai joint venture to sew fabric and leather seat covers, mainly to export to Toyota facilities in Thailand (ASEAN 2017: 31), and from the EU, there were Bosch and Thyssenkrupp (ASEAN 2017: 56).

The Lao PDR also has been the recipient of inward automotive investment. Local brand assembler, Kolao, was established by a Korean entrepreneur, Oh Sei Young, in 1997. Initial operations commenced with an official sales office in Laos importing from Kia. Since 2013, Kolao has also introduced the Daehan brand by means of assembling kits imported from China. It has 20,000 units of assembly capacity, and 3,264 units were sold in Laos in 2016 (Fourin 2017: 148 and 150). With regard to automotive suppliers, a Taiwanese electronics company established assembly of wire harnesses (ASEAN 2017: 36). Among the top 20 global component makers, Toyota Boshoku operates in Laos (ASEAN 2014: 157).

Thus, the other CMLV countries seem to be integrating into the ASEAN industry, aided by their geographical proximity to Thailand, possibly threatening some of Vietnam's automotive production. Yet Vietnam, already an exporter of components, has the potential to become an exporter of cars if there are large expansions by existing automotive multinationals in the country. It would need to expand its local (and ASEAN) content to do so within the ASEAN tariff-free area, though, as ASEAN rules of origin require a 40% ASEAN content (McClanahan *et al.* 2014: 6).

Notes

1 The authors are grateful to Nguyen Quang Loc at Ritsumeikan Asia Pacific University, Japan, for bringing to their attention some useful Vietnamese-language websites that can be machine-translated into English.

2 It is worth remembering here that in this book we use 'automotive' in the narrow sense so as to exclude motorcycles. This reminder is necessary because some of the literature on Vietnam includes the motorcycle and motorcycle components industry as 'automotive'. Also, although we do not focus on the motorcycle industry in this book, it should be noted that the auto parts industry in Vietnam has been somewhat linked to earlier developments in the production of motorcycle parts, in which Taiwanese inward investment was important (see Kobayashi 2017, Schröder 2017).

3 *Doi moi* is usually translated as (economic) 'renovation'. On *doi moi* and other economic developments in Vietnam, see Thoburn (2007 and 2013).

4 This derogation also applied to Myanmar, Cambodia, and Laos.

5 AFTA is more properly known from 2010 as ATIGA, the ASEAN Trade in Goods Agreement. ATIGA itself was a step towards the formation in 2015 of AEC, the ASEAN Economic Community. Where we discuss successive tariff changes up to 2018, the date of intra-ASEAN tariff-free trade for Vietnam, we refer for clarity (albeit rather clumsily) to AFTA/ATIGA/AEC and thereafter simply to AFTA or AEC, as appropriate.

6 As quoted by several interviewees in Hanoi in March 2015, as well as by many more recent sources. E.g. *Just Auto Plus* (1 March 2018), https://www.just-auto.com/analysis/vietnam-scraps-asean-tariffs-but-imports-crash-analysis_id181449.aspx. [accessed on 25 September 2019].

7 Interview with Ministry of Industry and Trade of Vietnam in Hanoi (5 March 2015).

8 However, Fourin (2017) lists 21 assemblers (refer back to Table 3.2), even though only 15 are listed in Table 9.1, derived from data in Fourin (2019). Some confusion in numbers of assemblers, and sometimes market shares too, appears to result from the fact that various major brands are produced by contract assemblers rather than the brand companies themselves.
9 VAMA's website: http://vama.org.vn [accessed on 25 September 2019].
10 MarkLines' website: https://www.marklines.com/en/statistics/flash_sales/salesfig_vietnam_2018 [accessed on 25 September 2019].
11 Pulse (24 January 2019), https://pulsenews.co.kr/view.php?year=2019&no=50694 [accessed on 25 September 2019].
12 See also Bao Anh Vietnam (20 September 2019), https://vietnam.vnanet.vn/english/hyundai-thanh-cong-vietnam-auto-jsc/38373.html [accessed on 25 September 2019], for more details of the Hyundai joint venture.
13 See *Vietnamnet News* (2 July 2018), https://english.vietnamnet.vn/fms/business/203412/veam-valuated-at-billions-of-dollars-despite-mounting-losses.html [accessed on 25 September 2019].
14 Hino's website: https://hino.vn/en/ [accessed on 25 September 2019].
15 Samco's website: http://samco.com.vn/en/main.html [accessed on 25 September 2019].
16 As we note elsewhere in the book, wiring harnesses are classified in trade data as electrical items (in the HS chapter 85), not as automotive (HS87).
17 http://ven.vn/automotive-industry-still-driven-mostly-by-foreign-content-35796.html [accessed on 17 October 2019].
18 Toyota's website: www.toyotavn.com.vn/en/toyota-vietnam/partners/suppliers [accessed on 25 September 2019].
19 Unlike the case for the ASEAN-4 producers, we do not have access to Vietnamese trade data in the Global Trade Atlas. In this chapter, therefore, all trade data are taken from comtrade.un.org/db/ [accessed in April 2019].
20 The gap of about $1 billion between total automotive exports (HS87) and exports of HS8708, however, is made up predominantly of exports of motorcycles (and cycles) (HS8711, $641 million) and of motorcycle and cycle parts (HS8714, $429 million), since the HS87 category includes these.
21 Of current (2017) HS8708 exports, the largest items are transmissions (HS870840) at 32% of the total, and safety airbags (HS870895) at 22%, followed by parts and accessories for auto bodies not otherwise specified (HS870829) at 13%. The other significant items (the only ones over 2% of the HS8708 total) are clutches and parts (HS870893, 7.4%), and steering wheels and columns (HS870894, 5.3%).
22 Less than US$3 million for every year in the 2010s up to 2017.
23 Imports of wiring harnesses (not shown) are quite small – hardly more than US$100 million since 2000 in any year but one (2011, when they were US$139 million).
24 This situation had started to change by the 2000s. State enterprises were being reformed and equitized, and from 2001, transformed into limited liability companies. Private enterprise development has been aided by the 2000 Enterprise Law, which simplified procedures for registering an enterprise, and the 2006 Enterprise Law, which brought state enterprises and private firms into a common regulatory framework. As a result, the share of the (non-household) private sector in industrial output in Vietnam increased from 6.4% in 1995, to 19.2% in 2005 (Thoburn 2013: 112–113).
25 As we discuss later in this chapter, local production of 'automotive' components was pioneered by the country's much more successful motorcycle industry (Hansen 2016).
26 In 1992, the country's early (post-1988) tariff schedule was replaced by one based on the standard HS system (as used throughout this book) and the use of quantitative restrictions was much reduced (Athukorala 2006: 163).

27 Using data from a JETRO survey, they estimated that the 48% excess of the Vietnamese car price compared that of Thailand could be decomposed into a parts cost gap accounting for 56% of the difference and a tax gap accounting for 44% (ibid.: 15).
28 Using input coefficients from the 2000 Vietnam input-output table.
29 Although Vietnam had already joined AFTA in 1995, by 2002, as Athukorala (2006: 167) notes, over 95% of imports entering Vietnam were still doing so at MFN tariff rates – with the countries with which VN had MFN status (the EU, Japan, most Asian countries outside ASEAN, Australia, and New Zealand. The US is not listed in this list as the US offer to Vietnam of MFN status under the USBTA did not come into force until December 2002).The CEPT rates under AFTA were applied to only to about 3.5% of total Vietnamese import value (or about 10% of imports from ASEAN countries). In addition, general tariff rates (that is, those that were neither CEPT nor MFN) were about 50% higher than MFN rates.
30 ERP is also affected by the value share of purchased inputs in total output, which, for motor vehicles, was 47.22 (%). In contrast to vehicles, motorcycles and accessories had a lower NRP than vehicles (60%) but a higher ERP (87.91%). This reflects the fact that although their average tariff on inputs was higher (32.39%) than for vehicles, their share of components in output was 68.59% compared to the only 47.22% in vehicles (Athukorala 2006: 182–184).
31 Interview with Ministry of Industry and Trade of Vietnam in Hanoi on 5 March 2015.
32 Interestingly, the Lao PDR was the fifth largest supplier in HS87, with 5%. Presumably, these imports from the Lao PDR were of automotive components, but imports for HS 8708 list 'Other Asian not otherwise included' as the second largest supplier of imports in 2000 (with a share of 28%, after Japan's 64%).
33 *Vietnamnet News* (6 December 2018), https://english.vietnamnet.vn/fms/business/213846/vietnam-needs-long-term-strategy-for-automobile-industry.html [accessed on 25 September 2019].
34 Note that a small number of agricultural, though not automotive, items will still be subject to 5% import duties under AEC. See *Vietnam Briefing* (10 January 2018), https://www.vietnam-briefing.com/news/vietnam-multiple-ftas-tariff-cuts-2018.html/ [accessed on 25 September 2019].
35 *Nikkei Asia Review* (8 August 2017), https://asia.nikkei.com/Economy/Vietnam-braces-for-zero-import-duties-on-vehicles-made-in-ASEAN [accessed on 25 September 2019].
36 More fully known as Clause 116/2017/ND-CP - 'on vehicle manufacturing/assembly, importation, maintenance, and warranty businesses' (https://www.just-auto.com/analysis/vietnam-scraps-asean-tariffs-but-imports-crash-analysis_id181449.aspx, [accessed on 20 March 2019].
37 See https://asia.nikkei.com/Economy/Vietnam-vexes-foreign-automakers-with-import-rules [accessed on 25 September 2019].
38 Unfortunately, Comtrade data for Thailand's exports for some reason do not include statistics for HS87 categories for 2017 – perhaps because of website problems in late April/early May 2019 – though (unlike for Vietnam) they do show data for 2018. Thai passenger vehicle (HS8703) sales to Vietnam did increase from US$147 million in 2016 to US$677 million in 2018. This 2018 figure can be compared to the figure in Vietnam's import statistics (see Figure 9.5) for 2017 of US$249 million for HS8703. Of course, the 'mirror' data of one country's exports compared to another's imports of the same product do not always match up precisely, even beyond differences caused by exports being valued FOB (Free on Board) and imports CIF (Cost Insurance and Freight) (Indonesia's HS8703 exports in 2017 to Vietnam were US$241 million and Vietnam's imports of HS8703 from Indonesia were US$262 million). Nevertheless, a substantial rise in Thai passenger vehicle exports to Vietnam from 2017 to 2018 does seem clear.

39 Vietnam's General Statistical Office website (www.gso.gov.vn) does give some monthly trade statistics, commodity by commodity, for Vietnam for 2018, and summed for the whole year, but individual commodity categories are not aggregated in a way comparable to the HS categories available for Vietnam on Comtrade or the GSO website up to and including 2017.

40 See Marklines' website: https://www.marklines.com/en/statistics/flash_sales/salesfig_vietnam_2018 [accessed on 25 September 2019].

41 See https://asia.nikkei.com/Economy/Vietnam-vexes-foreign-automakers-with-import-rules [accessed on 25 September 2019]. For further details, see *Reuters Business News* (28 June 2018), https://www.reuters.com/article/us-gm-vingroup/gm-to-transfer-vietnam-operation-to-vingroups-car-arm-eyes-sales-boost-idUSKBN1JO0QS [accessed on 25 September 2019].

42 See also the company's own website: https://vinfast.vn/en/vinfast-inaugurate-its-automobile-factory-june-2019 [accessed on 15 January 2020].

43 *Vietnamnet News* (14 June 2019), https://vietnamnet.vn/vn/oto-xe-may/thu-tuong-nguyen-xuan-phuc-vinfast-co-su-ung-ho-va-tiep-suc-cua-nguoi-viet-nam-541591.html [accessed on 25 September 2019].

44 *Tia Sang* (20 September 2017), http://www.tiasang.com.vn/-doi-moi-sang-tao/Huong-di-cho-VinFast-va-o-to-Viet--10923 [accessed on 25 September 2019].

45 *Vietnamnet News* (14 June 2019), https://vietnamnet.vn/vn/oto-xe-may/thu-tuong-nguyen-xuan-phuc-vinfast-co-su-ung-ho-va-tiep-suc-cua-nguoi-viet-nam-541591.html [accessed on 25 September 2019].

46 https://www.xeotodo.com/2018/10/bao-to-quoc-vinfast-va-tuong-lai-nganh.html [accessed on 25 September 2019].

47 World Bank's website: https://www.worldbank.org/en/country/vietnam/overview [accessed on 25 September 2019].

48 For a recent example, see the (Japanese) Institute for International Studies and Training piece on Vietnamese automotive policy on https://www.iist.or.jp/en-m/2015/0240-0960/ [accessed on 25 September 2019].

49 In addition, a large (non-Japanese) multinational assembler complained that market repression via the special consumption tax bears down more heavily on domestic producers than on importers. This is because it is based in the case of imported vehicles on the landed price, but for domestically produced vehicles, it is imposed at the stage when the wholesale vehicle is handed to the dealer, so the price includes the producer's sales and distribution costs (interview, Hanoi, 10 March 2015).

50 The 'special sales tax' in Vietnam on a wide range of goods was levied on 'automobiles having less than 24 seats' at rates ranging from 10% to a maximum of 150% (PWC 2018: 28).

51 Presumably, these include some second-tier suppliers, and the 18 suppliers listed on Toyota's own website (cited earlier) are first-tier.

52 On minimum efficient scale, see Schröder (2017: 45), Natsuda *et al.* (2015a: 48 and n.2) and our discussion here in Chapter 5, Note 1, p. 138.

53 See also *Nikkei Asian Review* (27 January 2019), https://asia.nikkei.com/Economy/Vietnam-vexes-foreign-automakers-with-import-rules [accessed on 25 September 2019].

54 *Hanoi Times* (22 June 2018), http://www.hanoitimes.vn/economy/industry/2018/06/81e0c8d5/toyota-vietnam-unveils-reasons-for-plant-expansion-plan/ [accessed on 25 September 2019].

55 *Vietnam Economic News* (1 November 2018), http://ven.vn/automotive-industry-still-driven-mostly-by-foreign-content-35796.html [accessed on 25 September 2019].

56 For a full list of agreements, actual and prospective, country by country (including Vietnam) see ADB's website: https://aric.adb.org/fta-country [accessed on 25 September 2019].

57 WTO's website: http://tariffdata.wto.org/default.aspx [accessed on 25 September 2019].

58 Note that this is a wider list than those in Table 3.10 based on Fourin (2017).

59 The WTO tariff database lists automotive products under HS 6-digit categories. Take the case of diesel cars under 1500 cc (HS 870331), one of 14 categories within HS 8703 (Motor Vehicles). Even such a specialised category as this has – under MFN – 25 tariff lines and 15 ***ad valorem import duties*** ranging from 15% to 70% (with an average of 53%). Under FTAs, to take the case of Japan, import duties range from 0% to 70%, with an average of 48% but with 15 tariff lines for diesel cars under 1500 cc being duty-free. The comparative figures for China are in the range 15% to 50% (average 28%), but no lines are duty-free, and for Korea, the range is 0-70%, average 52% and four lines duty-free.

60 See *Vietnam Briefing* (10 January 2018), https://www.vietnam-briefing.com/news/vietnam-multiple-ftas-tariff-cuts-2018.html/ [accessed on 25 September 2019].

61 But note that there are various ambitious plans to improve the country's infrastructure, such as those to connect Ho Chi Minh City by metro line to the nearby provinces of Dong Nai and Binh Duong, which may lessen the need for private cars to be used. See http://kenh14.vn/dong-nai-binh-duong-muon-ket-noi-metro-tphcm-20160417081405845.chn [accessed on 25 September 2019].

62 Focussing on exports of automotive components was one of the two main suggestions on future automotive policy made by Ohno and Mai The Cuong (2004: 11–12) in their comments on the 2004 Master Plan. Their other suggestion was to focus on assembly of models not assembled in Thailand that were suitable for small production runs and frequent modifications in specifications.

63 See Kobayashi and Jin (2013) on automotive developments in Myanmar, Cambodia, and Lao.

64 Nissan's website: https://newsroom.nissan-global.com/releases/release-ec4af64af22c94ff7dff33b08d000d64 [accessed on 25 September 2019].

65 *Nikkei Asian Review* (15 February 2019), https://asia.nikkei.com/Business/Business-trends/Hyundai-joins-fray-in-Myanmar-s-crowded-auto-market [accessed on 25 September 2019].

66 2018 figure, from Comtrade.

67 For company details see https://www.minebeamitsumi.com/english/corp/company/factories/cambodia/1186630_6770.html [accessed 31 January 2020].

68 Denso's website: https://www.denso.com/kh/en/ [accessed on 25 September 2019].

10 Conclusions

Introduction

In our Introduction, Chapter 1, three main aims of the book were identified

- within a detailed historical examination of the development of the automotive industry in Southeast Asia – and specifically within ASEAN, the Association of Southeast Asian Nations, where the industry is located – to look at the driving forces behind automotive development.
- among the drivers of automotive development, specifically to look at the role of industrial policy, both before and after the new set of the World Trade Organization rules on trade-related policies operative from the early 2000s.
- given that some 80% of vehicle production in ASEAN is in the hands of Japanese multinational companies, to consider the roles such companies have played in the industry's development in Southeast Asia, and their role in relation to the Japanese government and ASEAN's policy-makers.

This chapter now presents conclusions under each of these heading in turn, and then ends with a section discussing the challenges and prospects faced by ASEAN's automotive producers.

Drivers of automotive development in ASEAN

Market size and growth

One important factor has been the shift of both production and the growth of demand for vehicles away from North America, Western Europe, and Japan. This has been driven by the increasing saturation of American, European, and Japanese vehicle markets combined with the growing markets and rapidly rising incomes in much of less developed Asia, although there have been relocations to other areas too, such as Mexico and parts of Eastern and Central Europe. Lower labour costs in the less developed parts of Asia also have stimulated relocation to the region, as well as the reduction in transport costs from producing close to market. The most obvious beneficiary of such changes has been China, whose share of world vehicle production increased from 3.5% in 2000 to nearly 30% in

2018. India too has seen its production rise, and with a share of over 5% in 2018, it had overtaken Germany. Another important beneficiary has been Southeast Asia. The ASEAN-5 countries – Thailand, Indonesia, Malaysia, Vietnam, and the Philippines – had a combined 2018 world share of vehicle production of 4.6%, only a little behind Germany's and larger than Mexico's. ASEAN has received major relocations of production, particularly from Japan and to a limited extent from South Korea.

A country's market for vehicles depends primarily on a combination of population size and income per head, conveniently expressed as total GDP, although the distribution of income and the growth of middle-class urban populations are also influences (as is government tax policy towards vehicles and fuel). Conventionally in the industry, a minimum GDP per head figure of $3,000 (measured at market exchange rates) is thought to be the threshold at which vehicle ownership starts to become widespread and grows at a faster rate than GDP. *Motorisation* – conveniently expressed in terms of vehicles per 1,000 people – varies in ASEAN, from 23 in Vietnam to 439 in Malaysia. This higher figure, though, is still below that of major developed countries such as Japan (609). In ASEAN, Thailand and Malaysia, and more recently Indonesia and the Philippines, have passed the motorisation threshold, while Vietnam is approaching it. Growing domestic demand, however, is no guarantee of growing domestic vehicle production, as the case of the Philippines illustrates, where demand growth has been met by imports.

Successful vehicle producers, of course, do not simply depend on demand from the domestic market. Among ASEAN countries, two – Thailand and Indonesia – have become significant exporters of vehicles, while the others depend heavily on imports, especially the Philippines and Vietnam, though the latter is in too-early a stage of automotive expansion to rule out the likelihood of future export growth. Even the Philippines and Vietnam have grown their exports of certain automotive components, particularly transmissions and wiring harnesses.

Inward foreign investment, global value chains, and global production networks

Inward investment by multinational vehicle assemblers has been a crucial driving force for automotive development in all the vehicle-producing countries in ASEAN, and more than 80% of ASEAN vehicle production is now in the hands of Japanese MNCs. Even in Malaysia, famous for its national cars, the initial development of Proton was made in partnership with Mitsubishi. Proton now has almost 50% ownership by Geely of China, and there are hopes that this will help to remedy the deficiencies in Proton's performance, which is widely regarded as a failure, particularly in terms of exporting. Malaysia's second, and more successful, national car, was set up in 1993 as a joint venture between Toyota's affiliate Daihatsu and Malaysian companies. Vietnam's most recent new major automotive producer, and its first domestic automobile brand, VinFast, has a range of agreements with automotive multinationals, including from the USA and Europe, for technology.

The producer-driven global value chains that characterise the automotive industry have offered vehicle-producing ASEAN countries access to world and regional markets, and to the most advanced automotive technology. Inward investment has not only been made by assemblers but also by multinational Tier-1 suppliers, who, by organising assemblers' supply chains, have also exercised control – *governance* in GVC parlance – over local parts suppliers. Assemblers also include joint ventures between MNCs and local companies, and a range of contract assemblers, sometimes quite large such as Thaco in Vietnam. An issue of central concern to the GVC approach is whether local producers – in this case principally auto parts manufacturers – are able in these circumstances to *upgrade* their processes, products, and functions. Although various commentators have expressed doubt about this, even in the case of Thailand, we note that some parts producers, particularly Thai ones but also some from Malaysia, have developed overseas operations of their own. Various Thai producers have become significant multinationals, such as Thai Summit. The role of Japanese assemblers and Tier-1 suppliers in the upgrading of local suppliers is now left for discussion in the third section.

A common criticism of the GVC approach is that it concentrates too much on vertical relations between the various economic actors involved, and that it tends to neglect horizonal relations, which are important in the automotive industry. The global production network approach encourages a stronger focus on horizontal networks. In the ASEAN case, while using GVC and GPN insights, we stress that many economic relations in the industry are more regional than global, including producers making different models and different components in different ASEAN countries, and trading within the region. Such trading has been facilitated by the completion of tariff-free trade under the ASEAN Free Trade Area in 2010, covering all major automotive producing countries except Vietnam, whose tariff-free trade started in 2018 (though that country then imposed heavy non-tariff barriers to continue to protect its domestic market).

We have shown that the pattern of regional specialisation is quite varied, particularly in terms of specialisation in components. Take the case of two major examples, wiring harnesses and transmissions. A number of ASEAN countries export the electrical component, wiring harnesses, an increasingly important item as vehicles use more and more electronics for control functions. Yet these exports are mostly to outside of the ASEAN region in the case of major exporters of wiring harness like the Philippines, Indonesia, and Vietnam, though they have substantial exports to Japan. In the case of transmissions, Indonesia and (especially) the Philippines, for example, mainly export to other ASEAN countries (and very little to Japan), although Vietnam exports very little of its (non-electrical) components to ASEAN, with about two-thirds going to Japan, China, and the USA, and only 9% to Thailand. What is also clear, though, is that component exports can be established in their own right, relying very little on domestic automotive demand.

Industrial policy

Industrial policy has been a central concern of this book. The main focus has been on *hard* (directive, and usually sector-specific) policy, but *soft* (facilitative, and often not sector-specific) policy has also had some significance, for example, in Thailand.[1]

Import-substituting industrialisation before the WTO

The ASEAN-4 countries (the ASEAN-5 minus Vietnam) all were using import substitution policies starting from the 1950s or 1960s, protecting their domestic markets behind tariffs and quantitative restrictions. ISI can be viewed as an economy-wide *hard* industrial policy, but it is sector-specific in the sense that tariff rates and other import barriers typically differed between economic sectors. Usually the automotive sector was protected from imports, and based initially on local assembly of imported vehicles in kit form (CKD – 'completely knocked down' kits), which attracted lower rates of import duty, thus raising the effective protection (protection on value-added) on vehicle assembly to higher than the nominal tariff rates on assembly would indicate. Vietnam started to develop its motor industry using foreign investment only from the 1990s, having previously produced mainly military vehicles, and did so under heavy tariff protection.

As ASEAN-4 countries developed policies specific to the automotive sector, these were mainly to build on the possibilities of backward linkages from assembly into component production. Local content requirements (LCRs) were the typical methods, often backed up by mandatory deletion programmes (MDPs), mandating that certain individual components would be 'deleted' from imported kits and instead produced locally. Vietnam also used LCRs, though typically in the contracts of individual inward investors. Although LCRs (and MDPs) have been widely criticised as distorting – most recently in the World Bank's *World Development Report 2020* (World Bank 2020: 176) – we have found some quite positive effects, in the sense that component production encouraged by LCRs was usually able to survive when those requirements were withdrawn in the 2000s (outlawed by the WTO as part of its TRIMs, trade-related investment measures, agreement). Another successful policy, though we only know of the Philippines employing it among the ASEAN-4, was the use of foreign exchange balancing requirements, where assemblers were required to earn their own foreign exchange for imports. This policy encouraged assemblers to set up component production of their own for export, as most notably in the case of continuing exports of transmissions.

Countries of the ASEAN-4 introduced various measures to liberalise their economies and their trade regimes in the 1990s (at a time when many developing countries had already been doing so during the 1980s under the influence of the ultra-free-market Washington Consensus). However, the major change in the policy environment occurred in the 2000s, when the World Trade

Organization (set up in 1994 to replace the earlier organisation, the General Agreement on Tariffs and Trade, GATT) brought into force key rules to outlaw various trade-related policies. Of these, the rule on trade-related investment measures, TRIMs, was the most important for the automotive industry.

Hard industrial policies under the WTO from 2000

The banning of local content requirements and similar policies under TRIMs represented a serious potential challenge to the ASEAN-4 producers. What is striking is how component production initiated in the pre-WTO survived the end of formal policies to promote it. This survival, though, owes much to the decisions of automotive MNCs, mainly Japanese, in maintaining, for example, the Philippines' exports to other ASEAN countries of transmission initiated under foreign exchange balancing requirements.

An interesting feature of the 2000s is the role of *product champion* vehicles, which represented an attempt to promote particular types of vehicle rather than any particular companies. Thailand is the best-known example. Under the 'Detroit of Asia' plan of the populist government of Thaksin Shinawatra (2001–2006), it was planned for the country to become a regional hub for automotive exports. Its first product champion, the one-ton pickup truck, chosen in part for the already strong domestic demand for this type of vehicle, was aided by the government setting lower excise tax rates on such vehicles to strengthen the market demand by consumers. At the same time, the government provided tax concessions, such as low corporate tax, for attracting investors into product champion production. A second product champion, the Eco-car, followed in 2007, with both excise and corporate tax policy effectively linked to localisation of the automotive components industry as well as vehicles, particularly facilitating the growth of local engine production. A second Eco-car project started in 2013. An *Electric Vehicle Action Plan* has also been approved for the period 2016–2036.

Indonesia has followed Thailand's example to some extent with its low-cost green car (LCGC) initiative from 2013, with lowering of excise tax on LCGCs to stimulate market demand, though without the incentives to producers used by Thailand. In parallel to this, the Indonesian government also stated its aims to develop a low-carbon emission (LCE) programme by attracting investment in electric vehicles (EVs), hybrid electric vehicles (HEVs), and alternative-fuel cars such as biofuel and compressed natural gas (CNG).

In contrast to Thai and Indonesian policies, when faced with an opportunity to develop a market niche for a potential product champion – its Asian Utility Vehicle (AUV) – the Philippines in 2002 removed the previous excise tax exemption from AUVs. The Ministry of Finance appears to have seen AUVs as a good source of revenue. As a result, their domestic sales and their production decreased. Vietnam seems to have also seen policy conflicts between its Ministry of Industry wishing to stimulate automotive production and a more sceptical Ministry of Transport being less favourably disposed. Such conflicts, though, represent a deeper conflict between the stimulus of growing automotive production to general development, on the one hand, and the negative economic and social effects of increasing traffic without adequate infrastructure and public transport, on the other. Although such conflicts seem not to have attracted the same attention in the cases of the Philippines and Indonesia, one might think they would also be relevant there. Thailand, though, has made some such improvements with its light railway system in Bangkok.

Product champions have been important drivers of expanded exporting for both Thailand and Indonesia. Domestic policies towards *initiating* exporting seem to have been less important than other factors, however. In Thailand, automotive producers had first turned seriously to exporting after domestic demand fell drastically with the Asian financial crisis (AFC) of 1997. Exporting was aided by the large depreciations of the Thai baht that accompanied the AFC. In Indonesia, automotive exports grew slowly in the 2000s, but increased much faster after intra-ASEAN free trade was initiated in 2010 under AFTA, though the LCGC project has been an influence too. The Philippines did have an export policy, its Automotive Export Programme introduced in 2003 for five years, but only one company, Ford, took part, and Ford left the country in 2012.

While fiscal policies, particularly towards excise taxes, have been ways of re-introducing local content provisions as part of product champion development in ways that do not violate TRIMs rules, Malaysia has come closer to violating those rules. Malaysian automotive development has been characterised by its reliance on national champion *companies*, rather than types of vehicles, and it has given many discriminatory incentives to its national producers. While some liberalisation has occurred under the WTO, there remain certain policies that are contentious. For example, the Malaysian government's Industrial Adjustment Fund is linked with local content, under the National Automotive Policy first introduced in 2006, with incentives such as interest-free loans and grants based on scale and industry linkages and on *bumiputra* (indigenous, principally ethnic Malay) participation. An existing Industrial Linkage Programme is linked to local content, allowing access to refund of excise duty according to the level of locally added value.

Soft industrial policies

Thailand has been the most important user of soft policies in terms of facilitating technology transfer and human resource development. Thailand has been relatively successful among ASEAN automotive producers in establishing institutions for improving the quality of its labour force. This is important for coping with future challenges, particularly the impact of adopting new automotive technologies under Industry 4.0, like more advanced robotics (ILO 2016, Lee *et al.* 2019). These policies, unusual for soft policies internationally in being sector-specific, have been ones where Japanese MNCs have played a major role (as also in Malaysia – see later). Several industry-university links have been created, and R&D hubs have been created to aid technology transfer.

Promoting *clustering* can also been seen as a soft policy, designed to promote collective efficiency among producers located together. In Thailand, it was a policy emphasised under the Thaksin government, although it also is strongly driven by the automotive industry itself, where suppliers tend to locate close to their assembler customers, and had been occurring prior to the 2000s. Industrial zones set up by the government in new areas such as the Eastern Seaboard south of Bangkok, with its good port facilities, encouraged producers who were turning to exports after 1997 to set up there to avoid the congestion, rising land prices, and labour costs in the Bangkok area. In Malaysia's case, the Second Industrial Master Plan (1996–2005) aimed to develop industrial clusters in the automobile industry, so as to allow suppliers to enjoy the advantages of collective efficiency. In 1996, 'Proton City' had been proposed and was completed in 2002. In Indonesia, the government seems not to have effective soft industrial policy in relation to human resource development and technology transfer. It does have cluster networks, but these are not fully supported by the government and depend on the actions of (mainly) Japanese automotive MNCs. Similar comments seem to apply to the Philippines.

Japanese multinational automotive producers and the Japanese government

As noted, some 80% of automotive assembly is in the hand of Japanese MNCs, and even the national producers in Malaysia – Proton and Perodua – have strong MNC connections, as also does the large new Vietnamese company VinFast, although in VinFast's case, the connections are more with American and European MNCs. In such circumstances, domestic governments' policies must influence the operation and decisions of MNCs if such policies are to be effective. One good example is the way the Thai government's first *product champion* policy influenced Toyota and other Japanese producers such as Isuzu to transfer their pickup truck production from Japan to Thailand, and in some cases their R&D facilities too. Indonesia's low-cost green car product champion also saw significant support from Japanese automotive companies. In contrast, the Philippines' automotive export programme of 2003 attracted only one MNC, Ford, and was unsuccessful. The Philippines' new CARS programme of 2015 to develop the automotive industry relies on MNC participation from such MNCs as Mitsubishi and Toyota.

Japanese MNCs have strongly supported regional integration in Southeast Asia through ASEAN, and the Japanese government has represented the interests of Japanese industry, including the automotive sector, with ASEAN governments. The ASEAN Industrial Cooperation (AICO) scheme of 1996 raised some problems for Japanese automotive MNCs in the sense that several already had production in individual ASEAN countries that were in line with those countries' national requirements but conflicted with some provisions of AICO (particularly the requirement for producers to have at least 30% ASEAN equity).

However, the progressive tariff-cutting under the ASEAN Free-Trade Area arrangement, and later under the ASEAN Economic Community (in the case of Cambodia, Laos, Myanmar, and Vietnam), facilitated intra-regional specialisation in models and components and reinforced existing patterns driven by the MNCs themselves.

The Ministry of International Trade and Industry (MITI) (now METI, the Ministry of Economy, Trade and Industry) of Japan, together with the ASEAN Economic Ministers (AEM), set up the AEM-METI Economic and Industrial Cooperation Committee (AMEICC) in 1998, which has a working group on the automotive industry. This has been designed to facilitate automotive regional development, including fostering supporting industries and promoting regional automotive parts complementation. The Japanese government, through regional Economic Partnership Agreements, of which the agreement with Malaysia is a good example, and with strong Japanese automotive MNC participation, has provided training programmes both in-country and in Japan for workers in the industry. The Japan-Thailand EPA involved various agencies including JICA, JETRO, and the Japanese Chamber of Commerce in promoting human resource development.

Challenges and prospects

Challenges for policy-making

Although the ASEAN-4 automotive-producing countries used broadly similar policies during the years of import substitution up to the time of partial liberalisation in the 1990s, and Vietnam until more recently, various problems have arisen in the post-2000 WTO era. There have been policy conflicts between ministries in the Philippines and Vietnam: ministries of industry have wanted to identify and support 'product champion' types of vehicle with tax concessions along the successful lines of Thailand and Indonesia; finance ministries have wanted to tax such vehicles more heavily. And these conflicts may hide deeper conflicts, as we saw earlier in the case of Vietnam.

Of course, similar policies applied in different countries may generate different outcomes, as the work of Adam Fforde (2009) has argued. One issue is state capacity. We have identified Southeast Asian countries as *neo-developmental states*, which, though lacking the full strong state capacity of countries like Taiwan or South Korea, nevertheless are by no means simply *laissez-faire* in their policies. Some state capacity is still lacking, such as the Philippines' inability to control illegal imports of second-hand cars. In other cases, conflicts between economic objectives and social/political objectives are important, particularly Malaysia's decision to promote an inefficient 'national' automotive producer, Proton, partly as a national symbol but also has a means of exercising positive discrimination in favour of *bumiputra* workers and entrepreneurs, and neglecting the experienced firms owned by ethnic Chinese Malaysians.

Prospects

At present, at the start of the 2020s, the Philippines seems to be seriously lagging in its automotive development: its total vehicle production fell by 44% between 2017 and 2018, and is now less than half that of Vietnam. The Philippines' growth in motorisation, as its GDP and per capita incomes rise, is being met mainly by increased imports, although it remains a significant exporter of some major components. Its CARS policy aims to increase automotive production by recruiting major automotive MNCs to participate, but its impacts are as yet uncertain, to say the least. Malaysia's Proton has only recently gone into partnership with China's Geely company, and, again, the results are too early to predict. Vietnam is at an early stage of automotive production, but now has an important new producer, VinFast, and it will be interesting to see whether this company can become a more successful national champion than Malaysia's Proton. Vietnam's stellar overall economic performance in the 1990s, and subsequently, following its 1986 *doi moi* economic reform programme, gives some grounds for optimism about the country's state capacity for policy-making. For Thailand, as it has become a regional export hub for Japanese MNCs from the 2000s, these MNCs have invested in various 'more sophisticated activities beyond simple assembly', including advanced engineering and testing, and process and product design, thus helping to upgrade the country's automotive production capabilities (Lee *et al.* 2019: 12).

For ASEAN, the availability of new technologies such as vehicle electrification, the use of lightweight materials to improve fuel efficiency, advanced robotics, and autonomous driving present both opportunities and competitive threats (ILO 2016: 3–7). The prospects for the ASEAN automotive industry will depend heavily in the future on how it meets the global challenges to the use of petrol and diesel vehicles, including the need for greater fuel efficiency and lower emissions, and how well it can move towards electric and other kinds of 'green' energy-powered vehicles. The efficiency of the industry could be helped by moving towards 'Industry 4.0' technology, including more advanced robotics, whose use VinFast, for example, is stressing in its publicity. The moves towards robotics – in Tier-1 suppliers as well as assemblers - are driven in part to replace labour and reduce costs, but also to raise quality and reliability, especially in the case of electronic components, the smallness of which may be difficult to handle with human labour (ILO 2016). Lee *et al.* (2019) argue that these moves towards robotic automation have been made more in Thailand (and Malaysia in their case study of the Penang electronics cluster) than in Indonesia and the Philippines. They attribute this to the growing labour shortages and wage rises in Thailand (and Malaysia). Indonesia and the Philippines, they think, are likely to retain more labour-intensive methods and run the risk of later being squeezed into a middle-income trap where they will find it difficult to compete against either richer countries with more automated production or poorer countries with lower-wage costs. Indeed, for ASEAN countries more generally, a possibly challenging issue is whether the MNCs adopting Industry 4.0 technologies will be tempted to 're-shore' back to their home countries, or from one ASEAN country to another (ILO 2016, Lee *et al.* 2019). For the moment, though, we note that Indonesia is becoming a significant exporter of vehicles within ASEAN, and the ILO study of ASEAN transformation cites the decision of a major Tier-1 automotive supplier in Indonesia to automate much of its more 'mundane and repetitive tasks' (ILO 2016: 31).

As ASEAN automotive producers like Thailand move to more robotic automation, an important further challenge emerges in the labour market. Automation requires the use of more skilled and educated workers who, for example, can check the activities of robots and identify problems proactively. As noted earlier, soft industrial policies in terms of institutional developments in Thailand to improve training and skills development are underway, as also in the Malaysian automotive industry with strong support from Japanese companies and Japanese government aid. Nevertheless, much remains to be done within ASEAN, and this particularly is likely to emerge as a problem with the need also for basic developments in education (ILO 2016: 13–14).

Some relocation of automotive component production to the lower wage, so-called CLMV, countries of ASEAN – Cambodia, Laos, Myanmar, and Vietnam – has been happening. This is particularly true of Cambodia, Laos, and Myanmar, which have common borders with Thailand. These three CLMV countries have already started to produce some components and do some limited assembly,[2] generating a productive division of labour with Thailand, though also posing a threat to existing component producers in Thailand and more newly established producers in Vietnam.

Several ASEAN vehicle-producing countries are planning to encourage production of electric vehicles with government support programmes. In Thailand, the National Energy Policy Council approved an 'EV Action Plan (2016–2036)' in 2016, aiming for the production of 1.2 million electric vehicles, including plug-in hybrids, along with charging stands in the domestic market (an important factor in promoting domestic demand for EVs). A new development is that Toyota is reported as having secured permission from the Thai Board of Investment to produce both EVs and plug-in hybrids in Thailand, with tax privileges, including corporate tax exemption, if it starts production within three years of 7 January 2020 (*Bangkok Post*, 20 January 2020[3]). In Malaysia, energy efficient vehicles (EEVs) were part of the 2014 National Automotive Policy, but as of end-March 2019, only 5,403 EVs were registered in Malaysia, and the country suffered from a severe shortage of charging points.[4] Indonesia also has plans for EVs, under presidential decree 55/2019, with subsidies for vehicles with specified local content.[5] Toyota and Hyundai have expressed interest in building EV plants in Indonesia, and Toyota has committed to increase investment, including for production of EVs, over 5 years, according to the Indonesian Industry Minister.[6] Similarly to other ASEAN countries, the Philippines has plans for EVs, including electrification of Manila's famous fleet of 'Jeepney' mini-buses, and the tricycle motorcycle taxis.[7] Autonomous (self-driving) vehicles, however, seem a long way off, especially with the difficulties of busy roads crowded with motorcycles and street traders in Southeast Asia, though the ILO (2016: 6) notes that Singapore is testing their use for buses, taxis, and other utility vehicles, and that China is also experimenting with them.

While producing countries may hope that the existing large domestic firms like Proton or Perodua in Malaysia, or VinFast in Vietnam, may develop EV production with the help of their MNC partners and associates, it is likely that most production will be developed by multinational producers for the international market, and the issue then is whether the MNCs will choose to locate such production within ASEAN countries, converting or replacing their existing production. The development of hybrid electric vehicles (HEVs) is already advanced among MNCs, with HEV models made by Toyota and Hyundai, for example, already having substantial sales in the Western markets. Development of fully electric vehicles is less advanced, though Tesla from the USA, BMW from Germany, and Nissan from Japan are among companies now producing them commercially. Major problems for EVs include the development of batteries – the most costly component in EVs – which are powerful enough to generate ranges (travelling distances) comparable to that of cars with internal combustion engines, and at acceptable cost; electric charging infrastructure widespread enough to persuade consumers to switch to EVs; and in the longer run, increased national electricity generation to cope with the increased demand for electricity that the use of EVs creates.[8] The production of fully electric vehicles would also require considerable changes in supply chains: EVs have far fewer and sometimes different components than cars with internal combustion engines (some 11,000 individual parts compared to 30,000 – see ILO 2016: 11).

Product champions like Thailand's famous pickup trucks often have been developed on the basis of vehicles already popular in the country's domestic market. What are the prospects for EVs in ASEAN domestic markets? This raises several issues. One, as noted, is the need for far more extensive infrastructures of electric charging points than at present. Another, which could easily be based on the development of earlier product champions, is the use of tax concessions to promote domestic demand for EVs. More of a difficulty is that at the present time, EVs are typically more expensive than vehicles with internal combustion engines. Also, although some mass market EV models such as the Nissan Leaf already exist, more of current EV development takes place in more up-market ranges, beyond the means of many ASEAN middle-class consumers. In the longer run, EV prices are likely to fall and their ranges increase, but meanwhile hybrid electric vehicles may be more attractive as they generate less 'range anxiety' than do EVs.

Notes

1 One area of industrial policy which we did not consider is the application of rent-management theory to industrial development policy. This approach considers how rent-seeking and the generation of economic rents (excess returns over their competitive level) – often in the past regarded as entirely negative aspects of development – can be used productively to channel incentives to firms likely to innovate, and away

from more stagnant producers. This approach has only recently started to make its way into the industrial policy literature, but we think it is a promising area for future research. For an excellent introduction to rent-management, with applications to Vietnam, see Ngo (2020) (reviewed in Thoburn, 2020).

2 Adding Myanmar's tiny production of assembled vehicles (12,292 units) raises ASEAN's world share only very marginally, from 4.56% to 4.57%. Myanmar statistics from www.asean-autofed.com/files/AAF_Statistics_2018.pdf [accessed on 19 February 2020].

3 https://www.bangkokpost.com/business/1839769/toyota-gets-approval-for-ev-plug-in-hybrid-production-in-thailand [accessed on 22 January 2020].

4 See https://www.nst.com.my/cbt/2019/08/509085/5-reasons-why-you-shouldnt-dream-owning-electric-vehicle-malaysia [accessed on 21 January 2020].

5 See https://www.pv-magazine.com/2019/12/04/indonesia-plans-domestic-electric-vehicle-industry/ [accessed on 21 January 2020].

6 See https://www.reuters.com/article/us-indonesia-electric/indonesia-aims-to-start-electric-vehicle-production-in-2022-idUSKCN1UD1OG [accessed on 21 January 2020].

7 http://industry.gov.ph/industry/e-vehicles/ [accessed on 21 January 2020].

8 Indeed, Toyota itself was reported in the British press as being sceptical about purely EVs, citing problems of range anxiety, batteries, and the availability of electricity-charging infrastructure, and therefore preferring hybrids (*The Observer*, 19 January 2020), https://www.theguardian.com/business/2020/jan/18/if-the-uk-doesnt-act-now-the-car-industry-will-vanish [accessed on 19 January 2020].

References

Abbott, Jason (2003) *Developmentalism and Dependency in Southeast Asia: The Case of the Automotive Industry*. London: RoutledgeCurzon.

Abdulsomad, Kamaruding (1999) Promoting Industrial and Technological Development Under Contrasting Industrial Policies: The Automobile Industries in Malaysia and Thailand, in Jomo, K.S., Greg Felker and Rajan Rasiah (eds.) *Industrial Technology Development in Malaysia: Industry and Firm Studies*. London: Routledge, 274–300.

Abe, Masato (2009) *The Impact of the Crisis on the Global and Regional Value Chains: A Case Study of Excess Capacity in the Automotive Sector*. Vienna: United Nations Industrial Development Organization, Research and Statistics Branch (Paper delivered at the UNIDO conference on Rising to the Challenges of the Global Economic Crisis: Opportunities and Options for Competitive Asian Industries, Seoul, Korea, 12–13 November).

Abegglen, James (1958) *The Japanese Factory: Aspects of Its Social Organization*. New York: Free Press.

Abegglen, James (1994) *Sea Change*. New York: Free Press

Abegglen, James (2006) *21st-Centur Japanese Management: New System, Lasting Value*. New York: Palgrave Macmillan.

Abo, Tetsuo (1994) *Hybrid Factory: The Japanese Production System in the United States*. New York: Oxford University Press.

Abo, Tetsuo (2015) Researching International Transfer of the Japanese-Style Management and Production System: Hybrid Factories in Six Continents. *Asian Business & Management*, 14(1): 5–35.

Adachi, Fumihiko (1987) Jidosha Sangyo – Konnan na Kokusannka he no Michi (The Automobile Industry – Obstacles for Localisation Process), in Suhehiro, Akira and Yasushi Yasuda (eds.) *Tai no Kogyoka: NAIC he no Cyosen (Industrialisation in Thailand: Challenge for NAIC)*. Tokyo: Institute of Developing Economies, 256–277.

Alam, Samsul and Kaoru Natsuda (2016) The Competitive Factors of the Bangladeshi Garment Industry in the Post-MFA Era. *Canadian Journal of Development Studies*, 37(3): 316–336.

Alavi, Rokiah (1996) *Industrialisation in Malaysia: Import Substitution and Infant Industry Performance*. London: Routledge.

Alavi, Rokiah (2005) *Application of Special and Differential Treatment in TRIMs and TRIPs: A Case Study of Malaysian Automobile and Pharmaceutical Industries*. United Nations University. Mimeo.

Alavi, Rokiah and Syezlin Hasan (2001) The Impact of TRIMs on Malaysian Automotive SME Vendors. *Kajian Malaysia*, 19(2): 27–60.

Aldaba, Rafaelita (1997) *Micro Studies: Philippine Car Assembly Sector.* Discussion Paper Series No. 97-21. Quezon City: Philippine Institute for Development Studies.
Aldaba, Rafaelita (2000) *Increasing Globalization and AFTA in 2003: What Are the Prospects for the Philippine Automotive Industry?* Discussion Paper Series No. 2000–42. Quezon City: Philippine Institute for Development Studies.
Aldaba, Rafaelita (2007) *Assessing the Competitiveness of the Philippine Auto Parts Industry.* Discussion Paper Series No. 2007–14. Quezon City: Philippine Institute for Development Studies.
Aldaba, Rafaelita (2008) *Globalization and the Need for Strategic Government-Industry Cooperation in the Philippine Automotive Industry.* Discussion Paper Series No. 2008–21. Quezon City: Philippine Institute for Development Studies.
Aldaba, Rafaelita (2013) *Why a New Industrial Policy for the Philippines Is Critical.* PIDS Policy Note No.2013-01. Quezon City: Philippine Institute for Development Studies.
Amsden, Alice (1989) *Asia's Next Giants: South Korea and Late Industrialization.* New York: Oxford University Press.
Amsden, Alice and Tadashi Hikino (2000) The Bank Is Worse Than the Bite: New WTO Law and Late Industrialization. *Annals of the American Academy of Political Science*, 570(1): 104–114.
Aminullah, Erman and Richard Adnan (2012) The Role of Academia as an External Resource of Innovation for the Automotive Industry in Indonesia. *Asian Journal of Technology Innovation*, 20(S1): 99–110.
Anazawa, Makoto (1998) Mareisia Kukuminsha Purojekuto to Susono Sangyo no Keisei (Malaysian National Car Project and the Formation of Supporting Industry). *Ajia Keizai*, 39(5): 92–114.
Anazawa, Makoto (2006) Mareisia no Jidosha Sangyo (The Malaysian Automotive Industry), in Hiratsuka, Daisuke (ed.) *Higashi Ajia no Chosen (The Challenges to East Asia).* Chiba: Institute of Developing Economies, 295–325.
Anazawa, Makoto (2016) Mareisia no Jidosha Jidosha Buhin Sangyo (The Automotive and Auto Parts Industries in Malaysia), in Nishimura, Hidetoshi and Hideo Kobayashi (eds.) *ASEAN no Jidosha Sangyo (The Automotive and Auto Components Industries in ASEAN).* Tokyo: Keiso Shobo, 145–165.
Aoki, Takeshi (1997) AFTA to Nikkei Kigyo (AFTA and Japanese Corporations), in Aoki, Takeshi and Keiichi Umada (eds.) *Nihon Kigyo to Chokusetu Toshi (Japanese Corporations and Foreign Direct Investment).* Tokyo: Keiso Sobo, 75–105.
Asanuma, Banri (1997) *Nihon no Kigyo Soshiki (Corporate Organization in Japan).* Tokyo: Yuhikaku.
Aswicahyono, Haryo, Chatib Basri and Hal Hill (2000) How Not to Industrialise? Indonesia's Automotive Industry. *Bulletin of Indonesian Economic Studies*, 36 (1): 209–241.
Aswicahyono, Haryo and Pratiwi Kartika (2010) Production Linkages and Industrial Upgrading: Case Study of Indonesia's Automotive Industry, in Intarakumnerd, Patarapong and Yasushi Ueki (eds.) *Fostering Production and Science & Technology Linkages to Stimulate Innovation in ASEAN* (ERIA Research Project 2009, No 7-4). Jakarta: Economic Research Institute for ASEAN and East Asia, 57–86.
ASEAN Secretariat (2008) *ASEAN Economic Community Blueprint.* Jakarta: Association of Southeast Asian Nations.
ASEAN (2014) *ASEAN Investment Report 2013–2014: FDI Development and Regional Value Chains.* Jakarta: ASEAN Secretariat (co-published with UNCTAD, Geneva).
ASEAN (2017) *ASEAN Investment Report 2017: Foreign Direct Investment and Economic Zones in ASEAN.* Jakarta: ASEAN Secretariat (co-published with UNCTAD, Geneva).

ASEAN (2018) *ASEAN Investment Report 2018: Foreign Direct Investment and the Digital Economy in ASEAN*. Jakarta: ASEAN Secretariat (co-published with UNCTAD, Geneva).

Athukorala, Prema-Chandra (2006) Trade Policy Reforms and the Structure of Protection in Vietnam. *World Economy*, 29(2): 161–187.

Athukorala, Prema-Chandra (2011) Production Networks and Trade Patterns in East Asia: Regionalization and Globalization. *Asian Economic Papers*, 10(1): 65–95.

Athukorala, Prema-Chandra and Archanun Kohpaiboon (2010) *Thailand in Global Automobile Networks*. Geneva: International Trade Centre.

Attavanich, Witsanu (2017) *Impact of the First-Time Car Buyer Program on the Environmental Cost of Air Pollution in Bangkok*, MPRA Paper No. 83170.

Austria, Myrna (2012) Moving Towards an ASEAN Economic Community. *East Asia*, 29(2): 141–156.

Automotive World (2018) *Special Report: The ASEAN Auto Industry*. Penarth: Automotive World.

Auty, Richard (1994) Sectoral Targeting: Auto Manufacture in Korea and Taiwan. *Journal of International Development*, 6(2): 609–625.

Azmeh, Shamel and Khalid Nadvi (2014) Asian Firms and the Restructuring of Global Value Chains. *International Business Review*, 23(4): 708–717.

Bair, Jennifer (2005). Global Capitalism and Commodity Chains: Looking Back, Going Forward. *Competition & Change*, 9(2): 153–180.

Bair, Jennifer and Gary Gereffi (2001) Local Clusters in Global Chains: The Causes and Consequences of Export Dynamism in Torreon's Blue Jeans Industry. *World Development*, 29(11): 1885–1903.

Bamber, Penny and Gary Gereffi (2013) *Costa Rica in Aerospace Global Value Chain: Opportunities for Entry and Upgrading*. Center on Globalization, Governance & Competitiveness. Durham, NC: Duke University.

Barnes, Justin and Mike Morris (2008) Staying Alive in the Global Automotive Industry: What can Developing Economies Learn from South Africa Linking into Global Automotive Value Chains?. *The European Journal of Development Research*, 20(1): 31–55.

Basri, Chatib (2012) Indonesia's Role in the World Economy: Sitting on the Fence, in Reid, Anthony (ed.) *Indonesia Rising: The Repositioning of Asia's Third Giant*. Singapore: Institute of Southeast Asian Studies, 28–48.

Blazek, Jiri, Kaoru Natsuda and Jan Sykora (2018) Entrance-Exit Dynamics of Suppliers and the Repercussions for Reshaping the Structure of GVCs/GPNs. *European Planning Studies*, 26(12): 2364–2386.

Booth, Anne (1999) Initial Conditions and Miraculous Growth: Why Is South East Asia Different from Taiwan and South Korea?. *World Development*, 27(2): 301–321.

Bora, Bijit, Peter Lloyd and Mari Pangestu (2001) Industrial Policy and the WTO, in Hoekman, Bernard and Will Martin (eds.) *Developing Countries and the WTO: A Pro-Active Agenda*. London: Blackwell, 167–183.

Brewer, Thomas and Stephen Young (1998) Investment Issues at the WTO: The Architecture of Rules and the Settlement of Dispute. *Journal of International Economic Law*, 1(3): 457–470.

Brooks, Douglas, Emma Xiaoqin Fan and Lea Sumulong (2003) *Foreign Direct Investment in Developing Asia: Trends, Effects, and Likely Issues for the Forthcoming WTO Negotiations*. Manila: Asian Development Bank, Economics and Research Department Working Paper No.38, April 2003.

Busser, Rogier (2008) 'Detroit of the East Asia'? Industrial Upgrading, Japanese Car Producers and the Development of the Automotive Industry in Thailand. *Asia Pacific Business Review*, 14(1): 29–45.

Chalmers, Ian (1994) *Domestic Capital in the Evolution of Nationalist Auto Development Policy in Indonesia: From Instrumental to Structural Power*. Murdoch University Working Paper No.30.

Chandran, V.G.R., Rajah Rasiah, and Peter Wad (2009) *Malaysian Manufacturing Systems of Innovation and Internationalization of R&D*. CBDS Working Paper Series, Working Paper No.11 Copenhagen, Copenhagen Business School.

Chandran, V.G.R., V.P.K. Sundran, and Kalian Santhidran (2014) Innovation Systems in Malaysia: a Perspective of University – Industry R&D Collaboration. *AI & Society*, 29(3): 435–444.

Chang, Ha-Joon (2002) *Kicking Away the Ladder: Development Strategy in Historical Perspective*. London: Anthem Press.

Chatterjee, Sujit (1990) ASEAN Economic Co-operation in the 1980s and 1990s, in Broinowski, Alison (ed.) *ASEAN into the 1990s*. New York: St Martin's Press, 58–82.

Cheewatrakoolpong, Kornkuron, Chayodom Sabhasri, and Nath Bunditwattanawong (2013) *Impact of the ASEAN Economic Community on ASEAN Production Networks*. ADBI Working Paper 409. Tokyo: Asian Development Bank Institute.

Chia, Siow Yue (2011) Association of Southeast Asian Nations Economic Integration: Developments and Challenges. *Asian Economic Policy Review*, 6(1): 43–63.

Chia, Siow Yue (2013) *The ASEAN Economic Community: Progress, Challenges and Prospects*, ADBI Working Paper Series No.440. Tokyo: Asian Development Bank Institute.

Clark, Kim and Takahiro Fujimoto (1991) *Product Development Performance: Strategy, Organization, and Management in the World Auto Industry*. Boston, MA: Harvard Business School Press.

Contreras, Oscar, Jorge Carrillo and Jorge Alonso (2012) Local Entrepreneurship within Global Value Chains: A Case Study in the Mexican Automotive Industry. *World Development*, 40(5): 1013–1023.

Crain Communications (2018) *North America, Europe and the World, Top Suppliers*. Supplement to Automotive News (25 June 2018). Detroit, MI: Crain Communications.

Darby, James (2009) Liberalisation and Regional Market Integration: Turkish and Australian Automotive Sector Experience Compared. *The World Economy*, 32(3): 460–478.

Davies, Hugh, Liana M. Cipcigan, Ceri Donovan, Daniel Newman, and Paul Nieuwenhaus (2015) The Impact of Electric Automobility, in Nieuwenhuis, Paul and Peter Wells (eds.) *The Global Automotive Industry*. Chichester, UK: Wiley, 185–198.

Doner, Richard (1991) *Driving a Bargain: Automobile Industrialization and Japanese Firms in Southeast Asia*. Berkeley: University of California Press.

Doner, Richard (1992) Limits of State Strength: Toward an Institutionalist View of Economic Development. *World Politics*, 44(3): 398–431.

Doner, Richard, Patarapong Intarakumnerd and Bryan Ritchie (2013) University-Industry Linkage in Thailand: Source of Weakness in Economic Upgrading. *Science, Technology & Society*, 18(2): 213–229.

Doner Richard and Peter Wad (2014) Financial Crises and Automotive Industry Development in Southeast Asia. *Journal of Contemporary Asia*, 44(4): 664–687.

Doran, Desmond (2004) Rethinking the Supply Chain: An Automotive Perspective. *Supply Chain Management: An International Journal*, 9(1): 102–109.

Dunkley, Graham (1997) *The Free Trade Adventure: The WTO, the Uruguay Round and Globalism – A Critique*. London: Zed Books.

Economist, The (2019) *The World Is Not Flat: Special Report on Global Supply Chains*. London: The Economist (13 July 2019).

Egresi, Istvan (2007) Foreign Direct Investment in a Recent Entrant to the EU: The Case of the Automotive Industry in Romania. *Eurasian Geography and Economics*, 48(6): 748–764.

EIU (2005) *Country Report September 2005 (Malaysia)*. London: The Economic Intelligence Unit (EIU).

Erdogdu, Mustafa (1999) The Turkish and South Korean Automobile Industries and the Role of the State in Their Development. *METU Studies in Development*, 26(1–2): 25–73.

Evans, Peter (1995) *Embedded Autonomy: States and Industrial Transformation*. Princeton, NJ: Princeton University Press.

Fforde, Adam (2009) *Coping with Facts: A Skeptic's Guide to the Problem of Development*. Sterling, VA: Kumarian Press.

Fourin (1991) *Ajia Jidosha Sangyo (Asian Automotive Industry)*. Nagoya: Fourin.

Fourin (1994) *Ajia Jidosha Sangyo (Asian Automotive Industry)*. Nagoya: Fourin.

Fourin (1996) *Ajia Jidosha Sangyo (Asian Automotive Industry)*. Nagoya: Fourin.

Fourin (1999) *Ajia Jidosha Sangyo (Asian Automotive Industry)*. Nagoya: Fourin.

Fourin (2000) *2000 ASEAN Taiwan Jidosha Buhin Sangyo (ASEAN & Taiwan Automobile Components Industry)*. Nagoya: Fourin.

Fourin (2002) *Ajia Jidosha Sangyo (Asian Automotive Industry)*. Nagoya: Fourin.

Fourin (2004) *Ajia Jidosha Sangyo (Asian Automotive Industry)*. Nagoya: Fourin.

Fourin (2006) *Ajia Jidosha Sangyo (Asian Automotive Industry)*. Nagoya: Fourin.

Fourin (2008) *Ajia Jidosha Sangyo (Asian Automotive Industry)*. Nagoya: Fourin.

Fourin (2011) *Ajia Jidosha Sangyo (Asian Automotive Industry)*. Nagoya: Fourin.

Fourin (2012) *Ajia Jidosha Buhin Sangyo (Asian Automotive Parts Industry)*. Nagoya: Fourin.

Fourin (2015) *ASEAN Jidosha Sangyo (The ASEAN Automotive Industry)*. Nagoya. Fourin.

Fourin (2017) *ASEAN Jidosha Sangyo (The ASEAN Automotive Industry)*. Nagoya. Fourin.

Fourin (2018) *Sekai Jidosha Tokei Nenkan (Statistical Yearbook of World Automotive Industry)*. Nagoya. Fourin.

Fourin (2019) *ASEAN Jidosha Sangyo (The ASEAN Automotive Industry)*. Nagoya. Fourin.

Frederick, Stacey and Gary Gereffi (2011) Upgrading and Restructuring in the Global Apparel Value Chain: Why China and Asia Are Outperforming Mexico and Central America. *International Journal of Technological Learning, Innovation and Development*, 4(1/2/3): 67–95.

Fujimoto, Takahiro (1997) *Seisan System no Shinka Ron (The Evolutional Theory of Production System)*. Tokyo: Yuhikaku.

Fujimoto, Takahiro, Shoichiro Sei and Akira Takeishi (1994) Nihon Jidosha Sạngyo no Supplier System no Zentaizo to Sono Tamensei (The Total Perspective and Multifaceted Nature of the Supplier System in the Japanese Automotive Industry). *Kikai Keizai Kenkyu*, 24: 11–36.

Fujimoto, Takahiro, Seunghwan Ku and Yoshinori Konno (2006) *Jidosha Buhin Sangyo ni Okeru Torihiki Pattern no Hattuten to Henyo (Development and Change in the Trade Pattern in the Automotive Parts Industry)*. MMRC Discussion Paper No.85, Tokyo: 21 COE Monozukuri Keiei Center, University of Tokyo.

Fujita, Kuniko and Richard Child Hill (1997) Auto Industrialization in Southeast Asia: National Strategies and Local Development. *ASEAN Economic Bulletin,* 13(3): 312–332.

GAIKINDO (2010) *Enter the World Mobility Though Building Competitive Automotive Industry 2010–2013.* Jakarta: GAIKINDO.

Gallagher, Kevin (2005) *Putting Development First.* London: Zed Books.

Gentile-Ludecke, Simona and Axele Giroud (2009) Does the East Learn from the West? How Polish Automotive Suppliers Learn from Western MNEs. *Journal of East-West Business,* 15(3–4): 271–294.

Gentile-Ludecke, Simona and Axele Giroud (2009) Knowledge Transfer from TNCs and Upgrading of Domestic Firms: The Polish Automotive Sector. *World Development,* 40(4): 796–807.

Gereffi, Gary (1994) The Organization of Buyer-driven Global Commodity Chains: How U.S. Retailers Shape Overseas Production Networks, in Gereffi, Gary and Migrel Korzeniewicz (eds.) *Commodity Chains and Global Capitalism.* Westport, CT: Praeger, 95–122.

Gereffi, Gary (1999) International Trade and Industrial Upgrading in the Apparel Commodity Chain. *Journal of International Economics,* 48(1): 37–70.

Gereffi, Gary (2014a) Global Value Chains in a Post-Washington Consensus World. *Review of International Political Economy,* 21(1): 9–37.

Gereffi, Gary (2014b) A Global Value Chain Perspective on Industrial Policy and Development in Emerging Markets. *Duke Journal of Comparative and International Law,* 24: 433–458.

Gereffi, Gary, John Humphrey and Timothy Sturgeon (2005) The Governance of Global Value Chains. *Review of International Political Economy,* 12(1): 78–104.

Gereffi, Gary and Olga Memedovic (2003) *The Global Apparel Value Chain: What Prospects for Upgrading by Developing Countries?.* Vienna: United Nations Industrial Development Organization.

Goto, Kenta, Kaoru Natsuda and John Thoburn (2011) Meeting the Challenge of China: the Vietnamese Garment Industry in the post-MFA era. *Global Networks,* 11(3): 355–379.

Guiheux, Gilles and Yveline Lecler (2000) Japanese Car Manufacturers and Component Makers in the ASEAN Region: A Case of Expatriation under Duress - or a Strategy of Regionally Integrated Production?, in Humphrey, John, Yveline Lecler and Mario Segio Salerno (eds.) *Global Strategies and Local Realities: The Auto Industry in Emerging Markets.* London: Macmillan, 207–233.

Chang, Jae-Hee, Gary Rynhart, and Phu Huynh (2016) *ASEAN in Transformation: Automotive and Auto Parts – Shifting Gears.* Geneva: Bureau for Employers' Activities, Working Paper No.12.

Gutierrez, Rommel (2015) *The Philippine Automotive Industry: Roadmap Localization for Competitiveness.* Presented at the DTI-BOI Regional Conference, Tagaytay City, August 6 2015.

Hale, Christopher (2001) Indonesia's National Car Project Revised: History of Kia-Timor Motors and Its Aftermath. *Asian Survey,* 41(4): 629–645.

Hansen, John (1971) The Motor Vehicle Industry. *Bulletin of Indonesian Economic Studies,* 7(2): 38–69.

Hansen, Arve (2016) Driving Development? The Problems and Promises of the Car in Vietnam. *Journal of Contemporary Asia,* 46(4): 551–569

Hansen, Arve (2017) *Doi Moi* on Two and Four Wheels: Capitalist Development and Motorised Mobility in Vietnam, in Hansen, Arve and Kenneth Bo Nielsen (eds.) *Wheels of Change: Cars, Automobility and Development in Asia*. London: Routledge, 103–119.

Haraguchi, Masahiko and Upmanu Lall (2013) *Flood Risks and Impacts - Future Research Questions and Implication to Private Investment Decision-Making for Supply Chain Networks* (Background Paper prepared for the Global Assessment Report on Disaster Risk Reduction 2013). Geneva: The United Nations Office for Disaster Risk Reduction.

Hashiya, Hiroshi and Fangjing Jiang (2010) Global Jidai ni okeru Higasi Ajia Jidosha Sangyo no Saihen (The Reorganization of the East Asian Auto Industry in the Times of the Globalization). *Journal of Tokyo Keizai University*, 267: 73–113.

Hassler, Markus (2009) Variations of Value Creation: Automobile Manufacturing in Thailand. *Environment and Planning A*, 41(9): 2232–2249.

Hatch, Walter (1995) Japanese Investment and Aid Strategies in Vietnam, in Duffield, Barbara (ed.) *Vietnam and Japan*. Victoria, BC: University of Victoria Press, 288–306.

Hatch, Walter (2002) Regionalizing the State: Japanese Administrative and Financial Guidance for Asia. *Social Science Japan Journal*, 5(2): 179–197.

Hatch, Walter and Kozo Yamamura (1996) *Asia in Japan's Embrace: Building a Regional Production Alliance*. Cambridge: Cambridge University Press.

Hausmann, Ricardo and Dani Rodrick (2005) Self-Discovery in Developing Strategy in El Salvador. *Economia* 6(1): 43–101.

Hayashi Takubumi (2001) Technology Transfer in Asia in Transition: Case studies of Japanese companies, in Nakamura, Masao (ed.) *The Japanese Business and Economic System*. New York: Palgrave, 115–138.

Henderson, Jeffrey, Peter Dicken, Martin Hess, Neil Coe, and Henry Wai-Chung Yeung (2002) Global Production Networks and the Analysis of Economic Development. *Review of International Political Economy*, 9(3): 436–464.

Higashi, Shigeki (1995) Chapter 3 The Automotive Industry in Thailand: From Protective Promotion to Liberalization, in IDE Spot Survey - *The Automotive Industry in Asia: The Great Leap Forward?*. Tokyo: Institute of Developing Economies, 16–25.

Higashi, Shigeki (2000) Sangyo Seisaku (Industrial Policy), in Suehiro, Akira and Shigeki Higashi (eds.) *Tai no Keizai Seisaku: Seido, Soshiki, Akuta (Economic Policy in Thailand: The Role of Institutions and Actors)*. Chiba: Institute of Developing Economies, 115–178.

Hill, Hal (2000) *The Indonesian Economy* (Second Edition). Cambridge: Cambridge University Press.

Hoekman, Bernard (2005) Operationalizing the Concept of Policy Space in the WTO: Beyond Special and Differential Treatment. *Journal of International Economic Law*, 8(2): 405–424.

Hopkins, Terence and Immanuel Wallerstein (1986) Commodity Chains in the World Economy Prior to 1800. *Review* 10(1): 157–170.

Humphrey, John (2000) Assembler-Supplier Relations in the Auto Industry: Globalisation and National Development. *Competition and Change*, 4(3): 245–271.

Humphrey, John (2003) Globalization and Supply Chain Networks: The Auto Industry in Brazil and India. *Global Networks*, 3(2): 121–144.

Humphrey, John and Olga Memedovic (2003) *The Global Automotive Industry Value Chain: What Prospects for Upgrading by Developing Countries*. Vienna: United Nations Industrial Development Organization.

Humphrey, John and Hubert Schmitz (2002) How Does Insertion in Global Value Chain Affect Upgrading Industrial Cluster?. *Regional Studies*, 36(9): 1017–1027.

IFR (2018) *Executive Summary World Robotics 2018 Industrial Robots.* Frankfurt: International Federation of Robotics (IFR). https://ifr.org/downloads/press2018/Executive_Summary_WR_2018_Industrial_Robots.pdf [accessed on 29 August 2019].

Ikemoto, Yukio (1994) Tai no Jidosha Kumitate Sangyo to Jiyuka Seisaku (The Automobile Assembly Industry and Liberalisation Policy in Thailand), in Taniura, Taeko (ed.) *Sangyo Hatten to Sangyo Soshiki no Henka (Industrial Development and Transformation of Industrial Orgnisation).* Tokyo: Institute of Developing Economies, 169–190.

ILO (2016) *ASEAN in Transformation: Automotive and Auto Parts – Shifting Gears*, by Jae-Hee Chang, Gary Rynhart and Phu Huynh. Geneva: International Labour Office, Bureau for Employers' Activities, Working Paper No.12.

Inoue, Hiroshi (1990) Indonesia no Jidosha Kokusanka Seisaku to Nihon Jidosh Shihon (Localisation Policy for the Automotive Industry in Indonesia and Japanese Automotive Capitals). *Keizai Ronshu (Kyoto University)*, 146(3&4): 61–84.

Intarakumnerd, Patarapong and Kriengkrai Techakanont (2016) Intra-Industry Trade, Product Fragmentation and Technological Capability Development in Thai Automotive Industry. *Asia Pacific Business Review*, 22(1): 65–85.

Intarakumnerd, Patarapong and Nathasit Gerdsri (2014) Implications of Technology Management and Policy on the Development of a Sectoral Innovation System: Lessons Learned Through the Evolution of Thai Automotive Sector. *International Journal of Innovation and Technology Management,* 11(3): 1440009.

Intarakumnerd, Patarapong, Nathasit Gerdsri and Pard Teekasap (2012) The Role of External Knowledge Sources in Thailand's Automotive Industry. *Asian Journal of Technology Innovation*, 21(S1): 85–97.

Irawati, Dessy (2010) Challenges for the Indonesian Automotive Cluster. *Regional Insight*, 1(1): 6–8.

Irawati, Dessy (2012) *Knowledge Transfer in the Automobile Industry: Global-Local. Production Networks.* London: Routledge.

Irawati, Dessy and David Charles (2010) The Involvement of Japanese MNEs in the Indonesian Automotive Cluster. *International Journal of Automotive Technology and Management*, 10(2/3): 180–196.

Isaksen, Arne and Bo Terje Kalsaas (2009) Suppliers and Strategies for Upgrading in Global Production Networks: The Case of a Supplier to the Global Automotive Industry in a High-Cost Location. *European Planning Studies*, 17(4): 569–585.

Ito, Susumu (2014) Shashu Senryaku, Seisan Kaihatsu no Genchika to Rieki Kakudai: Toyota Jidosha no Shinkokoku taiou wo Chushin to shite (Model Development Strategy, Localisation of Production & Development and Enhancement of Profitability: Toyota Motor's Response to Emerging Countries). *Kyoto Management Review*, 24: 31–49.

Ivarsson, Inge and Claes Goran Alvstam (2004) International Technology Transfer through Local Business Linkage: The Case of Volvo's Truck and Their Domestic Suppliers in India. *Oxford Development Studies*, 32(2): 241–260.

Ivarsson, Inge and Claes Goran Alvstam (2005) Technology Transfer from TNCs to Local Suppliers in Developing Countries: A Study of AB Volvo's Truck and Bus Plants in Brazil, China, India, and Mexico. *World Development*, 33(8): 1325–1344.

JAMA (2008) *Hand-in-Hand: Partnership in the Auto Industry between ASEAN and Japan*. Singapore: Japan Automotive Manufacturers Association (JAMA).

JAMA (2016) *Driving Growth Towards the Future 2016: Hand in Hand between ASEAN and Japan*. Singapore: Japan Automotive Manufacturers Association (JAMA).

Jayasankaran, S. (1993) Made-In-Malaysia: The Proton Project, in Jomo, K.S. (ed.) *Industrialising Malaysia*. London: Routledge, 272–285.

JETRO (2015) *2014 Shuyokoku no Jidosha Seisan Hanbai Doko (Automotive Production and Sales in Major Countries in 2014)*. Tokyo: Japan External Trade Organization (JETRO).

JETRO (2016) *2015 Shuyokoku no Jidosha Seisan Hanbai Doko (Automotive Production and Sales in Major Countries in 2015)*. Tokyo: Japan External Trade Organization (JETRO).

JETRO (2018a) *2017 Shuyokoku no Jidosha Seisan Hanbai Doko (Automotive Production and Sales in Major Countries in 2017)*. Tokyo: Japan External Trade Organization (JETRO).

JETRO (2018b) *Survey on Business Conditions of Japanese Companies in Asia and Oceania 2018*. Tokyo: Japan External Trade Organization (JETRO), 20 December.

Johnson, Chalmers (1982) *MITI and the Japanese Miracle*. Stanford, CA: Stanford University Press.

Jomo, K.S. (1994) The Proton Saga: Malaysian Car, Mitsubishi Gain, in Jomo, K.S. (ed.) *Japan and Malaysian Development*. London: Routledge, 263–290.

Jomo, K.S. (2001a) *Growth After the Asian Crisis: What Remains of the East Asian Model?*. G-24 Discussion Paper, No.10. New York and Geneva: United Nations.

Jomo, K.S. (2001b) *Southeast Asia's Industrialization: Industrial Policy, Capabilities and Sustainability*. New York: Palgrave.

Jomo, K.S., Yun Chung Chen, Brian Folk, Ul-Hargue Irfan, Pasuk Phongpaicht, Simatupang Batara, and Mayuri Tateishi (1997) *Southeast Asia's Misunderstood Miracle: Industrial Policy and Economic Development in Thailand, Malaysia and Indonesia*. Boulder, CO: Westview Press.

Kamo, Kineko (1997) ASEAN ni Okeru Jidosha no Kokusai Buhin Hokan Taisei (The International Complementation Regime of Automotive Components in ASEAN). *Joho Kagaku Kenkyu*, 7: 61–81.

Kamo, Kineko (1999) Kokusai Bungyo no Shinten to Jidosha Sangyo (The Progress of International Division of Labour and the Automobile Industry), in Maruyama, Yoshinari, Takashi Sago and Hideo Kobayashi (eds.) *Ajia Keizaiken to Kokusai Bungyo no Shinten (Asia Economic Zone and the Progress of International Division of Labour)*. Kyoto: Minerva Sobo, 176–212.

Kaosa-ard, Mingsarn Santikarn (1993) TNC Involvement in the Thai Auto Industry. *TDRI Quarterly Review*, 8(1): 9–16.

Kaplinsky, Raphael and Mike Morris (2001) *A Handbook for Value Chain Research*. Institute of Development studies, Brighton: The University of Sussex.

Katayama, Hiroshi (2003) Kokusai Bungyo to Seisan Butsuryu Network System no Settukei (International Division of Labour and Deign of Production and Logistic Network), in Hiraki, Shusaku, Takaya Ichimura, Hiroshi Katayama, Kazuyoshi Ishii and Kineko Kamo (eds.) *Kokusai Kyoryoku ni yoru Jidosha Buhin Sogohokan System (Automotive Parts Mutual Complementation System through International Cooperation)*. Hiroshima: Keisuisha, 70–129.

Kawakami, Momoko (2011) Inter-Firm Dynamics in Notebook PC Value Chains and the Rise of Taiwanese Original Deign Manufacturing Firms, in Kawakami, Momoko and Timothy Sturgeon (eds.) *The Dynamics of Local Learning in Global Value Chains: Experiences from East Asia*. London: Palgrave MacMillan, 16–42.

Khai, Nguyen (2003) Foreign Direct Experience and Economic Development: The Vietnamese Experience, in Binh, Tran-Nam and Chi Do Pham (eds.) *The Vietnamese Economy: Awakening the Dormant Dragon*. London: Routledge, 176–198.

Khan, Shahrukh Rafi (2007) WTO, IMF and the Closing of Development Policy Space for Low-income Countries: A Call for Neo-Developmentalism. *Third World Quarterly*, 28(6): 1073–1090.

Kikuchi, Akifumi (2007) *A Flowchart Approach to Malaysia's Automobile Industry Cluster Policy*. IDE Discussion Paper No.120, Institute of Developing Economies.

Kim, Woosang and Yeonho Lee (2000) Prospects for East Asian Economic Regionalism in the 21st Century. *Global Economic Review*, 29(2): 83–102.

Kimura, Fukunari and Ayako Obashi (2011) *Production Networks in East Asia: What We Know So Far*. Tokyo: Asian Development Bank Institute, Working Paper No.320, November 2011.

Kimura, Fukunari and Shujiro Urata (2016) Jidosha-Jidosha Buhin Sangyo to Keizai Togo (The Automotive and Automotive Parts Industry and Economic Integration, in Nishimura, Hidetoshi and Hideo Kobayashi (eds.) *ASEAN no Jidosha Sangyo (The Automobile and Auto Components Industries in ASEAN)*. Tokyo: Keiso Shobo, 55–73.

Kishimoto, Chikashi (2004) Clustering and Upgrading in Global Value Chains: The Taiwanese Personal Computer Industry, in Schmitz, Hubert (ed.) *Local Enterprises in the Global Economy: Issues of Governance and Upgrading*. Cheltenham: Edward Elgar, 233–264.

Kobayashi, Hideo (2017) *Current Status and Traits of the Auto Parts Industry in Viet Nam*. Jakarta: Economic Research Institute for ASEAN and East Asia discussion paper, ERIA-DP-2017-06.

Kobayashi, Hideo and Yingshan Jin (2013) The CLMV Automobile and Auto Parts Industry, in Waseda University (ed.) *Automobile and Auto Components Industries in ASEAN: Current State and Issues*. ERIA Research Project Report 2013–17, 40–49. Available at: http:/www.eria.org/RPR_FY2013_No.7_Chapter_4.pdf [accessed on 5 September 2019].

Komura, Chikara (2000) Policies Towards Automobile Industries in Southeast Asia, in Hamada, Koichi, Mitsuo Matsushita and Chikara Komura (eds.) *Dreams and Dilemmas: Economic Friction and Dispute Resolution in the Asia-Pacific*. Singapore: Institute of Southeast Asian Studies, 173–197.

Kurasawa, Maki (2014) AREA Report: The Philippines: Kokunai Seisansha Kakudai heno Michi (Road to Expansion of Domestically Produced Vehicles). *JETRO Censor* (August): 58–59.

Kuroiwa, Ikuo, Fukunari Kimura and Shujiro Urata (2016) Jidosha, Jidosha Buhin Sangyo to Keizai Togo (The Automotive and Automotive Parts Industry, and Economic Integration, in Nishimura, Hidetoshi and Hideo Kobayashi (eds.) *ASEAN no Jidosha Sangyo (The Automobile and Auto Components Industries in ASEAN)*. Tokyo: Keiso Shobo, 55–119.

Kuroiwa, Ikuo, Bhandhubanyong Paritud and Yasuhiro Yamada (2016) Thai no Jidosha Buhin Sangyo (The Automotive and Parts Industry in Thailand), in Nishimura, Hidetoshi and Hideo Kobayashi (eds.) *ASEAN no Jidosha Sangyo (The Automobile and Auto Components Industries in ASEAN)*. Tokyo: Keiso Shobo, 75–119.

Lall, Sanjaya (1995) Malaysia: Industrial Success and the Role of the Government. *Journal of International Development*, 7(5): 759–773.

Lauridsen, Laurids (2004) Foreign Direct Investment, Linkage Formation and Supplier Development in Thailand during the 1990s: The Role of State Governance. *European Journal of Development Research*, 16(3): 561–586.

Lauridsen, Laurids (2008) ***State, Institutions and Industrial Development: Industrial Deeping and Upgrading Policies in Taiwan and Thailand Compared*** (in two volumes). Aachen: Springer.

Lauridsen, Laurids (2009) The Policies and Politics of Industrial Upgrading in Thailand during the Thaksin Era (2001–2006). ***Asian Politics and Policy***, 1(3): 409–434.

Lecler, Yveline (2002) The Cluster Role in the Development of the Thai Car Industry. ***International Journal of Urban and Regional Research***, 26(4): 799–814.

Lee, Kuen, Chan-Yuan Wong, Patarapong Intarakumnerd and Chaiyatorn Limapornvanich (2019) Is the Fourth Industrial Revolution a Window of Opportunity for Upgrading or Reinforcing the Middle-Income Trap? Asian Model of Development in Southeast Asia. ***Journal of Economic Policy Reform*** (online first version). DOI:10.1080/17487870.2019.1565411.

Lee, Sook-Jong and Taejoon Han (2006) The Demise of Korea, Inc.: Paradigm Shift in Korea's Developmental State. ***Journal of Contemporary Asia***, 36(3): 305–324.

Legewie, Jochen (2000a) Driving Regional Integration: Japanese Firms and the Development of the ASEAN Automotive Industry, in Blechinger, Verena and Jochen Legewie (eds.) ***Facing Asia: Japan's Role in the Political and Economic Dynamism of Regional Cooperation***. München: Indicium Verlag, 217–245.

Legewie, Jochen (2000b) The Political Economy of Industrial Integration in ASEAN: The Role of Japanese Companies. ***Journal of the Asia Pacific Economy***, 5(3): 204–233.

Lin, Justin, and Ha-Joon Chang (2009) Should Industrial Policy in Developing Countries Conform to Comparative Advantage or Defy It? - A Debate between Justin Lin and Ha-Joon Chang. ***Development Policy Review***, 27(5): 483–502.

Llanto, Gilberto and Ma Kristina Ortiz (2015) ***Industrial Policies and Implementation: Philippine Automotive Manufacturing as a Lens***. Discussion Paper Series No. 2015–39. Quezon City: Philippine Institute for Development Studies.

MAA (2010) ***Corporate Profile***. Selangor Darul Ehsan: Malaysian Automotive Association (MAA).

Machado, Kit (1994) Proton and Malaysia's Motor Vehicle Industry: National Industrial policies and Japanese Regional Production Strategies, in Jomo K.S. (ed.) ***Japan and Malaysian Development: In the Shadow of the Rising Sun***. London: Routlegde, 291–325.

MacIntyre, Andrew (1994) Power, Prosperity and Patrimonialism: Business and Government in Indonesia, in MacIntyre, Andrew (ed.) ***Business and Government in Industrialising Asia***. Ithaca, NY: Cornell University Press, 244–267.

MACPMA (2008) ***Malaysian Automotive Component Parts Manufacturers Directory 2008/2009***. Kuala Lumpur: Malaysian Automotive Component Parts Manufacturers Association (MACPMA).

Mayer, Jorg (2008) ***Policy Space: What, For What, and Where?***. Geneva: United Nations Conference on Trade and Development, Discussion Paper 191.

McClanahan, Paige, Alexander Chandra, Ruben Hattari, and Damon Vis-Dunbar (2014) ***Taking Advantage of ASEAN's Free Trade Agreements: A Guide for Small and Medium-Sized Enterprises***. Winnipeg: International Institute for Sustainable Development, produced jointly with ASEAN and the UK Foreign and Commonwealth Office.

METI (2011) ***Fukosei Boeki Hokokusyo 2011 (Report on Anti Fair Trade in 2011)***.Tokyo: Ministry of Economy, Trade and Industry of Japan (METI).

MIDA (2010) ***Business Opportunities, Malaysia's Automotive Industry***. Kuala Lumpur: Malaysian Investment Development Authority (MIDA).

MIDA (2018) ***Business Opportunities, Malaysia's Automotive Industry***. Kuala Lumpur: Malaysian Investment Development Authority (MIDA).

Miki, Toshio (2001) *Ajia Keizai to Chokusetu Toshi Sokusinron (Asian Economy and Promotion Theory of Foreign Direct Investment)*. Kyoto: Minelva Shobo.

Milberg, William, Xiao Jiang and Gary Gereffi (2014) Industrial Policy in the Era of Vertically Specialized Industrialisation, in Salazar-Xirinachs, Jose Manuel, Irmgard Nübler and Richard Kozul-Wright (eds.) *Transforming Economies: Making Industrial Policy Work for Growth, Jobs and Development*. Geneva: International Labour Organization, 151–178.

MITI (2009) *Review of National Automotive Policy*. Kuala Lumpur: Ministry of International Trade and Industry of Malaysia (MITI).

Moon, Chung-In and Sang-Young Rhyu (2000) The State, Structural Rigidity, and the End of Asian Capitalism: A Comparative Study of Japan and South Korea, in Robinson, Richard, Mark Besson, Kanishka Jayasuriya and Hyuk-Rae Kim (eds.) *Politics and Markets in the Wake of the Asian Crisis*. London: Routledge, 78–98.

Muslimen, Rasli, Sha'ri Mohd Yusaf and Ana Sakura Zainal Abidin (2011) Lean Manufacturing Implementation in Malaysia Automotive Components Manufacturer: A Case Study. *Proceeding of the World Congress on Engineering*, 1, July 6–8 2011, London, UK.

Nadvi, Khalid and John Thoburn (2004) Vietnam in the Global Garment and Textile Value Chain: Impact on Firms and Workers. *Journal of International Development*, 16(1): 111–123.

Nakata, Toru (2015) ASEAN Jidosha Sangyo dewa Seichyo Kikai to Risuku ga Kenzaika (Actualised Growth Opportunities and Risks in the ASEAN Automotive Industry). *Kaigai Toyushi* (May 2015): 14–17.

Natsuda, Kaoru (2008) Japan's Foreign Economic Policies towards East Asia in the Post War Era. *Asian Profile*, 36(5): 453–468.

Natsuda, Kaoru (2009) States, Multinational Corporations, and Institutional Arrangements: Economic Interdependence between Japan and Southeast Asia. *The Japanese Economy*, 36(3): 96–127.

Natsuda, Kaoru and Gavan Butler (2005) Building Institutional Capacity in Southeast Asia: Regional Governed Interdependence. *ASEAN Economic Bulletin*, 22(3): 331–339.

Natsuda, Kaoru, Kenta Goto and John Thoburn (2010) Challenges to the Cambodian Garment Industry in the Global Garment Value Chain. *European Journal of Development Research*, 22(4): 469–493.

Natsuda, Kaoru, Kunio Igusa, Aree Wiboonpongse, and John Thoburn (2012) One Village One Product - Rural Development Strategy in Asia: The Case of OTOP in Thailand. *Canadian Journal of Development Studies*, 33(3): 369–385.

Natsuda, Kaoru, Jan Sykora and Jiri Blazek (2020a) Transfer of Japanese-Style Management to the Czech Republic: The Case of Japanese Manufacturing Firms. *Asia Europe Journal*, 18(1): 75–97.

Natsuda, Kaoru, Kozo Otsuka and John Thoburn (2015a) Dawn of Industrialisation? The Indonesian Motor Industry. *Bulletin of Indonesian Economic Studies*, 51(1): 47–68.

Natsuda, Kaoru, Kozo Otsuka and John Thoburn (2015b) Indonesia's Automotive Industry Shifts up a Gear. *East Asia Forum* (2 May 2015). https://www.eastasiaforum.org/2015/05/02/indonesias-automotive-industry-shifts-up-a-gear/ [accessed on 5 September 2019].

Natsuda, Kaoru, Noriyuki Segawa, and John Thoburn (2013) Liberalization, Industrial Nationalism, and the Malaysian Automotive Industry. *Global Economic Review*, 42(2): 113–134.

Natsuda, Kaoru and John Thoburn (2013) Industrial Policy and the Development of the Automotive Industry in Thailand. *Journal of the Asia Pacific Economy*, 18(3): 413–437.

Natsuda, Kaoru, and John Thoburn (2014) How Much Policy Space Still Exists under the WTO? A Comparative Study of the Automotive Industry in Thailand and Malaysia. *Review of International Political Economy*, 21(6): 1346–1377.

Natsuda, Kaoru and John Thoburn (2018) Industrial Policy and the Development of the Automotive Industry in the Philippines. *Canadian Journal of Development Studies*, 39(3): 371–391.

Natsuda, Kaoru, John Thoburn, Jiri Blazek and Kozo Otsuka (2020b) Industrial Policy and Automotive Development: A Comparative Study between Thailand and Czechia. Mimeo.

Nehru, Vikram (2012) Modern Industrial Policy: Lesson from Malaysia's Auto Industry, *Carnegie Endowment for International Peace*, March 22, 2012. https://carnegieendowment.org/2012/03/22/modern-industrial-policy-lessons-from-malaysia-s-auto-industry-pub-47625 [accessed on 11 February 2019].

Ngo, Christine Ngoc (2020) *Rent Seeking and Development: The Political Economy of Industrialization in Vietnam*. London and New York: Routledge.

Nieuwenhuis, Paul and Peter Wells (2015) Impacts of Automobility, in Nieuwenhuis, Paul and Peter Wells (eds.) *The Global Automotive Industry*. Chichester, UK: Wiley, 153–162.

Nguyen Bich Thuy (2008) *Industrial Policies as Determinant of Localization: The Case of Vietnamese Automobile Industry*. VDF Working Paper No. 0810. Hanoi: Vietnam Development Forum: http://citeseerx.ist.psu.edu/viewdoc/download?doi=10.1.1.627.6560&rep=rep1&type=pdf [accessed 29 June 2020]

Nishimura, Hidetoshi and Hideo Kobayashi (2016) ASEAN Jidosha-Buhin Kigyo no Genjyo to Chiiki Togo (The Current Situation of The ASEAN Automotive and Parts Firms and Regional Integration, in Nishimura, Hidetoshi and Hideo Kobayashi (eds.) *ASEAN no Jidosha Sangyo (The Automobile and Auto Components Industries in ASEAN)*. Tokyo: Keiso Shobo, 3–53.

Nizamuddin, Ali (2008) Declining Risk, Market Liberalisation and State-Multinational Bargaining: Japanese Automobile Investments in India, Indonesia and Malaysia. *Pacific Affairs*, 81(3): 339–359.

Noble, Gregory, John Ravenhill, and Richard Doner (2005) Executioner or Disciplinarian: WTO Accession and the Chinese Auto Industry. *Business and Politics*, 7(2): 1–33.

Noda Shigenao (1999) Toshiba, in Kosei Boeki Senta (ed.) *AICO Sukimu ni Kansuru Chosa Kenkyu (Survey on the ASEAN Industrial Co-operation Scheme)*. Tokyo: Kosei Boeki Senta.

Nolan, Peter (2012) *Is China Buying the World?*. London: Polity Press.

Noland, Marcus and Howard Pack (2003) *Industrial Policy in an Era of Globalization: Lessons from Asia*. Washington, DC: Institute for International Economics.

Nomura, Toshiro (1996) Indonesia no Kukuminsha Keikaku to Humpuss, Kia no Jishosha Sannyu (National Car Plan and Humpuss and Kia's Entry into the Indonesian Automotive Industry). *ShoKei Ronshu*, 47: 23–69.

Nomura, Toshiro (2003) Indonesia Jidosha Sangyo no Kaihokatei (Liberalisation Process of the Indonesian Automotive Industry). *ShoKei Ronshu*, 53: 1–64.

Nomura, Toshiro (2007) Philippine no Jidosha Sangyo to IMV (The Automotive Industry in the Philippines and IMV). *Kenkyu Nenpo*, 39: 57–76.

Ofreneo, Rene (2007) Philippines, in *Elimination of TRIMS: The Experience of Selected Developing Countries*. New York: United Nations Conference on Trade and Development, 85–106.

Ofreneo, Rene (2008) Arrested Development: Multinationals, TRIMs and the Philippines' Automotive Industry. *Asia Pacific Business Review*, 14(1): 65–84.

Ofreneo, Rene (2016) Auto and Car Parts Production: Can the Philippines Catch Up with Asia?. *Asia Pacific Business Review*, 22(1): 48–64.

Ohno, Kenichi, and Mai The Cuong (2004) The Automobile Industry in Vietnam: Remaining Issues in Implementing the Master Plan. http://citeseerx.ist.psu.edu/viewdoc/download?doi=10.1.1.511.9927&rep=repl&type=pdf [accessed on 21 September 2019].

Ohno, Kenichi, and Nguyen Anh Nam (2006) *Supporting Industries in Vietnam from the Perspective of Japanese Manufacturing Firms*. Hanoi: Vietnam Development Forum Report.

Okada, Aya (2004) Skills Development and Interfirm Learning Linkages under Globalization: Lessons from the Indian Automotive Industry. *World Development*, 32(7): 1265–1288.

Onozawa, Jun (2008) Mareisia Jidosha Sangyo no Jiyuka to Nihon niyuru Jidosha Sangyo Kyoryoku (Liberalisation of the Malaysian Automotive Industry and Japan's Industrial Cooperatikon). *Kokusai Boeki to Toshi (International Trade and Investment)*, 74: 41–59.

Otsuka, Kozo and Kaoru Natsuda (2016) The Determinants of Total Factor Productivity in the Malaysian Automotive Industry: Are Government Policies Upgrading Technological Capacity?. *The Singapore Economic Review*, 61(4): 1550046.

Ozatagan, Guldem (2011) Shifts in Value Chain Governance and Upgrading in the European Periphery of Automotive Production: Evidence from Bursa, Turkey. *Environment and Planning A*, 43(4): 885–903.

Palpacuer, Florence, Peter Gibbon and Lotte Thomsen (2005) New Challenges for Developing Country Suppliers in Global Garments Chains: A Comparative European Perspective. *World Development*, 33(3): 409–430.

Pavlinek, Petr (2002) Transformation of the Central and East European Passenger Car Industry: Selective Peripheral Integration through Foreign Direct Investment. *Environment and Planning A*, 34(9): 1685–1709.

Pavlinek, Petr and Lubos Janak (2007) Regional Restructuring of the Skoda Auto Supplier Network in the Czech Republic. *European Urban and Regional Studies*, 14(2): 133–155.

Pavlinek, Petr and Jan Zenka (2011) Upgrading in the Automotive Industry: Firm-Level Evidence from Central Europe. *Journal of Economic Geography*, 11(3): 559–586.

Phongpaichit, Pasuk (1996) The Thai Economy in the Mid-1990s, in Institute of Southeast Asian Studies (ed.) *Southeast Asian Affairs 1996*. Singapore: Institute of Southeast Asian Studies.

Phongpaichit, Pasuk and Chris Baker (1995) *Thailand: Economy and Politics*. Oxford: Oxford University Press.

Pollio, Chiara and Lauretta Rubini (2019) Who Drives the Automotive Sector? Thailand Selective Policies. *International Journal of Emerging Markets*. vol. ahead-of-print. DOI:10.1108/IJOEM-02-2018-0084.

Porter, Michael (1990) *The Competitive Advantage of Nations*. New York: Free Press.

Purwaningrum, Farah, Hans-Dieter Evers and Yaniasih (2012) Knowledge Flow in the Academic-Industry Collaboration or Supply Chain Linkage? Case Study of the Automotive Industries in Jababeka Cluster. *Procedia-Social and Behavioral Sciences* 52(2012): 62–71.

PWC (2007) *Vietnam's Automotive Component Industry: Ready to Go Global*. PriceWaterHouse Cooper. www.pwc.com.vn [accessed on 5 September 2019].

PWC (2018) *Pocket Tax Book 2018*. PriceWaterHouseCooper. www.pwc.com.vn [accessed on 5 September 2019].

Quimba, Francis, and Maureen Rosellon (2012) Innovation in the Automotive Sector of the Philippines. *Asian Journal of Technology Innovation*, 20(1): 49–65.

Raikes, Philip, Michael Jensen and Stefano Ponte (2000). Global Commodity Chain Analysis and the French *filière* Approach: Comparison and Critique. *Economy and Society*, 29(3): 390–417.

Rasiah, Rajah (2005) Trade-related Investment Liberalization under the WTO: The Malaysia Experience. *Global Economic Review*, 34(4): 453–471.

Rasiah, Rajah (2009) Technological Capabilities of Automotive Firms in Indonesia and Malaysia. *Asian Economic Paper*, 8(1): 151–168.

Rasiah, Rajah and Ishak Shari (2001) Market, Government and Malaysia's New Economic Policy. *Cambridge Journal of Economics*, 25(1): 57–78.

Rock, Michael (2001) Selective Industrial Policy and Manufacturing Export Success in Thailand, in Jomo, K.S. (ed.) *Southeast Asia's Industrialization: Industrial Policy, Capabilities and Sustainability*. New York: Palgrave, 263–282.

Rodrik, Dani (2004) *Industrial Policy for the Twenty-First Century*. Available at http://www.hks.harvard.edu/fs/drodrik/Research%20papers/UNIDOSep.pdf [accessed on 5 September 2019].

Rodrik, Dani (2006) Goodbye Washington Consensus, Hello Washington Confusion? A Review of the World Bank's Economic Growth in the 1990s: Learning from a Decade of Reform. *Journal of Economic Literature*, 44(4): 973–987.

Rosellon, Maureen, and Erlinda Medalla (2012) *ASEAN+1 FTAs and the Global Supply Chain in East Asia; the Case of the Philippine Automotive and Electronics Sectors*. Discussion Paper Series No. 2012-38. Quezon City: Philippine Institute for Development Studies.

Rosli, Mohamad (2006) The Automobile Industry and Performance of Malaysian Auto Production. *Journal of Economic Cooperation*, 27(1): 89–114.

Rosli, Mohamad and Fatimah Kari (2008) Malaysia's National Automotive Policy and the Performance of Proton's Foreign and Local Vendors. *Asia Pacific Business Review*, 14(1): 103–118.

Rugraff, Eric (2010) Foreign Direct Investment (FDI) and Supplier-Oriented Upgrading in the Czech Motor Vehicle Industry. *Regional Studies*, 44(5): 627–638.

Sakurai, Masao (1997) *Kokusai Keizai Ho - Kokusai Toshi (International Economic Law - International Investment)*. Tokyo: Seibundo.

Sato, Yuri (1992) Jidosha Sangyo (The Automotive Industry), in Mihara, Norio and Yuri Sato (eds.) *Indonesia no Kogyoka (Industrialisation in Indonesia)*. Tokyo: Institute of Developing Economies, 336–361.

Schmitz, Hubert (2006) Learning and Earning in Global Garment and Footwear Chains. *European Journal of Development Research*, 18(4): 546–571.

Schmitz, Hubert and Khalid Nadvi (1999) Clustering and Industrialisation: Introduction. *World Development*, 27(3): 1503–1514.

Schröder, Martin (2017) *Viet Nam's Automotive Supplier Industry: Development Prospects under Conditions of Free Trade and Global Production Networks*. Jakarta: Economic Research Institute for ASEAN and East Asia discussion paper, ERIA-DP-2017-05.

Segawa, Noriyuki, Kaoru Natsuda, John Thoburn (2014) Affirmative Action and Economic Liberalisation: The Dilemmas of the Malaysian Automotive Industry. *Asian Studies Review*, 38(3): 422–441.

Shadlen Kenneth (2005) Exchanging Development for Market Access? Deep Integration and Industrial Policy under Multilateral and Regional-Bilateral Trade Agreements. *Review of International Political Economy*, 12(5): 750–775.

Shalev-Shwartz, Shai, Shked Shammah, and Amonon Shashua (2017) *On a Formal Model of Safe and Scalable Self-driving Cars.* eprint arXiv:1708.06374. https://arxiv.org/abs/1708.06374 [accessed on 29 August 2019].

Shimizu, Kazushi (1998) *ASEAN Ikinai Keizai Kyoryoku no Seiji Keizaigaku (The Political Economy of Economic Coorporation within ASEAN).* Kyoto: Minerva Shobo.

Shimizu, Kazushi (2011) ASEAN Ikinai Keizai Kyoryoku to Jidosha Buhin Hokan (ASEAN Economic Cooperation and Auto Parts Complementation Sheme). *Sangyo Gattukaki Kennkyuu Nenpo*, 26: 65–77.

Shimokawa, Koichi (2010) *Japan and the Global Automotive Industry.* Cambridge: Cambridge University Press.

Soete, Luc (2007) From Industrial to Innovation Policy. *Journal of Industry, Competition and Trade*, 7(3–4): 273–284.

Stanford, Jim (2017) When an Auto Industry Disappears: Australia's Experience and Lessons for Canada. *Canadian Public Policy*, 43(S1): ss.57–74.

Staples, Andrew (2008) *Responses to Regionalism in East Asia: Japanese Production Networks in the Automotive Sector.* Basingstoke: Palgrave Macmillan.

Stiglitz, Joseph (1998) *More Instruments and Broader Goals: Moving Toward the Post-Washington Consensus.* Helsinki: World Institute for Development Economics Research (WIDER) Annual Lecture.

Sturgeon, Timothy (1998) *The Automotive Industry in Vietnam: Prospects for Development in a Globalizing Economy*, Report for the Development Strategy Institute. Hanoi: Ministry of Planning and Investment.

Sturgeon, Timothy (2002) Modular Production Networks: A New American Model of Industrial Organisation. *Industrial and Corporate Change*, 11(3): 451–496.

Sturgeon, Timothy, Jack Daly, Stacey Frederick, Penny Bamber, and Gary Gereffi (2016) *The Philippines in the Automotive Global Value Chain.* Center on Globalization, Governance & Competitiveness. Durham, NC: Duke University.

Sturgeon, Timothy and Momoko Kawakami (2011) Global Value Chains in the Electronics Industry: Characteristics, Crisis, and Upgrading Opportunities for Firms from Developing Countries. *International Journal of Technological Learning, Innovation and Development*, 4(1/2/3): 120–147.

Sturgeon, Timothy and Richard Lester (2004) The New Global Supply-base: New Challenges for Local Suppliers in East Asia, in Yusuf, Shahid, Anjum Altaf and Kaoru Nabeshima (eds.) *Global Production Networking and Technological Change in East Asia.* Oxford: Oxford University Press, 35–87.

Sturgeon, Timothy, Olga Memedovic, Johannes Van Biesebroeck, and Gary Gereffi (2009) Globalisation of the Automotive Industry: Main Features and Trends. *International Journal of Technological Learning, Innovation and Development*, 2(1/2): 7–24.

Sturgeon, Timothy, Johannes Van Biesebroeck, and Gary Gereffi (2008) Value Chains, Networks and Clusters: Reframing the Global Automotive Industry. *Journal of Economic Geography*, 8(3): 297–321.

Sturgeon, Timothy and Johannes Van Biesebroeck (2011) Global Value Chains in the Automotive Industry: An Enhanced Role for Developing Countries?. *International Journal of Technological Learning, Innovation and Development*, 4(1/2/3): 181–205.

Suehiro, Akira (1989) *Capital Accumulation in Thailand 1855–1985.* Tokyo: The Centre for East Asian Cultural Studies.

Suehiro, Akira (1998) *Thai: Keizai Boom, Keizai Kiki, Kozo Chosei (Thailand: Economic Boom, Economic Crisis, Structural Adjustment).* Tokyo: Nippon Thai Kyokai.

Suehiro, Akira (2000) Thai no Keizai Kaikaku (Economic Reform in Thailand). *Shakai Kagaku Kenkyu*, 51(4): 25–65.

Suffian, Firdausi (2020) The Politics and Institutional Arrangements in Malaysia's Automotive Industry. *Journal of Southeast Asian Economies*, 37(1):47–64.

Tadjoeddin, Mohammad Zulfan, and Anis Chowdhury (2019) *Employment and Re-Industrialisation in Post Soeharto Indonesia.* London: Palgrave Macmillan.

TAI (2008) *10th Anniversary.* Bangkok: Thailand Automotive Institute (TAI).

Takehiro, Katsushi (2011) *JETRO's Achievements to Build Partnership with Malaysian Automotive Industry.* Kuala Lumpur: Japan External Trade Organization (JETRO) Kuala Lumpur Office.

Takeishi, Akira and Takahiro Fujimoto (2001) Modularisation in the Auto Industry: Interlinked Multiple Hierarchies of Product, Production and Supplier System. *International Journal of Automotive Technology and Management*, 1(4): 379–396.

Techakanont, Kriengkrai (2008) *The Evolution of Automotive Clusters and Global Production Network in Thailand.* Faculty of Economics of Thammasat University Discussion Papers Series, (No. 6, March).

Techakanont, Kriengkrai (2012) New Division of Labor between Thailand and CLMV Countries: The Case of Automotive Parts Industry, in Ueki, Yasushi and Teerana Bhongmakapat (eds.) *Industrial Readjustment in the Mekong River Basin Countries: Toward the AEC.* BRC Research Report (7). Bangkok: Bangkok Research Center, IDE-JETRO, 205–234.

Terdudomtham, Thamavit (2004) Thai Policies for the Automotive Sector: Focus on Technology Transfer, in Busser, Rogier and Yuri Sadoi (eds.) *Production Networks in Asia and Europe: Skill Formation and Technology Transfer in the Automobile Industry.* London: RoutledgeCurzon, 30–50.

Tham, Siew-Yean (2004) Malaysian Policies for the Automobile Sector, in Busser, Rogier and Yuri Sadoi (eds.) *Production Networks in Asia and Europe.* London: Routledge-Curzon, 51–70.

Thoburn, John (1973) Exports and the Malaysian Engineering Industry: A Case Study of Backward Linkage. *Oxford Bulletin of Economics and Statistics*, 35(2): 91–117.

Thoburn, John (1977 and 1984) *Primary Commodity Exports and Economic Development: Theory, Evidence and a Study of Malaysia.* London and New York: Wiley, 1977; Japanese-language edition Tokyo: Taga Shuppan, 1984.

Thoburn, John (2001) Becoming an Exporter of Manufactures: The Case of Indonesia, in Morrissey, Oliver and Michael Tribe (eds.) *Policy Reform and Manufacturing Performance in Developing Countries.* London: Elgar, 97–119.

Thoburn, John (2007) Viet Nam, in Chowdhury, Anis and Iyanatul Islam (eds.) *Handbook on the Northeast and Southeast Asian Economies.* London: Elgar, 224–242.

Thoburn, John (2013) Vietnam, in Fosu, Augustin (ed.) *Achieving Development Success: Strategies and Lessons from the Developing World.* London: Oxford University Press, 99–118.

Thoburn, John (2020) Review of Ngo (2020), *Journal of the Asia Pacific Economy* DOI:10.1080/13547860.2020.1786966.

Thoburn, John and Kaoru Natsuda (2017) Comparative Policies for Automotive Development in Southeast Asia, in Hansen, Arve and Kenneth Bo Nielsen (eds.) *Wheels of Change: Cars, Automobility and Development in Asia.* London: Routledge, 17–36.

Thoburn, John and Kaoru Natsuda (2018) How to Conduct Effective Industrial Policy: A Comparison of Automotive Development in the Philippines and Indonesia. *Journal of the Asia Pacific Economy*, 23(4): 657–682.

Thoburn, John and Mokoto Takashima (1992) *Industrial Subcontracting in the UK and Japan*. London: Avebury.

Tokatli, Nebahat and Omur Kizilgum (2004) Upgrading in the Global Clothing Industry: Mavi Jeans and the Transformation of a Turkish Firm from Full-Package to Brand-Name Manufacturing and Retailing. *Economic Geography*, 80(3): 221–240.

Torii, Takashi (1991a) Changing the Manufacturing Sector, Reorganizing Automobile Assemblers, and Developing the Auto Components Industry under the New Economic Policy. *The Developing Economies*, 29(4): 387–413.

Torii, Takashi (1991b) Jidosha Sangyo (the Automotive Industry), in Horii, Kenzo (ed.) *Mareisia no Kougyoka (Malaysian Industrialisation)*. Tokyo: Institute of Developing Economies, 273–293.

Truong, Thi Chi Binh and Nguyen Manh Linh (2011) Development of Automotive Industries in Vietnam with Improving the Network Capability, in Intarakumnerd, Patarapong (ed.) *How to Enhance Innovation Capability with Internal and External Sources*. ERIA Research Project Report 2010–9, Jakarta: ERIA, 273–307.

Ueda, Yoko (2007) Nihon no Cyokusetsu Toshi to Tai no Jidosha Me-ka- no Keisei (Japanese Foreign Direct Investment and the Development of Auto parts Industry in Thailand). *Doshisha University Economic Review*, 58(4): 87–117.

Ueda, Yoko (2009) *The Origin and Growth of Local Entrepreneurs in Auto Parts Industry in Thailand*, Center for Contemporary Asia Working Paper No.25, Doshisha University.

Ueki, Yasushi (2016) Nittukei Jidosha Buhin Kigyo Thai Seizo Kyoten no Kodoka Jiritsuka to Thai Purasu one gata Seisan Nettutowaku no Keisei (Upgrading and Self Reliance on Production Operations in Thailand of Japanese Autoparts Firms and the Establishment of Thai Plus One Type Production Networks). *Journal of Waseda University, Research Institute of Auto Parts Industries*, 18: 42–55.

UNCTAD (2001) *World Investment Report 2001: Promoting Linkage*. Geneva: United Nations Conference on Trade and Development (UNCTAD).

UNCTAD (2006) *Trade and Development Report 2006*. Geneva: United Nations Conference on Trade and Development (UNCTAD).

UNCTAD (2013) *World Investment Report 2013: Global Value Chains: Investment and Trade for Development*. Geneva: United Nations Conference on Trade and Development (UNCTAD).

UNCTAD (2014) *Trade and Development Report 2014*. Geneva: United Nations Conference on Trade and Development (UNCTAD).

UNDP (2005) *Human Development Report 2005. International Cooperation at a Crossroad: Aid, Trade and Security in an Unequal World*. New York: United Nations Development Programme (UNDP).

UNDP (2013) *Human Development Report 2013. The Rise of the South: Human Development in a Diverse World*. New York: United Nations Development Programme (UNDP).

UNIDO (2013) *Industrial Development Report 2013*. Vienna: United Nations Industrial Development Organization (UNIDO).

UNIDO (2018) *Global Value Chains and Industrial Development: Lessons from China, South-East Asia and South Asia*. Vienna: United Nations Industrial Development Organization (UNIDO).

Van Arkadie, Brian and Raymond Mallon (2003) *Viet Nam: A Transition Tiger*. Canberra: Asia Pacific Press.

Van Grunsven, Leo and Floor Smakman (2001) Competitive Adjustment and Advancement in Global Commodity Chains I: Firm Strategies and Trajectories in the East Asian Apparel industry. *Singapore Journal of Tropical Geography*, 22(2): 173–188.

Van Grunsven, Leo and Floor Smakman (2005) Industrial Restructuring and Early Industry Pathways in the Asian First-Tier Generation NICs: The Singapore Garment Industry. *Environment and Planning A*, 37(4): 657–680.

Wad, Peter (2006) The Automotive Supplier Industry between Localizing and Global Forces in Malaysia, India and South Africa, in Hansen, Michael and Henrik Schaumburg-Muller (eds.) *Transnational Corporations and Local Firms in Developing Countries – Linkages and Upgrading*. Copenhagen: Copenhagen Business School Press, 233–261.

Wad, Peter (2008) The Development of Automotive Parts Suppliers in Korea and Malaysia: A Global Value Chain Perspective. *Asia Pacific Business Review*, 14(1): 47–64.

Wad, Peter (2009) The Automobile Industry of Southeast Asia: Malaysia and Thailand. *Journal of the Asia Pacific Economy*, 14(2): 172–193.

Wad, Peter and Govindaraju, V.G.R.C. (2011) Automotive Industry in Malaysia: Assessment of its Development. *International Journal of Automotive Technology and Management*, 11(2): 152–171.

Wade, Robert (1990) *Governing the Market: Economic Theory and the Role of Government in East Asian Industrialization*. Princeton, NJ: Princeton University Press.

Wade, Robert (2003) What Strategies are Viable for Developing Countries Today? The World Trade Organization and the Shrinking of 'Development Space'. *Review of International Political Economy*, 10(4): 621–644.

Wakamatsu, Isao, Toshio Nomura and Norio Gomi (2001) AFTA, AICO to Jidosha Maker no Kyoten Senryaku (AFTA, AICO and Production Base Strategy of Automotive Producers), in Aoki, Takeshi (ed.) *AFTA*. Tokyo: Japan External Trade Organization, 101–129.

Wan, Hooi Lai (2001) Education and Training in the Auto Manufacturing Industry: A Comparative Analysis between Japan and Malaysia. *Human Resources Health Development Journal*, 5(1–3): 39–46.

Warwick, Ken (2013) *Beyond Industrial Policy: Emerging Issues and New Trends*. OECD Science, Technology and Industrial Policy Papers No.2. Paris: OECD Publishing.

Weiss, John (2016) Industrial Policy: Back on the Agenda, in Weiss, John and Michael Tribe (eds.) *Routledge Handbook of Industry and Development*. London: Routledge, 135–150.

Weiss, Linda (1995) Governed Interdependence: Rethinking the Government-Business Relationship in East Asia. *The Pacific Review*, 8(4): 589–616.

Williamson John (1990) What Washington Means by Policy Reform, in Williamson, John (ed.) *Latin American Adjustment: How Much Has Happened?*. Washington, DC: Institute for International Economics.

Witoelar, Wimar (1983) Ancilliary Firm Development in the Motor Vehicle Industry in Indonesia, in Odaka, Konosuke (ed.) *The Motor Vehicle Industry in Asia: A Study of Ancilliary Firm Development*. Manila: Council of Asian Manpower Studies, 17–84.

Woo-Cumings, Meredith (ed.) (1999) *The Developmental State*. Ithaca, NY: Cornell University Press.

World Bank (2017) *Global Value Chain Development Report 2017: Measuring and Analyzing the Impact of GVCs on Economic Development*. Geneva: World Trade Organization (produced jointly with the WTO, OECD, IDE-JETRO, UIBE).

World Bank (2019) *Global Value Chain Development Report 2019: Technological Innovation, Supply Chain Trade, and Workers in a Globalized World.* Geneva: World Trade Organization (produced jointly with WTO, OECD, IDE-JETRO, and UIBE).

World Bank (2020) *World Development Report 2020: Trading for Development in the Age of Global Value Chains.* Washington, DC: World Bank.

Yoshimatsu, Hidetaka (1999) The State, MNCs, and the Car Industry in ASEAN. *Journal of Contemporary Asia*, 29(4): 459–515.

Yoshimatsu, Hidetaka (2000) The Role of Government in Jump-Starting Industrialization in East Asia: The Case of Automobile Development in China and Malaysia. *Issues & Studies*, 36(4): 166–199.

Yoshimatsu, Hidetaka (2002a) Preferences, Interests and Regional Integration: The Development of the ASEAN Industrial Cooperation Arrangement. *Review of International Political Economy*, 9(1): 123–149.

Yoshimatsu, Hidetaka (2002b) Liberalisation Policy and International Competitiveness: The Experiences of the Automobile Industry in Taiwan and Thailand. *Asian Profile*, 30(2): 121–136.

Yoshimatsu, Hidetaka (2003) Japanese Policy in the Asian Economic Crises and the Developmental State Concept. *Journal of the Asian Pacific Economy*, 8(1): 102–125.

Zheng, Yanwei and Shihao Sheng (2006) Learning in a Local Cluster in the Context of the Global Value Chain: A Case Study of the Yunhe Wood Toy Cluster in Zhejiang, China, *Innovation: Management, Policy & Practice*, 8(1–2): 120–127.

Index

Note: **Bold** page numbers refer to tables; *italic* page numbers refer to figures, and page numbers followed by "n" denote endnotes.